The Encyclopedia of the Divine, Spiritual and Occult

The Encyclopedia of the Divine, Spiritual and Occult

Volume 2: H-P

by
Heather Eaton

One Spirit Press
Portland, Oregon

Copyright © 2012 Heather Eaton All rights reserved.
Printed in the USA

ISBN: 978-1-893075-50-4
LCCN: 2011939057

Book Design: Spirit Press, LLC/Alice Firpo

This book may not be reproduced by electronic or any other means which exist now or may yet be developed, without permission of Spirit Press, except in the case of brief quotations embodied in critical articles and reviews.

One Spirit Press,
onespiritpress@gmail.com
www.onespiritpress.com

Portland, Oregon

Dedication

For Love

Table of Contents

Introduction	ix
H: Ha Wen Neyu to Hyssop, James Hervy	1
I: I Ching to Izchup	43
J: Jabir ibn Hayyan, Abu Musa to Jyeshtha	61
K: Ka to Kye ne Bardo	73
L: LaBerge, Stephen to Lycanthropy	97
M: Maat to Mythological Places	123
N: Naadame to Nymphs	189
O: Oannes to Oxon, M.A.	217
P: PA to Pythias	237
Recommended Reading	291
Index	347
Art and Artists	366
Bibliography and Webography	371

"For those who believe, no proof is necessary.
For those who don't believe, no proof is possible."

Stuart Chase

"We live in matter.
We Exist in Spirit."

Heather Eaton

"True glory consists of doing what deserves to be written,
and writing what deserves to be read."

Pliny the Elder

Introduction

When I started my spiritual quest I discovered that there were many, many terms and words that I didn't understand, and people of whom I had never heard of. I started to keep a record of what I was learning while I was writing a book on herbs. Somehow that file turned into an Encyclopedia. I hope that this book will help others understand not only the terminology and the definitions but the spiritual concepts and the higher truths that accompany that knowledge as well.

This book is comprised of the main encyclopedic text, followed by a Recommended Reading section which includes a more detailed list of books (up to 15 for each) by authors described in the book as well as other recommended authors. This is followed by a section called Artists and Art, which lists the over 300 artists and works of art depicted herein. And lastly there are the reference files including the bibliography and webliography.

The main encyclopedic text includes around 4,000 entries. It gives a brief description or definition of each entry and tries to point the reader to the source of more information, such as books and websites or to other related entries. The people described herein, half of whom have passed on and half of whom are living are all people who in one way or another have spiritually influenced our world. You will find many highly educated people, as well as people with practically no education but with a spiritual gift to share or mystical message to impart. These entries include:

People

Among these (around 700) extraordinary people you will find are: alchemists, anthropologists, archeologists, astrologers, astronauts, Buddhists, best selling authors, channelers, Christians, consciousness researchers, clairvoyants, dream analysts, Egyptologists, Evangelists, Freemasons, futurists, Gnostics, Gurus, herbalists, Hermeticists, healers, Hindus, historians, holistic healers, human rights activists, hypnotherapists, Jews, journalists, Lamas, mathematicians, mediums,

Ministers, Mormons, mystics, Occultists, paranormal investigators, parapsychologists and psychic researchers, philosophical and medical doctors, philosophers, physicists, poets, prophets, psychics, psychologists, Priests, Qabbalists, quantum physicists, Rabbis, Reverends, Rosicrucians, Saints, Shamans, sound therapists, spiritual leaders, spiritual teachers, spiritualists, Swamis, therapists, Theosophists, theologians, Wiccans, and yogis, among others.

Gods and Goddesses

Over 650 Gods and Goddesses from the following traditions: Algonquin, Assyrian, Araucanian, Aztec, Babylonian, Celtic, Egyptian, Greek, Hawaiian, Hindu, Inca, Inuit, Iroquois, Maya, Navajo, Norse, Pawnee, Persian, Roman, Slavic, Sumerian, Tibetan and Zoroastrian.

Magical Methods

Including: Adjuration, Automatic Writing, Banishing, Bewitching, Binding, Ceremonial Magic, Channeling, Charging, Cone of Power, Depossession, Divination, Dowsing, Enchantment, Energy Ball, Evocation, Fumigation, Glamour, Godform, Incantation, Initiation, Invisibility, Invocation, Libation, Magical Circle, Natural Magic, Nature Worship, Offering, Pathworking, Philtre, Prediction, Radiesthesia, Rhabdomancy, Ritual, Sacrifice, Séance, Shape Shifting, Shield, Shroud of Concealment, Simulacrum, Slate Writing, Sympathetic Magic, Tattwas, Warding and White Magic.

Occult Orders, Brotherhoods and Secret Societies

Alpha et Omega, Benandanti, Cathars, Church of the Light, Fraternity of the Inner Light, Freemasonry, Germaeorden, Golden Dawn, Hermetic Brotherhood of Luxor, Illuminati, Knights Templar, Martinism, Order of Bards, Ovates and Druids, Order of Skull and Bones, Ordo Templi Orientis, Prieure de Sion, Rosicrucian Order, Servants of the Light, Society of Friends, Society of the Inner Light, Stella Matutina, Temple of Ara, Thelema and Theosophical Society.

Philosophical and Mystical Movements

Describing: Aesthetics, Ascension Movement, Bhakti, Carpocratians, Chaos Magic, Confucianism, Cosmic Movement, Deism, Druidry, Existentialism, Feng Shui, Gnosticism, Hasidism, Hermeticism, I Ching, Mysticism, Neo-Platonism, Orphism, Pantheism, Qabbalah, Quietism, Sacred Geometry, Shamanism, Spiritism, Spiritualism, Stoicism, Sufism, Taoism, Teleology, Thanatology, Thaumaturgy, Theology, Theosophy, Theurgy, Transcendentalism, Unanimism, and Zen.

Religions

Including: Brahamanism, Buddhism, Christian Science, Christianity, Church of Scientology, Confucianism, Dianic Wicca, Druse, Druidism, Eckankar, Gardnerian Wicca, Hinduism, Hoodoo, Huna, Islam, Judaism, Lamaism, Macumba, Manichaeism, Mormonism, Neopaganism, Obeah, Paganism, Santeria, Shinto, Taoism, Universal Religion, Voodoo, Wicca and Zoroastrianism.

Spiritual Goals

Describing: Absolute, Agape, Ahimsa, Ananda, Apocatastasis, Ascension, Attunement, Brahma-Viharas, Cosmic Humanism, Darshan, Dhyana, Empathy, Enlightenment, Globalism, Illumination, Jnana, Mimamsa, Moksha, Nirvana, Nyaya, Samadhi, Samkhya, Satori, Sunyata, Vaisheshika, Vedanta and Yoga.

Spiritual Techniques

Describing: Affirmation, Astral Projection, Autosuggestion, Blessing, Chanting, Contemplation, Consecration, Creative Visualization, Empathy, Empowering, Exorcism, Faith, Faith Healing, Herbal Magic, Grounding, Imagination, Inspiration, Lucid Dreaming, Mantra, Meditation, Monasticism, Positive Thinking, Prayer, Psychic Healing, Psychokinesis, Psychometry, Purification, Remote Viewing, Self-Healing, Self-Help, Self-Initiation, Sensory Deprivation, Smudging, Spiritual Cleansing, Sadhana, Supplication, Telethesia, Trance States, Transcendental Meditation, Unction, Visualization and Worship.

Spiritual Teachers

Adept, Acarya, Ascended Masters, Bodhisattvas, Buddhas, Clergymen, Great Bodhisattvas, Great White Lodge, Gurus, Hidden Masters, Houngan, Imans, Maggidins, Magis, Magicians, Magus, Maharishi, Mahatmas, Mambos, Masters, Ministers, Mullahs, Mystics, Old Souls, Paramahamsas, Preachers, Priests, Rabbis, Reverends; Rinpoches, Satgurus, Shamans, Siddhas, Silent Watchers, Swamis, Theurgists and Tulkus.

Therapeutic Systems

Including: Acupressure, Acupuncture, Aikido, Aromatherapy, Astrotherapy, Ayurveda, Bach Flower Therapy, Bau-Biologie, Biofeedback, Chiropractic, Chromotherapy, Core Energetics, Craniosacral Therapy, Crystal Therapy, Herbalism, Homeopathy, Lomi Lomi, Mesmerism, Naturopathy, New Thought, Qigong, Quantum Touch, Reflexology, Regression Therapy, Reiki, Sadhana, Shiatsu, Space Clearing, Somatic Disciplines, Spagyrics, Sound Therapy, Therapeutic Touch, Transcendental Meditation, Vastu, Vipassana, and Yoga.

You will also find descriptions of: (around) 100 Angels; 30 demons; 60 mythological creatures, 60 supernatural and spiritual beings; 90 New Age Associations and Societies; 50 types of divination; 10 types of divination tools; 20 magical tools, 50 sacred texts and writings; 20 elementals; 30 nature spirits; 20 types of fairies and nymphs; 30 astral bodies; 40 mythological places; 20 sacred sites; 10 haunted places; and much, much more.

May you enjoy reading this as much as I enjoyed writing it.

H

Ha Wen Neyu
From Iroquois mythology, Ha Wen Neyu is the Great Spirit. Also see Iroquois Gods and Goddesses.

Haamiah
Angel of the order of Powers, Haamiah rules over religious cults and protects all those who seek the truth. Also see Angels.

Hacavitz
In Maya mythology, Hacavitz is the God of the Hacavitz Mountain. Also see Maya Gods and Goddesses.

Hades
From the Greek word Aides meaning "the Unseen" Hades is the God of the Underworld. He rules over crops, minerals, gems, spring water, material gain and astral projection. Hades is the son of the Titans Cronus and Rhea and brother of Hestia, Zeus, Hera, Poseidon and Demeter. He is described as both the benign God of Prosperity and the terrifying God of Death because he supervises the trial and punishment of the wicked after death. He is also known as The Invisible One and the Absolute Master of the Underworld. He is also referred to as Pluto or Pluton. Hades is known to the Romans as Dis Pater. He is one of the Olympian Gods. Hades  is depicted here with Cerberus in a 1592 painting by Italian artist Agostino Carracci called Pluto.

Also see Greek Gods and Goddesses, Olympian Gods and Underworld Gods.

Hades

In Greek mythology, Hades is also the term used to describe the Underworld, also called the House of Hades, the Abode of the Departed Spirits and Kingdom of the Dead. The entrance is guarded by Cerberus, a three headed dog, who allows all to enter but none to leave. Hades is mentioned in The Bible and equated with hell. Shown here is a 1605 painting by German artist Joseph Heintz called The Abduction of Persephone. Also see Cerberus, Greek Gods and Goddesses, Mythological Places and Underworlds.

Hagalaz

As the 19th symbol of the runes, Hagalaz represents disruption. Other spellings include Hagalz. Also see Runes.

Hagelin, John

(1954-) American-born John Samuel Hagelin Ph.D. is a world-renowned quantum physicist, educator, author and third party candidate for President of the United States. He received his Ph.D. from Harvard University and is currently professor of physics and Director of the Institute of Science, Technology and Public Policy at the Maharishi University of Management, and President of the Global Union of Scientists for Peace. Dr. Hagelin conducted pioneering research at the Stanford Linear Accelerator Center (SLAC) and the European Center for Particle Physics (CERN), and formulated a successful Grand Unified Field Theory based on the superstring, which was featured in a cover story of Discover Magazine. Dr. Hagelin is one of the foremost researchers on the effects of meditation on brain development and higher states of consciousness, as well as phenomena of collective consciousness. He was awarded the Kilby Award for outstanding achievements in science and technology. He has written Manual for a Perfect Government: How TO Harness the Laws of Nature to Bring Maximum Success to Governmental Administration. Also see Physicists, Quantum Physics and Quantum Mechanics, Recommended Reading and hagelin.org.

Hagith

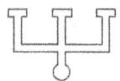

Olympian Spirit who governs Venus and other provinces of the Universe. See Olympian Spirits.

Hags

In the British Isles, the Hags are Nature Spirits who personify winter. They are described as old women in winter who turn into beautiful young women in spring. Shown here is a painting by American artist Lisa Hunt (lisahuntart.com) called The Sorceress. Also see Nature Spirits.

Hahaiah

Angel of the order of cherubim, Hahaiah influences human thoughts and when he so desires, may reveal hidden truths and mysteries to mortals. Also see Angels.

Hahbwehdiyu

Iroquois God of Creation, Hahbwehdiyu represents strength and victory. His evil counterpart is his twin brother Hahgwehdaetgah. Other spellings include Hahgwehdiyu. Also see Iroquois Gods and Goddesses.

Hahiniah

According to the Qabbalah, Hahiniah is one of the Throne Angels. Also see Angels.

Haich, Elisabeth

(1897-1994) Hungarian-born Elisabeth Haich was a child prodigy who even as a very young child was painting, sculpting and playing piano. After World War II she was forced to leave Hungary for Switzerland where she founded what is now the oldest and largest yoga school in Europe. Ms. Haich was a well known spiritual teacher, yogi and author of five books of spiritual matters. Her books are: Initiation (which has sold millions of copies in 17 languages); The Day With Yoga; Sexual Energy and Yoga; The Wisdom of the Tarot and Self-Healing, Yoga and Destiny. Also see Recommended Reading, Spiritual Teachers, Yogis and haich.de.

Hale, Susan Elizabeth

American-born Susan Elizabeth Hale, M.A. is internationally known as a pioneer in the fields of music therapy, creative arts therapy and sound healing. She received her M.A. in Creative Arts Therapy from Goddard College. Since the mid-70's she has been at the forefront of exploring music, sound, voice, word, and image as healing arts. Ms. Hale has also led pilgrimages to Sacred Sites including Avebury, Stonehenge and temples in the pyramids of Egypt. Ms. Hale currently is the director of the Songkeeper Apprenticeship and teaches therapeutic workshops throughout the United States, Britain and Canada helping people find and free their natural voice. She has written Song and Silence: Voicing the Soul and Sacred Space– Sacred Sound: The Acoustic Mysteries of Holy Places. Photograph from newfrontier.com. Also see Recommended Reading, Sacred Sites, Sound Therapy and songkeeper.net.

Halexandria Foundation

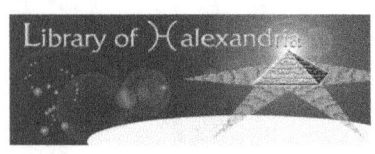

The Halexandria Foundation is (in their own words) dedicated to providing the means by which individuals will have the knowledge and understanding of themselves and the laws of the universe to make the choices that best benefit themselves and the world in which they live. For each Individual, the intent is: to know thyself, to develop the arts and sciences of living, to reach a state of mental alertness, emotional balance, physical action, and spiritual awareness, and to become, by example, a demonstration of what is best in humankind. Halexandria Foundation includes four main institutions: The Library of Halexandria, the Museion and University of Halexandria, the Temple of Halexandria, and the Pharos of Halexandria. As a living entity, the Foundation is also defined by the personnel or staff of the Library, Museion and University, Temple, and Pharos. These are the people who are currently donating their time to establish and structure the aims, goals, and destiny of the Foundation. Equally essential to the support structure are three groups, including: The Companions, The Fellowship, and The Community of Halexandria. Also see Daniel Ward and New Age and Societies.

Hall, Manly Palmer

(1901-1990) Canadian-born Manly Palmer Hall was a mystic, Minister, Freemason, Theosophist, occultist and author. At age 25 he published The Secret Teachings of All Ages: An Encyclopedic Outline of Masonic, Hermetic, Qabbalistic and Rosicrucian Symbolical Philosophy and he was well known as a leading scholar in mythology, mysticism, religion and the occult. While in his teens he joined the Theosophical Society, in 1923 he was ordained as a Minister in the Church of the People, in 1934 he founded the Philosophical Research Society in Los Angeles, California, and in 1973 he was recognized as a 33 degree Mason (the 2nd highest honor conferred by the Scottish Rite Supreme Council. Over 70 years he delivered over 8,000 lectures and wrote more than 200 books on occult

subjects, including: Initiates of the Flame; The Secret Destiny of America and The Secret Teachings of All Ages: An Encyclopedic Outline of Masonic, Hermetic, Qabbalistic and Rosicrucian Symbolical Philosophy. Also see Freemasons, Mystics, Mythology, Occultists, Qabbalists, Recommended Reading, Reverends and Ministers, Rosicrucians, Theosophists and manlyphall.org.

Hall of Maat

In Egyptian mythology the Hall of Maat is where the judgment of the dead takes place. Anubis accompanied the soul to the weighting of the heart ceremony where the heart is put on a scale on one side and a feather is placed on the other. If the heart is heavier than the feather then the soul is devoured by Ammut and if the heart weighs less the soul is admitted to the afterlife. The judgment of the soul is recorded by Thoth. The Hall of Maat is depicted here in a 1375 B.C.E detail scene from the Papyrus of Hunefer. Also see Ammut, Anubis, Maat, Mythological Places, and Thoth.

Hall of Records
See Akashic Records.

Hall of The Slain
See Valhalla

Halloween
See Samhain and Wicca.

Hallucination
A false perception of a sensory modality due to the absence of external stimulus, as opposed to an illusion which is a misperception of external stimulus. Hallucinations may be visual, gustatory, tactile, olfactory, auditory or proprioceptive and can include such alterations of perception as hearing flowers sing or seeing music. Shown here is a 20th Century painting by American artist Robert Venosa (venosa.com) called Hallucination. Also see Hallucinogens.

Hallucinogens
Hallucinogens (mind altering drugs) are psychoactive drugs that induce altered sensory perceptions or hallucinations, as well as altered states of consciousness. The people described herein who research hallucinogens include: Richard Alpert (Ram Dass), Stanislav Grof, Aldous Huxley, Luis Eduardo Luna, Robert E. Masters, Terence McKenna, Ralph Metzner, Marcia Moore, Claudio Naranjo, Jeremy Narby, Charles Tart, and Andrew Weil. Also see Ayahuasca and Hallucination.

Halo
Also called nimbus, the halo is described as a circular area or sphere of brightness, also seen sometimes as a bright white light that surrounds the head of a Holy person which represents the aura or spiritual character. Religious figures such as Jesus Christ, the Virgin Mary, Angels and Saints are usually depicted with halos. Halos are described in various religions and spiritual belief systems and are sometimes described as rays of bright light that emanate from the Holy person's head. Shown here stain glass window depicting Saint Anselm with a halo. Also see Aura, Celestial Light, and Nimbus.

Hamadryades

In Greek mythology, Hamadryades are Nymphs who live in and around trees. Hamadryades are born with a certain tree to watch over; they die when the tree dies. Also see Nymphs. A Hamadryad is depicted here in an 1895 painting by British artist John William Waterhouse (jwwaterhouse.com).

Hamakua

The Hamakua area in Hawaii is one of the twelve areas known as the Vile Vortices which are described as areas around the world said to have the same qualities as the famous Bermuda Triangle. In these areas strange phenomena are reported such as compasses and other instruments going crazy and ships and planes disappearing. Other spellings include Hamakulia. See Vile Vortices.

Hamblin, Henry Thomas

(1873-1958) British-born Henry Thomas Hamblin was born into a poor family from which he emerged to become a successful business man. He says that he had visionary experiences all his life where he felt a Divine Presence. As he became more successful he began to lose this ability and be haunted by nightmares as well. After turning towards a more spiritual life he founded The Science of Thought Review magazine. He became a prolific writer on self-help and spiritual matters. Among Hamblin's books are: Within You Is the Power; The Life of the Spirit; Divine Adjustment: How Divine Law Works in Our Life; Life Without Strain: The Strifeless Way to Harmony, Peace and Joy; and The Message of a Flower: The Divine Immanence in Nature. Also see Recommended Reading, Self-Help and henryrhomashamblin.wwwhubs.com.

Hameroff, Stuart

(1947-) American-born Stuart R. Hameroff, M.D. is an anesthesiologist, professor of anesthesiology and psychology, and Director of the Center for Consciousness Studies at the University of Arizona. He received his B.S. from the University of Pittsburgh and his M.D. from Hahnemann University Hospital (now part of Drexel University College of Medicine). He collaborated with mathematical physicist Roger Penrose in the development of the Orchestrated Objective Reduction model of consciousness. He also participated in the movie What the Bleep Do We Know? Dr. Hameroff has written over 150 papers and two books: Ultimate Computing: Biomolecular Consciousness and Nanotechnology and Toward a Science of Consciousness: The First Tucson Discussions and Debates. Photograph from whatthebleep.com. Also see Consciousness Researchers, Recommended Reading, quantumconsciousness.org and consciousness.arizona.edu.

Ham-sa

From Sanskrit meaning "I am That", ham-sa is a mantra designed on the sound of our own breath. Ham on the inhale and sa on the exhale, pronounced softly like breath.

Hamsa Hand

Also called the Hand of Fatima by the Muslims and the Hand of Miriam by the Jews, the Hamsa Hand is an amulet to ward off the evil eye. Also see Hand of Fatima, Hand of Miriam, Evil Eye, and Magical Amulets.

Hanan Pacha

In Inca mythology, Hanan Pacha is the Future World, one of three worlds that represent the Cosmos. Also see Inca Worlds, and Mythological Places.

Hand of Fatima

Muslim term for an amulet to ward off the evil eye. Image from handoffatima.com. Also see Evil Eye, Hamsa Hand, Hand of Miriam, and Magical Amulets.

Hand of Miriam

Jewish term for the Hamsa Hand the Hand of Miriam is an amulet to ward off the evil eye. Image from tattoosymbol.com. Also see Evil Eye, Hamsa Hand, Hand of Fatima, and Magical Amulets.

Hand of Mysteries

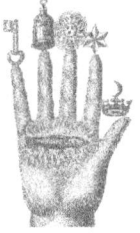

Also called the Hand of the Philosopher, the Hand of Mysteries is a Masonic talisman depicting the symbols of apotheosis, or transformation of man into God. It's alchemical symbolism is said to hold the keys to divinity. Manly Palmer said in his book The Secret Teaching of All Ages that the Hand of Mysteries played a role in the founding of the United States. Traditionally the images depicted are Suns, skulls, fish, keys, stars, crowns and other astrological symbols. Shown here is an 18th century depiction of the Hand of Mysteries by an unknown artist.

Handfasting

From Scottish and Irish traditions handfasting is a wedding or betrothal ritual where the couple's hands are clasped together and tied with a cord or ribbon. In modern Wiccan and Pagan traditions this ceremony is interpreted to be a spiritual marriage, either as a trial or as a permanent bondage. Photograph from spellworks.net. Also see handfasting.info and handfastings.org.

Hanged Man

The Hanged Man is one of the 22 major arcana of the tarot deck of cards. Its number is XII, its Qabbalistic title is The Spirit of The Mighty Waters and its meaning is: enforced sacrifice, loss, and suffering in general. Also see Tarot.

Hanh, Thich Nhat

(1926-) Vietnamese-born Nhat Hanh aka Thich Nhat Hanh is an expatriate Zen Buddhist monk, peace activist, teacher, poet and author. He founded the relief organization School of Youth for Social Services in Saigon in the 1960's. He traveled to the United States to study at Princeton University, and later to teach at Columbia University as well as lecture in others. Thich Nhat Hanh was nominated for the Nobel Peace Prize (nomination proposed by Reverend Dr. Martin Luther King Jr.) and led the Buddhist delegation to the Paris Peace Talks. He currently lives at the Plum Village Monastery in Southern France and travels giving talks and spiritual retreats internationally. Among Hanh's books are: Being Peace; Peace Is Every Step: The Path of Mindfulness in Everyday Life; Living Buddha, Living Christ; The Heart of the Buddha's Teachings; No Death, No Fear; and Touching the Earth: Intimate Conversations with the Buddha. Photograph from tnhvancouver2011.org Also see Buddhist Monks, Nobel Prize Laureates, Poets, Recommended Reading, Spiritual Retreats, interbeing.org.uk, nobelprizes.com, and plumvillage.org.

Haniel

From Hebrew meaning "Glory or Grace of God", Haniel is an Angel; chief of the order of principalities, virtues and innocents. Also see Angels.

Hanuman

Hindu Monkey God, son of Vayu (shown here), represents strength, wisdom and devotion to Dharma. Hanuman is usually shown carrying a club to destroy evil and holding one of his palms upwards to offer spiritual blessings. He is called the Monkey Hero in the Ramayana. Other spellings include Haunuman and Hanumat. Image from veerahanuman.com. Also see Hindu Gods and Goddesses.

Hapi

In Egyptian mythology, Hapi is the God of the Nile. He is a very ancient God who rules over fertility, crops, water and prosperity. Hapi is depicted as a man with a woman's breast and protruding belly. Other depictions include him wearing papyrus plants or lotus flowers on his head. Hapi rules over Upper Egypt and Lower Egypt. Other spellings include Hapy, Hep and Hap. Also see Egyptian Gods and Goddesses.

Harahel

In the Qabbalah, Harahel is an Angel in charge of the archives, libraries and rare scriptures. Also see Angels.

Hare

In Chinese Astrology, the Hare is one of the 12 animals of the Zodiac. People born in the year of the Hare are described as talented, lucky and articulate. Also see Chinese Zodiac.

Hariel

An Angel in the order of Cherubim, Hariel has dominion over tame beasts and he rules science and the arts. He is invoked against impieties. Other spellings include Behemial and Harael. Also see Angels.

Harman, Willis

(1909-1997) American-born Willis W. Harman Ph.D. was a futurist, visionary, social scientist and author. He earned his B.S. in electrical engineering at the University of Washington and his M.S. in physics and Ph.D. in electrical engineering from Stanford University. He taught for several years at the University of Florida. Dr. Harman was also the president of the Institute of Noetic Sciences, professor emeritus for Engineering Economic Systems at Stanford University, member of the Board of Regents of the University of California and Senior Social Scientist at SRI International for 16 years. Among his books are: Global Mind Change: The Promise of the Last Years of the Twentieth Century; Higher Creativity: Liberating the Unconscious for Breakthrough Insights; and An Incomplete Guide to the Future. Photograph from synearth.net. Also see Futurists, Scientists and Recommended Reading.

Harpies

Originally in Greek mythology the Harpies are described beautiful maidens with wings and in later Greek and Roman mythology the Harpies are described as ugly foul creatures with the heads and breasts of old women, the wings, beaks, and claws of a bird that fly through the skies and always leave a sickening odor in their wake. They are said to be extremely ill tempered and are associated with the Underworld where they are employed by the Gods to punish sin on Earth. Shown here is an 1874 depiction of harpies from Dr. Vollmer's Mythology book. Also see Cryptids, and Mythological Creatures.

Harris, Alexander

(1897-1974) Welsh-born Alexander "Alex" Frederick Harris was a well known spiritualist medium and channeler who was said to produce materializations. When his wife began to participate in séances he wanted nothing to do with them. Eventually Harris not only participated in them but discovered that he himself shown mediumistic abilities and could fall into trance states and channel spirits as well as produce materializations. He participated in séances with Helen Duncan where his sister and his wife's father materialized. He was said to have several spirit guides, among them Christopher and Jolkim. He lived in South Africa for many years conducting séances until his death. For a book about Harris, see Recommended Reading. Also see Channeled Spirit Guides, Channelers, Mediums and Spiritualists.

Harris, Bertha

(1900(?)-1981) British-born Bertha Harris was a well known spiritualist medium and psychic. From childhood she was said to see auras and fairies, as well as contacts spirits. She played chess with her father and beat him frequently until she said that it was her dead great grandfather who told her where to move the pieces. Once she described her uncle on a ship with a pretty doll that he threw into the sea. It was later revealed that her aunt had given birth to a still-born on board ship and the child was buried at sea. She was studying to become a pianist but was forced to work as a bookkeeper when her father died. She toured with Arthur Conan Doyle and reported visits with him after he died. She received the diploma of the Spiritualist National Union and later Minister. In London Ms. Harris' psychic abilities were much sought during Word War II by people such as Charles de Gaulle and Winston Churchill. She was of the organizers of the Spiritualist Association of Great Britain. Also see Mediums, Psychics and Spiritualists.

Hartmann, Franz

(1838-1912) German-born Franz Hartmann M.D. was a renowned physician, theosophist, astrologer, geomancer and a prolific author on occultism of his time. He immigrated to the United States in 1865 and became a traveling doctor. He lived for a time in India where he met Helena Blavatsky. He was president of the Theosophical Society for a while and later founded other societies. He translated the Bhagavad Gita into German. Among his books are: The Life and Doctrines of Philippus Theophrastus Bombast of Hohenheim Known as Paracelsus; An Adventure Among the Rosicrucians; The Life and Doctrines of Jacob Boheme; and The Principles of Astrological Geomancy: The Art of Divining by Punctuation, According to Cornelius Agrippa and Others and The Life of Jehoshua, the Prophet of Nazareth: An Occult Study and a Key to The Bible, Containing the History of an Initiate. Also see Astrologers, Recommended Reading, Theosophists and franzhartmann.org.

Hartmann Grids

The Hartmann Grids, named after Ernst Hartmann in the 1950's and are described as geopathic energy found in lines that form a grid around the Earth from North to South and East to West. Hartmann described these energy grid lines as appearing approximately every three meters on the North-South lines and every four meters on the East-West lines. The junction spots are called Hartmann knots and these are described as energetic hot spots where it is very harmful for humans or other living beings to be for long periods of time. Also see Earth's Grids.

Harvey, Andrew

(1952-) Indian-born British Andrew Harvey is a scholar, mystic and author who has dedicated the past 30 years to write about the world's spiritual and mystical traditions. He collaborated with Sogyal Rinpoche on The Tibetan Book of Living and Dying. Mr. Harvey is currently working on what he calls Sacred Activism; the fusion of mystical knowledge and radical action that he believes is essential for the world's survival. He has written over 30 books including: A Walk with Four Spiritual Guides: Krishna Buddha, Jesus and Ramakrishna; Hidden Journey: A Spiritual Awakening; The Divine Feminine: Exploring the Feminine Face of God Throughout the World; The Return of the Mother; A Journey in Ladakh: Encounters with Buddhism; and The Direct Path: Creating a Journey for the Divine Using the World's Mystical Traditions. Photograph taken by Kevin Abosch (kevinabosch.com). Also see Mystics, Recommended Reading and andrewharvey.net.

Hasidism

Jewish mystical movement, its name comes from the Hebrew hasid which means "the Pious Ones". Hasidism was founded in the 13th Century by members of the Kalonymos family, including Samuel ben Kalonymos (known as the Hasid), Judah ben Samuel and Eleazer ben Judah. It is based on the Qabbalah, Occultism and Talmudic and medieval Jewish Mysticism. A later revival of the movement in the 18th Century by the Baal Shem Tov is where the current trend of Hasidism stands today. The basic emphasis is on a loving relationship with God through prayer, study and contemplation and leading a life of compassion and good deeds. Other spellings include Chasidism. Shown here is a 20th Century painting by Isidor Kaufmann called Portrait of a Young Boy. Also see Philosophical and Mystical Movements.

Haskvitz, Sylvia

American-born Sylvia Haskvitz M.A., R.D. is a certified trainer with the Center for Nonviolent Communication, a registered dietitian and facilitator of Compassionate Communication seminars, health consultant and author. She received her M.A. in speech and communications studies at San Francisco State University in San Francisco, CA and her B.S. in nutrition and dietetics from the University of Texas Allied Health Science Center at Houston, TX. Ms. Haskvitz created the first –inpatient eating disorder program for Fairview Hospital and developed the Weight to Go program for the Northwest Racquet and Swim Club in Minneapolis, MN and offers a variety of vegetarian cooking classes. She presents Nonviolent Communication skills in conferences. She has written Eat by Choice, Not by Habit: Practical Skills for Creating a Healthy Relationship with Your Body and Food. Photograph from eatbychoice.net. Also see Mind-Body Energy Medicine, Recommended Reading, eatbychoice.net and nvcaz.com/tucson.

Hastsehogan

In Navajo mythology, Hastsehogan is the God of Houses. Also see Navajo Gods and Goddesses.

Hastsezini
In Navajo mythology, Hastsezini is the God of Fire. Also see Navajo Gods and Goddesses.

Hatha
From Sanskrit meaning "Union of Force", Hatha is a Hindu philosophy that teaches mastery over the body as the way of attaining spiritual enlightenment.

Hatha Yoga
The yoga which emphasizes the control and development of the physical body to free the mind for its search for enlightenment. Also see Yoga, hathayoga.net and hathayogalesson.com.

Hathor
Egyptian Mother Goddess, Mother of all Gods and Goddesses, Queen of the Heavens and the Sky and the Moon, Hathor is the personification of the great powers of nature. Wife of Ra, she is the protector of women and motherhood and marriage, of love, joy, flowers, beauty, prosperity, astrology, family, song, dance, and music. Hathor is also called the Lady of the West, Lady of the Sycamore and the Mistress of Heaven. Snakes are sacred to Hathor and she is also known as the Queen of the Underworld, Eye of Ra and the Serpent Lady. Hathor is shown here with an unnamed pharaoh. Other spellings include Athor, and Athyr. Also see Egyptian Gods and Goddesses, Gods of Heaven, and Underworld Gods.

Haumea
From Hawaiian mythology, Haumea is the Goddess of Procreation, Patroness of childbirth and Goddess of the Sacred Earth from whom the bodies of mankind descend. She is wife of the Sky Father Wakea and the mother of the Goddesses Pele, Kapo and Hi'iaka. She is also known as E Haumea, E Papa, E La'ila'i, E Kamehaikana and the Lonely One. Haumea is depicted here in a 1995 painting (engraved with a descriptive poem honoring her) by American artist Dawn M. Traina (merchantcircle.com). Also see Hawaiian Gods and Goddesses.

Haunting
A Haunting is the phenomena of paranormal activities within a certain place. Paranormal disturbances are usually attributed to the spirits of the dead or ghosts. The phenomena may include moving objects, strange noises, lights, cold spots, unpleasant smells, and the appearance of ghostly figures. Most Hauntings are attributed to discarnate spirits of those who have suffered some sort of violent death or to a place where violent acts occurred such as a battlefield. Also see Ghosts, Most Haunted, Spirit Photography, ghosthuntingsecrets.com, hauntedamericatours.com, headlesshorseman.co.uk and prairieghosts.com.

Haurvatat

In Persian mythology, Haurvatat is one of the six Amesha Spentas or benevolent and immortal beings created by Ahura Mazda as manifestations of himself. He protects water and vegetation and personifies integrity, health and salvation. Haurvatat is also known as Khurdad. See Ahura Mazda, and Amesha Spentas.

Hawaiian Gods and Goddesses

The following Hawaiian Gods and Goddesses are described herein: Akua, Hi'iaka, Haumea, Kanaloa, Kane, Kapo, Laka and Pele. Hawaiian Gods are depicted here in a painting by American artist Herb Kawainui Kane (herbkanestudio.com). Also see Hawaiian Gods and Goddesses.

Hawkes, Joyce

American-born Joyce Whiteley Hawkes Ph.D. is a biophysicist, past Postdoctoral Fellow at the National Institutes of Health, Fellow in the American Association for the Advancement of Science and founder of Healing Arts Associates. She received her Ph.D. in biophysics from Pennsylvania State University, was a postdoctoral fellow with the National Institutes of Health at the Oregon Regional Primate Research Center and worked as supervisory research scientist with the National Marine Fisheries in Seattle, WA and was honored with a U.S. National Achievement Award. Dr. Hawkes earned an international reputation for her contributions to the field of high-speed laser effects on cells and cellular pathology of fish exposed to water-borne toxins. She changed careers for the exploration of spiritual healing traditions after a near death experience in 1984. She currently works as a healer, author, and teacher presenting seminars nationally and internationally. Dr. Hawkes has written: Cell-Level Healing: The Bridge from Soul to Cell, now read in seven languages, and Resonance: Nine Practices for Harmonious Health and Vitality. Also see Healers, Near Death Experiences, Recommended Reading, Scientists, cellevelhealing.com and joycehawkes.com.

Hayagriva

In Tibetan mythology, Hayagriva, meaning "Horse Neck" (shown here) is one of the Wrathful Deities. Also see Tibetan Gods and Goddesses, and Wrathful Deities.

HB of L

See Hermetic Brotherhood of Luxor.

Hcoma

See Tablet of Union.

Healers

All healing is self healing. A healer is a person who has the ability to help others heal themselves. The people mentioned herein who are healers include: Rosemary Altea, Mary Baker Eddy, Franz Bardon, Daniel J. Benor, Rita Straus Berkowitz, Chrissie Blaze, **Rosalyn Bruyere**, Count Alessandro Cagliostro, John Cain, Ruth Carter-Stapleton, Sonia Choquette, Kenneth "Bear Hawk" Cohen, Grace Cooke, Gabriel Cousens, Gerard Croiset, Donna Eden, Marcia Emery, Joel Sol Goldsmith, Richard Gordon, Stuart Grayson, Joyce Hawkes, Daniel Dunglas Home, Sandra Ingerman, Shelley Kaehr, Charlotte Kasl, Deborah King, Daphne Rose Kingma, Dolores Krieger, Kathryn Kuhlman, Nina Kulagina, Denise Linn, Kristin Madden, Mani, Matthew Manning, Tricia McCannon, Lewis Mehl-Madrona, Franz Anton Mesmer, Eric Pearl, Michael Picucci, Phineas Parkhurst Quimby, William Samuel, Agnes Mary Sanford, Francis Schlatter, Betty Shine, Susan Shumsky, John Murray Spear, Chuck Spezzano, Hank Wesselman, Lisa Williams and Maria Yraceburu. Shown here is part of Michelangelo's (michelangelo.com) 1511 painting called The Creation of Adam. Also see Psychic Healing.

Healing Music

See Sound Therapy.

Heard, Gerald

(1889-1971) English-born Henry Fitzgerald Heard aka Gerald Heard was a philosopher, theologian, historian and writer. He studied history and theology at the University of Cambridge and was a council member of the Society for Physical Research. Heard later moved to the United States with his friend Aldous Huxley and held a chair of historical anthropology at Duke University. He settled in California and founded Trabuco College. He wrote over 35 books, including: The Ascent of Humanity: An Essay on the Evolution of Civilization from Group Consciousness Through individuality and Super-Consciousness; The Creed of Christ: An Interpretation of the Lord's Prayer; The Third Morality; The Emergence of Man; Training for the Life of the Spirit and The Five Ages of Man: The Psychology of Human History. Heard is shown here in a 1915 portrait by English artist Glyn Warren Philpot. Also see Philosophers, Recommended Reading, Theologians and geraldheard.com.

Heathen

Originally heathen was the term used to describe people who lived outside of cities, a person of the heath. Now the term is associated with Pagans. Also see Pagans.

Heaven

The term Heaven is generally used to describe the dwelling place of God, Gods, Angels and other spiritual beings, although different religions interpret the concept in different ways. According to the Old Testament Heaven is the abode of Yahweh, later described as the destination of the deceased righteous who would be resurrected to live with God. Jewish mystics regard the Heavens as contained in the seven spheres of the firmament. Christianity describes Heaven as the destination of the believers and followers of Christ. Islam preaches that Heaven is a place of joy to which the faithful Muslims to according to the will of Allah and also recognizes the existence of the seven Heavens of the firmament. Shown here is a painting by American artist Daniel B. Holeman (awakenvisions.com) called Welcome Home. Also see Afterlife, and Summerland.

Heavenly Host

The term used to describe the Angels of Heaven as a whole. Shown here is an 1880 painting by British artist Edward Burne-Jones called The Golden Stairs.

Hebe
See Juventas.

Hecate

Greek Goddess of the Underworld, Hecate is the Patroness of the Priestesses and Goddess. She rules over witches, dark magic, prophesy, charms, spells, transformation, reincarnation, weaving, charms and curses, Earth fertility, storms, revenge and regeneration. Her name comes from the Greek Hekate which means "She Who Works Her Will:" Hecate is the daughter of Perses and Asteria and also known as the Queen of the Witches, Most Lovely One, Queen of the Spirit World, Great Goddess of Nature and the Great Mother. She is often depicted with three heads and bodies. Hecate is depicted here by American artist Sandra Stanton (goddessmyths.com). Also see Greek Gods and Goddesses, and Triple Goddesses.

Hecate

Roman Goddess of Witchcraft, Hecate rules over dark magic, priestesses, charms and spells, riches, enchantment, victory and purification, also known as the Lady of the Wild Hunt, Goddess of Witchcraft and Queen of the Underworld. Other spellings include Hekate. Hecate is shown here in a 1795 painting by English poet and artist William Blake (william-blake.org) called Hecate or the Three Fates. Also see Roman Gods and Goddesses and Underworld Gods.

Hedge Witch
See Solitary Practitioner.

Heimdall

Norse God of Beginnings and Endings, Heimdall rules over seriousness, morning light and defense against evil. His name means "Rainbow", and he is also known as the White God and the Watchman of the Gods. He watches over the Bifrost Bridge which is the entrance to Asgard. Heimdall is one of the Aesir (Gods) of Odhin. Other spellings include Heimdallr and Heimdal. Shown here is an 1895 depiction of Heimdall by Danish artist Lorenz Froelich. Also see Aesir, Asgard, and Norse Gods and Goddesses.

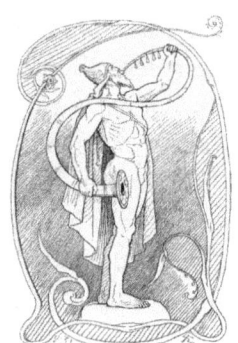

Heka

Ancient Egyptian term for magic.

Heket

Egyptian Moon Goddess, Heket rules over water, fertility and childbirth her giving each infant the breath of life before placing them in the womb. She is the wife of Khnum and is depicted as a woman with a frog's head or simply as a frog. Other spellings include Heqet. Also see Egyptian Gods and Goddesses.

Hel

In Norse mythology, Hel is the lowest of the Nine Worlds; an underworld and the abode of the dead. Hel is shown here in an 1882 depiction by German artist Karl Ehrenberg. Also see Mythological Places, Nine Worlds, Norse Gods and Goddesses, and Underworlds.

Hel

Norse Goddess of the Underworld Hel, Dark Magic, Revenge and Death, Hel is the daughter of Loki and Angerboda and sister of Jormungand and Fenrir Wolf. She is also known as the Queen of the Dead and Queen of the Underworld. Hel rules over Nifelheim or World of Darkness where the souls of those who die of disease or old age go. She is the Daughter of Loki and known as the personification of malice. She is sent by Odhin to live in the world beneath the worlds called Nifelheim. Hel is depicted here in an 1889 rendition by German artist Johannes Gehrts. Other spellings include Hela. Also see Mythological Places, Nine Worlds, Norse Gods and Goddesses and Underworld Gods.

Helios

Ancient Greek God of the Sun, Helios is the son of the Titans Hyperion and Thea, and brother of Eos, Goddess of Dawn and Selene, Goddess of the Moon. Helios rides his golden chariot across the sky every day, giving light to Gods and mortals and every evening he sinks back into the Western Ocean, from which he is carried in a golden cup back to his palace in the East. Shown here is a 1635 painting by Nicolas Poussin (nicolaspoussin.org) called Helios and Phaeton with Saturn and the Four Seasons. Also see Greek Gods and Goddesses.

Hell

The term hell is usually used to describe the abode of evil spirits and dammed souls in after-death punishment. Hell is the absence of God. The concept of hell as a place or a state of being that separates the good souls from the evil souls is found in most religions. Judaism describes hell as an infernal place of punishment for the wicked. Christianity views hell as the fiery domain of the devil and fallen Angels; a place of eternal damnation for those who lived a life of sin and died unrepentant. Hinduism describes hell as a stage in the progress of the soul where it must live until the evil accumulated during it life has been exhausted. Modern views of hell are mostly derived from Dante's Inferno, a part of The Divine Comedy, where Dante 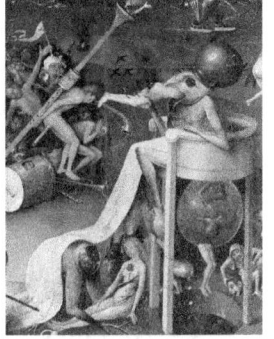 describes in detail, its different levels and punishments for every sin. Shown here is a 1510 painting by Dutch artist Hieronymus Bosch (hieronymus-bosch.org) called The Garden of Earthly Delights. Also see Dante Alighieri, Dante's Inferno and Hell.

Hellhound

See Cerberus.

Hells

The following versions of Hell are described herein: Christian Hell; Jewish Abbadon and Gehenna; and Theosophy's Avichi.

Hephaestus

Greek God of Fire, Forge and Metalwork, son of Zeus and Hera, Hephaestus has dominion over craftsmen such as blacksmiths, pottery makers, jewelry makers and metalworkers. He is also described as the God of Thunder, Lightning, Volcanoes, and Subterranean Fires. He is usually described as crippled, ugly and lame. Hephaestus is called Vulcan by the Romans. He is one of the Olympian Gods. Other spellings include Hephaistos and Hephaestos. Shown here is a 1757 painting by French artist Francois Boucher (francoisboucher.org) called Vulcan Presenting Venus with Arms for Aeneas. Also see Greek Gods and Goddesses, and Olympian Gods.

Heptascopy

Divination by liver, heptascopy examines the liver of sacrificed animals. This form of divination was practiced by the ancient Babylonians, Chinese and Etruscans. Also see Divination.

Hera

Greek Goddess of Heaven, Queen of the Gods, Hera rules over the protection of the home, women, childbirth, children and marriage and of all other aspects of female life. She is the daughter of the Titans Rhea and Cronus, the sister and wife of Zeus and the mother of Hephaestus. Her other siblings are Hestia, Hades, Poseidon and Demeter. Snakes are sacred to her. Hera is also known as the Lady, the Holy One, Mother and Queen of the Gods, Queen of Heaven, Earth Goddess and Great Mother. Hera is called Juno by the Romans. She is one of the Olympian Gods. Other spellings include Here. She is shown here in a 5th Century B.C.E. sculpture by an unknown artist. Also see Greek Gods and Goddesses, Gods of Heaven, and Olympian Gods.

Heracles

See Hercules.

Herb

An herb is a plant or tree that has specific properties and specific uses in medicine, food, religion and magic.

Herbal Magic

Herbal magic can be defined as a process or art that harnesses and directs the natural energies of herbs for magical or healing purposes. Shown here is a young woman gathering narcissus flowers at dawn in a 1912 painting by British artist John William Waterhouse (jwwaterhouse.com) called Narcissus.

Herbalism

Also known as phytotherapy, Herbalism and one of the oldest forms of natural medicine, making use of fresh herbs and natural herb extracts for the process of healing. Shown here are the front and back pages of the 1749 version of Materia Medica, by Greek physician and botanist Pendanius Dioscorides, which describes more than 675 plants and their use in medicine. The original version was written in the 12th Century in Arabic. Also see Therapeutic Systems.

Herbalists

An Herbalist is a person who studies herbs for magical or healing purposes. The people described herein who are considered herbalists include: Paul Beyerl, Stephanie Rose Bird, Nicolas Culpeper, Scott Cunningham, Simon Forman, Geber and Jeanne Rose. Also see Herbal Magic and Herbalism.

Hercules

Greek Demi-God, son of Zeus and legendary hero with superhuman strength, Hercules protects travelers and rules over courage, wine and women. He is also known as Heracles. Shown here is a 1611 painting called The Drunken Hercules by Flemish artist Peter Paul Rubens (peterpaulrubens.org). Also see Greek Gods and Goddesses.

Hereditary Witch

In Wicca hereditary witch is the term used to describe a sensitive who was born into a family of witches. Be these parents, grandparents or aunts and uncles.

Heresy

Heresy is a religious or theological doctrine or opinion maintained contrary to any church, creed or religious system considered orthodox.

Heretic

A heretic is a person whose beliefs differ from the accepted beliefs of their religion. Also see Heresy.

Hermes

Greek God of Magic and Philosophy, son of Zeus and Maia, Hermes is the Patron of the Alchemists. He rules over roads, fertility, fortune, profit, commerce, occult wisdom, astronomy, astrology, divination, music, reincarnation and diplomacy. He is often depicted as wearing winged sandals and a winged hat, carrying a golden caduceus. As the Leader of Souls, He takes the dead to the Underworld and influences the dreams of mortals. He is also known as the Messenger of the Gods and the Ram Bearer. Hermes is known to the Romans as Mercury. He is one of the Olympian Gods. He is depicted here in a

1585 painting by Flemish artist Bartholomaeus Spranger called Hermes and Atenea (Athena). Also see Greek Gods and Goddesses, Olympian Gods and Underworld Gods.

Hermes Trismegistus

Meaning "Hermes the thrice great", Hermes Trismegistus was the mythical founder of Hermeticism, supposedly an Egyptian priest and occultist, (or the Greek God Hermes and the Egyptian God Thoth merged into one figure), alleged author of the 42 books that are collectively known as Hermetic Literature. These writings deal with mysticism, religion, philosophy, astrology, medicine, magic and alchemy. Hermes Trismegistus has also been described as the Egyptian God Toth. Depicted here is a portrait of Hermes Trimegistus from a 1488 mosaic on the floor of the Siena Cathedral attributed to Italian artist Sassetta called Tabula Smaragdina. Other spellings include Hermes Trimegistos. Also see Hermeticism.

Hermetic Brotherhood of Luxor

Also called H.B. of L., the Hermetic Brotherhood of Luxor was an occult brotherhood founded in 1870 by Max Theon who was the Grand Master of the Exterior Circle of the Order. Prior to the Hermetic Order of the Holden Dawn the Hermetic Brotherhood of Luxor was the only order that taught practical occultism in the Western Mystery Tradition and among its members were many Theosophists, spiritualists and occultists. The order was one of the first to use correspondence courses and in 1886 when the knowledge became public that two of its members had been convicted for mail fraud the order became all but extinct. Also see Occult Orders, Brotherhoods and Secret Societies and Max Theon.

Hermeticism

Relating to Hermes Trismegistus and the 42 works ascribed to him. Hermeticism, also called Hermetic Magic, is a system of magic based on the Hermetic Literature probably dating from the 1st Century B.C.E. It is divided into two classes, the first class deals with the Occult, especially Ceremonial Magic, Alchemy and Astrology, and the second class deals with Philosophy, Mysticism and Theology. This doctrine, which is mainly Greek in origin, includes some Christian Mysticism and makes references to Egyptian magic and healing techniques. Other spellings include Hermetica. Also see Philosophical and Mystical Movements, gnosis.org, hermetic.com, and hermeticfellowship.org.

Hermeticists

Relating to Hermeticism, the Hermeticists described herein include: Mary Ann Atwood, Franz Bardon, John Dee, Edward Kelly, Anna Kingsford, Heinrich Khunrath, Sir Isaac Newton and Valentin Tomberg. Also see Hermeticism.

Hermit

From the Greek meaning "desert" a hermit is a person who lives in seclusion from society. Shown here is an 1888 painting by Russian artist Mikhail Nesterov called the Spiritual Hermit.

Hermit

The Hermit is one of the 22 major arcana of the tarot deck of cards. Its number is IX, its Qabbalistic title is The Prophet of the Gods and The Magus of the Voice of Light and its meaning is: divine inspiration and wisdom. Also see Tarot.

Hermod
In Norse mythology, Hermod is the Messenger of the Gods. He is the son of Frigga and Odhin and is called the Valiant in Combat, Hermod the Bold and Hermod the Swift. He wears a helmet and coat of mail that were given to him by Odhin and carries his magic staff Gambantaein. Hermod is shown from in a 16th Century Icelandic Text. Also see Norse Gods and Goddesses.

Hespere
In Greek mythology, Hespere is a nymph, one of three sisters called the Hesperides. Shown here is an 1870 painting by British artist Sir Edward Burne-Jones called Hesperus, The Evening Star. Also see Greek Gods and Goddesses, and Hesperides.

Hesperides
In Greek mythology the Hesperides are Triple Goddesses, sister nymphs, daughters of Atlas and Hesperis. They guard the golden apple tree given to Hera as a wedding present, but are later replaced by a dragon, when Hera realizes they have been stealing the apples. They are: Aegle, Erytheis, and Hespere, depicted here in an 1873 painting by British artist Sir Edward Burne-Jones called The Garden of Hesperides. Also see Greek Gods and Goddesses, and Triple Goddesses.

Hestia

Greek Virgin Goddess of the Hearth and Fire, Hestia rules over humility, prudence, modesty, continuity and service to others. She is the eldest daughter of the Titans Cronus and Rhea and sister of Zeus, Hera, Hades, Poseidon and Demeter. Her name means "home and hearth" and she presides over all sacrificial altar fires, including the sacred fire on Mount Olympus. Hestia is known as Vesta by the Romans. She is one of the Olympian Gods. Her Roman counterpart is Vesta. Shown here is a painting of Vesta-Hestia by American Artist Sandra Stanton (goddessmyths.com). Also see Greek Gods and Goddesses, and Olympian Gods.

Hex
See Curse.

Hexagram

Also called the Star of David, the hexagram is a geometric figure with six points, formed from two interlocking triangles. In Hermetic literature the Hexagram symbolizes the principle of "as above, so below". It was defined by the Golden Dawn as a "Powerful symbol representing the operation of the seven planets under the presidency of the Sephiroth and the name Ararita". The hexagram is used in rituals to invoke or banish planetary forces. It is also used in the I Ching divinatory system. Also see I Ching and Star of David.

Hexagrams

The hexagrams according to the Chinese I Ching divinatory system are 64 symbols made from 8 basic triagrams. These are then cast in lots of six hexagrams six times to determine the oracle of I Ching. Image from sacred-texts.com. Also see I Ching, Triagrams, iching.com and zhouyi.com.

Hidden Masters

The Hidden Masters, also called the Great White Brotherhood were described by Madame Blavatsky as an Esoteric Brotherhood of superhuman beings with mystical powers, who live hidden in Tibet, who watch over humanity. The Golden Dawn also professes the existence of Hidden Masters and describes them as Adepts in the Occult arts, interested in the welfare of humanity and who intervene to guide and assist the human race in its spiritual evolution. Dion Fortune called the Hidden Masters as the Inner Plane Adepti and said that they ultimately ran her own order, the Society of the Inner Light. Shown here is a 2008 painting by American artist Gilbert Williams (gilbertwilliams.com) called The Old Man. Also see Ascended Masters, Spiritual Teachers, Wrathful Deities, and Silent Watchers.

Hierarch

A Hierarch is a High Priest, one in position of authority in a religious hierarchy.

Hieroglyphics

See Egyptian Hieroglyphs.

Hierophant

In Occultism the Hierophant is described as the Chief of the Adepts who delivers the knowledge of the sacred mysteries to the neophytes at initiations.

Hierophant

From the Greek Hierophantes meaning "displayer of Holy things" the Hierophant is described as the interpreter and discloser of sacred Esoteric Mysteries and principles. In ancient Greece the Hierophant was the chief of the Eleusian cult, whose job was to chant sacred hymns during magical rituals and celebrations. Also see Eleusian Mysteries.

Hierophant

The Hierophant is one of the 22 major arcana of the tarot deck of cards. Its number is V, its Qabbalistic title is Chief Among the Mighty and its meaning is: divine wisdom, manifestation, teaching, explanation and occult wisdom. Also see Tarot.

Hierophany

From the Greek hieros meaning "sacred" and epiphaneia meaning "appearance, hierophany is a manifestation or encounter of the sacred.

High Priestess

The High Priestess or Female Pope is one of the 22 major arcana of the tarot deck of cards. Its number is II, its Qabbalistic title is Priestess of the Silver Star and its meaning is: change, alteration, fluctuation, increase and decrease. Also see Tarot.

High Priestess

A High Priestess is a female follower of the Wicca religion (and other Pagan and nature based religions) who has reached a high status within the religion, usually involving at least three initiations. Also see Wicca.

Higher Self

Occultism describes the higher self as the inner conscience or God within, as the part of the personality which survives death and may eventually reincarnate and the part of the spirit which is direct contact with the Divine. From a Qabbalistic point of view, the higher self is the personification of the transcendent spiritual self which acts as a mediator and communicator between the divine self, and the lower personality. The higher self is also called the inner genius. Shown here is a painting by Canadian artist Mario Duguay (marioduguay.com) called Being Light.

Hi'iaka

In Hawaiian mythology, Hi'iaka is the patron Goddess of Hawaii and Hawaiian hula dancers. She is the daughter of Haumea and Kane and sister of Pele. Shown here is a 20th Century painting by American artist Linda Rowell-Stevens (lindaspaintings.com) called Hi'iaka and Hopoe. Also see Hawaiian Gods and Goddesses.

Hill, Napoleon

(1883-1970) American-born Napoleon Hill was a bestselling author of self-help books including a few of the all time bestsellers. As part of his research for his books, he interviewed some of the most famous people of the time including: Alexander Graham Bell, Andrew Carnegie, Thomas Edison, John D. Rockefeller, Theodore Roosevelt, William H. Taft, Woodrow Wilson and Henry Ford. Hill was also an informal advisor to Presidents Franklin Roosevelt and Woodrow Wilson. He also dealt with many controversial subjects in his books such as slavery, revolution, war, poverty and racism. Among his books are: Think and Grow Rich (one of the all time best selling books); How to Sell Your Way Through Life; Success Through a Positive Mental Attitude; The Law of Success; Grow Rich Through Persuasion and The Master Key to Riches. Also see Recommended Reading, Self-Help and naphill.org.

Hillfolk
See Trolls.

Hindu Gods and Goddesses

The following Hindu Gods and Goddesses are described herein: Aditi, Agni, Bhaga, Brahma, Brihaspati, Chandra, Devi, Diti, Durga, Ganesha, Ganga, Hanuman, Indra, Indrani, Jnana-Dashinamurti, Jyeshtha, Kali, Kama, Kami, Karttikeya, Ketu, Krishna, Kubera, Laksmi, Madira, Mangala, Maru, Nidra, Parvati, Puchan, Rahu, Rati, Rudra, Sarasvati, Shakti, Shani, Shiva, Shukra, Siva Lingodbhava, Surya, Tara, Tvashtar, Uma, Varuna, Vayu, Vishnu and Visvakarman. Image from scriptures.ru.

Hinduism

Religion and philosophy based on the teachings of the Indian Vedas, Upanishads and Bhagavad-Gita (Holy Books) and the doctrines of karma and reincarnation. Hinduism differs from other religions in that it doesn't have a single founder and has evolved from many different religions for over 3,000 years. A few the main mystic teachings of Hinduism are the belief in karma and the practice of Yoga, and its ultimate goal is mystical transcendence to escape from the world of maya (illusion) through the union with Brahma, the divine. The main Deities of Hinduism are Brahma, the Creator, Vishnu, the Savior and Shiva, the Destroyer/Restorer, but there are also many other Gods, spirits and devils. Hindu festivals vary by area. The main ones are: Maha Shivratri is the night of Shiva when from midnight to dawn Lord Shiva is prayed to and honored. People give offerings of milk and flowers in the temples at sunrise; Holi is a very happy celebration where people through dyes at each other and dance and play tricks; Ram Naumi celebrates the birthday of Lord Rama, the incarnation of Lord Vishnu. For 8 days leading to the birthday there is a continual recital of Ramayana in pious homes, with final offerings made to Lord Rama in the temples on the day; Rakhi or Raksha Bandhan is the festival when sisters tie a thread or string with flowery decorations on the wrists of their brothers and in return the brothers give the girls presents and money. The Rakhi is kept on the wrist for a week with a promise of protection for the sisters and the vow is renewed each year; Janmashtami is the birthday of Lord Krishna and it is celebrated by bathing an image of Lord Krishna in milk and honey and people pray and sing hymns, Ganesh Chauth or Ganesh Charurthi is a celebration of Lord Ganesha's day; Dussehra marks the victory of Lord Rama over King Ravana who had kidnapped Sita. People burn Ravana's huge effigies and celebrate with plays performed in every town and fun fairs that last for a week; Diwali or Deepwali is the largest festival and celebrates the homecoming of Lord Rama from the 14 year exile after his victory over the evil forces. People celebrate by lighting lamps and burning fireworks. It is also the day when the Goddess Laksmi, representing wealth, is prayed to and the houses are left lit at night to welcome her. Other spellings include Hindooism. Also see Religions, atributetohinduism.com, hindu.com, hindubooks.org, hinduism.net, hinduofuniverse.com, indiadivine.org, mudrashram.com, om-guru.com, om-sweet-om.net and religioustolerance.com.

Hino

In Iroquois mythology, Hino is the God of the Sky and Thunder. He is a benevolent God whose consort is the Rainbow. Hino destroys evil beings with his arrows. Also see Iroquois Gods and Goddesses.

Hippocampus

In Roman mythology the Hippocampus is a mythical creature, half horse half fish that draw Neptune's and Amphitrite's chariots. Other spellings include Hippocampos. Shown here is an 18th Century depiction of a Hippocampus. Also see Mythological Creatures.

Hippogriff

In Greek mythology the hippogriff, also called Buckbeak is the offspring of a griffin and a mare. In medieval legends the hippogriff appears as a familiar to either a sorcerer or a knight and is said to fly as fast as lightning. Shown here is an 1819 painting of a hippogriff by French artist Jean Auguste Dominique Ingres called Roger Delivering Angelica. Other spellings include Hippogryph and Hippogryphe. Also see Familiars, and Mythological Creatures.

Hippomancy

Divination by horses, hippomancy interprets omens from the appearance, behavior, and neighing of horses. Also see Divination.

Hismael

In Occult and Qabbalistic literature, Hismael is the Spirit of the planets Jupiter and Venus and who rules over the zodiac signs of Sagittarius and Pisces. Also see Planetary Spirits.

Historical Apparitions

Historical Apparitions refer to the manifested presence of Ghosts in a historical context. Such apparitions are more commonly found around battlefields and sites of massacres or great historical violence and may include visions of battles with auditory phenomena. These apparitions are considered as psychic imprints on space and time rather than Ghosts per se. Shown here is a 20th Century painting called Knight of the Valley by American artist John Paul Strain (johnpaulstrain.com). Also see Apparition, Anniversary Ghosts, Gettysburg, Ghosts, Hauntings and Imprinting.

Historians

The historians herein include: Cornelius Agrippa, Riane Tennenhaus, Sir James Frazer, Andrew Lang, Robert Moss, John G. Neihardt, Ross Nichols, Posidonius, Richard Tarnas and Dame Francis Yates.

Hnossa

Norse Goddess, one of the Vanir Gods that live in Vanaheim. She is shown here with Heimdall in a 1920 rendition by Hungarian artist Willy Pogany called Heimdall and Little Hnossa. Also see Norse Gods and Goddesses, and Vanir.

Hobgoblins

In Scottish and Irish mythology, Hobgoblins are described as friendly Earth Elementals. Other spellings include Robgoblin and Hobbolinet. Hobgoblins are shown here in a 1799 depiction by Spanish artist Francisco Jose de Goya (franciscodegoya.net). Also see Elementals.

Hocus Pocus

Term used since the 17th Century as a preface of a bogus spell or conjuring tricks. It may have come from a corruption of the Latin hoc est corpus, meaning "this is my body", words of the act of transubstantiation in the Roman Catholic Mass.

Hod

The eighth Sephirah on the Qabbalistic Tree of Life whose symbols are mantras, mandalas and the eight pointed star and who represents splendor. See Tree of Life.

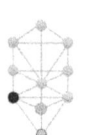

Hoder

Norse God of Darkness, Hoder is a blind God; he is the son of Frigga and Odhin and twin brother of Balder. He is the God of Winter, night and snow. He is one of the Aesir (Gods) of Odhin. Other spellings include Hodur and Hod. Hoder is shown here in an 1840 painting of Norse Gods by Danish artist Christopher Wilhelm Eckersberg called The Death of Balder. He is the one with the outstretched arms. Also see Aesir, and Norse Gods and Goddesses.

Hoenir

Norse God, Hoenir is the God of Silence. He is one of the Aesir (Gods) of Odhin. Hoenir is shown here in a 18th Century Icelandic manuscript with Loki and Hoenir. Also see Aesir, and Norse Gods and Goddesses.

Holda

Norse Goddess of Fate, Holda rules over children, witchcraft, dark magic and revenge. She is also called White Lady, Goddess of winter and witchcraft and Black Earth Mother. Shown here is an 1893 painting by French artist William Adolphe Bouguereau (bouguereau.org) called Alma Parens. Other spellings include Holde, Holle and Hulda. Also see Norse Gods and Goddesses.

Holi

One of the main Hindu festivals and also known as the Festival of Colours, Holi is a very happy celebration where people throw dyes at each other and dance and play tricks. Also see Hinduism.

Holism

From Greek holos meaning, "entire", "total", Holism refers to all the properties of a given system, meaning the system as a whole determines how the parts behave. It can also be defined as a theory that all reality is one and everything in the universe is interrelated and interdependent. Shown here is the Ptolemaic System from Dutch cartographer Andreas Cellarius' 1660 Harmonia Macrocosmica showing the signs of the zodiac and the solar system with the world in the center.

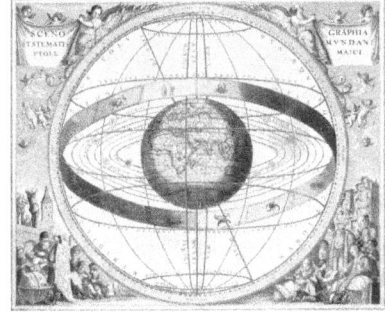

Holistic

The consideration of a whole being or thing to be more than a collection of pieces or parts; such as treating a person as a whole, (mentally, physically and spiritually) and not just the symptoms of a disease. Also see Disease, Healers, Holistic Healing Naturopathy, Therapeutic Systems, holistic-alt.com, holisticlearningcenter.com, holisticmedicine.org, holisticonline.com, holisticpr.com and holisticuniversity.org.

Holistic Healing

Holistic healing is a philosophy that deals with the whole human being, as in mind, body and spirit when treating a disease. The people described herein who study and or practice holistic healing include: Hunter "Patch" Adams, Ted Andrews, Rudolph Ballentine, Fadel Behman, Daniel J. Benor, Harvey Bigelsen, Chrissie Blaze, Annemarie Colbin, Gerald Epstein, Richard Gordon, Shelley Kaehr, Leonard Laskow, Elizabeth Lipski, Nancy Mramor, Christiane Northrup, Michele O'Donnell, Kenneth R. Pelletier, John C. Pierrakos, Swami Rama, Linda Salvin, Norman Shealy, David Simon and Andrew Weil. Also see Holistic and Therapeutic Systems.

Holmes, Ernest

(1887-1960) American-born Ernest Shurtleff Holmes was a spiritual teacher, founder of Religious Science and author of several books. He was the last student accepted by Emma Curtis Hopkins, founder of New Thought. He developed a simple technique of healing prayer and through his Institute of Religious Science and School of Philosophy trained others in his methods in what came to be known as Science of Mind. His best known books are Creative Mind: Tapping the Power Within; Can We Talk to God?; This Thing Called Life; Mind Remakes Your World: How to Think Yourself Into Better Health, Greater Happiness, and More Success as Proved by 36 Leading Exponents of New Thought and New Thought Terms and Their Meanings: A Dictionary of the Terms and Phrases Commonly Used in Metaphysical and Psychological Study. Also see New Thought, Recommended Reading, Spiritual Teachers and ernestholmes.wwwhubs.com.

Holotropic Communication

Holotropic communication is communication with the infinite, a message that is so understood and intuited that it leads to no further questions breaking through self-imposed barriers of beliefs to impress the knowledge of total consciousness. This communications comes from infinite knowledge, complete and perfect, from oneness.

Holos University Graduate Seminary

Founded by Dr. C. Norman Shealy, the Holos University Graduate Seminary (or HU) **(in its own words) prepares students to integrate Universal Principles of Spirituality and Holistic Health through self-development, scholarly exploration and research, and compassionate service.** The mystical traditions of virtually all religions contain substantial references that address the subtle physical energies of

the body, the transpersonal aspects of the mind, and the expressive activity of the spirit. These traditions exist at the very core of holistic mysticism, spiritual direction, counseling intuition, transformational psychology, and integrative healthcare. Holos University Graduate Seminary emphasizes ecumenical spiritual approaches that fulfill a growing need for an inclusive, holistic, and creative approach to life in contemporary communities. Also see New Age Associations and Societies, Norman Shealy, holosuniversity.org and holosuniversity.net.

Holotropic Breathwork

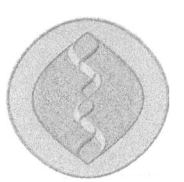

Founded by Cristina and Stanislav Grof, Holotropic Breathwork is (in their own words) a powerful approach to self-exploration and healing that integrates insights from modern consciousness research, anthropology, various depth psychologies, transpersonal psychology, Eastern spiritual practices, and mystical traditions of the world. The name Holotropic means literally "moving toward wholeness" (from the Greek "holos"=whole and "trepein"=moving in the direction of something). The process itself uses very simple means: it combines accelerated breathing with evocative music in a special set and setting. With the eyes closed and lying on a mat, each person uses their own breath and the music in the room to enter a non-ordinary state of consciousness. This state activates the natural inner healing process of the individual's psyche, bringing him or her, a particular set of internal experiences. With the inner healing intelligence guiding the process, the quality and content brought forth is unique to each person and for that particular time and place. While recurring themes are common, no two sessions are ever alike. Also see Christina Grof, Stanislav Grof, New Age Associations and Societies, and breathwork.com, grof-holotropic-breathwork.net and holotropic.com.

Holy

Belonging to, derived from, or associated with divine power; sacred. Holiness is the state of being Holy, or, set apart for the worship or service of God or Gods. The term Holy can be ascribed to people as well as objects, times, or places. The concept is found in almost all religions.

Holy Chalice

In Christian literature and religious tradition, the Holy Chalice is the cup that Jesus Christ used at the Last Supper. This particular chalice was made in 2439 by Russian goldsmith Ivan Fomin. Also see Holy Grail.

Holy Friday

See Good Friday.

Holy Ghost

According to Christianity the Holy Ghost, also called Holy Spirit, is the third being in the Holy Trinity, the others being God the Father and his son (Jesus Christ). The Holy Ghost is usually regarded as female and is also called Paraclete. Shown here is a 1732 painting by French artist Jean Restout called Pentecost, showing the descent of the Holy Ghost.

Holy Grail

The Holy Grail, also called Sangreal, is in medieval Christian literature, the vessel that caught Jesus Christ's blood during his crucifixion. Some legends that surround this vessel are much much older than the advent of Jesus Christ. A few hold that the Holy Grail is an emerald from the crown of Lucifer, the Light Bringer, others say that Seth, son of Adam and Eve found it in the Garden of Eden when he was searching for medicine to cure his father. A few Christian historians believe that the Holy Grail was taken from Palestine to Britain by Joseph of Arimathea and hidden near Glastonbury. Various other tales of the Grail are related to Arthurian legend. There are even other theories including one that says that the Holy Grail was Mary Magdalene and suggests that she had a child with Jesus (hence Holy Grail) and had to flee to with the child to France to escape persecution. Shown here is an 1857 painting by British artist Dante Gabriel Rossetti (rossettiarchive.org) called The Holy Grail.

Holy Saturday

Christian Holy day that celebrates the Sabbath on which Jesus rested in the grave. See Christianity, and Holy Week.

Holy Thursday

Christian Holy day that celebrates the Last Supper of Jesus and the apostles and the betrayal of Jesus by Judas. Shown here is a 1955 rendition of the Last Supper by Spanish surrealist painter Salvador Dali (dali-gallery.com). See Christianity, and Holy Week.

Holy Week

In Christianity the Holy Week is the week before Easter, commemorating events in the last days of Christ's life. It begins on Palm Sunday and ends on Easter Monday and includes: Palm Sunday (also called Passion Sunday), the entrance of Jesus into Jerusalem; Holy Thursday (also called Maundy Thursday),Last Supper and the betrayal of Jesus by Judas; Good Friday (also called Holy Friday), the arrest, trial, crucifixion, death and burial of Jesus Christ; and Holy Saturday, the Sabbath on which Jesus rested in the grave.

Holzer, Hans

(1920-2009) Austrian-born Hans Holzer was a well known parapsychologist and prolific author. He wrote more than 140 books on the occult as well as documentaries, films plays and musicals. He worked with psychics such as Sybil Leek and investigated many prominent haunted places. Some of his books include: Ghosts I've Met; The Psychic Side of Dreams; The Aquarian Age: Is There Intelligent Life on Earth?; Love Beyond the Grave; Life Beyond:

Compelling Evidence for Past Lives and Existence After Death; The Directory of Psychics: How to Find, Evaluate, and Communicate with Professional Psychics and Mediums and Are You Psychic: Unlocking the Power Within. Also see Parapsychologists and Psychic Researchers, Recommended Reading and hauntingholzer.com.

Home, Daniel Dunglas

(1833-1886) Scottish-born Daniel Dunglas Home was a famous spiritualist, healer and medium of his time. He was born into a family with a history of mediumship and clairvoyance. His mother foretold her own death soon after immigrating to the United States, correctly so. He was asked to leave the house where he lived with an aunt at age 18 due to poltergeist phenomena including rapping because it was believed that he was producing it. Home could also reportedly levitate himself, furniture and handle hot coals without injury, claims that were made by several people over time. Home conducted hundreds of séances in 25 years including for Napoleon III and Queen Sophie of the Netherlands. He accepted payment because he believed he was on "a mission to demonstrate immortality", although he did accept gifts and lodging. He was investigated by several people who stated that they did not believe he was fraudulent. Also see Healers, Levitation, Mediums, Poltergeist and Spiritualists.

Homeopathy

Term coined by Christian Hahnemann in the late 1700's to describe an alternative medicine system which aims to treat "like with like". Homeopathic treatment consists of giving the patient extremely small doses of substances that produce the same symptoms in healthy people. The people described herein who study Homeopathy include: Harvey Bigelsen, Melanie J. Grimes, Christine Page, Paracelsus, Beverly Rubik and Edward Christopher Whitmont. Photo from nativeremedies.com. Also see Therapeutic Systems, abchomeopathy.com, homeopathic.org, homeopathyhome.com and wholehealthnow.com.

Honorian Alphabet
See Theban Alphabet.

Hoodoo
Ancient African magical tradition, Hoodoo was "exported" when West African slaves where brought to the United States in the 1800's. Also see Religions.

Hoodoo Sea
See Bermuda Triangle.

Hope
See Virtues.

Horae
In Greek mythology the Horae, meaning "hours" are three Goddesses who represent Spring, Summer and Winter. They are daughters of Zeus and Themis. They are: Dike, Goddess of Justice and Winter; Eirene, Goddess of Peace, Springtime and Riches; and Eunomia, Goddess of Good Order and Summer. Other spellings include Horai. Also see Greek Gods and Goddesses, and Triple Goddesses. They are shown here in an 1894 painting by British artist Sir Edward John Poynter called Horae Serenae.

Horaios
In to Gnosticism and Orphics, Horaios is one of seven Archons or planetary spirit rulers. See Archons.

Horn
In Norse mythology, Horn is one of the Vanir Gods that live in Vanaheim. Also see Norse Gods and Goddesses, and Vanir.

Horned God
In Wiccan and Pagan traditions the Horned God is the God of Nature, consort to the Goddess. The Horned God is one of the oldest forms of male Gods. Shown here is the Celtic God Cernunnos on the 100 Century B.C.E. Gundestrup Cauldron (a richly decorated silver vessel) by an unknown artist, housed in the National Museum of Denmark in Copengagen. Also see Wicca.

Horniman, Annie

(1860-1937) Irish-born Annie Elizabeth Fredericka Horniman was a well known dramatist, theatre manager, occultist and diviner of her time and member of the Golden Dawn. She was the granddaughter of a wealthy Quaker tea merchant (who invented the tea bag) and the daughter of a Member of Parliament. After she received a substantial inheritance from her grandfather she became a major financial backer of MacGregor Mathers. She also established the Abbey Theatre in Dublin and the Gaiety Theatre in Manchester. She later resigned from the Golden Dawn and joined the Quest Society formed by George R.S. Mead. She was friends with several famous people of her time including George Bernard Shaw and W. B. Yeats. From a conservative upbringing she rebelled and explored alternative religions, smoked in public and lectured on subjects including women's suffrage. She was awarded an honorary M.A. by Manchester University. Also see Diviners, Golden Dawn and Occultists.

Horoscope

A horoscope is the astrological delineation of the planets position and the signs of the zodiac at a particular time and place, as in birth, that reflects on a person's character and destiny. It is described by a circle, called an ecliptic which is the plane on which the Earth orbits the Sun. A natal horoscope is also referred to as an Astral Chart or a Birth Chart. See Astrology, Zodiac, astro.com, astrology.com, daily-horoscopes.com, horoscope.com and zodiac-signs-astrology.com.

Horse

In Chinese Astrology, the horse is one of the 12 animals of the zodiac. People born in the year of the horse are described as attractive, impatient and popular. Also see Chinese Zodiac.

Horse Whispering

As a method for communicating with horses, horse whispering is used by certain persons who are then able to manage horses. Gypsies have been traditionally reputed to be excellent horse whisperers. Photograph by Carol Walker (livingimagescjw.com). Also see Animal Communication Specialist, horsewhisperer.com, montyroberts.com and wayofthehorse.org.

Horus

Egyptian Falcon headed Sun and Sky God. He is the son of Osiris and Isis, and is described as being fair haired and having blue eyes. Horus is commonly associated with the sacred cats. He is the ruler of mankind and Heaven and God of Light and Goodness. He is also called He Who is Above and Lord of Prophesy. Other spellings include Hor or Har. The symbol of the Eye of Horus is considered a powerful amulet. Also see Egyptian Gods and Goddesses, Eye of Horus and Gods of Heaven.

Hoturu

In Pawnee mythology, Hoturu is the Wind Spirit. Also see Pawnee Gods and Goddesses.

Houngan

A Priest of the Voodoo religion who acts as shaman, teacher, healer and spiritual guide to the living, a Houngan is an expert magician. See Spiritual Teachers and Voodoo.

Houses of Heaven

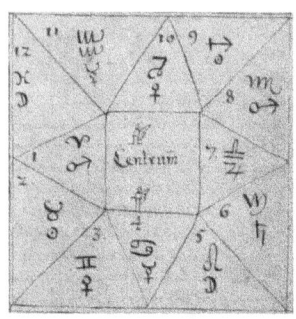

In Astrology, the whole of Heaven is divided into four equal parts by the Meridian and Horizon, and again into four quadrants, and every quadrant again into three parts, according to other circles drawn by points of sections of the aforesaid Meridian and Horizon; so the whole Heaven is divided into twelve equal parts, which the Astrologers call Houses or Mansions. The Houses of Heaven are shown here from a 1747 Icelandic manuscript. Also see Astrology. There are twelve Houses of Heaven with the following descriptions: the first house refers to life, health and questions; the second house refers to money, prosperity and personal wealth; the third house refers to brothers, sisters, news, and short journeys; the fourth house refers to father, property, inheritance, the grave and the end of matter; the fifth House refers to children, pleasure, speculation and feasts; the sixth house refers to uncles and aunts, servants, illnesses and small animals; the seventh house refers to love, marriage, husband and wife, associations and partnerships, law suits and public enemies; the eighth house refers to deaths, legacies, wills, pain, and anxiety; the ninth house refers to voyages, long journeys, science, art, religion, visions and divinations; the tenth house refers to rank and honor, mothers, professions, authority, employment and worldly position; the eleventh house refers to hopes, wishes and friends; and the twelfth house refers to punishments, fears, sorrows, secret enemies, prisons and hospitals, restrictions and dangers. The houses of heaven are shown here from an 18th Century Icelandic manuscript.

Howard, Vernon

(1918-1992) American-born Vernon Linwood Howard was a spiritual teacher, speaker, philosopher and author. Although he did not teach a specific philosophical or spiritual school of thought, he drew from what he called "common thread" among Christianity, Eastern Mysticism, Gospels of the New Testament, teachings of Gurdjieff, Jungian psychology and American Transcendentalism. He founded the non-profit learning center New Life Foundation where he taught until his death. Among his books are: Cosmic Command; The Mystic Path to Cosmic Power; Psycho-Pictography: The New Way Use the Miracle Power of Your Mind; Treasury of Positive Answers; Esoteric Encyclopedia of Eternal Knowledge; and Pathways to Perfect Living. Photograph from superwisdom.com. Also see Jungian Analysts, Philosophers, Recommended Reading, Spiritual Teachers, anewlife.org and vernonhoward.wwwhubs.com.

HU

See Holos University Graduate Seminary.

Huacas

In Incan mythology, Huacas are stone forms and or carvings inhabited with nature spirits of who watch over fields. Shown here is the Huacas del Arcoiris (rainbow) found in Trujillo, Peru. Also see Nature Spirits and huacas.com.

Huaillepenyi

In Araucanian (Chile) mythology Huaillepenyi is the God of Fog. Also see Araucanian Gods and Goddesses.

Huallepen

In Araucanian (Chile) mythology a Huallepen is an amphibious creature with the head of a cow and the body of a sheep. Legend says that if a pregnant woman dreams about a Huallepen for three nights in a row, she will bear a defective baby. Other spellings include Guallipen. Also see Mythological Creatures.

Hubbard, L. Ron

(1911-1986) American-born Lafayette Ronald Hubbard, known as L. Ron Hubbard was a prolific writer, founder of a self-help system called Dianetics. He created the Hubbard Dianetics Research Foundations which grew into the Church of Scientology. Hubbard received his M.A. in civil engineering at the George Washington University. During World War II Hubbard served in the U.S. Navy with the rank of lieutenant, working briefly in navel intelligence. His most famous books are Dianetics: The Modern Science of Mental Health; Scientology: A New Slant on Life and Scientology: The Fundamentals of Thought. Also see Church of Scientology, Dianetics, Recommended Reading, Self-Help, dianetics.org and lronhubbard.com.

Huehuecoyotl

Aztec God of Gaiety, Uninhibited Sexuality and Irrational Fun, known as a mischievous Deity, a shape-shifter and trickster God who plays tricks on other Gods and humans. Huehuecoyotl means "old, old coyote". He is often depicted laughing and shaking a rattle and a flower. Other spellings include Ueuecoyotl. Huehuecoyotl is depicted here in a 16th Century rendition from the Codex Telleriano-Remensis. Also see Aztec Gods and Goddesses.

Huehueteotl

Aztec God of Fire; domestic, ritual and spiritual fire, Huehueteotl rules the calendar. He is Patron of Warriors and Kings and represents wisdom and experience. His name means "old, old God" but he is also called the Turquoise Lord. He is often depicted as an old man with wrinkled skin sitting with a bowl of incense on his head. Other spellings include Xiuhtecuhtli. Also see Aztec Gods and Goddesses.

Huginn

In Norse mythology, Huginn is one of the two (the other being Muninn) ravens of the God Odhin. Huginn is the raven who represents "thought" while Muninn represents "memory". Huginn and Muninn travel the world from dawn to dusk and then perch on Odhin's shoulders and whisper the news in his ear. Shown here is a 2009 painting by British artist Andy Paciorek (batcow.co.uk) called Corpse Birds. Other spellings include Hugin. Also see Mythological Creatures and Odhin.

Hugo, Victor

(1802-1885) French-born Victor Marie Hugo was an essayist, novelist, poet and human rights activist. He was considered the leader of the French literary school known as the Romanticists. He was good friends with Charles Nodier with whom he traveled to Switzerland. He had a lifelong interest in Occultism, Gnosticism and Hermeticism. The shortest correspondence in history is said to have happened between Hugo and his publisher, when while on vacation, his book Les Miserables was published. He telegraphed '?' to his publisher who answered '!'. Hugo was elected a member of the Legion of Honor in 1845. He is mentioned in the Dossier Secrets as Grand Master of the Prieure de Sion. Photograph taken by French photographer Etienne Carjat. Also see Dossier Secrets, Gnostics, Human Rights Activists, Poets, Prieure de Sion and hugo-online.org.

Huitzilopochtli

Aztec War God who rules over the Sun, Huitzilopochtli is the son of Coatlicue and the brother of Quetzalcoatl. He presides over warriors, death, war, young men, storms and safe journeys. Huitzilopochtli's name derives from the Aztec huitzilin, meaning "hummingbird" and he is also called the Left Handed Humming Bird. Prisoners of war and warriors were sacrificed to him each year, under the belief that after four years they would incarnate as hummingbirds. Other spellings include Uitzilopochtli. Huitzilopochtli is depicted here in a 16th Century rendition from the Codex Telleriano-Remensis. Also see Aztec Gods and Goddesses.

Human Rights Activists

The people described herein who deal (or dealt) with human rights include: Leonardo Boff, Raphael Cushnir, Victor Hugo and John Shelby Spong.

Hun Pic Tok

Maya War God also called Eight Thousand Stone Knives. One of the most important pyramid temples in Izamal, Yucatan was built in his honor. Also see Maya Gods and Goddesses.

Huna
Huna is the native religion, ancient secret science and philosophy of the people of the Hawaiian Islands. The priests, known as Kahunas, meaning "Keepers of the Secrets", are practitioners of traditional ancient magic and are said to have the ability to heal or to curse and to see and change the future. There are many similarities between ancient Egyptian initiation and Huna initiation. The essence of Huna teachings is that every human being is composed by three selves, a conscious mind, and unconscious mind and a higher self which lives on a higher plane of consciousness and communicates with the conscious mind during sleep and meditation. The seven principles of Huna are: Aloha, (also used as a greeting) meaning "to love is to be happy with"; Ike, meaning "reality is what you believe it is"; Kala, meaning "everything is possible, there are no limitations"; Makia, meaning "where your mind goes your energy flows"; Mana, meaning "the moment of power is now"; and Pono, meaning "effectiveness is the measure of truth". Also see Kahuna, Religions, huna.com and huna.org.

Hunab Ku
Maya Supreme God, Hunab Ku is the Father of Itzamna. He is called the Eyes and Mouth of the Sun and he exists only in Spirit. Also see Maya Gods and Goddesses.

Hurakan
Maya God who created the Earth, fire, people and animals. Hurakan is the God of spiritual illumination, thunder, storms, whirlwinds and hurricanes. He is also called the Triple Heart of the Universe. Also see Maya Gods and Goddesses.

Huxley, Aldous

(1894-1963) English-born novelist, poet essayist, pacifist, humanist and spiritual teacher, Aldous Leonard Huxley studied mysticism, alternative medicine and altered states of consciousness. He advocated the ingestion of psychedelics. He published two books on the nature of psychedelic experience and mysticism, The Doors of Perception and Heaven and Hell along with more than 40 other books. Huxley believed that the brain acted as a reducing valve for what he called 'mind at large' ensured that in a normal state of awareness we are only able to receive information that is useful for physical survival. He studied Vedanta, meditation and other spiritual practices with J. Krishnamurti and Swami Prabhavananda who initiated him. Later in life he gave lectures on Human Potentialities at the Esalen institute. His books include: Brave New World; Ends and Means; Tomorrow and Tomorrow and Tomorrow; The Art of Seeing; and The Perennial Philosophy. Photograph taken by G. Paul Bishop (gpaulbishop.com). Also see Hallucinogens, Meditation, Poets, Recommended Reading, Spiritual Teachers and somaweb.org.

Huznoth
In The Greater Key of Solomon, Huznoth is an Angel invoked in exorcism of water. Also see Angels.

Hydra

In Greek mythology, the Hydra is a seven-headed monster that dwells in a marsh, with fatally poisonous breath. If one of its heads is severed, two will grow back in its place. The Hydra is the guardian of the golden apples of Hesperides and the guardian of Tartarus. The Hydra is finally destroyed by Hercules and his nephew Iolaus. Image from pantheon.org. Also see Mythological Creatures.

Hydromancy

Divination by water, Hydromancy interprets water's color, ebb, ripples and flow or tide. Also see Divination.

Hygeia

In Greek mythology, Hygeia is the Goddess of Health and Cleanliness. She is the daughter of Asclepius. Shown here in a 1615 painting called Hygeia, Goddess of Health by Flemish artist Peter Paul Rubens (peterpaulrubens.org). Also see Greek Gods and Goddesses.

Hylic

From Greek hulikos meaning "matter" hylic is the opposite of psychic. Another term for hylic is somatic. Also see Somatics.

Hymen

In Greek mythology, Hymen is the Goddess of Marriage. She is also called Hymenaeus. Hymen is shown here in an 1868 painting by British artist Sir Edward Burne-Jones called Hymenaeus. Also see Greek Gods and Goddesses.

Hymn

A hymn is a song or prayer that is usually addressed to a God. Shown here is part of the 1779 hymn called Amazing Grace by John Newton.

Hyperborean

In Theosophy Hyperborean refers to one of humanities Root Races, described by Helena Blavatsky said to have originated some 25 to 30 million years ago in regions around the North Pole, the Arctic Circle and northern Asia. See Root Races.

Hyperion
In Greek mythology, Hyperion is a Titan, son of Uranus and Gaea and the father of the Dawn, the Sun and the Moon. Shown here is a 1753 painting by French artist Francois Boucher (francoisboucher.org) called The Rising of the Sun. Also see Greek Gods and Goddesses, and Titans.

Hyperesthesia
Hyperesthesia is defined as an actual or apparent exaltation of the perceptive faculties or a super acuity of the normal senses that is characteristic of the hypnotic or hypnagogic states.

Hypnagogic State
Term coined by British researcher Frederick Myers to describe the state of mind present immediately before going to sleep and immediately after awakening, while still in a half dreamy state of mind. In this state the consciousness, comparable to altered states of consciousness, the conscious mind may receive intermittent images from the unconscious mind. A hypnagogic state is very similar to a semitrance state of consciousness. Shown here is an 1880 painting by French artist Pierre-Auguste Renoir (pierre-auguste-renoir.org) called Girl With a Cat. Also see Altered States of Consciousness.

Hypnos
Greek and Roman God of Sleep, Hypnos causes people to sleep by touching their eyelids and fanning them with his dark wings; he has a human body during the day and the body of a bird at night. He is shown here in an 1874 painting by British artist John William Waterhouse (jw-waterhouse.com) called Hypnos and Thanatos. Also see Greek Gods and Goddesses, and Roman Gods and Goddesses.

Hypnotherapy
Hypnotherapy is therapy performed while the subject is under hypnosis. Under hypnosis people display hyper-suggestibility which is useful in modifying behavior, attitudes, anxiety and fear, pain management, personal development and dysfunctional habits. Also see spiritualregression.org.

Hyslop, James Hervey
(1854-1920) American-born James Hervey Hyslop Ph.D. was a psychologist, professor of logic and ethics and a well known psychical researcher. He studied medium Leonora Piper who he said conveyed messages from his deceased father and relatives. Of 205 incidents he was able to verify 152. He wrote extensively on the subject of life after death and once said "I regard the existence of

discarnate spirits as scientifically proved and I no longer refer to the skeptic as having any right to speak on the subject. Any man who does not accept the existence of discarnate spirits and the proof if it is either ignorant or a moral coward." Among his books are: Life After Death: Problems of the Future Life and Its Nature; Enigmas of Psychical Research; Science and a Future Life; and Contact with the Other World: The Latest Evidence as to Communication With the Dead. Also see Parapsychologists, Psychic Researchers, Recommended Reading and Reincarnation (Life After Life).

I

I Ching

Also known as the Book of Changes and the Holy Book of Mutations, the I Ching is an ancient Chinese system of profound philosophy and method of divination. Both the Confucians and the Taoists claim the I Ching as theirs, but traditionally the work has been attributed to Wen Wang (sage and father of the Chou dynasty). The basic principle of the I Ching is the subdivision of phenomena into the negative and positive forces or yin and yang. It is based on 64 symbolic hexagrams which are broken down into triagrams. There are 8 basic triagrams each named for a natural phenomenon. The book of I Ching is then consulted by casting lots of hexagrams six times to determine the appropriate hexagram. The oracle then reads the current state of yin and yang. Other spellings include Yi Ching and Pinyin Yi Jing. People described herein who practice I Ching include: Herbert Brennan, Mary-Margaret Moore and Asoka Selvarajah. Also see Divination Tools, Hexagrams, Philosophical and Mystical Movements, Sacred Writings, Triagrams, Yin/Yang, iching.com and zhouyi.com.

Iadabaoth

In Gnosticism and the Orphics, Iadabaoth is the first of seven Archons or planetary spirit rulers. He created six other Archons. See Archons.

Iamblichus

(255-333 C.E.) Syrian-born Neo-Platonist philosopher, theurgist and mystic of the 4th Century C.E., Iamblichus was known as The Inspired and The Divine. He was considered the intellectual equivalent of Plato and was the first Neo-Platonist to dislodge Plotonius mysticism in favor of Theology and Theurgy. Occultists have described his works and being of much importance in the development of ceremonial magic. Iamblichus is most known for his works: On the Egyptian Mysteries, Theological Principles of Arithmetic, On The Mysteries, An Exhortation to Philosophy and On the Pythagorean Life. Shown here is an 1801 illustration from Galerie der alten Griechen und Rumer. He was also called Iamblichus of Chalcis. Also see Mystics and Philosophers.

IANDS
See International Association for Near Death Studies.

Iao
In Gnosticism and the Orphics, Iao is one of seven Archons or planetary spirit rulers. See Archons.

Iapetus
In Greek mythology, Iapetus is a Titan, the father of Prometheus. Also see Greek Gods and Goddesses, and Titans.

IASD
See International Association for the Study of Dreams.

Ibn al-'Arabi, Muhyi al-Din

(1165-1240) Arab-born Muhyi Al-Din Ibn al-'Arabi (full name Abu abd-Allah Muhammad ibn-Ali ibn Muhammad ibn al-Arabi al-Hatimi al-T Taai) was a visionary mystic, prophet and prolific writer, considered the greatest Sufi theorist of his time. After living for almost 30 years in Spain he lived in Mecca and Antolia and later settled in Damascus where he lived until his death. He claimed to have had very lucid metaphysical visionary experiences, to have explored altered states of consciousness and lucid dreaming. Ibn al'Arabi stated that "this power of the active imagination developed in me visually in a bodily, objective, extra-mental figure just as the Archangel Gabriel appeared bodily to the eyes of the Prophet." His writings include: The Spiritual Conquests of Mecca; The Book of Annihilation in Contemplation; The Mecca Illuminations; The Interpreter of Desires; and Contemplation of the Holy Mysteries. Also see Dream Analysts, Lucid Dreaming, Mystics, Prophets and Sufism.

Ic Zod Heh Chal
Enochian Great King of the North.

Ica Stones
In a private museum in the village of Ica in Peru there is a massive collection of ancient caved stones owned by Dr. Javier Cabrera. He calls these stones Gliptoliths and he believes that

they were carved to depict the history of an ancient advanced civilization. He has over 11,000 carved stones. The depictions on the stones include medical depictions showing blood transfusions, cesarean sections, amputations and brain transplants, men overcoming dinosaurs, strange looking animals, and many images of Earth from space showing what looks like the continents of Atlantis and Lemuria as well as images of people observing space. There are believed to be over 15,000 of these stones in existence. These stones have also been called Dinostones. Also see Gliptoliths and Unsolved Mysteries.

Ichthus

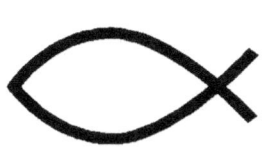

From the Greek meaning "fish", ichthus is a symbol which consists of two intersecting arcs that resemble the profile of a fish. Also known as the Jesus Fish the ichthus is used by the Christian to symbolize Christ. Other spellings include Ichthys, Icthus and Ikhthus.

Ichthyomancy

Divination by fish, Ichthyomancy interprets the appearance and behavior of fish. Also see Divination.

Icon

From the Greek eikon meaning "image", an icon in the Eastern Orthodox Church refers to images, pictures, representations or likenesses of Christ, or Saints or the Virgin Mary. Shown here is a 1626 painting of an icon called Assumption of the Holy Mary by Flemish artist Peter Paul Rubens (peterpaulrubens.org).

Ida

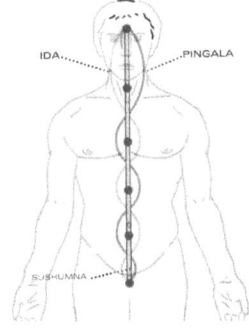

In Buddhism and Hinduism, Ida is the left hand nadi or channel in each human being that, when awaken, moves kundalini energy inward through the chakras. Ida is also called the Moon Current. The right hand channel is called Pingala and the central channel is called Shushumna. Image from alquimistadeconsciencias.blogspot.com. Also see Chakras, Kundalini, Nadis, Pingala, and Shushumna.

Ideoplasm

Another term for Ectoplasm. See Ectoplasm.

Idlirvirissong

In Inuit mythology, Idlirvirissong is the demon cousin of the Moon who dances in the sky. Also see Demons.

Idol

In Wiccan traditions an idol is an object that is consecrated or blessed to represent a God or a spirit.

Idunn

Norse Goddess of Immortality and Eternal Youth, Idunn rules over spring, rejuvenation, long life and beauty. She is the wife of Bragi and known as Keeper of the Golden Apples of Immortality which the Aesir Gods must eat to preserve their youth. Other spellings include Idun, Iduna, Ithun and Ithunn. Idunn is depicted here in an 1890 painting by British artist James Doyle Penrose called Idun and the Apples. Also see Norse Gods and Goddesses.

Ietuqiel

In Occultism, Ietuqiel is an Angel invoked at childbirth. Also see Angels.

Igaluk

Inuit God of Natural Phenomena, Igaluk rules over animals and sea creatures. He is also called Supreme God and Moon God. Also see Inuit Gods and Goddesses.

Ignis Fattus

See Will o' the Wisp.

Ike

From Hawaiian religion Huna, Ike is one of its seven philosophical principles and it means "reality is what you believe it is". Also see Huna.

Ilamatecuhtli

Aztec Mother Goddess in her negative aspect, Ilamatecuhtli is also called the Old Princess. Also see Aztec Gods and Goddesses.

Ilaniel

In Jewish tradition, Ilaniel is an Angel with dominion over fruit-bearing trees. Also see Angels.

Illapa

Incan God of Thunder, Illapa (shown here) rules over the weather and he is worshiped mostly during the growing season. Traditionally male children born during a thunderstorm were declared priests of Illapa and accepted with reverence by even the eldest priests themselves. Illapa is also called Chiqui Illapa. Other spellings include Yllapa and Ilyap'a. Image from geocities.ws. Also see Inca Gods and Goddesses.

Illuminati

From Latin meaning "enlightened ones" and also called the Order of the Illuminati, the Illuminati Order and the Bavarian Illuminati, the Illuminati was originally an Occult Brotherhood founded in 1776 in Bavaria by Adam Weishaupt as a Secret Society within a Secret Society. Its goal was to achieve spiritual enlightenment from direct contact with the Divine Reason. Many other orders have since called themselves Illuminati. Also see Occult Orders, Brotherhoods and Secret Societies, Trinacria and illuminati-news.com.

Illumination

To understand, realize or comprehend the meaning of the union with the divine. Illumination can be described as a complete understanding of the divine plan of spiritual evolution. This illumination then frees the soul from all karma and the need for reincarnation. Also see Enlightenment, Nirvana and Spiritual Goals.

Illuminism

Archaic term from French Illuminer, Illuminism refers specifically to the form of enlightenment or illumination that is a part of advancement in the ranks of various Secret Societies that originate with the Bavarian Illuminati. Also see Enlightenment, and Adam Weishaupt.

Imagination

According to Occultism imagination is the "creative faculty of the human mind". When we use our imagination we create forms and images on the astral planes, the more concentration and imagination used in conjunction with the will, will create a more dense and or powerful form or image. Many things have been said about the imagination. Albert Einstein said "Imagination is more important than knowledge. Knowledge is limited. Imagination encircles the world." Paracelsus said "Man has a visible and invisible workshop. The visible one is his body; the invisible one is his imagination." It is said that the spirit is the master, imagination is the tool and the body is the means to material realization. Imagination has also been described as the powers of the higher soul. Also see Spiritual Techniques.

Imans

In Islam, Imans are religious and spiritual teachers. Also see Islam, Religious Teachers and Mullahs.

Imbolc

Wiccan, Druidical and Pagan Festival of the Maiden celebrated on February 2nd for growth and renewal and the mark the first appearance of spring. The Celtic (Druidical) version of Imbolc was called Oimelc (celebrated on the 31st of January) marking the loosening of the grip of winter. Shown here is a 1918 painting by Scottish artist John Duncan entitled The Coming of the Bride. Also see Druidism, and Wicca.

Imhotep

Egyptian vizier, sage, architect, astrologer and chief Minister to the King of Egypt, considered by many as the "grandfather of western civilization". He was the architect of the first pyramid and an extremely gifted physician. Imhotep was later worshiped as the God of Knowledge, who presided over learning, medicine, magic, healing, herbs, drugs and suffering and pain by both Egyptians and Greeks. Imhotep means "He Who Comes in Peace". Other spellings include Imhetep. Shown here is a statuette of Imhotep housed in the Louvre museum in Paris, France. Also see Egyptian Gods and Goddesses.

Immortality

Without cease; forever; eternal, referring to life, immortality means either spiritual immortality in which, despite the demise of the physical, the spirit lives forever or, it means a never-ending infinite form of physical life.

Imperator

Spirit guide said to be channeled through medium Leonore Piper. Also see Channeled Spirit Guides, Channelers, and Leonore Piper.

Imprinting

Also called place memory, imprinting is the term used to describe how emotions, especially extreme negative emotions can "imprint" a memory of a traumatic event in a specific location. This type of imprinting is most common in battlefields and places of mass massacres. Also see Anniversary Ghosts, Gettysburg, Ghosts, Hauntings and Historical Apparitions.

In Between Worlds

In many religious, theosophical and mystical traditions In Between Worlds refer to planes of existence where souls reside until they reincarnate into physical matter again. The following In Between Worlds are described herein: Afterlife, Avichi, Chionyid Bardo, Devachan, Seventh Heaven, Sipa Bardo and Summerland. Shown here is a photograph from tgstars.blogspot.com called Heaven Can't Wait. Also see Greeters, Life Review, Near Death Experience, Reincarnation, afterlife101.com, lifeafterlife.com, litesofheaven.com, near-death.com, neardeathsite.com, nderf.org and victorzammit.com.

Inanna

From Sumerian mythology, Inanna is the Supreme Goddess who is dually associated especially with love, fertility, procreation and warfare and destruction. She is also called the Queen of Heaven, the Mistress of Heaven and the Queen of Beasts and she is related to Venus and the Moon. Her temples housed priestesses also called Sacred Women who performed ancient sacred sexual rituals and practices. She is, in later mythology, described as the daughter of Nanna and Ningal. Other spellings include Innin and Innini. Also see Gods of Heaven, Sacred Women, and Sumerian Gods and Goddesses.

INARS
See International Association of Rubenfeld Synergists.

Inca

South American Indian empire which flourished for many centuries until the Spanish conquest in 1532, the Inca domain reached as far North as Ecuador and as far South as the Maule river in central Chile. At its peak of power, the Inca empire was the largest nation on earth. According to the Inca, the founder of their dynasty was Manco Capac. They were ruled by an emperor called the Inca who was regarded as the son of the Sun God Inti and was considered a God on Earth. They had a highly organized form of government and were very skilled in astrology, farming, architecture, engineering and gold and silver handcrafting. They had no form of writing but kept accurate records on quipus, an intricate system of knotted cords. They are most known for their impressive stone buildings, terraced farms and extensive roads (45,000kilometers, still standing) and complex irrigations systems located high in the Andes. The only remaining Incas are the Q'ero. Shown here a painting by American artist Meredith Miller (meredithmillerart.com) called Machu Picchu. Also see Machu Pichu, Q'ero and incaglossary.org.

Inca Gods and Goddesses
The following Inca Gods and Goddesses are described herein: Amaru (dragon), Catequil, Chasca, Chuichu, Coniraya, Cuycha, Ekkeko, Illapa, Inti, Kilya, Mama Allpa, Mama Coca, Mama Cocha, Mama Quilla, Mama Zara, Manco Capac, Pachacamac, Pacha Mama, Pariacaca, Supay, Taguacipa, Tuapaca, Urcaguary, Viracocha, Wacas and Yaku Mama.

Inca Worlds

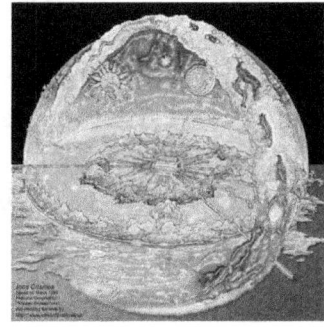

In Inca mythology the world is made up three worlds represented as concentric circles and inhabited by spiritual beings. These worlds are: Hanan Pacha, which is the World of the Future; Kay Pacha, the World of the Present; and Uku Pacha, the World of the Past; and Underworld. Shown here is a 1990 depiction of the Inca cosmos by Edward T. Babinski (edward-t-babinski.blogspot.com).

Incantation

A mantra, phrase or text, chanted, spoken or intoned as part of religious or spiritual rituals. Incantations are often used to banish evil spirits and to summon good ones. Also see Magical Methods.

Incarnation

An incarnation, which literally means "enfleshment", is the embodiment of the spirit in flesh for the duration of the lifetime of the physical body as material manifestation of a spiritual being. Also see Reincarnation.

Incarnation

Christianity explains incarnation as the doctrine that God became flesh and assumed a human nature and became a man in the form of Jesus Christ.

Incorporeal

From Latin meaning without body or substance, incorporeal means without a body or bodiless.

Incubus

A male demon or spirit believed to sexually tempt and have intercourse women in their sleep. According to some medieval legends, intercourse with incubi is supposed to result in the birth of demons, witches and deformed offspring. According to other medieval legends, the incubus could only impregnate women with the seed of men resulting in human offspring. The female version is called succubus. Shown here is an 1800 painting by Dutch painter Nicolai Abraham Abidgaard called Nachtmahr (Nightmare). Also see Demons, and Succubus.

Indigo Children

New age term used to describe the souls of some entities who are choosing to incarnate now with special abilities to help humankind These children are said to be born with an special connection to Earth and are empathic to others thoughts and emotions. Special abilities shown by indigo children include such things as empathy, telepathy, and extra sensory perception. Also see Crystal Children, indigolife.org and starchild.co.za.

Indra

Hindu and Vedic God of the Atmosphere, Indra rules over thunder, lightning, rain, the sky, rivers, rainbows, fertility, warriors, war, strength, reincarnation, horses, elephants, love, law, magic powers, opposition to evil, offerings, creativity and the Sun. He is depicted with four arms riding a white elephant and carrying a thunderbolt. Indra is known as King of the Gods, Lord of Storm, Great God and the Thousand-Eyed and described as champion of all Gods. He is also referred to as Svargapati and Parjanya. Indra is one of the Lokapalas as Guardian of the Eastern Quarter. Shown here is a 19th Century drawing by French artist Louis Thomas Bardel called Indra on Devendran. Also see Hindu Gods and Goddesses, and Lokapalas.

Indrani

In Hindu mythology, Indrani is the consort of Indra. Indrani personifies the evolution of the senses. Other spellings include Aindri and Indrini. Image from omsakthi.org. Also see Hindu Gods and Goddesses.

Inedia

Inedia is defined as the ability to live without food.

Inferno

See Dante's Inferno.

Infinity

From the Latin infinitas, meaning "unboundedness" infinity refers to the concept of never ending.

Ingerman, Sandra

American-born Sandra Ingerman MA is a licensed marriage and family therapist, leading practitioner of soul revival and mental health counselor. She holds an MA in counseling psychology from the California Institute of Integral Studies and she teaches and conducts workshops internationally on shamanism, healing and reversing environmental pollution using spiritual methods. Ms. Ingerman was the Educational Director of the Foundation for Shamanic Studies and she founded an international alliance of medicine for the shamanic and earth teachers called Shamanic Teachers. She has written: Soul Retrieval: Mending the Fragmented Self; Welcome Home: Following Your Soul's Journey Home; Medicine for the Earth: How to Transform Personal and Environmental Toxins; Shamanic Journeying; How to Heal Toxic Thoughts and Awakening to The Spirit World: The Shamanic Path of Direct Revelation; and How to Thrive in Changing Times: Simple Tools to Create True Health, Wealth, Peace, and Joy for Yourself and the Earth. Also see Healers, Recommended Reading, Shamans, sandraingerman.com, shamanicteachers.com and shamanicvisions.com.

Inguz

As the 8th symbol of the runes, Inguz represents fertility. Other spellings include Ingwaz. Also see Runes.

Initiation

Initiation means "to begin", "to start something new". Described in Occultism and Theosophy as a ritual or period of instruction in which a new member or neophyte is admitted or initiated into an Organization, Society or Order. According to the one tradition, "Initiation is the preparation for immortality". On a personal level initiation is basically an individual transformation involving a transition from one level of awareness to another higher more spiritual level. Shown here is a 1759 depiction of a Masonic Initiation ceremony. Also see Magical Methods.

Inner Genius
See Higher Self.

Inner Plane Adepti
See Hidden Masters.

Inner Visions

Founded in 1998 by Iyanla Vanzant Inner Visions is (in their own words) a network of spiritual and holistic practitioners who believe that all individuals must be empowered. We believe that empowerment is a function of knowing who you are, why you are on the planet and the role you play in the divine order of life.

We believe that with spiritual knowledge, all individuals are equipped to demonstrate in their lives the glory we know as God. Inner Visions is not a religious organization. We are a multi-cultural, multi-ethnic network of individuals who embrace various spiritual philosophies. Our desire is to provide access to information that will assist and support spiritual growth and evolution of all people. Persons of all religious faiths and philosophies are welcome to participate in our activities and to utilize our services. We do, however, encourage study and application of universal principles and spiritual laws to every aspect of living. Our work is based on the concept that through the development and the discipline of the mind, everyone learns to recognize and acknowledge their life's purpose. When an individual is on purpose s/he is empowered to control the events in his/her daily living and will ultimately make valuable contributions to the world. We believe that empowerment begins with healing. We believe that living the principles activates the spiritual laws which support the evolution of humanity. We are, therefore, teachers dedicated to spreading knowledge of God. Also see, New Age Associations and Societies, Iyanla Vanzant and innervisionsworldwide.com.

Inspiration

Inspiration has been defined as a psychic state in which a person becomes susceptible to spiritual and creative influences and becomes an instrument for through-flowing ideas. Also see Spiritual Techniques.

Institute for the Study of Human Knowledge

The Institute for the Study of Human Knowledge (or ISHK) is (in their own words) an educational institution dedicated to bringing important research on human nature to the general public. It takes a multi-disciplinary approach to the questions of who we are, where we came from, and what we might become. The programs highlight contributions from contemporary psychology, education, anthropology, medicine, evolutionary biology, neuroscience, and ecology - as well as from traditional systems of knowledge and learning with ancient roots. For more than 30 years, the Institute for the Study of Human Knowledge's publishing, book distribution, and educational programs have been reaching thousands of professional and lay persons, contributing to important shifts in public attitudes and policies. Aided by the Institute's programs, the role of the mind in health is now an integral part of medical education and health care. Many educators and public policy makers now recognize the need to train more flexible ways of thinking and responding if mankind is to adapt successfully to the challenges of the modern world. Also see New Age Associations and Societies and ishk.com.

Institute of Core Energetics

The Institute of Core Energetics was created and founded by John Pierrakos and Alexander Lowen in 1980 as a trademark therapeutic program and holistic healing method, promoted as a bridge between psychology and spirituality. Core Energetics combines psychotherapy, bodywork and spiritual processes to improve a person's state of consciousness including the body, mind, emotions and spirit. Also see New Age Associations and Societies, John Pierrakos and coreenergetics.org.

Institute of Noetic Studies

The Institute of Noetic Sciences (or IONS) is a nonprofit organization, founded in 1973 by former American astronaut Edgar Mitchell and others and headquartered in Petaluma, California. Its purpose is to encourage and conduct research and education programs on mind-body relationships to expand knowledge on the mind, consciousness and spirit. This research includes consciousness, meditation, alternative healing, spiritual energy, spirituality, psychic abilities, human potential, lucid dreaming, and life after death, among others. Also see Edgar Mitchell, New Age Associations and Societies, noetic.org and shiftinaction.com.

Institute of Transpersonal Psychology

Founded in 1975 by Robert Frager, the Institute of Transpersonal Psychology is a private, non-sectarian graduate school accredited by the Western Association of Schools and Colleges. The Institute focuses its approach to holistic psychological studies to include the intellectual, spiritual, emotional, physical, social and creative aspects of life. Also see Robert Frager, New Age Associations and Societies, and itp.edu.

Instrumental Transcommunication

Also called ITC, instrumental transcommunication is the New Age term used for the phenomena of electronic recording of spirit voices and the photographs of the images of spirits or ghosts. Also see Electronic Voice Phenomena, Spirit Photography, atransc.org, spiritcommunicator.com and transcommunication.org.

Interconnectedness

Interconnectedness refers to the recognition that all life is linked and connected on a physical, mental and spiritual level; that All is One and One is All.

Interdependence

In Buddhism Interdependence is explained as the phenomena of nature and all objects in nature as organically joined together and internally dependent on each other as well as mutually affecting and conditioning each other.

International Association for Near Death Studies

The International Association for Near Death Studies (or IANDS) is (in their own words) the only membership organization in the world devoted exclusively to providing information about near death and related experiences to experiencers, researchers, educators, health care providers, and the interested public. In addition to maintaining this information-rich website, it publishes a peer-reviewed scholarly journal and a member newsletter, sponsors conferences and other programs, works with the media, and encourages the formation of regional discussion and support groups to become a part of this mission and keep up to date on what is known about this fascinating subject. Its purpose is to promote responsible, multi-disciplinary exploration of near death and similar experiences, their effects on people's lives, and their implications for beliefs about life, death, and human purpose. Also see New Age Associations and Societies, and iands.org.

International Association for the Study of Dreams

The International Association for the Study of Dreams (or IASD) is (in their own words) is a non-profit, international, multidisciplinary organization dedicated to the pure and applied investigation of dreams and dreaming. Its purposes are to promote an awareness and appreciation of dreams in both professional and public arenas; to encourage research into the nature, function, and significance of dreaming; to advance the application of the study of dreams; and to provide a forum for the eclectic and interdisciplinary exchange of ideas and information. Also see New Age Associations and Societies, and asdreams.org.

International Association of Rubenfeld Synergists

The International Association of Rubenfeld Synergists (or INARS) is (in its own words) the professional association of Certified Rubenfeld Synergists, founded in 1996 and licensed by the Rubenfeld Center, Inc. It is dedicated to supporting Rubenfeld Synergists in their professional growth and in development of their practices as well as to educating the general public and other professionals about the Rubenfeld Synergy Method. The Rubenfeld Synergy Method is an alternative healing method which combines touch and talk together to help people deal with the stresses in their lives. It uses the body as the starting point, because the body is home to our thoughts, our feelings, and our spirit. By exploring these relationships, we can claim a greater role in our own physical and emotional wellness. Also see Ilana Rubenfeld, New Age Associations and Societies and rubenfeldsynergy.com.

International Holistic Health Energy Institute

The International Holistic Health Energy Institute was founded by Dr. Fadel Behman after decades of teaching and therapy using four specific energy approaches. He developed The Behman Technique of Vibrant Living which enhances physical, emotional, mental and spiritual well-being. In addition to his practice and research, Dr. Behman teaches courses Energy Bodies and Chakras, Holistic Health, Cranio-Sacral Therapy, Expansion of Consciousness, Meditation, and Awakening Intuition, among others. Also see Fadel Behman, New Age Associations and Societies, and 4energies.org.

Interspecies Telepathic Communicator

See Animal Communication Specialist.

Inti

Incan Sun God, consort and brother of the Moon Goddess Mama Quilla and father of Viracocha, Pachacmac and Manco Capac. Inti is the God of Fertility and Crops and considered to be the ancestor of the Incas. He soars across the sky every day, plunges into the ocean and swims under the Earth to soar in the sky the next day. Inti is also called Apu-Punchau. Also see Inca Gods and Goddesses.

Intuition

Intuition may be defined as a direct perception or inner knowing of a truth, independent of a conscious reasoning process. A feeling or sensation, sometimes described as an inner voice that communicates something of importance. Knowledge that arrives spontaneously, without conscious thought. Also see Methods of Prediction, and Psychic Abilities.

Inuit Gods and Goddesses
The following Inuit Gods and Goddesses are described herein: Agloolik, Alignak, Anguta, Aningan, Igaluk, Pinga, Sedna, Sun and Torngasak.

Invisibility
In Occultism and other magical traditions, invisibility is the magically empowered act of fading from the physical or exterior environment in such a manner as to create the illusion to others that the person is no longer present or by leading them to forget that they have seen the person. This process is also called the "Shroud of Concealment". Also see Magical Methods.

Invisibles, The
Spirit guides said to be channeled through medium Stewart White, his wife and others. Also see Channeled Spirit Guides, Channelers and Stewart White.

Invocation
The act of invoking or calling upon a specific spiritual entity Deity, Elemental, Angel, spirit or other entity for protection, inspiration or aid, or to request their appearance. Also described as potent formula, prayer or ritual used to invoke a deity or to establish communication with higher spiritual entities. Shown here is a 19th Century painting of a magician invoking an elemental spirit by American artist J. A. Knapp. Also see Adjuration, Evocation, Ritual Magic, and Magical Methods.

Involution
In Gnosticism, involution is the descent of the Spirit into matter.

Inward Light
See Society of Friends.

Inward Bound
Founded by David Cumes, Inward Bound leads inner journeys mostly to Southern Africa to connect with ancient models of healing and the primal African bush. In its own words, its intention is to explore the inner or healing journey into wilderness. This implies using the experience of nature as medicine and the itinerary for the trek differs vastly from most wilderness adventures. During and after these journeys the participants have profound restorative and healing experiences. Many of them who have done wilderness trips for years admit that this inner journey is quite different and even life-altering. Also see David Cumes and New Age Associations and Societies.

IONS
See Institute of Noetic Sciences.

Ioskeha

Iroquois Creator God, Ioskeha is the Defeater of Demons and he rules over magic, herbs, rituals and healing. Also see Iroquois Gods and Goddesses.

Iris

Greek Rainbow Goddess, Iris carries messages between the Gods (especially Zeus and Hera) and humans. She is the daughter of the Titans Thaumas and Electra and sister of the Harpies. Iris can travel with the speed of the wind and go from one end of the earth to the other, to the bottom of the sea and to the depths of the Underworld. She is described as a beautiful maiden, with wings and robes of beautiful colors and a halo of light on her head. Iris leaves rainbows in her wake when she travels. Shown here is a painting by British artist Josephine Wall (josephinewall.com) called Iris, The Keeper of the Rainbow. Also see Greek Gods and Goddesses.

Isa

As the 23rd symbol of the runes, Isa represents standstill. Also see Runes.

Iroquois Gods and Goddesses

The following Iroquois Gods and Goddesses are described herein: Adekagagwaa, Big Heads, Ga-Oh, Gohone, Ha Wen Neyu, Hahbwehdiyu, Hino, Ioskeha, Keneun and Onatha. Shown here is a depiction of the Iroquois creation myth by American artist Marcine Quenzer (marcinequenzer.com).

Isa

See Upanishads.

ISHK

See Institute for the Study of Human Knowledge.

Ishtar

Main Goddess of the Babylonians and the Assyrians, Ishtar is the Goddess of Heaven, Fertility, Love, Beauty, Hunting, Warfare and Destruction. Her name means "giver of light" and she is both a beneficent Goddess and a demonic Deity and she rules over vegetation, animals, sexuality, wedlock, maternity, and the laws of the Earth. Although she rules the Moon and morning and evening stars, Ishtar is related to the planet Venus and is also called Goddess of All Things, Great Mother, She Who Directs the Oracles, the Queen, Lady of Sorrow and Battles, Lady of Heaven and Earth, Goddess of the Universe and the Queen of Heaven. Ishtar is also the protector of rulers. She is the daughter of Sin, sister of Shamash and Adad and later, the wife of

Anu. Other spellings include Athtar, Ashtart, Astar and Istar. Her temples housed priestesses also called Sacred Women who performed ancient sacred sexual rituals and practices. Shown here is a 2000 B.C.E. statuette of Ishtar housed in the Louvre Museum in Paris, France. Also see Assyrian Gods and Goddesses, Babylonian Gods and Goddesses, Gods of Heaven, and Sacred Women.

Isis

Supreme Egyptian Goddess; Isis is called Mistress of Magic, Speaker of Spells, Great Mother, Great Goddess, Giver of Life, Goddess from whom All Becoming Arose, Great Lady, Mistress of the House of Egypt, Lady of the East, Mistress of Heaven, Mistress of the Perfect Black and Moon Goddess. She is the daughter of Geb and Nuit, sister of Seth and Nephthys, sister-wife of Osiris, and mother of Horus. She described as having dark hair, fair skin and blue eyes. Cats are sacred to Isis and her sistrum is carved with the image of a cat that represents the Moon. As the High Priestess she is considered a powerful magician. As Patroness of Priestesses, Isis also rules over women, motherhood, fertility, magic, alchemy, divination, initiation, purification and healing. Her temples housed priestesses also called Sacred Women who performed ancient sacred sexual rituals and practices. She is also called Aset and Eset. Her original name in Egyptian is Au Set. Shown here is a painting by American artist Susan Seddon Boulet (turningpointgallery.com) called Isis and Osiris. Also see Egyptian Gods and Goddesses, Gods of Heaven, and Sacred Women.

Islam

Muslim monotheist religion founded by the Prophet Muhammad in the 7th Century B.C.E. Allah is the sole God, and is described in the sacred scriptures or Qur'an. Muhammad was given the message of Islam by the Angel Gabriel. The term Islam means "to surrender" and expresses the fundamental religious ideal that the believer accepts to "surrender to the will of Allah". It also teaches that the path to spiritual enlightenment is open to all. Islam is also called Mohammedism. The main Islamic festivals are: Eid ul-Fitr is a huge celebration at the end of Ramadan which is the thirty day fast and Eid-ul-Adha is to remember the time when Abraham was to sacrifice his own son to prove his obedience to God. Also see Qur'an, Religions, islam.com, islam101.net and religioustolerance.com.

ITC
See Instrumental Transcommunication.

Itzamna
Maya Sky God, creator and father of humankind, Itzamna is the Principal God of Mayan civilization, ruling over heaven, day and night, writing and books, healing, fertility, water, regeneration and medicine. He is the son of Hunab Ku and he is married to Ixchel and is also known as the Sky God, the Father of the Gods and the Lord of Day and Night. Also see Gods of Heaven, and Maya Gods and Goddesses.

Itzpapalotl

Aztec Goddess of Fate, Itzpapalotl rules over the stars and agriculture. She is described as a beautiful female demon, a mixture of sensuality and death; she is the female counterpart of Itzcoluihqui. She is also called the Obsidian Butterfly. Shown here is a depiction of Itzpapalotl from the Codex Borgia believed to have been written before the Spanish conquest of Mexico. Also see Aztec Gods and Goddesses, and Demons.

Itztlacoliuhqui

Aztec God of Darkness, Itztlacoliuhqui rules over disaster, cold and volcanic eruptions, he is the male counterpart of Itzpaplotl. He is also called the Twisted Obsidian One and the Curved Obsidian Knife. Itztlacoliuhqui is depicted here from the 16th Century Codex Telleriano-Remensis. Other spellings include Itzcoliuhqui. Also see Aztec Gods and Goddesses.

Ivunches

In Araucanian (Chile) mythology Ivunches are familiars. Also see Familiars.

Ixchel

Maya Goddess of the Moon, Ixchel rules over magic, creativity, sexuality, health, water, floods, tides, medicine, weaving, domestic arts, pregnancy and childbirth. She represents the healing powers of the elder women. She is the wife of the Sun God Itzamna and the mother of all the Mayans. Ixchel is also called the Our Mother, White Lady, Goddess of Becoming, Rainbow and Lady Rainbow. Ixchel is depicted here from the 12th Century Codex Dresden. Other spellings include Ix Chebel Yax, Ix Chel and Ix Chel. Also see Maya Gods and Goddesses.

Ixchup

Maya Goddess, wife of the Sun God Ah Kinchil, Ixchup is also called Young Moon Goddess. Also see Maya Gods and Goddesses.

J

Jack o' Lantern
See Will o' the Wisp.

Jacob's Ladder
In the Bible, Jacob's Ladder which was disclosed to him in a dream was a vision of Angels ascending and descending a ladder which extended from Earth to Heaven. According to Qabbalistic interpretation this ladder symbolized the metaphorical powers of alchemy operating through the visible nature. Shown here is an 1800 painting of Jacob's Ladder by English poet and artist William Blake (william-blake.org).

Jaegers, Beverly

(1935-2001) American-born Beverly "Bevy" Jaegers was a well known psychic who specialized in remote viewing. She earned a B.A. and M.A. at St. John's University. Ms Jaegers wrote over 20 books dealing with her psychic experiences and was a popular teacher and lecturer for over 40 years. She formed the US Psi Squad with a group of her students which, internationally assists police with criminal cases. She was described as a highly-successful, self-taught remote viewer with an exceptional natural talent. She never charged anything for her psychic work. Among her books are: Beyond Palmistry: The Art and Science of Modern Hand Analysis; The Magic Power of Healing: Learn to Heal Yourself; The Psychic Paradigm; and Psychometry: The Science of Touch. Also see Remote Viewing and US Psi Squad. Also see Palmistry, Psychics, Recommended Reading, Remote Viewing and uspsisquad.com.

Jaina Cross
See Swastika.

James, William

(1842-1910) American-born William James M.D. psychologist, author, philosopher and parapsychology investigator, also M.D. at Harvard Medical School where he spent his whole academic career, although he never practiced medicine. He was a champion of alternative healing methods. Dr. James developed the Philosophy of Pragmatism. He was a founding member of the American Society for Psychical Research, where he tested many mediums and psychics. Among James' books are: Varieties of Religious Experience: A Study in Human Nature; The Principles of Psychology; The Will to Believe and Other Essays in Popular Philosophy; Talks to Teachers on Psychology: and to Students on Some of Life's Ideals; Some Problems of Philosophy: A Beginning of an Introduction to Philosophy and A Pluralistic Universe. Also see Mind-Body Energy Medicine and Parapsychologists and Psychic Researchers, Recommended Reading and williamjames.com.

Janmashtami
One of the main Hindu festivals, Janmashtami is the birthday of Lord Krishna and it is celebrated by bathing an image of Lord Krishna in milk and honey and people pray and sing hymns. Other spellings include Janmaashtami and Janam Ashtami. Also see Hinduism.

Janus

Roman God of Beginnings, Janus rules over doorways, gateways, journeys, departure and return, communications, navigation, victory, endings, the seasons and the rising and setting of the Sun. He is described as a bearded old man with two heads or faces, each looking in the opposite direction. Janus is also called Janus Pater. Also see Roman Gods and Goddesses.

Jarnsaxa
In Norse mythology Jarnsaxa is a Wave Maiden, daughter of Aegir and his wife-sister Ran. She is one of nine sister Goddesses. Shown here is a 1908 painting by French artist Guillaume Seignac called The Wave. Also see Norse Gods and Goddesses, and Wave Maidens.

Jarnvidjur
In Norse mythology, the Jarnvidjur are a race of witches or magicians who live in Jarnvid. Also see Supernatural and Spiritual Beings.

Jarow, Rick

American-born E. H. Rick Jarow, Ph.D. is a practicing alternative career counselor, yogi, author and professor. At age 19 he left Harvard University to travel thought Europe and India for seven years, seeking a higher truth and was initiated in yoga disciplines and meditational arts as he continued to study in India and the United States for several years. He is currently associate professor of Religious Studies at Vassar College in Poughkeepsie, New York. His books include: Creating the Work You Love: Courage, Commitment and Career, Self-Expression and Freedom; Alchemy of Abundance: Using the Energy of Desire to Manifest Your Highest Vision, Power and Purpose and Tales for the Dying: The Death Narrative of the Bhagavata-Purana. Photograph by Dan Stein (dansteinphotography.com). Also see Meditation, Recommended Reading, Yogis, alchemyofabundance.wordpress.com and rickjarow.com.

Jehovah

From Hebrew Yahweh, Jehovah is the most sacred of names given to God and has been the name of the God of Israel since the 14th Century. Also see Yahweh.

Jenkins, John Major

(1964-) American-born John Major Jenkins is an independent researcher and author who dedicates his time to the reconstruction of ancient Mayan philosophy and cosmology. He teaches, as a visiting scholar at the Institute of Maya Studies in Miami, The Esalen Institute, Naropa University, The Maya Calendar Congress in Mexico and others. Among his books are: The Mirror in the Sky; Maya Cosmogenesis 2012: The True Meaning of the Maya Calendar End-Date; Galactic Alignment: The Transformation of Consciousness According to Mayan, Egyptian and Vedic Traditions; Pyramid of Fire: The Lost Aztec Codex: Spiritual Ascent at the End of Time; and The 2012 Story: The Myths, Fallacies, and Truth Behind the Most Intriguing Date in History. Also see Recommended Reading and alignment2012.com.

Jera

As the 13th symbol of the runes, Jera represents harvest. Also see Runes.

Jerusalem

Sacred Site and capital and largest city of the modern state of Israel; Jerusalem is a Holy city for Jews and Christians and Muslims. According to Midrash, Jerusalem was founded by Shem and Eber, ancestors of Abraham. Jerusalem became the capital of the Jewish kingdoms of Israel, Judah and Judea. Jerusalem is depicted here in a 15th Century drawing by German artist Michael Wohlgemut. Also see Sacred Sites, sacred-destinations.com and sacredsites.com.

Jesodoth

In Jewish tradition, Jesodoth is the Angel who receives wisdom and knowledge directly from God for transmission to mankind. Also see Angels.

Jesus Fish

See Ichthus.

Jesus of Nazareth

Major Prophet and Messiah of our times, Christianity derives from the life and teachings of Jesus of Nazareth, who became The Christ or Christ The Anointed when he was baptized by John the Baptist. The Christian New Testament written by the disciples of Jesus narrates his life and teachings. The Islamic Qur'an frequently mentions and recognizes Jesus as a Prophet. He was called The Prince of Peace by the late medium Edgar Cayce. Jesus is shown here with his disciples in a reproduction of the famous Italian artist Leonardo da Vinci's 1498 painting The Last Supper. Also see Christianity, Prophets and Spiritual Leaders.

Jewish New Year

See Roshanah and Judaism.

Jinni

In Islamic mythology a Jinni is a spirit, lower than an angel, Jinni are composed of fire and air and can assume both animal and human form and become visible or invisible at will. They may be either good or evil; if good, they are beautiful; if evil, they are ugly. Jinni are said to be found in the air, in flames, under the ground and even in rocks and trees. As mischievous spirits they produce accidents and disease. Other spellings include Genie, Jinn and Jinnee. Also see Supernatural and Spiritual Beings.

Jinx

In popular terminology, a jinx is a person, animal or object which is believed to cause bad luck or to be cursed by a large number of minor misfortunes.

Jnana

From Sanskrit meaning "knowledge", in Hindu philosophy Jnana refers to spiritual knowledge acquired through meditation that is a total experience in relation to its object, especially the supreme reality or divine being and can be considered the opposite of "practical knowledge". This philosophy is explained as that the complete cognitive experience of the supreme will set the soul free from the transmigratory life and polarities that this imposes upon thought. Jnana is also called Brahamajnana. Also see Illumination, and Spiritual Goals.

Jnana-Dakshinamurti

Hindu God of all Wisdom and Rewarding Meditation. Also called Dakshinamurthi (which means facing south), Jnana-Dakshinamurti is an aspect of Shiva as a jnana guru, teaching knowledge and awareness through music and yoga. His image is always placed on the southern side of the path around the sanctum sanctorum. Shown here is Lord Shiva as Jnana-Dakshinamurti. Also see Hindu Gods and Goddesses.

Jnana Yoga

Esoteric yoga which calls for the study and knowledge of the Vedas. See Yoga and jnanayoga.org.

Joey Sandy

Spirit guide said to be channeled through medium William Eglinton. Also see Channeled Spirit Guides, Channelers, and William Eglinton.

Johannes

Spirit guide said to be channeled through medium Hester Dowden. Johannes claimed to have lived 200 B.C.E. and to have studied in the Alexandrian Library. His teachings were compared to the Neoplatonic philosophy of Plotinus. Also see Channeled Spirit Guides, Channelers, and Hester Dowden.

Johnson, Robert A.

(1921-) American-born Robert A. Johnson D.Hum., is a world renown lecturer and well known author. He studied at the University of Oregon, Stanford University and the C. G. Jung Institute in Zurich, Switzerland. Johnson also spent four years in a Benedictine monastery in Michigan. After he left the monastery he founded the retreat the Saint Johns House. He later settled in California making annual trips to India for over 20 years. Among his books are: Ecstasy: Understanding the Psychology of Joy; Femininity Lost and Regained; Lying with the Heavenly Woman: Understanding and Integrating the Feminine Archetypes in Men's Lives; She: Understanding Feminine Psychology; He: Understanding Masculine Psychology and We: Understanding the Psychology of Romantic Love. Also see Recommended Reading and jerryruhlrobertjohnson.com.

Jolkim

Spirit guide said to be channeled through medium Alexander Harris who claimed that he was a Russian soldier who died in World War I. Also see Channeled Spirit Guides, Channelers, and Alexander Harris.

Jones, Marc Edmund

(1888-1980) American-born Marc Edmund Jones Ph.D. was a well known astrologer and writer on astrological and occult subjects. He was a pioneer motion picture writer and author of over 200 original screen plays. Jones was ordained a Minister of the United Presbyterian Church and founded the Sabian Assembly. He later received a Ph.D. from Columbia University. Dr. Jones is acclaimed for reformulating the study of astrology. Among books are: Occult Philosophy; Astrology: How and Why It Works; Essentials of Astrological Analysis; Key Truths of Occult Philosophy: An Introduction, the Major Concepts and a Glossary – Key Truths of Occult Philosophy Completely Rewritten and Expanded; Scope of Astrological Prediction: An Introduction to the Dynamic Horoscopy; Essentials of Astrological Analysis: Illustrated in the Horoscopes of One Hundred and Seventy-Four Well-Known People and The Ritual of Living: An Occult Manual. Photograph from sabian.org. Also see Astrologers, Recommended Reading, Reverends and Ministers and sabian.org.

Jord

Nordic Earth Goddess, Jord is the first wife of Odhin and Mother of Thor. She is one of the Vanir Gods that live in Vanaheim. Jord is also called Fyorgyn, Erda and Lork. Other spellings include Jordh. Shown here is a 1912 image by British artist Arthur Rackham (rackham.art-passions.net) called Erda Bids Thee Farewell. Also see Norse Gods and Goddesses, and Vanir.

Jormungand

In Norse mythology, Jormungand is a giant snake, son of Angerboda and brother of Fenrir and Hel. Sent by Odhin, he lives in heaven, surrounding the world of men as the Midgard Serpent. Also see Midgard Serpent.

Jotunheim

In Norse mythology, Jotunheim or home of the giants is one the nine worlds make up the universe and are guarded by Odhin. Also see Mythological Places, and Nine Worlds.

Journalists

The people mentioned herein who are journalists include: Margot Anand, Algernon Blackwood, James Herbert Brennan, Paul Brunton, Paulo Coelho, Daniel Goleman, Andrew Lang, Guido von List, Lynne McTaggart, Robert Moss, James Morgan Pryse Jr., Ruth Montgomery, D. Scott Rogo, Harold Morrow Sherman, Alfred Percy Sinnet, Thomas Spence, William Thomas Stead and Jess Stearn.

Joyce-Swaim, Elizabeth

American-born (Ridgewood, New Jersey) Elizabeth Joyce-Swaim is a well known clairvoyant, psychic, author, spiritual teacher and radio and television talk show personality. She studied hypnotherapy and behavior modification and is a member and contributing writer to the Association of Research and Enlightenment, Self-Realization Fellowship, the New Jersey Metaphysical Society, Wisdom Magazine, the International Association for Counselors and Therapists and the National Guild of Parapsychologists among others. Ms. Joyce-Swaim is the founder of Visions of Reality (1981) which teaches classes and seminars to improve your intuition and psychic abilities in Doylestown, Pennsylvania. She has also assisted police and FBI as psychic consultant for over 25 years. She has written: Psychic Attack - Are You A Victim? and Ascension - Accessing The Fifth Dimension: The Truth About 2012. Also see Clairvoyants, Psychics, Recommended Reading, Spiritual Teachers and new-visions.com.

Judaism

The religion and culture of the Jewish people, Judaism was founded by Abraham and Moses 3,500 years ago. The Tanakh (Old Testament) is the main religious text, and along with the Torah and the Talmud describe the commandments of God and determine the basic beliefs and values to live by as well as religious statements and concepts. For thousands of years, up until the mid eighteen hundreds, Judaism included the concept of Gilgul, or reincarnation, concept which is still held by the contemporary Orthodox and Chasidic communities. The main festivals are:

Purim (Festival of Lots) is a one-day festival takes place four weeks before Passover and usually falls in late February or early March. It recalls the story of Esther, a Queen who foiled a plot by one of her advisors, Haman, to kill all the Jews;

Pesach (Passover) takes place around March/April, and commemorates Moses freeing the Israelites from their enslavement under the Pharaoh in Egypt. This festival lasts for eight days and during that time no 'leavened' food may be consumed;

Shavuot (Pentecost) takes places seven weeks after Passover (usually around late May or early June) and it commemorates Moses being given the ten commandments by God after the Exodus from Egypt. This festival lasts for two days;

Rosh Hashanah (Jewish New Year) takes place around September/October, and is considered to be one of the most important holidays in the Jewish calendar. As well as a time for celebration Rosh Hashanah is also a time for reflection and repentance for sins committed in the previous year;

Yom Kippur (Day Of Atonement) is the day on which the fates of the Jews are sealed for the following year. This High Holy day is considered the most solemn and serious day in the Jewish calendar, and it involves 25 hours of fasting and praying for forgiveness for sins and afflicting oneself as punishment for those committed in the past year;

Succot (Tabernacles) is an eight day festival which begins five days after the end of Yom Kippur and commemorates the booths the Israelites constructed and lived in after their exodus from Egypt;

Simchat Torah (Rejoicing Of The Law) celebrates the end of the reading of the Torah, in synagogue - and the fact that it can now be re-read from the beginning. It is considered one of the happiest festivals in the Jewish calendar;

Chanukah (Festival of Lights) is an eight-day festival, celebrated in December. The story of Chanukah goes back to when Jews were forbidden to follow their faith and many were made to convert or were killed for not converting. That's when some Jews called the Maccabees formed an army and revolted against the Greeks and won, albeit at a very high price because their temple and way of life was almost destroyed. These men cleaned up the temple and attempted restore the faith by lighting the Menorah, with only enough oil for one day. A miracle is then said to have happened when the Menorah continued to remain lit for seven days on only one day's supply of oil. Also see Religions, jewishpeople.com, jewishvirtuallibrary.org and religioustolerance.com.

Judge, William Quan

(1851-1896) Irish-born William Quan Judge was a theosophist, occultist and mystic and co-founder of the original Theosophical Society. He immigrated with his family to the United States where he became a lawyer, specializing in commercial law and American citizen at age 21. He became the General Secretary of the Theosophical Society in 1884 and wrote articles for several theosophical magazines along with writing many books on the occult, all the while having a successful practice as a lawyer. Some of his best known books are: The Ocean of Theosophy; Echoes from the Orient; Bhagavad-Gita combined with Essays on the Gita; The Bhagavad-Gita: The Book of Devotion; Occult Tale; and An Epitome of Theosophy. Also see Mystics, Occultists, Recommended Reading, Theosophical Society, Theosophists, iswara.com and theosophical.org.

Judgement

Judgement is one of the 22 major arcana of the tarot deck of cards. Its number is XX, its Qabbalistic title is The Spirit of the Primal Fire and its meaning is: judgment, sentence, determination and final decision. Also see Tarot.

Jung, Carl

(1875-1961) Swiss-born Carl Gustav Jung Ph.D. was a famous psychologist, psychoanalyst, student of the Occult and author. He was a friend and colleague of Sigmund Freud but differed from Freudian psychoanalysis in his ideas of the unconscious mind and universal or collective unconsciousness. He traveled extensively and studied Gnosticism, Alchemy and the Qabbalah. He was fluent in ancient languages including Latin, Greek and Sanskrit and was a firm believer in parapsychology, astrology, clairvoyance, psychokinesis and telepathy. Dr. Jung had premonitory visions and dreams about World War I and a Near Death Experience. Some of his books are: Synchronicity; Psychology and Alchemy; The Psychology of the Transference; The Interpretation of Nature and the Psyche - Synchronicity: An Acausal Connecting Principle Collective Unconscious; and Memories, Dreams, Reflections. Also see Consciousness Researchers, Dream Analysts, Gnostics, Near Death Experience, Occultists, Qabbalists, Recommended Reading and cgjungpage.org.

Jungian Analysts

Jungian Analysts are psychologists and psychoanalysts who follow Carl Jung's psychoanalytical ideas. People described herein who are Jungian Analysts include: Jean Shinoda Bolen, Stuart Grayson, Vernon Howard, Arnold Mindell, Robert L. Moore, Joseph Chilton Pearce, Konstantin Raudive, Edward Whitmont and Roger J. Woolger. Also see Carl Jung.

Juno

Roman Principle Goddess of Heaven, the Sky and the Moon, Juno is the protector of women, marriage, home and childbirth, fertility, purification, death, pain and punishment. She is also known as the Moon Goddess, the Goddess of Childbirth, the Queen of Heaven, the Great Mother and the Earth Goddess. Juno is the daughter of Saturn and the sister, wife and female counterpart of Jupiter, representing the female principle of life. She is also called Juno Pronuba, Juno Lucina and Juno Regina. She is Hera to the Greeks. Shown here is an 1881 painting by French artist Gustave Moreau (gustavemoreau.com) called The Peacock Complaining to Juno. Also see Gods of Heaven, and Roman Gods and Goddesses.

Jupiter

Roman God of Heaven and the Sky, Lord of rain, wind, thunder, lightning, and mountain tops, Jupiter is also God of the elements, of agriculture, honor, friendship, oaths, treaties, riches and protection. He is the son of Saturn and is also called Jupiter Optimus Maximus (Best and Greatest), the Supreme God, the Great God and the Lord of the Heavens. The Romans considered that lightning was struck by Jupiter and considered sacred ground and circular walls were erected to protect the areas. Other spellings include Jove, Iuppiter, and Iovis. Jupiter is Zeus to the Greeks. He is also called Diespiter. Shown here is a 1613 painting called Jupiter and Callisto by Flemish artist Peter Paul Rubens (peterpaulrubens.org). Also see Gods of Heaven, and Roman Gods and Goddesses.

Jupiter

In Occultism and Theosophy, as the planet or celestial body affecting aspects of human life, Jupiter represents finances, banks, bankers, prestige and reputation, wagers, horses and horse races, luck in general, religions and philosophies, riches, royal courts, lawyers and judges, the law, universities and higher education, benefits and expansion, wisdom, editorials and authors, foreigners and foreign relations, discovery voyages, insurances, children, dreams, ceremonies, rituals and parades, liver and blood. See Planets.

Jurgenson Frequency

The radio reception frequency 1485.0 kHz is called the Jurgenson Frequency for Freidrich Jergenson who discovered Electronic Voice Phenomena. Also see Electronic Voice Phenomena and Friedrich Jurgenson.

Jurgenson, Friedrich

(1903-1987) Russian-born Friedrich Jurgenson was a Swedish painter, singer, polyglot (he could speak at least 10 languages) and film producer who discovered and researched Electronic Voice Phenomena (or EVP) that has also been called Raudive voices. In 1959 he recorded the song of a finch and on playback heard what appeared to be a message from his dead mother. With the help of psychologist Konstantin Raudive he continued to research paranormal voices on tape recordings. In 1960 one of the voices told him to "use the radio". From then on he connected a microphone and a radio receiver to the tape recorder and could have real time conversations. The radio reception frequency 1485.0 kHz is now called the Jurgenson Frequency. He also received the Order of Commendatore Gregorio Magno from Pope Paul VI for his documentary The Fisherman from Gallilea – On the Grave and Stool of Peter. Upon his death Jurgenson left several hundred tapes of recorded material. Also see Electronic Voice Phenomena and aaevp.org.

Justice

Justice is one of the 22 major arcana of the tarot deck of cards. Its number is XI, its Qabbalistic title is The Holder of the Balances and Daughter of the Lord of Truth and its meaning is: eternal justice and balance, force and strength. Also see Tarot.

Justice

See Virtues.

Juventas

In Roman mythology, Juventas, who is also known as Hebe is the Goddess of Youth. She is the daughter of Zeus and Hera and sister of Ares. Juventas helps Hera with her horses and her chariot and serves nectar to the Gods. She is depicted as a beautiful woman wearing beautiful garments. Shown here in a 1753 painting by French artist Jean-Marc Nattier of the Duchess of Orleans called Madame de Caumartin as Hebe. Also see Roman Gods and Goddesses.

Jyeshtha

Hindu Goddess of Bad Luck, Revenge and Dark Magic. She is described as hideous with a black face smeared with blood and with bared teeth and a protruding tongue. Also see Hindu Gods and Goddesses.

K

Ka

According to the ancient Egyptians, the Ka is the vehicle or astral body also known as the life force of humans which is believed to survive the death of the physical body. The Ka together with the Ba (soul) and Khaibit (shadow) are the three components of the human body and soul. This vehicle according to the Egyptians visits the mummified body once in a while and wanders through the Underworld after death. The Ka lives in the physical world and has the same needs as the physical body which is why the offerings of food and drink were left in the tombs. Other spellings include Koi. Also see Astral Bodies.

Ka'aba

In the Holy Islamic city of Mecca there is the sacred stone of the Islamic faith called the Ka'aba. It is considered a massive black meteorite and in 630 B.C.E. the prophet Muhammad deemed it a sacred stone. Muslims always pray towards Mecca and the Ka'aba and every Muslim must make a pilgrimage to the Ka'aba once in their lifetime to represents the ultimate in spiritual fulfillment. While they worship at the Ka'aba pilgrims circle the shrine seven times and then kiss the sacred shrine. Other spellings include Ka'ba. Shown here is a photograph of the Ka'aba from sabrodiesel2000.wordpress.com. Also see Islam, and Mecca.

Ka Akua Po
See Kapo.

Kabalah
See Qabbalah.

Kabat-Zinn, Jon

(1944-) American-born Jon Kabat-Zinn Ph.D. is a bestselling author and professor of medicine. He is the founding Executive Director of the Center for Mindfulness in Medicine, Health Care, and Society at the University of Massachusetts Medical School, founding Director of its renowned Stress Reduction Clinic and Professor of Medicine emeritus at the University of Massachusetts Medical School.. He received his Ph.D. in molecular biology from MIT in the laboratory of Nobel Laureate, Salvador Luria. He is a board member of the Mind and Life Institute and teaches mindfulness and Mindfulness-Based Stress Reduction in various venues around the world. Among Dr. Kabat-Zinn's books are: Full Catastrophe Living: Using the Wisdom of Your Body and Mind to Face Stress, Pain and Illness, Wherever You Go, There You Are: Mindfulness Meditation in Everyday Life; Coming to Our Senses: Healing Ourselves and the World Through Mindfulness; Arriving at Your Own Door: 108 Lessons in Mindfulness; and Letting Everything Become Your Teacher: 100 Lessons in Mindfulness. Photograph from esseresostenibili.it. Also see Center for Mindfulness in Medicine, Health Care and Society, Meditation, Mind-Body Energy Medicine, Recommended Reading, umassmed.edu and mindfulnesstapes.com.

Kachinas

In Hopi mythology, Kachinas, or Katsinas, are Nature Spirits who inhabit everywhere. They animate and control the weather the animals and even the spirits of dead ancestors. Kachinas are known to come down to Earth and interact with human beings to help with agriculture and wisdom. Kachina dolls are a physical vehicle for communication with the Gods. Shown here are Kachina costumes. Image by twofeathers.co.uk. Also see Nature Spirits.

Kaehr, Shelley

(1967-) American-born Shelley Kaehr Ph.D. is considered one of the world's leading authorities on mind-body medicine and energy healing. She specializes in past life regression, grief counseling and future memory journeys. She began her career as a hypnotherapist after the death of a close friend and has conducted over a thousand sessions of hypnosis all over the world where she works with future current life memories and parallel universes. She holds a Ph.D. in Parapsychic Science from the American Institute of Holistic Theology. She has written over 15 books. Among Dr. Kaehr's books include: Gemstone Journeys; Edgar Cayce Guide to Gemstones; Minerals, Metals and More; Origins of Huna: Secrets Behind the Sacred Science; Lifestream: Journey into Past and Future Lives; Divination of God: The Obscure Ancient Tool of Prophecy Revealed; Explorations Beyond Reality: Living Evolution Through Genetic Memory; and Damned: True Tales of the Cursed, Hexed and Bewitched. Also see Healers, Holistic Healing, Mind-Body Energy Medicine, Recommended Reading and shelleykaehr.com.

Kahuna

A traditional Hawaiian practitioner of the Hawaiian magical and philosophical traditions, the Kahuna serves as a priest(ess), teacher and magician of the Huna religion. Kahuna literally means "Keeper of Secrets". Also see Huna, huna.com and huna.org.

Kaku, Michio

(1947-) American-born Michio Kaku Ph.D. is a Japanese American theoretical physicist, advisor to NASA and author of numerous books. He received his B.S. from Harvard, his Ph.D. from the University of California Berkeley, and he also held a lectureship at Princeton University. He currently holds the Henry Semat Chari and Professorship in theoretical physics at City College of New York and the Graduate Center of the City University of New York, where he has taught for 30 years. Among Dr. Kaku's books are: Hyperspace: A Scientific Odyssey through Parallel Universes; Time Warps, and the Tenth Dimension; Parallel Worlds: The Science of Alternative Universes and Our Future in the  Cosmos; Physics of the Impossible: A Scientific Exploration Into the World of Phasers, Force Fields, Teleportation, and Time Travel; and his latest book Physics of the Future: How Science Will Change Daily Life by 2100. Photograph by Andrea Brizzi (andreabrizzi.com). Also see Physicists, Recommended Reading and mkaku.org.

Kala

From Hawaiian religion Huna, Kala is one of its seven philosophical principles and it means "everything is possible, there are no limitations". Also see Huna.

Kali

From the Sanskrit kala meaning "time", Kali is a Hindu Goddess, consort of Siva, who has a dual personality, on one side she is gentle and loving and on the other revengeful and hateful. Kali is the Patron of Witches. She is also known as The Black Mother, the Dark Goddess, the Goddess of Death and the Mother of Karma. She is the embodiment of Mother Nature and rules over revenge, regeneration, dark magic and sexual activities but at the same time she is considered the destroyer of evil spirits and the protector of the devotees. As the female in the Holy Trinity, Kali is called Parvati and represents Nature and embodies the past, present and future. Other spellings include Kali Ma. Shown here is a 1770 depiction of Kali by Richard B. Godfrey. Also see Hindu Gods and Goddesses.

Kali Yuga
See Yugas.

Kaliya
In Hindu mythology, Kaliya is an evil serpent king who is overpowered by Krishna, who pardons his life but sends him to live elsewhere. Shown here is a 1979 depiction of Kaliya called Krishna Chastises the Kaliya Serpent. Also see Mythological Creatures.

Kalki
In Hinduism, Kalki is the last of the ten Avatars, or incarnations of the God Vishnu. Kalki is the only Avatar to have not incarnated yet, he is expected to incarnate at the end of the Kali Yuga or end of time. Kalki is also spelled Kalkin. See Avatar.

Kama
In Theosophy, Kama is the vehicle or body of desire. Also see Astral Bodies.

Kama
In Hindu mythology, Kama is the God of Love and Erotic Desire; he personifies cosmic desire and creative energy. Consort of Rati, he is described as a handsome young man, attended by heavenly nymphs who shoot love-producing flower-arrows. Other spellings include Kandarpa. Also see Hindu Gods and Goddesses.

Kama Rupa
In Theosophy, Kama Rupa is the thought form or thought body created by the physical desires, passions and thoughts in connection to matter which survives the death of the physical body. The Kama Rupa will "dissolve" over time under normal circumstances in the Kamaloka or semi material plane. Other spellings include Kamarupa. Also see Astral Bodies, Kamaloka, Second Death, Thought Forms and Tulpa.

Kamaloka
In Theosophy, Kamaloka is the semi material plane where the Kama Rupas or thought forms remain until they dissolve. Also see Kama Rupa.

Kami
Hindu Goddess of Physical Love, Kami rules over pleasure, sensual desire, spring, flowers and women. She is also called Dipka. Also see Hindu Gods and Goddesses.

Kan
Meaning Water, Dui is the sixth of the eight Gua in Ba Gua. It is the exact opposite of the Li Gua. Its direction is North and it represents Career. See Ba Gua and Triagrams.

Kan Xib Chac
In Mayan mythology, Kan Xib Chac is the yellow man of the South, a facet of the God Chac. Also see Chac, and Maya Gods and Goddesses.

Kanaloa
In Hawaiian mythology Kanaloa is the God of the Sea and the Underworld. He rules over magic the forces of nature and is closely associated with Kane. He is sometimes symbolized by the squid or octopus. Kanaloa is also called the Ocean God. Shown here is a wood carving of Kanaloa by Coco Joe's. Also see Hawaiian Gods and Goddesses, and Underworld Gods.

Kane
In Hawaiian mythology Kane is the God of Forests and Trees. He is closely associated with Kanaloa. He rules over the sun, the sky and dawn. Shown here is a carving of Kane housed in the Bishop Museum of Hawaii. Also see Hawaiian Gods and Goddesses.

Kano
As the 14th symbol of the runes, Kano represents opening. Other spellings include Kenaz. Also see Runes.

Kapo
From Hawaiian mythology, "Ka Akua Po" or Kapo is the Goddess of Night. She guides Earth's children, keeping them safe in the darkness of night. She is sister of Pele and the daughter of Haumea. Kapo lives a double life, on one side she is an angel of grace and beauty, but on the other she also is described as a demon of darkness and lust. Also see Hawaiian Gods and Goddesses.

Kardec, Allan

(1804-1869) French-born Hippolyte Leon Denizard Rivail aka Allan Kardec was a teacher, author and spiritualist. He became interested in Spiritualism and claimed that he had been a Druid named Allan Kardec in a previous life, and adopted the name. Kardec was fluent in several different languages and taught mathematics, astronomy, chemistry, anatomy, physiology, physics and French. He is called the Father of Spiritism. Among his books are: Book on Mediums: or, Guide for Mediums and Invocators: Containing the Special Instruction of the Spirits on the Theory of All Kinds of Manifestations, the Means of Communi-

cating with the Invisible World, the Development of Mediumship, the Difficulties and Dangers That are to Be Encountered in the Practice of Spiritism and Gospel According to Spiritism: Contains Explanations of the Moral Maxims of Christ in Accordance With Spiritism and Their Application in Various Circumstances of Life. Shown here is a 19th Century depiction of Kardec by an unknown author. Also see Spiritualists and allan-kardec.org.

Karma

From Sanskrit, meaning "action" or "deed", in Hinduism, Buddhism and Occultism, karma is the spiritual law of cause and effect that plays itself out in the psychic, moral and physical aspects of life. The law of karma says that every action reaps a like reaction and that the influence of an individual's past incarnations affects his present and future incarnations. Thus, neither unmerited pleasure nor undeserved suffering exists, but rather a universal justice that works through a natural moral law rather than through divine judgment. Good and bad karma have their effect through many lifetimes, as the soul evolves slowly learning from its mistakes and growing wiser, reaping the rewards of good karma and paying off the dept of bad karma until a state of grace is reached and incarnation is no longer needed. Also see Buddhism, Hinduism, Reincarnation, and Yoga.

Karma Yoga

The yoga that preaches the way of good deeds to end bad karma. See Yoga and karma-yoga.net.

Karmic Debt

Karmic debt is the emotional and spiritual dept we owe to people who we have harmed or neglected in previous incarnations. Also see Karma.

Karmic Tie

See Astral Link.

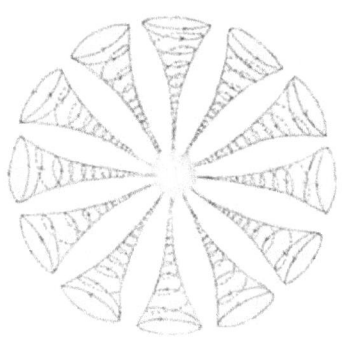

Kartikeya

Hindu God of War, Kartikeya rules over revenge, bravery, battle and black magic. He is called Defender of the Gods, and Chief Battle God. Women are not allowed in his temples. Karttikeya is also known as Subramanya and Skanda. Other spellings include Karttikeya and Karthikeyar. Image by Thiruvavaduthurai Aadheenam. Also see Hindu Gods and Goddesses.

Kasl, Charlotte

American-born Charlotte Sophia Kasl Ph.D. is a psychotherapist, lecturer, author, Quaker and Reiki healer. She holds an M.A. in music from the university of Michigan and a Ph.D. in counseling psychology from Ohio University. She is also a certified addiction specialist and has served on several advisory boards including the Women's Action Alliance for Alcohol and Drug Education, the Organization for Secular Sobriety and the Women's Recovery Network. Dr. Kasl is also a founding member of The Association for the Teaching and Training in the Attachment of Children. Among her books are: If the Buddha Married: Creating Enduring Relationships on a Spiritual Path; If the Buddha Dated: Handbook for Find Love on a Spiritual Path; Many Roads, One Journey: Moving Beyond the Twelve Steps; Women, Sex and Addiction: A Search for Love and Power; and Zen and the Art of a Happier Life: A Handbook for Change on a Spiritual Path. Photograph from discovermbn.com. Also see Healers, Recommended Reading and charlottekasl.com.

Kataskion
See Ephesia Grammata.

Katha
One of the texts of the Upanishads. See Upanishads, and Vedas.

Katie King
Spirit guide said to be channeled through medium Florence Cook. Also see Channeled Spirit Guides, Channelers, and Florence Cook.

Kausitaki
One of the texts of the Upanishads. See Upanishads.

Kay Pacha
In Inca mythology, Kay Pacha is the Present World, one of three worlds that represent the Cosmos. Also see Inca Worlds and Mythological Places.

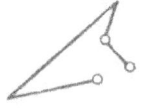

Kedemel
According to Occult and Qabbalistic literature, Kedemel is the spirit of the planets Venus and Jupiter and rules over the zodiac signs of Taurus and Libra. Also see Planetary Spirits.

Kelly, Edward
(1555-1597) Irish-born Thomas Allen Edward Kelly aka Edward Talbot hermetic scholar, alchemist, scryer, lawyer, mathematician and author, as well as convicted criminal and self-declared spirit medium. He worked for seven years as a diviner and scryer with John Dee supposedly deciphering the Enochian system of magic, using ritual magic, scrying and angelic communications with an Angel named Ave. He was imprisoned by the Holy Roman Emperor Rudolf II for failing to produce gold he promised and died trying to escape. Kelly published three works on alchemy: The Stone of the Philosophers, The Theatre of Terrestrial Astronomy and The Humid Way. Shown here is a

mid 19th Century drawing of Edward Kelly by an unknown artist. Also see Alchemists, Diviners, Hermeticists, Mathematicians and Scrying.

Kelpie

A Scottish mischievous or evil mythological creature found around waterfalls, rivers, lakes and streams, and especially near Loch Ness. Kelpies are described as a handsome black or brown horse that can shape-shift into a human being at will, although they said to usually lure their victims by letting them ride on their backs (as a horse) and then plunge them into the lakes or rivers and either scare them or drown them. A Kelpie is also called Aughisky and Each-uisg. Other spellings include Kelpy. Shown here is a 1913 painting by British artist Herbert James Draper called The Kelpie. Also see Mythological Creatures, and Phooka.

Kemet
The ancient name for Egypt, Kemet literally means "black land".

Kena
One of the texts of the Upanishads. See Upanishads.

Keneun
From Iroquois mythology, Keneun is an invisible spirit, chief of the Thunderbirds. In a storm the thunder is the sound of his beating wings and lightning is his eyes flashing. Also see Iroquois Gods and Goddesses.

Kether
The first Sephirah on the Qabbalistic Tree of Life, representing the crown or unity with the Divine, whose symbol is a brilliant glowing crown. See Tree of Life.

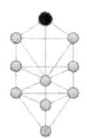

Ketu

In Hinduism Ketu is a celestial deity who rules over the descending lunar node or South lunar node. He is called a "shadow" planet and is said to have an enormous impact on human lives. He is one of the nine Navagrahas and is often depicted with a gem on his forehead to symbolize a mystery light. Other spellings include Kethu. Also see Hindu Gods and Goddesses and Navagrahas.

Key of Solomon
Also known as Clavicula Salomonis, and The Greater Key of Solomon, the Key of Solomon is an ancient planetary magic grimoire

dating back from the 5th Century by an unknown artist. It includes formulae on how to create and consecrate planetary talismans and how to invoke higher spiritual beings such as Angels and other intelligences.

Key to the Mysteries of the Universe
See Archeometre.

Khaibit

According to the ancient Egyptians, the Khaibit is the soul's shadow, or essence of immortal individuality, which, together with the Ka, the astral body and the Ba, the soul, form the Higher Triad. See Ba and Ka. The Khabit is also known as the Akh and is called the blessed dead, the form the deceased takes when the Ba and Ka are united. Shown here is an ancient Egyptian wall painting depicting the Khaibit.

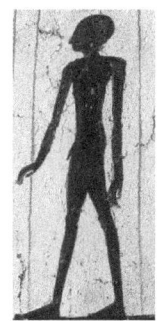

Kharitidi, Olga

Russian-born Olga Kharitidi aka Olga Yahontova M.D. is a doctor, psychiatrist and author. She was born in Siberia and after working in a mental hospital she traveled to Kazakhstan, Uzbekistan and Siberia researching shamanic teachings and ancient magical healing practices. Dr. Kharitidi later moved to the United States living first in Minneapolis, MN and currently in Santa Barbara, CA where she runs Cliffhouse Publications, and presents her thoughts on trauma in her blog Breaking the Walls. She has written: Entering the Circle: Ancient Secrets of a Siberian Wisdom Discovered by a Russian Psychiatrist and The Master of Lucid Dreams: In the Heart of Asia a Russian Psychiatrist Learns How to Heal the Spirits of Trauma. Photograph from 123people.co.uk. Also see Lucid Dreams, Recommended Reading and Shamans.

Khem
Khem is an ancient name for Egypt.

Khepera

Egyptian God of Transformations, Khephera's symbol is the scarab beetle and he rules over beginnings, healings, literary abilities, creative energy and eternal life. He is the God of reincarnation and rebirth, of exorcism, healing and of miracles and compassion. Other spellings include Khepra and Khepri. Khepera is depicted here from a mural on the walls of the tomb of Queen Nefertiti from around 1,250 BCE, located in the Valley of the Queens near Thebes, Egypt. Also see Egyptian Gods and Goddesses.

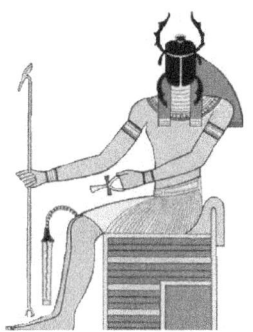

Khnemu

Egyptian Ram Headed God of the Nile Khnemu watches over the sources of the Nile and makes each human form and their Ka on his potter's wheel. Khnemu is considered a creator, an architect, a builder and a controller of water. Other spellings include Khnum, Khenmew and Khenmu. Also see Egyptian Gods and Goddesses, and Ka.

Khonsu

Egyptian Moon God, Khonsu crosses the sky in a boat. He is the son of Amun and Mut, he is worshiped at Karnak and his statue is believed to have healing powers. Khonsu rules over female fertility, the crescent and full moon and cattle. Other spellings include, Chons, Chunsu and Khons. Shown here is a carving of Khonsu in Karnak, Egypt. Also see Egyptian Gods and Goddesses.

Khopun

Slavic River God who drowns bad men. Also see Slavic Gods and Goddesses.

Khshathra-Vairya

In Persian mythology, Khshathra Vairya is one of the six Amesha Spentas or benevolent and immortal beings created by Ahura Mazda as manifestations of himself. He helps the lost souls overcome evil and personifies God's might. Khshathra-Vairya is also known as Shahrevar. See Amesha Spentas, and Ahura Mazda.

Khunrath, Heinrich

(1560-1605) German born Heinrich Khunrath M.D. was a physician, spiritual alchemist, Hermetic philosopher, author and illustrator. He wrote around 10 books on spiritual alchemy and mysticism, most published after his death. Dr. Khunrath's most famous book was the Amphitheatrum Sapientiae Aeternae (Amphitheater of Eternal Wisdom) aka the Alchemist's Laboratory. Disciple of Paracelsus, Dr. Khunrath received his M.D. from the University of Basel in Switzerland in 1588 and practiced medicine in Magdeburg, Hamburg, Dresden and Leipzig. He traveled extensively and met John Dee while Dee was imprisoned at the Imperial court in Prague. Dr. Khunrath was later appointed court physician in Trebona to Count Rosemberk. He is shown here is a 16th Century depiction by an unknown author. Other spellings include Kunrath. Also see Alchemists, Hermeticists and Philosophers.

Kikimora

In Slavic mythology, Kikimora is a female Nature Spirit who lives behind the stove or fireplace. She looks after the poultry and when she likes the woman of the house she helps her with household chores, but when she doesn't like her she makes noises at night and interferes with the household by breaking and hiding things. Kikimora is married to Domovoi. She is depicted here in a 1934 rendition by Russian illustrator Ivan Bilibin. Also see Domovoi, and Nature Spirits.

Kilya
In Inca mythology, Kilya is the Goddess of Marriage. Also see Inca Gods and Goddesses.

King Arthur
Legendary prince and hero of ancient Briton, King Arthur holds his court at Camelot with his noble knights of the round table, his Queen Gwynevere and his counselor and magician Merlin. His legend is closely related to Avalon, the Sword in the Stone and the Holy Grail. Shown here is a 1903 painting of King Arthur by English artist Charles Ernest Butler. Also see Avalon, Holy Grail, Merlin, arthurian-legend.com and celtic-twilight.com.

King, Deborah
American-born Deborah King is a health and wellness expert, attorney, national keynote speaker, frequent TV commentator and a "healer to the stars" as well as a featured blogger for The Huffington Post. She holds a doctorate in law from the University of California and has studied many different modalities of alternative healing. Her amazing recovery from cancer in her twenties lead her to leave the corporate arena for the alternative medical field, where she mastered ancient and modern healing systems and ultimately developed a powerful technique of her own. She has written Truth Heals – What You Hide Can Hurt You, which explores the powerful relationship between the suppression of painful emotions and their impact on our health and happiness and Be Your Own Shaman: Heal Yourself and Others with 21st Century Energy Medicine. Through celebrity profiles and the telling of her own remarkable story of recovery from an eating disorder, depression, various addictions, sexual abuse and cancer. Ms. King hosts seminars across the country where she leads thousands to recovery. Also see Healers, Mind-Body Energy Medicine, Recommended Reading and deborahkingcenter.com.

King of the Witches
See Alex Sanders.

King Solomon
(?-931 B.C.E.) King of Israel, son of King David. King Solomon was the third King of Israel and noted for his wisdom. He was described as The Wisest of Men and was considered a powerful occultist who used magic to defeat his enemies. One of King Solomon's great achievements was the building of the

Temple of Jerusalem that his father King David had wanted to build. This temple is now known as the Temple of Solomon. Shown here is an 1854 painting of King Solomon by British artist Simeon Solomon (simeonsolomon.com). Also see Occultists.

Kingma, Daphne Rose

American-born Daphne Rose Kingma is a psychotherapist, author, teacher, spiritual healer, motivational speaker and workshop leader. She was dubbed "The Love Doctor" by the San Francisco Chronicle and has written many books. She presents seminars throughout the United States and Europe and is considered an expert of matters of the heart. Ms. Kingma's books include: The Future of Love: The Power of Soul in Intimate Relationships; The; Loving Yourself: Four Steps to a Happier You; Weddings from the Heart: Contemporary and Traditional Ceremonies for an Unforgettable Wedding; True Love: How to Make Your Relationship, Sweeter, Deeper, and More Passionate; A Life Time of Love: How to Bring More Depth, Meaning and Intimacy Into Your Relationship; and The Ten Things to Do When Your Life Falls Apart: An Emotional and Spiritual Handbook. Also see Healers, Recommended Reading, Spiritual Teachers and daphnekingma.com.

Kingsford, Anna

(1846-1888) English-born Anna Bonus aka Anna Kingsford M.D. was one of the first female physicians in England. She was a precocious child and married her cousin Algernon Godfrey Kingsford when she was 21. She later studied medicine in Paris. She was a president of the Theosophical Society for a while and founded her own Hermetic Society. Dr. Kingsford was a well known advocate of women's rights and vegetarianism. She claimed to receive insights in trance-like states of sleep. She wrote several books including; The Perfect Way in Diet: A Treatise Advocating a Return to the Natural and Ancient Food of Our Race; Health, Beauty, and the Toilet: Letters to Ladies from a Lady Doctor; and "Violationism", Or, Sorcery in Science. Also see Hermeticists, Theosophists and anna-kingsford.com.

Kingston, Karen

English-born Karen Kingston is considered to be the leading authority in the Feng Shui art of Space Clearing and she tours the world give lectures and teaching workshops. Ms. Kingston coined the term Space Clearing in 1989 and it has been a common New Age term since. She has lived in Bali since 1990 and she built a hotel and conference center based on Feng Shui called Dancing Dragon Cottages, which has become a popular tourist destination. She has written: Creating Sacred Space with Feng Shui and Clearing Your Clutter with Feng Shui, which has been translated into 26 languages, Clear Your Clutter with Feng Shui; and Clutter Free in Seven Days. Also see Feng Shui, Space Clearing and Recommended Reading and spaceclearing.com.

Kinich-Ahau
Maya Sun God who rules the lighting of sacrificial fires and he commands disease and drought. He is Itzamna during the daytime. Kinich-Ahau is also known as Sunface Fire Macaw and Golden Bird. Other spellings include Kinich-Ahaw and Kinich-Ajaw-Pakal. Also see Maya Gods and Goddesses.

Kircher, Athanasius

(1602-1680) German born Athanasius Kircher was a Jesuit priest, mathematician and scholar who published over 40 books in oriental studies, geology and medicine. He studied at the Jesuit College in Fulda and took philosophy and theology at Paderborn. He was one of the first to observe microbes and propose that the plague was caused by them. He taught mathematics, Hebrew and Syriac at Heilingenstadt and was professor of ethics and mathematics at the University of Wurzburg. He studied Egyptian hieroglyphics and designed a variety of machines including a speaking tube, a perpetual motion machine and an Aeolian harp. He even tried to decipher the Voynich Manuscript. He was considered one of the last renaissance men and was described as the first scholar with a global reputation. He wrote over 35 books including Mundus Subterraneus in 1664 where he describes the continent of Atlantis. Other spellings include Kirchner. Shown here is a 1664 depiction of Kircher by Dutch artist Cornelius Bloemart. Also see Atlantis, Mathematicians, Philosophers, Recommended Reading, Reverends and Ministers and Voynich Manuscript.

Kirlian Photography

A form of photography invented by Semyon Kirlian in 1939 that uses high frequency, high voltage and low amperage electrical fields that reveals the electro-magnetic field, or aura of plants, animals and people. This type of photography is also called Electrography. Also see Aura, Gas Discharge Visualization Technique, kirlian.com and kirlian.org.

Kishar

In Assyrian and Babylonian mythology, Kishar, meaning "Whole Earth" is the Mother of the Gods. She is the daughter of Apsu and Tiamat and she rules with her brother and consort Anshar. She rules the Earth while he rules the Sky. Kishar is shown here in an ancient Babylonian relief with Anshar. Also see Assyrian Gods and Goddesses, and Babylonian Gods and Goddesses.

Kisin

In Maya mythology, Kisin is the evil God or Spirit of Earthquakes, known as "the Stinking One". He lives underground where the spirits of the dead spend some time, and suicides are doomed to his realm for eternity. Other spellings include Cizin. Image from dailygalaxy.com. Also see Maya Gods and Goddesses.

Kitcki Manitou

In Algonquin mythology, Kitcki Manitou is the Supreme God and Great Spirit. He is called Father of Life and the Uncreated. Also see Algonquin Gods and Goddesses.

Knight, Gareth

(1930-) British-born Basil Wilby aka Gareth Knight is a well known British Qabbalist and Occultist who trained as a member of Dion Fortune's Society of the Inner Light where he was the librarian. Later with W.E. Butler he created the Helios Course in Practical Qabbalah for the Esoteric Order, the Servants of the Light. Knight later established his own Esoteric Order. He has written over 30 books including: Practical Guide to Qabbalistic Symbolism; Occult Exercises and Practices: Gateways to the Four 'Worlds' of Occultism; The Practice of Ritual Magic; The Occult: An Introduction; The Secret Tradition in Arthurian Legend; Magical Images and the Magical Imagination: A Practical Handbook for Self Transformation Using the Techniques of Creative Visualization and Meditation; The Experience of the Inner World; and Yours Very Truly –Gareth Knight Selected Letters. Photograph from lojasaojorge.blogspot.com. Also see Occultists, Qabbalists, Recommended Reading, Servants of the Light and garethknight.blogspot.com.

Knight, JZ

(1946-) American-born Judith Darlene Hampton aka Judy Zebra Knight and JZ Knight is a spiritual channel and founder of Ramtha's School of Enlightenment. Ms. Knight channels an entity called Ramtha the Enlightened One, the great Ram of many ancient cultures and traditions, including Egypt and India. It was Ramtha, channeled through JZ Knight, who coined the term "channeling" in 1978, which later became very popular. Ramtha made a clear distinction between a channel and a medium. Ms. Knight submitted herself to rigorous scientific testing by independent scholars and scientists who published their findings in the Journal of the American Parapsychological Society. She has published many books CD's and DVD's of her work and teachings recorded live while channeling Ramtha. Among her books are: Ramtha: The White Book; JZ Knight: A State of Mind – My Story; A Beginner's Guide to Creating Reality; A Masters Key for Manipulating Time; and Changing the Timeline of Our Destiny. Photograph from ramisrael.com. Also see Channeled Spirit Guides, Channelers, Ramtha, Ramtha's School of Enlightenment, Recommended Reading, jzknight.com and ramtha.com.

Knights Templar

Order of Knights and monks, also known as the Templars, the Order of the Poor Knights of Christ and the Knights of the Temple of Solomon. They were a religious military order founded in Jerusalem in 1118, during the Crusades, by Hugh de Payens, Godfrey of St. Omer and seven others, allegedly as administrative and military branch of an older Secret Order called the Prieure de Sion. Officially recognized by the Pope in 1129, their mission was to protect people on their pilgrimages to the Holy Land. They were divided into four classes: knights, sergeants, chaplains and servants headed by a Grand Master. Only the knights wore the distinctive regalia of the order, a red cross. They were a formidable army, the greatest since the Romans, partly because they took vows of poverty and believed that being killed in battle would make up for all their sins. They became vital in the defense of the Christian Crusades in the Holy Land and at their height numbered around 20,000 or more. For political and monetary gain King Philip IV of France with the aid of Pope Clement V had all members of the Knights Templar arrested in 1307 and accused of heresy and immorality. The order was suppressed by the Pope in 1312 and in 1314 the Order's last Grand Master, Jaques de Molay, was burned at the stake. Shown above is a 19th Century depiction of the Knights Templar by Irish artist Thomas Keightley. Also see Jacques de Molay, Occult Orders, Brotherhoods and Secret Societies, Prieure de Sion, knightstemplar.org and templarhistory.com.

Kolisko Effect

In the 1920's a young follower of theosophist Rudolf Steiner named Lili Kolisko began a series of experiments to test claims of the society's astrological teachings that certain planets rule certain metals. The tradition says that the Sun rules gold, the Moon rules silver, Mercury rules mercury, Venus rules copper, Mars rules iron, Jupiter rules tin and Saturn rules lead. Ms. Kolisko carried out a series of experiments in which metallic salts were dissolved and the solutions dried on filter paper. She hypothesized that if the position of the planets affected the metals than the patterns of the resulting crystals would have to change as the planets shifted. After hundreds of tests she was able to show that indeed the rates of the crystallization were either blocked all together or significantly delayed during the occultation in which Saturn is behind the Sun or Moon. Ms. Kolisko also conducted experiments to test the traditional belief that planting should occur while the moon is waxing and she found that in fact plants sown before the full Moon grow more rapidly and are healthier in general than those planted prior to the new Moon.

Koran
See Qur'an.

Kornfield, Jack

(1945-) American-born Jack Kornfield Ph.D. is a Buddhist monk, teacher and author. He holds a Ph.D. in clinical psychology. He trained as a Buddhist monk in the monasteries of Thailand, India and Burma and has taught meditation internationally since 1974. He founded the Insight Meditation Society and Spirit Rock Meditation Center. Among Dr. Kornfield's books are: A Path with Heart: The Classic Guide Through the Perils and Promises of Spiritual Life; Buddha's Little Instruction Book; Teachings of the Buddha; The Art of Forgiveness, Lovingkindness and Peace and The Wise Heart: A Guide to the Universal Teaching of Buddhist Psychology. Photograph by Jerushalom. Also see Buddhist Monks, Meditation, Recommended Reading, Spirit Rock Meditation Center, Spiritual Retreats, spiritrock.org and jackkornfield.org.

Korotkov, Konstantin

Russian-born Konstantin Korotkov Ph.D. is the director of the St. Petersburg Research Center on Medical and Biological Engineering and professor of physics at St. Petersburg State Technical University in Russia. He is also an inventor, holding 12 patents on biophysics inventions, author of four books and scholar in philosophy. His invention, known as the Gas Discharge Visualization technique is the next step in Kirlian photography, allowing real-time viewing of the aura. Dr. Korotkov has written Light After Life: A Scientific Journey Into the Spiritual World; Human Energy Field: Study with GDV Bioelectography; Aura and Consciousness: New Stage of Scientific Understanding; Energy Fields Electrophotonic Analysis in Humans and Nature and The Energy of Consciousness. Photograph from reconnectyourself.it. Also see Aura, Gas Discharge Visualization Technique, Kirlian Photography, Recommended Reading, korotkov.org and gdvusa.org.

Korrigan

In Celtic mythology, Korrigan is a female fairy or Elemental who lives in the woods near a spring or stream and seeks mortal lovers among those who drink from her waters. Other spellings include Korigan and Corrigan. She is also called Ozeganned and Ozegan. Korrigan is also called The Lady of the Lake and The Lady of the Fountain. Shown here is an 1863 painting by British artist Herbert James Draper called The Water Nymph. Also see Elementals.

Kovelman, Joyce

American-born Joyce Kovelman Ph.D. anatomy and Ph.D. psychology is an internationally renowned motivational speaker, scientist, TV and radio speaker, and author. She also holds a NIMH post-doctoral fellowship in psychiatry and biobehavioral sciences. She taught at the Medical School and the University of California Los Angeles and currently practices psychology in Chatsworth, California. Dr. Kovelman serves as an official ECOSOC representative to the United Nations for the Institute of Global Education as is the President of the Millennium Project, foundation dedicated to "Peace on Earth, Peace with

Earth." She has written: Namaste: Initiation and Transformation: A How to for Those Who Wish to Embrace ASOUL and One Upon a Soul: The Story Continues… Science, Psychology and the Realms of Spirit. Also see Recommended Reading, Scientists and essentialsforasoul.com.

Koven, Jean-Claude

French-born Jean-Claude Gerard Koven is a well known entrepreneur, award-winning author and speaker. He was educated in New York public schools and attended M.I.T. He also studied for many years with spiritual masters and is the author of over 100 published articles and the book Going Deeper: How to Make Sense of Your Life When Your Life Makes No Sense, the recipient of the best metaphysical book of the year award from both Allbooks Reviews and USA Book News. He has lead awareness-expanding workshops all over the world. He is a feature columnist for United Press International's Religion and Spirituality Forum. Also see Recommended Reading, Self-Help and goingdeeper.org.

Kowalski, Gary

(1953-) American-born Gary Kowalski D.D. is a Unitarian Universalist and author of spiritual matters. He studied at Harvard College and graduated from Harvard Divinity School. Reverend Kowalski served in churches in Seattle, Washington and Memphis, Tennessee before serving the First Unitarian Universalist Society of Burlington, Vermont. Among his books are: Revolutionary Spirits: The Enlightened Faith of America's founding Fathers, The Souls of Animals; The Bible According To Noah: Theology As If Animals Mattered; Science and the Search for God; Understanding the World's Religions: A Story Guide to Huston Smith's The World's Religions; Goodbye Friend: Healing Wisdom For Anyone Who Has Ever Lost a Pet; and Questions You Might Ask. Also see Recommended Reading, Reverends and Ministers, Spiritual Teachers and uusociety.org.

Kraken

In Western European mythology, a Kraken is an enormous sea snake or creature. The Kraken is said to be so big that sailors mistake it for islands but when they come near it the Kraken becomes all heads and tentacles and sinks the ship. Shown here is a 20th Century depiction of a Kraken by American artist Bob Eggleton (bobeggleton.com). Also see Cryptids, and Mythological Creatures.

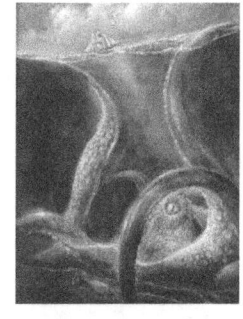

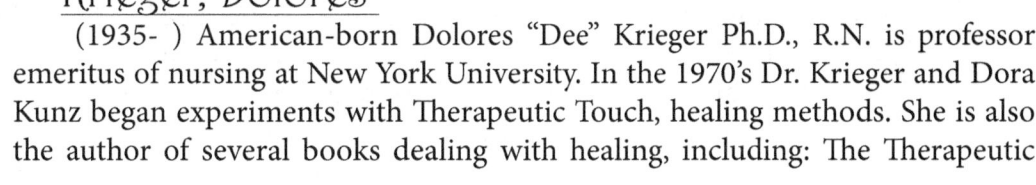

Krieger, Dolores

(1935-) American-born Dolores "Dee" Krieger Ph.D., R.N. is professor emeritus of nursing at New York University. In the 1970's Dr. Krieger and Dora Kunz began experiments with Therapeutic Touch, healing methods. She is also the author of several books dealing with healing, including: The Therapeutic

Touch: How to Use Your Hands to Help and Heal; Spiritual Healing; Accepting Your Power To Heal: The Personal Practice of Therapeutic Touch and The Spiritual Dimension of Therapeutic Touch. Also see Therapeutic Touch. Photograph taken by Crystal Hawk. Also see Clairvoyants, Healers, Recommended Reading, doloreskrieger.com, pumpkinhollow.org and therapeutictouch.org.

Krippner, Stanley

(1932-) American-born Stanley Krippner Ph.D. is one of the best known and most respected parapsychological researchers in the world today. He served as president of the Parapsychological Association, the Association for Humanistic Psychology, and both the Psychological Hypnosis and the Humanistic Psychology Divisions of the American Psychological Association. Dr. Krippner is also a former president of the International Association for the Study of Dreams and the 2002 recipient of the American Psychological Association's Award for Distinguished Contributions to the International Advancement of Psychology. Among his books are: Dream Telepathy: Experiments in Nocturnal ESP; Becoming Psychic: Spiritual Lessons for Focusing Your Hidden Abilities; Song of the Siren: A Parapsychological Odyssey; Healing States: A Journey Into the World of Spiritual Healing and Shamanism; The Mythic Path: Discovering the Guiding Stories of Your Past and Mysterious Minds: The Neurobiology of Psychics, Mediums and Other Extraordinary People. Photograph from123people.com. Also see Dream Analysts, Parapsychologists and Psychic Researchers, Recommended Reading and stanleykrippner.weebly.com.

Krishna

Hindu Savior God also known as The Dark One, the Stealer of Hearts and the Savior from Sin. Krishna is known as the most famous incarnation of Vishnu and the eighth of the Avatars. The Hindus refer to Krishna as the Firstborn, the Redeemer, the Sin Bearer, the Liberator and the Universal Word. He is also believed to be the author of the Bhagavad-Gita. Krishna is the God of Sexual Pleasures, Erotic Delights, Music and Love. It is written that he returns at the end of each age to establish goodness and destroy sin. Image from iloveulove.com. Also see Avatar, Hindu Gods and Goddesses, krishna.com, and iskcon.com.

Krishnamurti, Jiddu

(1895-1986) Indian-born Jiddu Krishnamurti was a well known author, speaker, spiritual teacher in human relationships, mind, meditation and psychological revolution. In 1909 he met Charles Leadbeater and was subsequently raised by Leadbeater and Annie Besant groomed to be a World Teacher. He eventually disavowed the Theosophical traditions and went on to tour the world given speeches for the next 60 years claiming allegiance to no country, cast, philosophy or religion. Krishnamurti addressed the United Nations on the subject of awareness and peace at age 90 and was awarded the United Nations Peace Medal. Among his books are: At the Feet of the Master; The Immortal Friend; Life in Freedom; The Wholeness of Life; The Way of Intelligence and Freedom from the Known. Photograph from sentientpublications.com. Also see Recommended Reading, Spiritual Teachers and jkrishnamurti.org.

Kriya Yoga
The yoga that preaches religious observance through ritual acts. See Yoga, kriya.org and kriyayoga.com.

Krita Yuga
See Yugas.

KRN
See Kundalini Research Network.

Krumm-Heller, Arnold

(1876-1949) German-born Arnold Krumm-Heller aka Huiracocha was an occultist, doctor and Rosicrucian best known for being an important figure in Latin American occultism. At age 16 he moved to Argentina and instead ended up in Chile where he married and lived for the next 20 years. After that he returned to Germany and traveled extensively. In Germany Krumm-Heller studied with Franz Hartmann and later he visited with Papus and Rudolf Steiner. He moved to Mexico in 1910 studied medicine and founded the Fraternitas Rosicruciana Antiqua. Krumm-Heller was member of several occult orders, including the Ordo Templi Orientis (OTO). In Peru he received the magical name of Huiracocha, by which he would be known in esoteric circles. A decade later he moved back to Germany and established a printing business. He wrote and published many books in German and Spanish. Photograph taken by Dionisio Rios Ballester in 1939. Also see Occultists, Ordo Templi Orientalis and Rosicrucians.

Kshandada-chara
In Hindu mythology, Kshandada-chara are evil spirits and ghosts that roam in the night. They are also called Night Walkers. Also see Supernatural and Spiritual Beings.

Kshitagarbha
In Tibetan Buddhism, Kshitagarbha is one of the eight Great Bodhisattvas or enlightened ones who spiritually ministers to humanity. He is also called the Great Vow Bodhisattva. In China he is considered the God of Mercy. Also see Bodhisattvas, Great Bodhisattvas, and Buddhas.

Kubera

Hindu dwarf Earth God, Kubera is the King of the Yakshas, semi-divine beings and Guhyakas, lesser spirits and guardians of treasures. He rules over of fertility, minerals, earth, mountains, gold, jewels, silver, pearls, precious stones and wealth in general. He is also called the Lord of Riches. Brahma gave Kubera a magic vehicle made of flowers (palace included) called the Pushapaka. Kubera is depicted as a man covered in ornaments and jewels. Other spellings include Kuvera. Kubera is also called Dhanapiti, Vaisravana, Jambhala and Khanapait. Kubera is one of the Lokapalas as Guardian of the Northern Quarter. Shown here is a 19th Century drawing by French artist Louis Thomas Bardel called Kuvera. Also see Hindu Gods and Goddesses, and Lokapalas.

Kubera

The Tibetan Kubera is a version a God of riches, one of the Wrathful Deities. Kubera is also called Vaisravana. Also see Tibetan Gods and Goddesses, and Wrathful Deities.

Kubler-Ross, Elisabeth

(1926-2004) Swiss-born Elisabeth Kubler-Ross M.D. studied psychiatry in Zurich before moving to the United States in 1958. She worked at several major hospitals in several different cities. In the 1980's she bought a large farm in Head Waters Virginia which she called Healing Waters for her workshop and healing center. Dr. Kubler-Ross proposed the now famous "Five Stages of Grief" (denial, anger, bargaining, depression, and acceptance) and wrote more than 20 books on death and dying, including: On Death and Dying; On Children and Death; To Live Until We Say Good-Bye; Death: The Final Stage of Growth; The Tunnel and the Light: Essential Insights on Living and Dying; Life Lessons: Two Experts of Death and Dying Teach Us About the Mysteries of Life and Living and Remember the Secret. Dr. Ross has received 23 honorary doctorates. Photograph from verleih.polyfilm.at. Also see Elisabeth Kübler-Ross Foundation, Recommended Reading, Thanatology and ekrfoundation.org.

Kuhlman, Kathryn

(1907-1976) American-born Kathryn Johanna Kuhlman was a well known Christian faith spiritual healer and Pentecostal evangelist. She had a religious experience at 13 to become a Minister and dropped out of school at 15 to preach, eventually becoming an itinerant evangelist, traveling extensively around the United States on "healing crusades" for over 30 years. She held regular services in the Carnegie Auditorium at Pittsburgh for the next 20 years where a number of healings were reported. Ms. Kuhlman claimed that she experienced astral projection during her trancelike conditions in which she would become aware of illnesses among her audiences in her healing services. Photograph from weaton.edu. Also see Astral Projection, Evangelists, Healers, Recommended Reading and kathyrnkuhlman.com.

Kukulcan
Maya and Toltec Supreme God, Kukulcan rules over the four elements, resurrection and reincarnation, light, learning, culture, healing, law and order and the calendar. According to the legend he emerged from the ocean and helped build and name the city of Mayapan which later became the capital of the Mayan territory, he then disappeared into the ocean again. He is also known as the Feathered Serpent. Other spellings include Kulkulcan. Also see Maya Gods and Goddesses.

Kulagina, Nina
(1926-1990) Russian-born, Ninel "Nina" Sergeyevna Kulgarina was a famous psychic who demonstrated extraordinary psychokinetic, psychic and healing abilities and was studied and tested extensively by the Russians who, to hide her identity called her Nelya Mikhailova, name by which she was known outside of Russia. Ms. Kulgarina reportedly could identify colors with the tips of her fingers; heal open wounds by placing her hand over the affected area and move objects with her mind under laboratory conditions. She said she required time to meditate and clear her mind before she could focus and that storms interfered with her abilities. Also see Healers, Psychics and Psychokinesis.

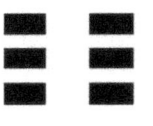
Kun
Meaning Earth, Kun is the first of the eight Gua in Ba Gua. It contains all Yin and represents the Mother. Its direction is Southwest and it also represents Love and Marriage. See Ba Gua and Triagrams.

Kundalini
Sanskrit meaning "serpent of power" or "serpent of fire", kundalini is described as the dormant spiritual or cosmic energy stored in the root chakra which, when adequately aroused through meditation, rituals or yoga techniques, rises through channels called the ida and the pingala to the other chakras until it reaches the crown chakra where it produces spiritual enlightenment and activates the psychic abilities. Shown here is a painting by American artist Cynthia Re Robbins (art4spirit.com) called Kundalini Rising. Also see Chakras, Ida, Pingala and fire-serpent.com.

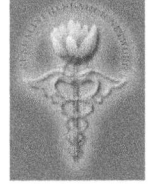
Kundalini Research Network
The Kundalini Research Network (or KRN) is in its own words: welcomes interested individuals from around the world. We are not restricted to any religious tradition or spiritual discipline. The common thread is an interest in ancient streams of traditional wisdom, as well as in the flow of scientific information pertinent to Kundalini

phenomena. We are dedicated to expanding and deepening this pool of knowledge and making it accessible to all. The Kundalini process and spiritual transformation are often misunderstood and even pathologized. Therefore, a primary goal is to bring accurate information and research findings related to Kundalini processes to health care professionals, researchers, and individuals experiencing such processes. The Kundalini Research Network is dedicated to making these awesome and complex processes more understandable and more widely recognized. Also see New Age Associations and Societies, and kundalininet.org.

Kundalini Yoga

Yoga that deals with awakening of Kundalini. See Kundalini Yoga, kundaliniyoga.com and kundaliniyoga.org.

Kunz, Dora

(1904-1999) Javanese-born Dora van Gelder Kunz, was an American Theosophist, psychic, clairvoyant and psychic diagnostician (medical intuitive). She was President of the Theosophical Society in America from 1975 to 1987. She claims to have communed with fairies and elementals her whole life and as a young woman she wrote about those experiences. Ms. Kunz was said to have the ability to see psychic energy patterns (auras) and their relationship to the health of the body. In the 1970's she and Dolores Krieger began experiments with Therapeutic Touch healing methods. Her books include: The Real World of Fairies: A First Person Account; Spiritual Aspects of the Healing Arts; The Spiritual Dimension of Therapeutic Touch and Spiritual Healing. Photograph from cwlworld.info. Also see Psychic Diagnosticians, Psychics, Recommended Reading, Auras, Theosophists, Therapeutic Touch, and therapeutictouch.org.

Kupala

Slavic Goddess of Water and Springs, Kupala rules over plants and herbs, flowers, trees, prosperity, riches, purification and protection. Kupala is the counterpart of Kupalo. Kupala is depicted here in an 1897 rendition by Polish artist Wojciech Gerson. Also see Slavic Gods and Goddesses.

Kupalo

Slavic God of Water and Springs, Kupalo rules over plants and herbs, flowers, trees, prosperity, riches, purification and protection. Kupalo is the counterpart of Kupala. Other spellings include Kypalo. Also see Slavic Gods and Goddesses.

Kurma

In Hinduism, Kurma, the tortoise is the second incarnation or Avatar of the God Vishnu in the Satya Yuga. See Avatar and Yuga.

Kurma Purana

In Hinduism, Kurma Purana, which deals with the Kurma or tortoise incarnation of Vishnu and his revelations, is one of the texts which explain the myths and rituals of the Gods. Also see Puranas.

Kushner, Lawrence

(1943-) American-born Rabbi Lawrence Kushner is a well known author and the Emanu-El Scholar in residence at the Congregation Emanu-El of San Francisco, California. He graduated from the University of Cincinnati and was ordained Rabbi from the Hebrew Union College. Rabbi Kushner also serves as Adjunct member of the faculty of the Hebrew Union College in Los Angeles. He has written over fifteen books. His most notable book is: Kabbalah: A Love Story. He also wrote among others: The River of Light: Spirituality, Judaism, and the Evolution of Consciousness; Sparks Beneath the Surface: A Spiritual Commentary on the Torah; Invisible Lines of Connection: Sacred Stories of the Ordinary; The River of Light: Jewish Mystical Awareness; The Book of Miracles: A Young Person's Guide to Jewish Spiritual Awareness; Book of Letters: A Mystical Hebrew Alef-Bait; and I'm God, Your Not: Observations on Organized Religion and Other Disguises of The Ego. Photograph from jccdet.org. Also see Rabbis, Recommended Reading, lawrencekushner.com and rabbikushner.org.

Kutiel

In Jewish magical traditions, Kutiel is an Angel invoked in connection with the use of the divining rods. Also see Angels.

Kybalion, The

One of the most important books on Occultism, published anonymously in 1912 as the work of "Three Initiates". Also see Sacred Writings. This book explains the seven hermetic principles: The principle of mentalism, which says that all phenomena is the result of mental and that physical mater is the result of the universal Mind; The principle of correspondence, which says that the same patterns and principles are true on every level of existence; The principle of vibration, which says that all the different levels of existence are different levels of vibration which emanate from one basic mental source; The principle of polarity, which says that all things have two opposing aspects and all opposites are aspects of some unity; The principle of rhythm, which says that all things have a rhythm between their opposing aspects and this, gives rise to an infinite number of cycles of rhythm of action and reaction. The principle of cause and effect, which says that all things are the cause of some effect and the effect of some cause, so nothing happens by chance; and The principle of gender, which says that everything and every plane has male and female principles and that all creation takes place between the contacts of the genders.

Kye ne Bardo

In Tibetan Yoga and Buddhist traditions Kye ne Bardo is the plane of the normal waking. See Bardo.

L

LaBerge, Stephen

(1947-) American-born Stephen LaBerge Ph.D. is a psychophysiologist, bestselling author and world renowned leader in the scientific study of lucid dreaming. He received his B.A. in mathematics from the University of Arizona and his Ph.D. in psychophysiology at Stanford University. In 1987 Dr. LaBerge founded The Lucidity Institute to continue his research with his most notable techniques called MILD technique (mnemonic induction of lucid dreams) and DreamLight. He has taught courses on sleep and dreaming, altered states of consciousness and psychobiology at the California Institute of Integral Studies, Stanford University and San Francisco State University. Dr. LaBerge has written: Lucid Dreaming; Exploring the World of Lucid Dreaming; and Lucid Dreaming: A Concise Guide to Awakening in Your Dreams and in Your Life; Controlling Your Dreams. Also see Dream Analysts, Lucid Dreams, Recommended Reading and lucidity.com.

Lachesis

One of the three Greek Goddesses who determine human destiny, Lachesis is the Dispenser of Lots who decides the life span and assigns to each their own destiny. Lachesis is shown here with her sisters in an 1887 painting by American artist Elihu Vedder (elihuvedder.org) called The Fates Gathering the Stars. See Fates, and Greek Gods and Goddesses.

Lad, Vasant

Indian-born Vasant Dattatray Lad B.A.M. & S., MASc is a well known Ayurvedic physician and author, founder of the Ayurvedic Institute and considered the foremost expert of Ayurveda in the United States. He received the degree of Bachelor of Ayurvedic Medicine and Surgery (B.A.M.&S.) in 1968 from the University of Pune, in Pune, India and a Master of Ayurvedic Science (MASc.) in 1980 from Tilak Ayurved Mahavidyalaya in Pune. He worked for three years as a medical doctor for the Ayurveda Hospital in Pune, India and was professor of clinical medicine at the Pune University College. In 1979 he began teaching Ayurveda throughout the United States and in 1984 he founded and began as director of The Ayurvedic Institute. Among Dr. Lad's books are: Ayurveda: The Science of Self-Healing: The Complete Book of Ayurvedic Home Remedies; Secrets of the Pulse; Ayurvedic Cooking for Self-Healing and The Textbook of Ayurveda series (four volumes). Photograph from joyfulbelly.com. Also see Ayurvedic Institute, Recommended Reading, Self-Healing and ayurveda.com.

Lada

From Slavic mythology, Lada is the Goddess of Marriage, and wife of Lado, God of Marriage. Together they rule over happiness. Shown here is a 1991 painting of Lada by Russian artist Alex Fantalov (fantalov.narod.ru). Also see Slavic Gods and Goddesses.

Lado

From Slavic mythology, Lado is the God of Marriage, and husband of Lada, Goddess of Marriage. Together they rule over happiness. Image from slavpagan.hit.bg. Also see Slavic Gods and Goddesses.

Lady Lovibond

The Lady Lovibond is one the most famous of the Phantom Ships. She was shipwrecked on February 13th 1748 on the Goodwin Sands off the Kent coast of England and is said to appear every fifty years. According to sea folklore it was bad luck to bring women on board ships and Lady Lovibond's captain Simon Reed had brought his new bride Annetta on board on the fatal voyage. The legend says that the first mate John Rivers who had been a rival for the young woman's hand in marriage was seized with a jealous rage and drove the ship into the Goodwin Sands, killing everyone aboard. Other spellings include Luvibond. Also see Phantom Ships.

Lady of the Lake

In Arthurian legends the Lady of the Lake is the Water Spirit or Deity who gave the sword Excalibur to Arthur. She now guards the same sword he gave back to her before he died. The Lady

of the Lake lives in her underwater castle. She is also called Nimue, Niniane, Nyneve and Viviane. The Lady of the Lake is depicted here in a 1919 painting by British artist Lancelot Speed. Also see Supernatural and Spiritual Beings.

Laetitia
As a Qabbalistic geomantic figure, Laetitia represents good for joy, current or future and is used in the ancient art of Geomancy. Also see Divination, and Geomancy.

Laguz
As the 18th symbol of the runes, Laguz represents flow. Also see Runes.

Lailah
In Jewish tradition, Lailah is a demonic being of the night, called the Prince of Conception. Other spellings include Layla, Liaila, Lailahel, and Leliel. Also see Demons.

Laka
From Hawaiian mythology, Laka is the Goddess of Song and Dance. Shown here is a photograph by Kirk Lee Aeder (kirkaederphoto.com). Also see Hawaiian Gods and Goddesses.

Laksmi
Hindu Goddess of Love and Beauty, Laksmi rules over good fortune, prosperity, abundance and success. She is the wife of the God Narayana, an incarnation of Vishnu and she was born to be with him in each of his incarnations; as Sita when he was Rama, as Rukmini when he was Krishna and as Padmavati when he was Venkateshwara. Laksmi is associated with elephants and is usually depicted with the lotus flower. The Festival of the Lights is held in September in her honor. She is called the Daughter of the Milky Ocean. Other spellings include Laxsmi and Laxmi. Laksmi is also called Rukmini and Sri. Also see Hindu Gods and Goddesses.

Lama
Buddhist senior monk and spiritual teacher belonging to the Lamaic religion of Tibet, the term Lama comes from the Tibetan bla-ma meaning "superior one". Many Lamas are considered to be reincarnations of their predecessors. The term Lama in itself means "One who perceives all other beings with the same compassion that a mother shows her child" and it is applied to certain enlightened Buddhist monks. Shown here is a 19th Century painting of Lama Monke Bormanshinov (1855-1919) by Alexander Burtschinow. Also see Dalai Lama and Lamas.

Lamas

The people described herein who are Lamas include: Alexandra David-Neel, Dalai Lama, Sogyal Rinpoche and B. Alan Wallace. Also see Buddhist Monks, Lama and Religious Teachers.

Lamaism

Esoteric Buddhism of Tibet and Mongolia derived from Mahayana Buddhism and the Shamanistic Bon religion, Lamaism is divided into two sects, the Red Hats and the Yellow Hats. Lamaic worship consists mostly in reciting sacred texts and prayers and chanting hymns to the accompaniment of trumpets, horns, and drums. Religious rituals performed by the Lamas involve the use of rosaries, prayer wheels, and prayer flags, in addition to Holy relics, talismans, and such mystical incantations as the frequently repeated Mantras. Shown here is the Universe of the Lamas from the 1899 book The Buddhism of Tibet by L. Austine Waddell. Also see Religions.

Lamassu

In Assyrian and Babylonian mythology, Lamassu is a protective demon with the body of a bull, the wings of an eagle and a human head. Monumental statues of Lamassu were placed at the entrances of royal palaces as gateway guardians. Shown here is a Lamassu from Khorsabad housed in the Louvre Museum in Paris, France. Also see Demons.

Lamassu

In Assyrian, Sumerian and Jewish traditions, Lamassu is a protective female spirit who is appealed to at the end of an invocation for the exorcism of evil spirits. Also see Supernatural and Spiritual Beings.

Lamen

A Lamen is a magical symbol of Occult authority worn as a collar on the chest supported by cords or ribbons during rituals or ceremonial magic. It has also been described as a round plate of metal or wood with magical words or symbols inscribed upon it. Shown here is Achad's Lamen (named for Charles Stansfeld Jones aka Frater Achad). Also see Magical Amulets.

Lamia

From Greek mythology, Lamia is a beautiful woman, mistress of Zeus whose children were killed by Zeus's wife Hera. She turned into a creature that can remove her eyes at will and who eats human flesh and sucks their blood. She is often described in the form of a serpent with the head of a woman. Lamia is depicted here in a 1909 painting by British artist John William Waterhouse (jwwaterhouse.com). Also see Greek Gods and Goddesses.

Lampadomancy

Divination by light, lampadomancy interprets movement of flames from candles, torches and lamps, and is also a form of pyromancy. Also see Divination, and Pyromancy.

Lane, Belden C.

American-born Belden Curnow Lane Ph.D. is a professor of theological studies, Presbyterian theologian, author and storyteller. He received his B.A. Florida State University, his B.D. at Fuller Theological Seminary and his Ph.D. at Princeton Theological Seminary. He is currently professor of theological studies at Saint Louis University in Saint Louis, Missouri. His books include: The Solace of Fierce Landscapes: Exploring Desert and Mountain Spirituality; Storytelling Study Guide; Storytelling, The Enchantment of Theology; Merton's Hermitage and the Deconstruction of the Self: A Topoanalysis Using Gaston Bachelard's The Poetics of Space and Landscapes of the Sacred: Geography and Narrative in American Spirituality. Photograph from slu.edu. Also see Recommended Reading and Theologians.

Lang, Andrew

(1844-1912) Scottish-born Andrew Lang was a poet, scholar, historian, journalist and author of many books about mythology, folklore, anthropology, history, ghosts and fairy tales, among others. He studied at the Edinburgh Academy, St. Andrews University, and Balliol College, Oxford. He later became an honorary fellow of Merton College. He joined the Society for Psychical Research and later became its president and wrote several articles on psychic research for the Encyclopaedia Britannica. Lang's books include: The Blue, Brown, Crimson, Green, Grey, Lilac, Olive, Orange, Pink, Red, Violet, and Yellow Fairy Books; Magic and Religion; The Book of Dreams and Ghosts; Custom and Myth; and Myth, Ritual and Religion. Lang is depicted here in an 1855 painting by British artist Sir William Blake Richmond. Also see Historians, Journalists, Mythology, Poets and Recommended Reading.

Lao Tzu

(6th Century B.C.E.) Chinese sage and philosopher who is believed to be the founder of Taoism. Lao Tzu aka Laozi wrote 81 poems in his Holy book, the Tao Te Ching, also known as The Book of the Way. Contemporary of Confucius, Lao Tzu was venerated as a philosopher by Confucians and as a God or Saint by others. According to legend he was the keeper of the archives at the imperial court. He was reported to have said "I have just three things to teach: simplicity, patience, compassion. These are your greatest three treasures." Other spellings include Lao Tun, Laotze, Lao Zi, Lao Tan and Li Erh. Shown here is a depiction of Lao Tzu from an ancient Chinese book. Also see Philosophers, Taoism, tao.org and taopage.org.

Laozi
See Lao Tzu and Tao Te Ching.

Lares

In Roman mythology Lares are spirits or household Gods called lares familaris (spirits or Gods of the crossroads are called lares compitales). Every family has a lar familiaris, sometimes the spirit of a dead ancestor, and they are the center of the family worship. The Romans would keep images or dolls representing the Lares and would greet them every morning at breakfast and dinner and an offering of the food would be left for them along with incense and flowers. Shown here is an 1880 painting by British artist John William Waterhouse (jwwaterhouse.com) called The Household Gods. Also see Roman Gods and Goddesses.

Laskow, Leonar

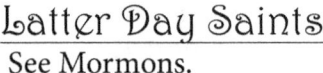

(1954-) English-born Leonard "Len" Laskow M.D. is an OB-GYN physician, author and researcher who, in his own words "has studied the healing power of love for the past 33 years". He completed residency at Stanford Medical Center and post-doctoral fellowship in Psychosomatic Medicine at the University of California, San Francisco. He developed a process he calls Holoenergetic Healing which means healing with the energy of the "whole". Dr. Laskow was a founding member of the American Board of Integral Holistic Medicine. He is a Life Fellow of the American College of Obstetrics and Gynecology and former Chief of Ob-GYN at the Community Hospital of the Monterey Peninsula in Carmel, California. He taught internationally at universities, holistic institutes and medical centers and now teaches as a consultant in Behavioral and Energy Medicine in Ashland, Oregon. He has written Healing With Love: A Physician's Breakthrough Mind/Body Medical Guide for Healing Yourself and Others: The Art of Holoenergetic Healing. Also see Holistic Healing, Mind-Body Energy Medicine, Recommended Reading, laskow.net and holisticboard.org.

Latis
Celtic Goddess of Water and Beer. Shown here is an 1877 painting of a young Goddess by British artist Dante Gabriel Rossetti (rossettiarchive.org) called A Sea Spell. Also see Celtic Gods and Goddesses.

Latter Day Saints
See Mormons.

Lauday
In the Grimorum Verum, Lauday is an Angel invoked in the blessing of the Salt. Also see Angels.

Laveau, Marie

(1801-1881) Born a Free Woman in New Orleans, Louisiana, Marie Laveau was a beautiful, famous, powerful, respected and feared practitioner of Voodoo. She was known as the Voodoo Queen of New Orleans. Ms. Laveau was a well known Mambo, or Voodoo priestess and she was said to help you find a lover, keep a lover or get rid of a lover just as easily. At age 25 she married Jacques Paris and when he disappeared 6 months later she became known as The Widow Paris. A year later she became a common law wife to Christopher Glapion and had 15 children with him. She was reported to have helped the wounded during the Battle of New Orleans and frequently visited the sick in New Orleans' prisons. Among other curiosities she had a big snake named Zombi, whom the locals also feared. Her daughter Marie Laveau (1827-1895) was also a well known Voodoo practitioner and they are often confused. Shown here is a 20th Century painting of Marie Laveau by American artist DiMitri Fouquet (kristinfouquet.blogspot.com). Also see Mambo, Voodoo and mysticvoodoo.com.

Law of Attraction

The law of attraction is a New Age theory that proposes that we attract what we think of and says that no one should dwell on negative thoughts because the law of attraction will attract negative things. On the contrary to attract positive things into one's life, one should strive to think positively, with thoughts of love and gratitude to attract good things into one's life. Image from sassywomeninspired.com. Also see Affirmation, Autosuggestion, Creative Visualization, Positive Thinking, and law-of-attraction-info.com, thesecret.tv, powerlawofattraction.com and themastersofattraction.com.

Laya

From Sanskrit, laya means "point of dissolution".

Laya Center

The laya center is described by Occultists as the mystical (or cosmic) point where matter disappears from one plane or dimension and passes onwards to exist on another plane. It is also descrybed as a cosmic vortex between parallel universes.

Laya Yoga

The yoga that practices the awakening of the chakras using sound mantras. See Chakras, Mantras, Yoga and layayoga.com.

LCC

See Liberal Catholic Church.

LDS
Latter-Day Saints. See Mormons.

Lea
Spirit guide said to be channeled through William A. Guillory Ph.D. Also see Channeled Spirit Guides, Channelers, and William A. Guillory.

Leadbeater, Charles

(1854-1934) English-born occultist, clairvoyant and psychic, Charles Webster Leadbeater D.D. was a contemporary, collaborator and friend of Annie Besant and Helena Blavatsky. He was an Anglican priest when he joined the Theosophical Society in 1883. He was also a founding member and Bishop of the Liberal Catholic Church in Australia and was initiated into Co-Masonry. Reverend Leadbeater published more than 30 books on Occultism, some of his best are: The Inner Life; The Chakras: A Monograph; The Real Astral Plane; Dreams: What They Are and How They are Caused; The Masters and the Path; Life after Death, and How Theosophy Unveils It; Man Visible and Invisible: Examples of Different Types of Men as Seen by Means of Trained Clairvoyance; The Inner Mysteries of Isis and Osiris; and The Science of Sacraments. Also see Clairvoyants, Dream Analysts, Liberal Catholic Church, Occultists, Psychics, Reincarnation (Life After Life), Recommended Reading, Reverends and Ministers, charlesleadbeater.net and liberalcatholic.org.

Leanan-Sidhe

In Irish mythology Leanan-Sidhe is described as a beautiful female fairy vampire or a muse of poetry. She is said to be invisible to everyone except the man she enchants. Other spellings include Leanansidhe. Leanan-Sidhe is depicted here by British artist Brian Froud (worldoffroud.com). Also see Supernatural and Spiritual Beings.

Lecanomancy

Divination by a basin of water, Lecanomancy interprets ripples in the water after dropping gems or stones in it or studies the surface, as in scrying. Photograph from manataka.org. Lecanomancy is also called Water Witching. Also see Divination, and Scrying.

Leek, Sybil

(1917-1983) English-born Sybil Leek was a self-proclaimed witch, psychic, author of the occult and astrologer. She was dubbed Britain's Most Famous Witch by the BBC. Ms. Leek worked as a Red Cross volunteer in England during World War II and was awarded several medals. She moved to the United States in the 1960's where she also became very well known. Ms. Leek worked with Hans Holzer in New York investigating psychic phenomena. Later she moved to Los Angeles where she met Israel Regardie with whom she learned Golden Dawn rituals. She wrote more than 60 books on occult subjects but is best known for her autobiography Diary of a Witch. Among her books are: The Complete Art of Witchcraft The Jackdaw and The Witch: A True Fable; Sybil Leek's Book of Herbs; Reincarnation: The Second Chance; Telepathy: The Respectable Phenomenon and The Night Voyagers: You and Your Dreams. Also see Astrologers, Occultists, Recommended Reading, Reincarnation (Life After Life), Wicca, Wiccans and witchcraftandwitches.com.

Leffas

According to Occultists, leffas are the astral bodies of plants and trees. Also see Astral Bodies. Shown here is a 2004 photograph by Jonathan J. Stegeman.

Left Hand Path

See Black Magic.

Legomena

Occult knowledge taught by spoken word.

Lemegeton

Also known as the Lesser Key of Solomon, the Lemegeton is a grimoire of ceremonial magic from the 17th Century. Also see Sacred Writings. It contains four separate texts, which are: Almadel, which talks about the Angels that rule the four quarters; Goetia, which deals with the summoning of Qlipothic demons and evil spirits; Pauline Arts, which lists the Angels of day and night and deals with the zodiac; and Theurgia, which deals with spirits that control the directions.

Lemures

In Roman mythology, Lemures are evil spirits of the dead who are said to appear as skeletons. In Occult terminology, Lemures are noisy obnoxious elementals or elementaries. Shown here is the 1493 Dance of Death by German artist Michael Wolgemut. Also see Supernatural and Spiritual Beings.

Lemuria

Legendary lost continent whose civilization is said to have preceded that of Atlantis. Lemuria was also called Mu and Pacifica and was supposedly located in the Pacific Ocean. Many occultists and Theosophists say that Lemuria along with Atlantis were the cradle of human civilization some 10 million years ago. The Hawaiian Islands, Rapa Nui (Easter Island)

and several other islands are said to be all that is left of the lost continent. People herein who describe Lemuria include: Madame Blavatsky, Edgar Cayce, James Churchward, Charles Leadbeater, Ramtha (spirit channeled by JZ Knight), Thomas Spence and Rudolf Steiner. Shown here is a 1927 depiction of Lemuria (Mu) by James Churchward. Also see Atlantis, Ica Stones, Recommended Reading, Root Races and lemuria.net.

Lemurian

In Theosophy Lemurian refers to one of humanities Root Races, described by Helena Blavatsky said to have occurred around 10 million years ago in the lost continent of Lemuria as well as parts of California, Australia, and South America. See Root Races and Lemuria.

Lenormand, Marie-Anne

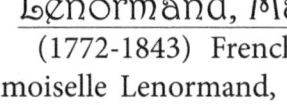

(1772-1843) French-born Marie-Anne Adelaide Lenormand aka Mademoiselle Lenormand, is considered in France the greatest cartomancer of French history. She was a famous professional diviner, and cartomancer who was consulted by Napoleon I and others including the Empress Josephine and Robespierre and Russian Czar Alexander. She published several books on the tarot, palmistry and divining. Ms. Lenormand was imprisoned several times but never for long. She is best known for The Famous Parlour Game and Secret Practices; and Historical and Secret Memoirs of the Empress Josephine (Marie Rose Tascher de la Pagerie): First Wife of Napoleon Bonaparte. Mademoiselle Lenormand is shown here in an 18th century painting by French artist Jeanne-Philiberte Ledoux housed in The Bowles Museum in England. Also see Cartomancy and Palmistry.

Lent

Christian period of forty days which comes before Easter in the Christian calendar, traditionally a time of fasting and reflection. It begins with Ash Wednesday. Also see Christianity.

Leo

One of the twelve signs of the zodiac, Leo is ruled by the Sun and symbolized by the lion. Also see Astrology, and Zodiac.

Leonard, Gladys Osborne

(1882-1968) British-born Gladys Osborne Leonard was a singer and famous trance medium and channeler of her time. She was said to have showed psychic abilities from the time she was a child and later as a medium channeling an entity called Feda. She also wrote about her experiences in: My Life in Two Worlds where she also speaks about her out of body experiences. She spent three months being studied exclusively by the Society for Psychical Research and later was also studied by the Reverend Charles Drayton Thomas for many years. He wrote two books on her story: Some New Evidence for Human Survival and Life Beyond Death with Evidence. She also met and cooperated with the parapsychologist Herewood Carrington. Also see Astral Projection, Channelers, Channeled Spirit Guides, Diviners, Mediums and Recommended Reading.

Leonardo da Vinci

(1452-1519) Italian-born Leonardo di ser Piero da Vinci (later Leonardo da Vinci, the Maestro or simply Leonardo) was a genius and one of the most talented persons in history. He was an architect, musician, anatomist, botanist, writer, inventor, engineer, sculptor, geometer, and painter and he was also involved in hydrodynamics, mechanics, mathematics, optics and occultism. Born an illegitimate son of a notary and a peasant woman, in Florence, Italy, he was educated by the Florentine painter Andrea del Verrocchio. Leonardo is considered one of the greatest artists that ever lived. Two of his most famous paintings are the Mona Lisa and The Last Supper. As a scientist he advanced the fields of anatomy, optics, hydrodynamics and civil engineering and his technological ingenuity included designing, long before his time, machines such as helicopters, tanks, concentrated solar power and others. He is also mentioned in the Dossier Secrets as Grand Master of the: Prieure de Sion. In 1998 Lynn Picknett and Clive Prince published The Templar Revelation: Secret Guardians of the True Identity of Christ which proposes that the Turin Shroud is a photographed image of Leonardo de Vinci made by him. Leonardo is shown here in a 15th Century self-portrait. Also see Dossier Secrets, Mathematicians, Prieure de Sion, Scientists, Turin Shroud and davincilife.com.

Leprechaun

In Irish folklore a Leprechaun is a mischievous Earth Elementals who guards treasures. They are described as small beings with tiny male humanlike figures who fix shoes. They are also described as solitary beings that live in barns and wine cellars. Other spellings include Lepracaun, Leprecaun and Luchorpain. Shown here is an image of a Leprechaun by Jean-Noël Lafargue (hyperbate.com). Also see Elementals.

Leshy

Slavic God or spirit of the forests considered dangerous. Leshy is said to be the offspring of a woman and a demon. He enjoys playing tricks on people, substituting ugly babies for beautiful ones and seducing young girls. Although Leshy is seldom seen he can be heard in the forests laughing, singling or whistling. He is described as a man without eyebrows, eyelashes and a missing his right ear. He is known as a shape-shifter who can take on any form of animal, plant or person. Leshy is said to be averted by wearing clothes backwards. Other spellings include Lesiye, Leshiy, Lechy, Lesovik and Leszi. Image from fullimage.ru. Also see Slavic Gods and Goddesses.

Leucosia

In Greek mythology, Leucosia is a sea nymph, one of the three sirens along with Ligeia and Parthenope. Shown here is an 1864 painting by British artist Sir Edward John Poynter called The Siren. Also see Greek Gods and Goddesses, and Sirens.

Levanah
See Luna.

Levi, Eliphas

(1810-1875) French-born Eliphas Levi (pen name of Alphonse-Louis Constant) was considered an important figure in the Occult Revival of the 19th Century and well known author and Occultist. He studied at Saint-Sulpice monastery, where he became a deacon before he was expelled, some said for his heretic ideas and others because he fell in love. Although he was largely a theorist in Occultism, he was known to have had some encounters with ritual magic with alleged extraordinary results. His best known book, Transcendental Magic: Its Doctrine and Ritual, greatly influenced the Golden Dawn. He wrote several other books including: The Key to the Great Mysteries; The Science of Spirits; The Book of Splendours: The Inner Mysteries of Qabalism: Its Relationship to Freemasonry, Numerology and Tarot; and The Great Secret or Occultism Unveiled. Shown here is an 1874 portrait of Eliphas Levi by Charles Revel. Also see Occultists and Recommended Reading.

Leviathan

In traditional Christian demonology, Leviathan is a demon who represents one of seven deadly sins; envy. Shown here is a depiction of Leviathan often found in grimoires by an unknown artist. Also see Demon, and Demons.

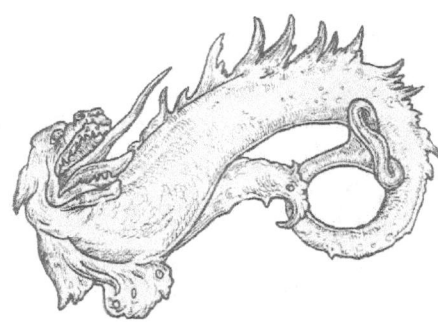

Leviathan

In Jewish traditions Leviathan is a great sea monster or sea dragon, described in the bible in five places.

Levine, Stephen

(1937-) American-born Stephen Levine is a poet, teacher of meditation healing techniques and bestselling author. He and his wife have counseled the dying and their loved ones for over 30 years. He attended the University of Miami, worked as a writer and editor in New York City where he founded the first hospice, and founded the San Francisco Oracle. Levine worked with the dying with meditation methods along with Richard Alpert and Elizabeth Kubler-Ross. Among Levine's books are: A Gradual Awakening; Who Dies?: An Investigation of Conscious Living and Conscious Dying; Meetings at the Edge:

Dialogues with the Grieving and the Dying, the Healing and the Healed; Healing into Life and Death; A Year to Live: How to Live This Year as if It Were Your Last; Turning Toward the Mystery: A Seeker's Journey; and Embracing the Beloved: Relationship as a Path of Awakening. Photograph taken by Chris Gallo (chrisgallophoto.com). Also see Poets, Recommended Reading, Thanatology and warmrocktapes.com.

Levitation

Levitation has been described as the ability to defy gravity, referring most commonly to self-levitation or the lifting of the body off the ground by supernatural means. This can also apply to furniture and other objects that rise through the air during séances or other situations where mediums or saints are present. Other terms include Psychokinesis and Transvection. The people described here who were said to have the ability to levitate include: Florence Cook, William Eglinton, Agnes Guppy-Volkman, Daniel Dunglas Home, Saint John of the Cross and Saint Teresa of Avila. Shown here is a depiction of the levitation of Daniel Dunglas Home from French artist Louis Figuier's 1887 Les Mysteres de la Science. Also see Aethrobacy and levitation.org.

Leviticus

Leviticus is the third book of the Hebrew Old Testament. See Torah.

Lewis, Harvey Spencer

(1883-1939) American-born Harvey Spencer Lewis Ph.D. was a famous mystic, occultist, author and founder of the Ancient Mystical Order Rosae Crusis (AMORC), the New York Institute for Psychical Research and the Rosicrucian Egyptian Museum in San Jose, California. His magical name was Sar Alden and he was one of the three Imperators of the Federation Universelle des Odres et Societes Iniatiques (FUDOSI). He held several earned and honorary titles and degrees, many for humanitarian work. Among Dr. Spencer's books are: A Thousand Years of Yesterdays: A Strange Story of Mystic Revelations; The Secret Doctrines of Jesus; The Mystical Life of Jesus; Rosicrucian Questions and Answers with Complete History of the Order; Rosicrucian Manual and Mansions of the Soul: The Cosmic Conception. Also see Mystics, Occultists, Recommended Reading, Rosicrucian Egyptian Museum, Rosicrucians, amorc.org, egyptianmuseum.org and rosicrucian.org.

Lewis, Ralph Maxwell

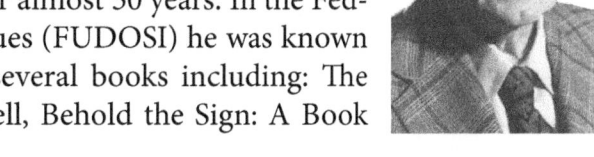

(1904-1987) American-born Ralph Maxwell Lewis was the son of Harvey Spencer Lewis and imperator of the Rosicrucian organization Ancient and Mystical Order of the Rosae Crusis (AMORC) for almost 50 years. In the Federation Universelle des Odres et Societes Iniatiques (FUDOSI) he was known by the magical name Sar Validivar. He wrote several books including: The Sanctuary of the Self, Yesterday has Much to Tell, Behold the Sign: A Book on Ancient Symbolism, The Conscious Interlude; Whisperings of Self: A Collection of Aphorisms Designed to Uplift and Inspire Each Day of the Year; and a biography of his father entitled Cosmic Mission Fulfilled. Also see Recommended Reading, Rosicrucians, amorc.org and rosicrucian.org.

Ley Lines

Also called leys, ley lines are said to be lines of powerful earth energy connecting sacred sites such as temples, megaliths, Holy wells, Churches, burial sites and others. First described by Alfred Watkins in 1925 in, The Old Straight Track, and later in 1969 in The View Over Atlantis by John Michell in which he describes ley lines found around the pyramids and other monuments. He says that the ley lines are channels of polar magnetism or telluric energy currents from all over the world. Others claim that ley lines are associated with paranormal activity or are gateways for other dimensions. Shown here is the St. Michael/St. Mary alignment map showing the ley lines stretching across England. Also see Earth's Grids, psychicchildren.co.uk and stonesofwonder.com.

Lha-Mo

In Tibetan Buddhism, Lha-Mo is the Goddess who protects the capital of Tibet, Lhasa, as well as the ruling Dalai Lama. She is the only female of the Wrathful Deities and is also known as the Great Queen and the Queen of the Warring Weapons. She is also called Palden Lhamo, DMagz and Rgyal-Mo. Other spellings include Lhamo. Also see Tibetan Gods and Goddesses, and Wrathful Deities.

Li

Meaning Fire, Li is the third of the eight Gua in Ba Gua. It contains Yang rising from the bottom towards the middle. Its direction is South and it also represents Fame and Reputation. See Ba Gua and Triagrams.

Li-Sung

Spirit guide said to be channeled through medium Alan Vaughan. Also see Channeled Spirit Guides, Channelers, and Alan Vaughan.

Libanomancy

Divination by incense, Libanomancy interprets figures and movement of smoke. Also see Divination.

Libation

A libation is a very ancient universal ritual pouring of a beverage as an offering to a God or poured on the ground itself as an offering to the Earth or the God who represents the Earth. Even today in places such as Chile and Peru a small amount of one's drink is poured on the ground before toasting and drinking to honor Pachamama (Mother Earth). Also see Magical Methods, Offering, and Sacrifice.

Liberal Catholic Church

Founded in 1918 the Liberal Catholic Church, also called LCC was formed by independent bishops from the Old Catholic Church of Holland and several well known Theosophists such as Charles Leadbeater. Leadbeater became a bishop of the Liberal Catholic Church in 1916 and wrote The Science of the Sacraments which became its handbook. The Liberal Catholic Church draws from Christianity and Theosophy. Also see Religions and liberalcatholic.org.

Liberation

Liberation is described as freedom from karmic conditioning or reincarnation. Also see Moksha.

Libitina

From Roman mythology, Libitina is an ancient Goddess who presides over the death ceremonies and is the recipient and custodian of corpses. Her temples housed the mortuary records and death registers. She is sometimes called Venus Libitina. Shown here is a dead gladiator being dragged through the Gate of the Goddess of Death. Also see Roman Gods and Goddesses.

Libra

One of the twelve signs of the zodiac, Libra is ruled by Venus and is symbolized by balance. Also see Astrology, and Zodiac.

Life after Death

See Reincarnation.

Life Between Life

See In Between Worlds.

Life Reading

A life reading is a clairvoyant review of the current life or past lives.

Life Review

A life review refers to the spiritual review of a person's whole life alongside a spiritual being, guide or Angel where the person reviews his actions, emotions and thoughts of the life they are leaving. Shown here is a 1998 painting by American artist Thomas Kinkade (thomaskinkade.com) called Stairway to Paradise. Also see Afterlife, Greeters, and Near Death Experience.

Ligeia

In Greek mythology, Ligeia is a sea nymph, one of the three sirens along with Leucosia and Parthenope. Ligeia is shown here in an 1873 painting by British artist Dante Gabriel Rossetti (rossettiarchive.org) called the Ligeia Siren. Also see Greek Gods and Goddesses, and Sirens.

Lightworker

Lightworker refers to people who spiritually help others though meditation, prayer, teaching, healing, speaking and unconditional love regardless of their spiritual traditions and religious backgrounds. Many people believe that the choice to become a lightworker was made before incarnating here on Earth. The term lightworker was popularized by Doreen Virtue in her book The Lightworker's Way. Also see angeltherapy.com, lightworkers.org and planetlightworker.com.

Lilith

In Gnostic literature Lilith is the Queen of the Elementals. Also see Elementals.

Lilith

In Sumerian and Middle Eastern mythology, Lilith is the Goddess of the Moon and the Patroness of Witches. She rules over wisdom, fertility, agriculture, knowledge, death and regeneration, magic and dreams. She is assigned to help Inanna by finding young men who she takes to Inanna's temple for sacred sexual rituals. Shown here is an 1800 B.C.E. terracotta plaque of Lilith called The Burney Relief (for the antiquities dealer who owned it until 1935). Also see Sumerian Gods and Goddesses.

Lilith

In Jewish folklore, Lilith is a female demon, who dwells in deserted places and is the enemy of infants and children. In Rabbinic literature, Lilith predates Eve as Adam's first wife, but after having marital relations with Adam she leaves him due to their incompatibility. Lilith is sometimes described as the mother of Adam's demonic offspring. She is also called the Bride of Satan and the Night Hag. She is frequently compared to a Succubus. Shown here is an 1892 painting of Lilith by British artist John Maler Collier (john-collier.org). Also see Demons.

Lilly, William

(1602-1681) English-born astrologer and occultist, William Lilly is considered one of the most important figures in astrology. He was a very popular figure in his time and accurately predicted the Great Fire of London, the battle of Naseby and the violent death of King Charles I. His wrote many books but his Christian Astrology was the first book published in English on the subject and remained unrivaled until the late 19th Century. It is considered one of the classic books for traditional astrology, specifically horary astrology. Shown here is a 17th Century engraving of William Lilly by Czechoslovakian artist Wenceslaus Hollar. Also see Astrologers, Occultists and renaissanceastrology.com.

Limbo

From the Latin limbus, meaning "edge" and in Roman Catholic theology, Limbo is a state or place where souls who die in original sin go, instead of hell. Shown here is a 1468 painting by Italian artist Andrea Mantegna called Christ's Descent into Limbo. Also see Mythological Places.

Lincoln Theatre

In Decatur, Illinois stands the Lincoln Square Theatre built in 1916. Built of fireproof materials the Lincoln resembles a turn of the Century opera house. During its prime time the theatre was used for movies, plays and vaudeville acts. Reports of ghost sightings and other strange activities have been reported since the 1930's. To this day strange sounds and sightings are still reported, especially on the balcony and the metal staircase in the back of the theatre. Also see Most Haunted and haunteddecatur.com.

Lingam

From Hinduism, Lingam is a representation of the sacred phallus of Shiva. Some Hindi who worship the phallus, wear a Lingam around their necks the way that Christian's wear crosses or the Jewish wear the star of David. The opposite of the Lingam is the Yoni or vagina. Also see Yoni.

Lingam Purana

In Hinduism, Lingam Paruna, which is devoted to the worship of the Lingam (sacred phallus) of Shiva, is one of the texts which explain the myths and rituals of the Gods. Also see Puranas.

Linn, Denise

American-born Denise Linn is a well known healer, lecturer and author on New Age subjects. After a near death experience, where she survived a gunshot wound and helped heal her own body, Ms. Linn has traveled all over the world lecturing on spiritual matters, Feng Shui and space clearing She has been called America's Best Kept Secret. Among her books are: Sacred Space: Clearing and Enhancing the Energy of Your Home; Feng Shui for the Soul: How To Create a Harmonious Environment That Will Nurture and Sustain You; Past Lives: Present Dreams: How to Use Reincarnation for Personal Growth; Space Clearing A-Z: How to Use Feng Shui to Purify and Bless Your Home; and her latest book: The Hidden Power of Dreams: The Mysterious World of Dreams Revealed. Photograph from charjung.com. Also see Dream Analysts, Feng Shui, Healers, Near Death Experience, Recommended Reading, Reincarnation (Life After Life), deniselinn.com and interioralignment.com.

Lipski, Elizabeth

American-born Elizabeth "Liz" Lipski, Ph.D., CCN CHN is an expert in the fields of nutrition, holistic and mind-body medicine and digestive and auto-immune conditions as well as author and co-author of many health books. She is Director of Doctoral Studies at Hawthorn University, Executive Director of Access to Health Experts, currently a member of the Board of Directors for the National Association of Nutrition Professionals, a member of the Clinical Nutrition Certification Board Scientific Council, and on the Nutrition Advisory Board of the Institute of Functional Medicine. Dr. Lipski's books include: Digestive Wellness: How to Strengthen the Immune System and Prevent Disease  Through Healthy Digestion; and Digestive Wellness for Children: How to Strengthen the Immune System and Prevent Disease Through Healthy Digestion. Photo from mnupetm.tumblr.com. Also see Holistic Healing, Mind-Body Energy Medicine, Recommended Reading, innovativehealing.com and lizlipski.com.

Lipton, Bruce

(1944-) American-born Bruce Harold Lipton Ph.D. is the director of the Institute for Cellular Communication, researcher, lecturer, author and internationally known authority in bridging science and spirit. He received his Ph.D. from the University of Virginia at Charlottesville before joining the Department of Anatomy at the University of Wisconsin's School of Medicine. Dr. Lipton later conducted epigenetics research for Stanford University School of Medicine for five years where he studied the influence of thoughts on our genes and cells and examined the principles of quantum physics and how they might affect epigenetics. He is regarded as one of the leading voices of the new biology and leading- edge science and how it interacts with body medicine and spiritual principles. He is currently a sought after workshop presenter and keynote speaker to lay audiences as well as conventional and complementary medical professionals. Among his books: The Biology of Belief: Unleashing the Power of Consciousness, Matter and Miracles; and Spontaneous Evolution: Our Positive Future (And a Way to Get There From Here). Photograph from enhancedpotential.com. Also see Quantum Physics and Quantum Mechanics, Recommended Reading and brucelipton.com.

List, Guido von

(1848-1919) Austrian-born Guido Karl Anton von List was a well known and highly respected journalist, author, poet, mystic and occultist. He was considered one of the most important figures of his time in Germanic mysticism. The most well known of his books on the occult is The Secret of the Runes. Also see Journalists, Mystics, Occultists, Poets and Recommended Reading.

Lithomancy

Divination by the observation of precious stones and crystals, lithomancy in its oldest tradition uses seven stones which represent the astrological signs of the Sun, Moon, Mercury, Venus, Mars, Jupiter and Saturn. These stones are either cast in lots and interpreted (sortilege) or held to a flame or light to study the reflections (scrying). Also see Divination, Magical Gems, Scrying and Sortilege.

Lix

See Ephesia Grammata.

Lludd

Celtic Sea God who rules over healing, water, the Sun, childbirth, youth, beauty, poets, sorcerers, magic and incantations. Lludd is also known as the Cloud Maker, the Silver Hand and He Who Bestows Wealth. Lludd is depicted here from the 11th Century Mabinogion. Other spellings include Llud, Lud and Ludd. Also see Celtic Gods and Goddesses.

Llyr

Celtic God of the Sea and Water, Llyr is the father of Bran the Blessed and Branwen. He is also one of the Tuatha de Dannan. Other spellings include Lear, Leir, Ler, and Lir. Llyr is depicted here from the 11th Century Mabinogion. Also see Celtic Gods and Goddesses.

Loa

From Haitian Voodoo, the Loa is defined as a spirit of the dead which is called forth by a Houngan or Mambo to take possession of a person and control all their actions, of which they will have no later recollection. Also see Voodoo.

Loch Ness Monster

Also known as Nessie, the Loch Ness monster is an unidentified creature that looks like a dinosaur which supposedly inhabits Scotland's Loch Ness. Many, many sightings of the Loch Ness monster have been reported for many, many years. Many people have claimed to have photographed the monster. This is one of the most famous photographs taken by Ian Wetherell in 1972 which supposedly shows the Loch Ness monster. Also see Cryptids, Mythological Creatures and nessie.co.uk.

Lodge

A lodge is an organization in the physical world or on the astral planes that works on behalf of human spiritual evolution.

Lodge, Sir Oliver

(1851-1940) British-born Sir Oliver Joseph Lodge Ph.D. was a physicist and author was well known for his involvement in the development of the wireless telegraph. He received a B.A. from the University of London and his Ph.D. from the University College in Liverpool where he taught physics and mathematics. Sir Oliver later worked as the principal of Birmingham University. He was knighted by King Edward VII and received the Rumford Metal of the Royal Society. He was also known for his studies on life after death. After his son Raymond was killed in WWI he visited several psychics and wrote over 40 books including: Raymond, or Life and Death: With Examples of the Evidence for Survival of Memory and Affection After Death: Reason and Belief; Why I Believe in Personal Immortality; The Ether of Space; Christopher: A Study in Human Personality and Phantom Walls. Sir Oliver Lodge is shown above in a 19th Century painting by Scottish artist Sir George Reid. Also see Physicists, Recommended Reading and Reincarnation (Life After Life).

Logos

Logos comes from the Greek term that means "word" or "reason". The Gnostics used Logos to define the Deity manifest in the Universe, the Creative Principle and Creator of the Universe. Referred to also sometimes as the "Soul of the Universe", Logos has also been called the Oldest Angel and is identified with the concept of the Holy Ghost. Christian doctrines use Logos to describe the role of Jesus Christ as the active principle of God. Plato described the Logos as both immanent in the world and at the same time the transcendent divine mind. The Greek philosopher Heraclites used the term Logos in a Metaphysical sense when he defined it as a divine force that produces the order and pattern in the flux of nature.

Lokapalas

From Hindu mythology, the Lokapalas (shown here) are the four guardians of the quarters of the Earth, they are: Indra; Guardian of the Eastern Quarter; Kubera; Guardian of the

Northern Quarter; Varuna; Guardian of the Western Quarter; and Yama; Guardian of the South Quarter

Loki

Norse God of Earthquakes and Fire, Loki rules over stealth, mischief, daring, deceit, trickery, revenge, destruction, death, lies, evil and dark magic. He is also known as a shape-shifter and is called the Trickster, the Father of Lies and the Shape Changer. Loki is described as a giant who possessed extraordinary beauty and is said to have the ability to change his sex and shape at will. He is said to be very handsome but of a very evil disposition. Loki is the foster brother of Odin and one of the Aesir. Shown here in a 1910 painting by British artist Arthur Rackham (rackham.artpassions.net) called Loki and the Rhine Maidens. Also see Aesir, and Norse Gods and Goddesses.

Lombroso, Cesare

(1835-1909) Italian-born Cesare Lombroso was a criminal anthropologist, psychiatrist and psychic investigator. He began his career as a psychiatry professor at Pavia, went on to direct an insane asylum at Pesaro followed by teaching forensic medicine and psychiatry at Turin and finally he became a professor of criminal anthropology. He became involved in psychic investigations to prove them wrong but after attending sittings with the medium Eusapia Palladino he openly declared "I am ashamed and grieved at having opposed with so much tenacity the possibility of the so called spiritualistic facts, I say the facts because I am still opposed to the theory. But the facts exist, and I boast of being a slave to facts." He wrote several books on criminal anthropology and After Death What?: Spiritistic Phenomena and Their Interpretation. Also see Anthropologists, Parapsychologists and Psychic Researchers and Recommended Reading.

Lomi Lomi

Ancient Hawaiian art of healing, Lomi Lomi uses coconut based oils for healing massages and is based on the philosophies of Huna. Also see Huna, Therapeutic Systems, lomilomi.com and lomilomi.org.

Lost Continents

See Atlantis and Lemuria.

Lotus Sutra

The most read of Buddhist scriptures in the Orient, the Lotus Sutra preaches salvation for all creatures and its principle is "One is All and All is One".

Lourdes

Lourdes, France is one of the Sacred Sites of this world. Lourdes is considered sacred because in 1858 a young peasant girl named Bernadette Soubirous had 18 mystical visions in which she spoke with Virgin Mary and discovered a spring in the grotto which is held in high regard for its healing waters. Photograph from famouswonders.com. Also see Sacred Sites, lourdes-france.org, sacred-destinations.com and sacredsites.com.

Lovers

The Lovers is one of the 22 major arcana of the tarot deck of cards. Its number is VI, its Qabbalistic title is The Oracles of the Mighty Gods and Children of the Voice Divination and its meaning is: inspiration, motive, power and action. Also see Tarot.

Lower Spirits

See Elementals.

Loyalty Islands

The Loyalty Islands off the coast of Fiji are one of the twelve areas known as the Vile Vortices which are described as areas around the world said to have the same qualities as the famous Bermuda Triangle. In these areas strange phenomena are reported such as compasses and other instruments going crazy and ships and planes disappearing. See Vile Vortices.

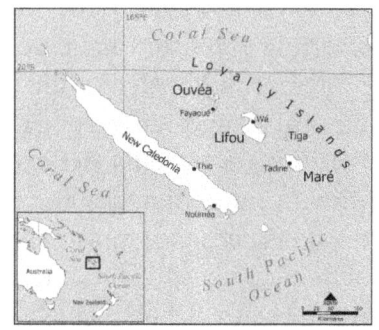

Lucid Dreaming

Lucid dreaming is the ability to identify the fact that one is dreaming and to control the dream. Several historical figures including Aristotle, Muhyi Al-Din Ibn al-'Arabi and Saint Thomas Aquinas reported having lucid dreams as well as contemporaries such as Carlos Castaneda, Stephen LaBerge and Olga Kharitidi. Also see Lucidity Institute, Spiritual Techniques, dreamviews.com, lucidity.com, explorations-in-consiousness.com, and world-of-lucid-dreaming.com.

Lucidity Institute, The

Founded in 1987 by Stephen LaBerge, The Lucidity Institute (or TLI) is (in their own words) the leading scientific research institute dedicated to lucid dreaming. Its mission is to advance research in the nature and potentials on consciousness using lucidity. Becoming adept at lucid dreaming requires focused attention and practice - something that is difficult to maintain during our busy lives. So The Lucidity Institute has created an ideal opportunity to cultivate your

lucid dreaming skills and enhance your mindfulness in everyday life. Using the most effective techniques and technology, derived from both Tibetan Dream Yoga and Western science, Stephen LaBerge and his team present methods to develop the mental skills that foster lucidity and direct your consciousness within both dreaming and waking states. Also see Stephen LaBerge, Lucid Dreaming, New Age Associations and Societies and world-of-lucid-dreaming.com.

Lucifer

Meaning "Light Giver", and according to Occult literature, Lucifer is a spiritual being who has been erroneously equated with Satan, the fallen Angel. Originally Lucifer was the Angel of the morning and evening star (Venus), described as the Brightest Angel and Child of the Light. Lucifer is also called Eosphoros and Phosphorus. Shown here is an 1871 painting by British artist Simeon Solomon (simeonsolomon.com) called Autumn. Also see Supernatural and Spiritual Beings.

Lucifer

In Christian demonology, Lucifer is a demon who is equated with the deadly sin of pride. The name Lucifer originally referred to the Morning Star. Shown here an 1868 painting by French artist Alexandre Cabanel called Fallen Angel. Also see Demon, and Demons.

Lucimi

See Santeria.

Luel

In Jewish magical tradition, Luel is an Angel invoked before using divining rods. Also see Angels.

Lugh

Celtic Druid God of War, son of Arianrhod, Lugh rules over, reincarnation, magic, lightning, arts and crafts, sorcerers, healing, history, initiation, prophesy, poetry, journeys and revenge. He is also known as The Shining One, God of War, the Bright One, the Fair Haired One, the Sun God and Lugh of the Long Arm. In Ireland Lugh is associated with ravens and in Wales with the white stag. Other spellings include Lamhfada, Llew, Lug, Luga and Lugus. He is depicted here in a painting by American artist Mickie Mueler (mikiemuellerart.com). Also see Celtic Gods and Goddesses.

Lughnasadh

See Lunasa.

Luminaries
In Astrology, the Sun and the Moon are luminaries.

Luminous Phenomena
Luminous phenomena refers to strange lights that glow in the sky and around people or places. Also see Aura, Ecto Mist, and Will o' the Wisp.

Lumisial
In Gnosticism, Lumisial is "a place of light", a generator of spiritual energy.

Luna
Roman Goddess who personified an aspect of the Moon as Lover and Bride, Luna is considered the Goddess of Enchantments and Love Spells. Luna is shown here in an 1885 painting by British artist Evelyn de Morgan (demorgan.org.uk). Luna is also known as Levanah and Selene. Also see Roman Gods and Goddesses.

Luna, Luis Eduardo
(1947-) Colombian-born Luis Eduardo Luna Ph.D. is an anthropologist, ayahuasca researcher and author. He studied philosophy and literature at the Complutense University of Madrid while teaching Spanish and Latin American Literature at the Department of Romance Languages of Oslo University. He received his Ph.D. from the Institute of Comparative Religion at Stockholm University and an honorary Ph.D. from Saint Lawrence University in New York. Dr. Luna is currently a language teacher at the Swedish School of Economics and Business Administration in Helsinki, Finland. He is also the director of Wasiwaska, Research Center for the Study of Psychointegrator Plants, Visionary Arts, and Consciousness in Florianopolis, Brazil. Dr. Luna has written Vegetalismo: Shamanism Among the Mestizo Population of the Peruvian Amazon; Ayahuasca Visions: The Religious Iconography of a Peruvian Shaman and Ayahuasca Reader: Encounters With the Amazon's Sacred Vine. Also see Anthropologists, Ayahuasca, Hallucinogens, Recommended Reading, Shamans and wasiwaska.org.

Lunasa
Wiccan, Druidical and Pagan festival celebrated on August 1st to mark the first harvest and the symbolic ebbing of the Sun's energies, the turning point in Mother Earth's cycle. To the Celtic Druids, Lunasa was called Lughnasadh and was celebrated on July 31st and celebrated high summer. Shown here is an 1878 painting by French artist William-Adolphe Bouguereau (bouguereau.org) called Return From the Harvest. See Druidism, and Wicca.

Luria, Isaac

(1534-1572) Born in Jerusalem to German parents, Rabbi Isaac ben Solomon Luria aka Holy Ari was a Jewish mystic and the most important scholar of modern Qabbalah. After his fathers death when he was a child he grew up with his mother in the house of her brother in Egypt. He was a child prodigy who, at age eight was already a respected authority on the Talmud. He later revolutionized the study of Jewish mysticism through the Qabbalah. In Hebrew he is known as Yitzhak Lurya, Yitzhak Ben Shlomo Ashkenazi and Yitzhak Ashkenazi. He later taught and lived in the famous center of Qabbalistic studies Safed. Luria believed that he could speak with deceased teachers including Elijah the prophet. Other spellings include Loria. Also see Mystics, Qabbalists, Rabbis and Recommended Reading.

Lustration

A Wiccan term for a ritual purification with water, lustration also includes ritual baths and baptisms. Shown here is a 19th Century painting by British artist Evelyn de Morgan (demorgan.org.uk) called Daughters of the Mist.

Lycanthropy

From the Greek lukos, meaning "wolf" and anthropos, meaning "man", Lycanthropy refers to a condition or state in which human beings can shape-shift into animals, specifically wolfs. Shown here is an image by Italian artist Massimo Righi (massimorighi.com) called Howling. Also see Shape Shifting, and Werewolf.

Maat

Egyptian Goddess of Truth, Order and Justice, daughter of Ra, Maat rules over the law, fairness, integrity, righteousness, cosmic order and final judgment of the human soul and divine order. She weighs the souls of the departed against an ostrich feather at the time of death. She is also known as The Mother and Lady of the Judgment Hall and The Eye of Ra. Snakes are sacred to Maat. Other spellings include Ma'at, Maa, Maet, Maut and Mayet. Also see Hall of Maat, and Egyptian Gods and Goddesses.

Mabinogion, The

Welsh collection of eleven, 11th Century anonymous medieval prose. The Mabinogion is a collection of tales based on mythology, folklore and legends, containing elements from pre-Christian myths of Celtic Britain. These tales include the earliest surviving material related to the Arthurian legend. The best known of the tales are the four related stories known as The Four Branches of the Mabinog". These tales are preserved in two manuscripts, the White Book of Rhydderch and the Red Book of Hergest. Mabinogion literally means "Tales of Youth". Also see Sacred Writings and mabinogion.info.

Mabon

Wiccan and Pagan festival celebrated on the Autumn equinox to honor rest after the completion of the harvest, when the hours of the day and night are in balance and darkness is increasing. Also see Wicca.

Mabon

From Celtic mythology, Mabon is a Sun God who is famous for his hunting, his fast horse and his hound. Also see Celtic Gods and Goddesses.

Macha

Celtic Goddess of War and Death, Macha rules over shear physical force, sexuality and fertility. She is considered as a protector in war and in peace, and she is also known as the Great Queen of Phantoms, the Great Earth Mother, the Mother of Life and Death and Mother Death. Other spellings include Mania, Mana, Mene, Minne Dana and Badb. Shown here is a 1904 drawing by British artist Stephen Reid called Macha Curses the Men of Ulster. Also see Celtic Gods and Goddesses.

Machen, Arthur

(1863-1947) Welsh-born Arthur Llewelyn Jones aka Arthur Machen was a well known author of the occult. He studied at the Hereford Cathedral School and later tried to attend medical school in London but failed the exams. He was a close friend of Arthur Waite and Evelyn Underhill and short time member of the Golden Dawn. Although he was raised an Anglican in the Church of England (son of a clergyman) he held a life-long fascination with mysticism, Hermeticism and the occult, which is reflected in his writing. His books include: The Three Imposters; The Hill of Dreams; The Secret Glory; Far Off Things; Dreads and Drolls; and The House of Souls. He was the first person to use the idea that the Holy Grail survived into modern times in the book The Secret Glory. Also see the Golden Dawn, Occultists, Recommended Reading and machensoc.demon.co.uk.

Machu Picchu

From Quechua (ancient Inca language still in use today), Machu Picchu means "Old Mountain". Nestled high in the Peruvian Andes, Machu Picchu was the center of the Incan civilization. It contains over 200 stone buildings and terraced agricultural areas were built with such precision that even knives will not fit between the stones. Machu Picchu was the center of religious worship and astronomical observations and is considered a Sacred Site. Photograph from traveltoenlightenment.com. Also see Sacred Sites, machupicchu.org, sacred-destinations.com and sacredsites.com.

Macumba

Afro-Brazilian religion, Macumba is a combination of old African religions, Brazilian Spiritualism, Roman Catholicism and traditional Brazilian magical systems that have been molded together. The belief in magic, spirits and spirit possession is principal to its philosophy. Of the several Macumba sects the most well known are Candombe (or Candomble) and Umbanda which include common elements as outdoor ceremonies, animal sacrifices, dance rituals, drumming and spirit offerings. Macumba rituals are led by mediums, who in states of trance, communicate with spirits. Also see Religions.

Macy, Mark

(1949-) American-born Mark Macy is a pioneer in ITC (Instrumental Transcommunication) research. An atheist for most of his life Macy had a bout with cancer in 1988 which almost killed him. Consumed with the question of what happens after death he was introduced to the work of ITC researchers. In his books Macy recounts years of work capturing communications with spirits and angels through telephones, radios, televisions, computers and other electronic devices. He has received many honors including the 2001 Swiss Prize for Epipsychology and he participates in seminars and conferences all over the world. He has written: The Project: the Past, Present, and Future of Humanity; Miracles in the Storm: Talking to the Other Side With the New Technology of Spiritual Contact; Solutions for a Troubled World; Healing the World and Me; and Spirit Faces: Truth About the Afterlife. Also see Electronic Voice Phenomena, Instrumental Transcommunication, Recommended Reading, macy-afterlife.wordpress.com, spiritfaces.com and worlditc.org.

Madden, Kristin

American-born Kristin Madden is former environmental chemist and raptor biologist and current Druid, teacher, author, healer, deathwalker, homeschooling mother and wildlife rehabilitator. She is a tutor in the Order of Bards, Ovates and Druids and a member of the Druid College of Healing. Ms. Madden was raised in a shamanic home and assumed the roles that were handed down in her family for generations. Her books include: Pagan Parenting: Spiritual, Magical and Emotional Development of the Child; Festival Feasts: Pagan Celebration Cookbook, Pagan Homeschooling: A Guide to Adding Spirituality to Your Child's Education; The Book of Shamanic Healing; Exploring the Pagan Path: Wisdom from the Elders and The Shamanic Guide to Death and Dying: Meditations, Exercises, Rituals and Ceremonies. Also see Druidism, Healers, Recommended Reading, Shamans and kristinmadden.com.

Madira

In Hindu mythology, Madira is the wife of Varuna and Goddess of Wine. She is also called Varuni. Image from iskcon.com. Also see Hindu Gods and Goddesses.

Maenads

In Greek mythology the Maenads, are female followers of Dionysus. Maenads means "raving ones" and they are known to be wild women who could not be reasoned with. They are depicted here in an 1887 painting by Dutch-born English painter Sir Lawrence Alma-Tadema (alma-tadema.org) called The Women of Amphissa. They are called Bacchantes in Roman mythology.

Maeve

Celtic Goddess of War, Earth Fertility and Femininity, and also known as Queen Meave, Maeve is known to have a legendary sexual appetite. She rules over war and sexual love and she endows the Celtic sovereign with his powers. Other spellings include Medb. Maeve is depicted here in a 1916 rendition by American illustrator Joseph Christian Leyendecker. Also see Celtic Gods and Goddesses.

Mafdet

Egyptian Goddess invoked for protection against dangerous animals and snakes. Mafdet is sometimes depicted as a woman with the head of a cheetah with braided hair ending in scorpion tails. She is a very old Goddess whose cult is later supplanted by that of Bast. Also see Egyptian Gods and Goddesses.

Mage

A mage is a wise person who practices magic. Shown here is a 1631 painting by Dutch artist Rembrandt (rembrandtpainting.net) called A Scholar. Also see Sage.

Maggidim

Maggidim were itinerant Jewish preachers in Russia in the 17th and 18th centuries. Also see Spiritual Teachers.

Maggidim

According to Occultists and from Hebrew meaning "preacher", the Maggidim (singular Maggid) are spirits or angels who appear to a chosen few to reveal spiritual teachings and secrets of the future. Shown here is a 1602 painting by Italian artist Caravaggio (caravaggiogallery.com) called The Inspiration of Saint Matthew. Also see Supernatural and Spiritual Beings.

Magi

In the Christian New Testament the Magi were the three wise men who visited Mary and Joseph when Jesus was born. Shown here is a 1660 painting by Spanish artist Bartolomeo Esteban Murillo called The Adoration of the Magi.

Magi

Magi were priests, astrologers and magicians from ancient Persia who taught Zoroastrianism. Magi are shown here in an 1894 painting by French artist James Jacques Joseph Tissot (jamestissot.org) called The Journey of The Magi. Also see Spiritual Teachers.

Magic

The word Magic comes from the Greek word magus meaning "wise". Occultists mostly agree in its definition. Dion Fortune defined it as "The art of producing changes of consciousness in accordance with the Will". MacGregor Mathers said that Magic is "The science of the control of the secret force of nature". James Herbert Brennan said that Magic is "the art of generating synchronistic effects or meaningful coincidences to order". All of these statements are generally accepted by Occultists. Magic is also called to as magick by some to distinguish it from the conventional definition of magic.

Magic Circle

In Wiccan and Occult traditions the magic circle is a sacred space or sphere of personal energy which is projected by the magician to protect him or herself and the environment during a ritual against negative forces or evil influences. The magic circle or sphere may be physically drawn on the floor or envisioned on the astral planes, either way it symbolically extends above and below ground, the ground being the middle of the sphere. The magic circle is the place where Gods and Goddesses are invoked and rituals are performed. Shown here is a magic circle depicted in an 1886 painting by British artist John William Waterhouse (jwwaterhouse.com) called The Magic Circle. Also see Magical Methods and Ouroboros.

Magic Mirror

A magic mirror is a tool used in scrying. A magic mirror may be simply a mirror or a black mirror for basic scrying or elaborately decorated and ritually consecrated mirrors for more complex or ceremonial forms of scrying. Shown here is a 1553 painting by Italian artist Titian called Venus in Front of the Mirror. Also see Divination Tools.

Magical Amulets

Magical amulets are passive magical empowered objects, used to deflect negative energy and carried to ward off evil, illness or misfortune, and to bring good fortune and health. Of the many different types of amulets, the following are described herein: Ankh, Calundronius, Charm, Dream Catcher, Eye of Horus, Gris-Gris,

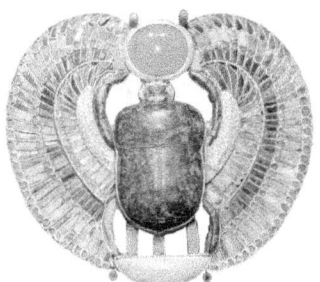

Hamsa Hand, Hand of Fatima, Hand of Miriam, Lamen, Mandala, Mojo, Mudra, Seal of Solomon, Witch Ball, Witch Bottle and Yantra. Shown here is Pharaoh Tutankhamen's scarab amulet. Also see Magical Tools.

Magical Correspondences

Magical correspondences refers to days, moon phases, colors, herbs, angels, oils or objects that are ritually chosen and used to match or "correspond" to the intent of the ritual.

Magical Methods

Of all the different magical methods used in esoteric and occult practices, natural magic and ritual magic, the following are described herein: Adjuration, Automatic Writing, Banishing, Bewitching, Binding, Ceremonial Magic, Channeling, Charging, Cone of Power, Depossession, Divination, Dowsing, Enchantment, Energy Ball, Evocation, Fumigation, Glamour, Godform, Incantation, Initiation, Invisibility, Invocation, Libation, Magical Circle, Natural Magic, Nature Worship, Offering, Pathworking, Philtre, Prediction, Radiesthesia, Rhabdomancy, Ritual, Sacrifice, Séance, Shape Shifting, Shield, Shroud of Concealment, Simulacrum, Slate Writing, Sympathetic Magic, Tattwas, Warding and White Magic.

Magical Name

Also known as magical motto and craft name, the magical name is a name or phrase chosen by the magician for personal use in a Brotherhood, Lodge or Occult Order. The original purpose of the name was for anonymity but it is currently used to disassociate oneself from the material world during rituals or magical work.

Magical Sword

One of the standard tools in ritual magic, the magical sword is used to command and banish spirits. One of the most famous medieval grimoires, The Key of Solomon, describes the magical process of consecrating four different kinds of magical swords. A more contemporary description of a magical sword can be found in Eliphas Levi's book Doctrine and Ritual of High Magic and Israel Regardie's book The Complete Golden Dawn System of Magic. Shown here is an 1845 painting called Bertuccio's Bride by British artist Edward Robert Hughes. Also see Magical Tools.

Magical Temple

In Occultism the magical temple is the space or room in which ceremonial rituals are carried out. These Temples exist on astral planes as well as on the physical plane. Shown here is a painting by American artist Gilbert Williams (gilbertwilliams.com) called The Gathering.

Magical Tools

Magical Tools, also called Ritual Tools are active tools used in ritual or ceremonial magic. Of the many magical tools, the following are described herein: Altar, Athame, Baculum, Bell, Besom, Boline, Cauldron, Censer, Chalice, Dagger, Elemental Weapons, Magical Sword, Seal of Solomon, Simulacrum, Talisman, Thurible and Wand. Photograph from myarmoury.com. Also see Divination Tools and Magical Amulets.

Magician

From the Sanskrit word maha, meaning "great", a magician is a person well versed in the secret or esoteric knowledge or the occult sciences and who practices and teaches magic. Also see Spiritual Teachers.

Magician

The Magician or Juggler is one of the 22 major arcana of the tarot deck of cards. Its number is I, its Qabbalistic title is The Magus of Power and its meaning is: skill, wisdom, craft, cunning and occult wisdom. Also see Tarot.

Magnetic Currents

Magnetic currents are lines of electromagnetism which flow in and around the Earth caused by the iron-nickel core of the Earth. Photograph taken by Eric Henze of NASA. Also see Becker-Hagens EarthStar, Curry Lines, Earth Energy, Geopathic Stress, Geopathic Zones, Sacred Geometry and Vile Vortices.

Magnetic Center

In Gnosticism, the Magnetic Center refers to the interests at the heart of a personality and the laws of attraction related to them. The Magnetic Center of a scientist would be all things related to science and therefore the person will be interested and attracted to scientific things, such as books, laboratories, and like minded people. The occultist will have a Magnetic Center related to esoterism and the occult, and so on. Also see Law of Attraction.

Magus

From Greek magos meaning "magician", magus is defined as a skilled or adept magician. The term originally referred to a member of the Zoroastrian priesthood of the ancient Persians. Shown here is a 1642 painting by Dutch artist Rembrandt (rembrandtpainting.net) called The Rabbi. Also see Spiritual Teachers.

Mah

In Persian mythology, Mah is the Goddess of the Moon who shines her lights to make the plants and herbs grow. Shown here is the Moon Goddess depicted by British artist Josephine Wall (josephinewall.com). Also see Persian Gods and Goddesses.

Maha

In Sanskrit, Maha means "great".

Maha Shivratri

One of the main Hindu festivals, Maha Shivratri is the night of Shiva when from midnight to dawn Lord Shiva is prayed to and honored. People give offerings of milk and flowers in the temples at sunrise. Also see Hinduism.

Mahabharata

From Sanskrit Mahabharata means "Great Epic of the Bharata Dynasty" and it is one of the two major Sanskrit epics of India. It is composed of the Bhagavad-Gita, the Narayaniya, the Anugita and the Harivamsa. It consists mostly of an exposition on dharma, including the proper conduct of Kings, warriors and men and for the attainment of emancipation from rebirth. Other spellings include Maha-bharata. Also see Sacred Writings.

Mahakala

In Tibetan mythology Mahakala, whose name means "Great Black One", is one of the Wrathful Deities. Shown here is an 18th Century painting of Mahakala by an unknown artist housed in the Asian Art Museum of San Francisco, California. Also see Tibetan Gods and Goddesses, and Wrathful Deities.

Mahamudra

From Sanskrit meaning "The Great Symbol", the mahamudra is, in Vajrayana Buddhism, the term for the realization of the true nature of mind. It refers to the methods and that state of enlightenment that it produces. Also see Enlightenment, Nirvana and mahamudracenter.org.

Maharishi

In Hinduism, Maharishi, from the Sanskrit maja meaning "great" and rishi meaning "seer", is the term used to describe Holy men or the title given to a spiritual teacher. Also see Spiritual Teacher.

Maharishi Mahesh Yogi

(1917(?)-2008) Indian-born Mahesh Prasad Varma aka Maharishi Mahesh Yogi was the founder of Transcendental Meditation which has taught millions of people around the world and The Spiritual Regeneration Movement. Maharishi Mahesh Yogi became a well known name in the 1960's when The Beatles and the Beach Boys became his students and visited him in India. He wrote over 15 books including: Meditation: Easy System Propounded by Maharishi Mahesh Yogi; On the Bhagavad-Gita: A New Translation with Commentary with Sanskrit Text; Love and God; Building for the Health and Happiness of Everyone: Creating Ideal Housing in Harmony with Natural Law; Meditations of Maharishi Mahesh Yogi; and The Science of Being and the Art of Living. Also see Meditation, Recommended Reading, Transcendental Meditation, Yogis and maharishi.org.

Mahasaya, Lahiri

(1828-1898) Indian-born Shyama Charon Lahiri aka Lahiri Mahasaya was an Indian yogi, disciple of Manabatar Babaji who was instrumental in reviving the science of Kriya Yoga. He studied Hindi, Urdu, Bengali, Sanskrit, Persian and English along with the Vedas. He lived an unconventional life for a Holy man, marrying, raising a family, working for a living and living at home rather than a monastery or temple. Lahiri lived most of his life in Varanasi, India where he organized study groups and meditation groups and gave regular lectures on the Bhagavad Gita and Kriya Yoga. He became known in the West through the book Autobiography of a Yogi by Paramahansa Yogananda. Also see Meditation, Recommended Reading, Yogis and kriyayogalahiri.com.

Mahatma

From Sanskrit meaning "great soul" a Mahatma is an adept, an exalted being, one who has reached a very high degree of esoteric knowledge and spiritual perfection. The name is given to great ones, "Masters of Wisdom and Compassion" in India and Tibet. A mahatma is also described as a spiritually evolved soul who chooses to stay with humankind to help in its spiritual evolution. Also see Spiritual Teachers.

Mahatma Gandhi

(1869-1948) Indian-born Mohandas Karamchand Gandhi aka Mahatma Gandhi was a mystic and major political and spiritual leader of India and the Indian independence movement. His philosophy was firmly founded upon ahimsa (total non-violence) and he led India to independence through pacific mass civil disobedience and inspired civil rights movements across the world. Honored in India as the Father of the Nation he led a very simple life living in a self-sufficient residential community where he ate vegetarian foods and undertook long periods of fasting. Although he was born a Hindu and practiced

Hinduism all his life, he was an avid theologian and when he was asked if he was a Hindu he replied "Yes I am. I am also a Christian, a Muslim, a Buddhist and a Jew". Mahatma Gandhi believed that at the core of all religions was truth and love. He is officially honored in India where his birthday is considered a national holiday and worldwide as the International Day of Non-Violence. Photograph from photos-room.com. Also see Mystics, Spiritual Leaders, Theologians and mkgandhi.org.

Mahayana

The Mahayana is a Buddhist doctrine that states that the body of man is of a three-fold nature. It considers that once such appearance of a body of transformation was the incarnation of Prince Siddhartha Gautama who later came to be known as the Buddha. Another important concept in Mahayana is that of the Bodhisattva or "enlightenment being", as the ultimate ideal toward which Buddhists should aspire. Also see mandalamagazine.org. The Mahayana describes these bodies as: the body of communal bliss, which represents the essential Buddha nature in a heavenly form; the body of essence, which represents the ultimate nature of the Buddha; and the body of transformation, which is the body taken by Buddha on earth among humankind.

Mahish

In the Bhagavad-Gita, Mahish is a mighty Angel who, together with the Gods Vishnu and Brahma, sprang from one of the primary properties. Also see Angels.

Maia

Greek Goddess of Fertility, Maia is the eldest and most beautiful of the Pleiades (seven sisters) and the mother of Hermes by Zeus. She rules over youth, life, rebirth, love and sexuality. As the Goddess of Plants and of the Spring, she is also called Flora and Bona Dea. Shown here is a 1482 painting by Italian artist Sandro Botticelli (sandrobotticelli.net) called Primavera. Also see Greek Gods and Goddesses, and Pleiades.

Maiden

Celtic Goddess, one of the aspects of the triple Goddess along with the Mother and the Crone. The Maiden represents new beginnings, birth, youth, health, enchantment, the waxing Moon and the female principle. Shown here is a 1903 painting of a maiden by British artist John William Waterhouse (jwwaterhouse.com) called Windflowers. Also see Triple Goddess.

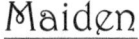

Maier, Michael

(1568-1622) German-born Michael Maier M.D. was a physician, philosopher and alchemist who served as personal physician, astrologer, imperial counselor and secretary to Emperor Rudolf II Habsburg, and later the court of James I and Landgrave Moritz of Hesse-Kassel. He studied philosophy and medicine in Rostock, Frankfurt and Padua and obtained his doctorate in medicine at Basel and returned to Rostock to practice. He wrote extensively and was also involved in the Rosicrucian movement of his time. Shown here is a 1617 engraving by of Michael Maier by Swiss engraver Matthaus Merian. Also see Alchemists, Astrologers, Philosophers and Rosicrucians.

Maimonides, Moses

(1135-1204) Spanish-born Moses ben Maimon aka Moses Maimonides was a Jewish Rabbi, philosopher and theologian and considered one of the greatest Torah scholars of all time. He was educated by Arabic teachers in Cordova and then lived for five years in Morocco where he studied at the University of Al Karaouine, after that he moved to Egypt where he was physician of the Grand Vizier Alfadhil and Sultan Saladin. His writing influenced the Jewish community as well as the non Jewish community and even today his work is considered a cornerstone of Jewish study and thought. Shown here is an 19th Century depiction of Maimonides by an unknown artist. Also see Philosophers, Rabbis, Theologians and mosesmaimonides.com.

Maitreya

Tibetan name for the future Buddha who is believed to reside in the Tusita Heaven, he is known as The Benevolent One and the Buddha of the Future. His name is derived from the Sanskrit maitri which means "friendliness". Maitreya is one of eight Great Bodhisattvas. According to Occultists and Theosophists, Lord Maitreya replaced Jesus Christ by taking his body and living his last three years of life on earth. He is said to have incarnated in the past and that he will reincarnate again to help humanity on its quest for spiritual enlightenment Maitreya is also called The Buddha Who Is to Come and Master of Masters. Other spellings include Metteyya. and Maitreyia. Image from dharma-media.org. Also see Bodhisattvas, Great Bodhisattvas, Gods of Heaven, and Buddhas.

Maitri

See Upanishads.

Majestas

In Roman mythology, Majestas is the Goddess of Majesty who rules over honor and reverence. Shown here is a 20th Century painting by French artist Guillaume Seignac called A Moment's Pause. Also see Roman Gods and Goddesses.

Makara

In Buddhist and Hindu mythology, Makara is a fantastic mythological animal ridden by Varuna. It is depicted as an aquatic creature something like a crocodile or as a mixture of an elephant and a fish. Shown here is a carving of a Makara from the Sambor Prei Kuk temple in Kampong Thom City, Cambodia. Photograph by Vassil. Also see Mythological Creatures, and Varuna.

Makia

From Hawaiian religion Huna, Makia is one of its seven philosophical principles and it means "where your mind goes your energy flows". Also see Huna.

Malachy Prophecies

In the 1140's an Irish-born medieval bishop named Malachy O'More was said to have foretold a succession of 112 Popes from Celestinus II to a Pope yet to come. These predictions, called the Malachy Prophecies are written in Latin character mottos and not actual names. These mottos start with Ex Castro Tiberis (meaning "from a castle on the Tiber") which may refer to Celestinus II who came from near the Tiber and later Flos Florum (meaning "flower of flowers") which may refer to Pope Paul VI who had a fleur de lis on his armor. The last Pope mentioned is said to be Petrus Romanus (meaning "Peter the Roman") after which Rome will be destroyed and the world purified by fire. Also see Prophets.

Mal'ak

Hebrew term for Angel or messenger.

Malak

Arabic term for Angel or messenger. Shown here is an 1871 painting of an angel by British artist Simeon Solomon (simeon-solomon.com) called Dawn.

Maleficia

From Latin meaning "evil doings" maleficia was a term used in medieval literature to describe evil magic that was punishable by law. During the Burning Times (inquisition) maleficia became synonymous for witchcraft. The singular of maleficia is maleficium.

Malkuth

The tenth sephiroh on the Qabbalistic Tree of Life whose symbols are magic circles, altars, temples and equal-armed crosses and represents beauty. See Tree of Life.

Malleus Maleficarum

Infamous document published in Latin 1486, during the Inquisition and the Burning Times, by Dominicans Heinrich Kramer and Johann Sprenger. It was considered the standard handbook on witchcraft. The writing and publication of this document requested by Pope Innocent VIII provoked almost two centuries of witch-hunting hysteria in Europe and the Americas. Its contents was divided into three parts, the first describing the depravity of witches, the second part the activities of witches (diabolic contracts, sexual relations with devils and other aberrations) and the third part describing of the legal procedures to be followed in witch trials, including the tortures to be used as a means to extract confessions. It was also referred to as The Hammer of Witches, its title in Latin. Also see Sacred Writings and Burning Times.

Mama

According to the Inca, mama is a general name for a Goddess or female spirit. They believe that all things and events such as mountains, rivers, plants, animals and meteorological phenomena have mamas.

Mama Allpa

Inca Earth Goddess, Mama Allpa is a fertility Goddess invoked for good harvests. She is depicted with many breasts to symbolize fertility and powers of nourishment. Other spellings include Mamallpa. Also see Inca Gods and Goddesses.

Mama Coca

In Inca mythology, Mama Coca (shown here) is Goddess of Health and Joy. She rules over the Coca plant from which she allows men to chew only after bringing a woman to orgasm. Other spellings include Cocomama and Mamacoca. Image from bigsoccer.com. Also see Inca Gods and Goddesses.

Mama Cocha

Inca Sea Goddess, Mama Cocha rules over fishing and the sea, maintained the fertility of the sea; she supplies all the fish and protects the fishermen and sailors. She is the wife of Viracocha and is also known as Mother Sea and the Mother of the Sea. Mama Cocha is depicted here by American artist Lisa Hunt (lisahuntart.com). Other spellings include Mamacocha and Mama Qocha. Also see Inca Gods and Goddesses.

Mama Quilla

Inca Moon Goddess, wife and sister of the Sun God Inti, Mama Quilla is the Time Keeper of the Heavens and she rules over married women, religious festivals and the calendar. Mama Quilla is represented by silver, in contrast to her husband Inti is represented by gold. She is also known as Mother Moon. Other spellings include Mamaquila, Mama Killa, and Mama Kilya. Mama Quilla is depicted here by American artist Lisa Hunt (lisahuntart.com). Also see Gods of Heaven, and Inca Gods and Goddesses.

Mama Zara

In Inca mythology, Mama Zara is Goddess of Grain, Corn and Willow Trees. Other spellings include Mama Sara and Zaramama. Image from incaglossary.org. Also see Inca Gods and Goddesses.

Mambo

A Priestess of the Voodoo religion who acts as shamanistic healers, teachers and spiritual guides to the living, a Mambo is considered an expert magician. Also see Marie Laveau, Spiritual Teachers, and Voodoo.

Mammon

In traditional Christian demonology, Mammon is a demon who represents the deadly sin of avarice. Shown here in a 1909 painting by British artist Evelyn de Morgan (demorgan.org.uk) called The Worship of Mammon. Also see Demon and Demons.

Mana

From Hawaiian religion Huna, Mana is one of its seven philosophical principles and it means "the moment of power is now". Also see Huna.

Mana

From Polynesian and Melanesian meaning "Great Power", Mana describes the supernatural force or energy ascribed to persons, spirits and inanimate objects. Mana may be good or evil and is never spoken of by itself, only in connection with powerful beings or things.

Managarm

In Norse mythology, the Managarm is an evil giant wolf also called the Moon's Dog. Image from fanpop.com. Also see Mythological Creatures.

Manannan

Celtic God of the Sea, Manannan is the son of Llyrr and he rules over storms, weather at sea, navigators, sailing, fertility, weather forecasting, magic, shape shifting, arts, commerce and rebirth. He is also the ferryman who carries the souls of the dead to the Underworld. Manannan is also called Manawydan Ap llyu, Mannan Mac Llyr, Manannan Mac Lir and Manawydden. Other spellings include Mananaan. Manannan is depicted here by Miranda Gray (mirandagray.co.uk), R.J. Stewart from Celtic Gods, Celtic Goddesses, R.J. Stewart, 1990. Also see Celtic Gods and Goddesses, and manannan.net.

Manas

From Sanskrit meaning "mind" or "thought", Manas is the individual mind, reason and intelligence, that which receives sensory impressions before it reaches the consciousness.

Manco Capac

Incan God of Magic and Fire, Manco Capac is the youngest son of the Sun God Inti and said to be the founder of the city of Cuzco (Peru). Together with his sister and Queen, Mama Oello Huaco, are called The Children of the Sun. Manco Capac is also called Mythical Father of the Incas. Manco Capac is depicted here in a 16th Century rendering by an unknown artist. Also see Inca Gods and Goddesses.

Mandala

Sanskrit meaning "circle", the mandala in Hindu and Buddhist Tantrism is an intricate mystical and symbolic diagram used in religious rites as a meditation tool and to gather spiritual energies. This tool works by mentally entering the mandala and meditating or proceeding towards the center. The mandala is primarily a graphic representation of the spiritual universe (or God) and is considered a consecrated area which is used as a collection point for universal forces. Mandalas are frequently represented in Chinese, Tibetan and Japanese art. Dr. Carl Jung frequently wrote about mandalas in his works. Also see Magical Amulets, Yantra and mandalaproject.org.

Mandino, Og

(1923-1996) American-born Augustine "Og" Mandino was a sales guru and author many of bestselling motivational self-help books. He was president of Success Unlimited magazine and inducted into the National Speakers Association's Hall of Fame. Among his books are: The Greatest Salesman in the World (which has sold over 50 million copies and been translated into 25 languages); The Greatest Secret In The World; The Greatest Miracle In The World; The God Memorandum: From The Greatest Miracle in the World; A Better Way To Live; The Twelfth Angel; Spellbinder's Gift; and The Ten Ancient Scrolls for Success: From the Greatest Salesman In The World. Photograph from corbisimages.com. Also see Recommended Reading, Self-Help and ogmandino.com.

Mandukya

See Upanishads.

Manes

In Roman mythology, Manes are souls or spirits of the dead who reside in the other world and good spirits who preside over graves and monuments. The ancient Romans celebrated the festival of Parentalia observed in praise of the Manes. Shown here is an ancient Roman relief of Manes. Also see Supernatural and Spiritual Beings.

Mangala

In Hinduism, Mangala is the God of War and Occult sciences and is a celestial deity who rules over Mars. He is also called Angaraka and Bhauma. He is one of the nine Navagrahas. Also see Hindu Gods and Goddesses and Navagrahas.

Mani

(216-276 C.E.) Persian-born prophet Mani was the founder of Manichaeism. He was renowned for his spiritual healings and exorcisms and his followers called him the new Jesus. He was also known as Apostle, Savior, Raiser of the Dead, Illuminator and Helmsman. Mani taught that everything in the universe was a conflict of light and darkness and he believed in the doctrine of reincarnation. He regarded Buddha, Zarathustra and Jesus as his forerunners. Mani was tortured to death by the Zoroastrian priesthood and his Church was persecuted by the Persians, Romans and Chinese. Also see Healers, Manichaeism, Prophets and Reincarnation (Life After Life).

Mani Wheel
See Prayer Wheel.

Manichaeism

Religion founded by the Persian prophet Mani around 240 C.E. in what is now Iraq. There were branches all over Eurasia and China. Manichaeism was essentially Gnostic although it has elements from Zoroastrianism, Taoism and Buddhism. Also see Religions.

Manifestation

Manifestation refers to the belief that we can, by force of will, desire and focusing energy, make something come true or "manifest" on the physical level. An apport is an example of manifestation. Also see Thought Forms and Tulpa.

Manipura

From Sanskrit meaning "diamond", or Solar Plexus, Manipura is the chakra corresponding to the pancreas. It governs emotions and the emotional and mental bodies. It is associated with the seat of energy and identity and the perceptions of freedom, control and power, its color is yellow and its element is fire. This chakra has also been called the center of power. See Chakras.

Manjusri

In Tibetan Buddhism, Manjusri is one of the eight Great Bodhisattvas or enlightened ones who spiritually ministers to humanity. Manjushri is known as the personification of the Wisdom of Buddha and as the Annihilator of Yama and Lord of Death. His name in Sanskrit means "sweet" or "gentle glory". Manjusri is also called Vagisvara. Other spellings include Majughosa and Manjushi. Also see Bodhisattvas, Great Bodhisattvas, and Buddhas.

Mannaz

As the 1st symbol of the runes, Mannaz represents the self. Other spellings include Mannuz. Also see Runes.

Manning, Matthew

(1955-) British-born Matthew Manning is a world famous psychic healer. He also demonstrates psychokinetic abilities such as bending spoons and affecting clocks and watches. He is frequently mentioned in the media and lectures and demonstrates his techniques all over the world and has been involved in more scientific research and testing and any other psychic healer. Among his books are: In the Mind of Millions, The Strangers; The Healing Journey: Discover Powerful New Ways to Beat Cancer and Other Serious Illnesses; No Faith Required; Your Mind Can Heal Your Body: How Your Experiences and Emotions Affect Your Physical Health; and The Link: Matthew Manning's Own Story of His Extraordinary Psychic Gifts. Photograph from lotuskrystallen.com. Also see Healers, Psychokinesis, Recommended Reading and matthewmanning.com.

Mansions of Heaven

See Houses of Heaven.

Mansions of the Moon

According to Occultism and Astrology, the Mansions of the Moon (shown here) are the 28 days of the lunar cycle, each day assigned to a portion of the Zodiac. Each of these mansions (days) have a specific influence or energy that is used by Occultists in ceremonial magic. Image from yeatsvision.com. Also see Zodiac.

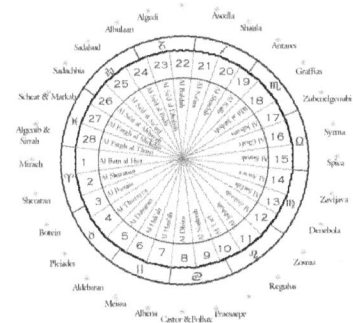

Mantra

From the Sanskrit meaning "mind protector" or "instrument of thought" and in both Hinduism and Buddhism, a Mantra is described as the sacred sound of a syllable, word, verse, incantation, prayer or magic phrase that is repeated over and over for the purpose of stilling the mind and raising it to a higher state of consciousness or spiritual awareness. Used mostly by Oriental Esoteric and Mystic traditions, Mantras have also been defined as either a prayer to the Gods or a magical charm. Mantras are even used to protect a person or place from evil psychic powers. Mantras are found in the Vedas and the Atharva-Veda. Other spellings include Mantram. Also see Spiritual Techniques, Om, om-sweet-om.net and sanskritmantra.com.

Mantra Yoga

The yoga that uses chants or mantras to focus the attention, activate energies and awaken higher states of consciousness. See Yoga and mantra-yoga.com.

Mara

Mara is the Hindu and Buddhist Master Magician of Black Magic and Illusion, the Satan of Buddhist mythology. He is also known as the Lord of the Senses. Legend says that Mara appeared to Prince Gautama to try and tempt and confuse him while he was meditating for enlightenment, even to the extent of challenging his right to sit under the Bodhi tree and sending his daughters Trsna, Raga and Rati (Thirst, Delight and Desire) to seduce the future Buddha to no avail. Shown here is a painting called The Temptation of Buddha by Mara.

Marah

Egyptian Goddess of the passive principal of nature, Marah is also the Great Goddess of Space, Earth and Water. She is also known as the Great Mother, the Bitter One and the Wise One. Also see Egyptian Gods and Goddesses.

Marden, Orison Swett

(1850-1924) American-born Orison Swett Marden M.D., L.L.B. was a successful businessman, author of New Thought and self-help books and founder of Success Magazine. He obtained his M.D. and his L.L.B from Harvard and he also studied at the Boston School of Oratory. Dr. Marden was president of the League for Higher Life (a New Thought organization in New York City). His books include: Character: The Grandest Thing in the World; He Can Who Thinks He Can, and Other Papers of Success in Life; Do It To a Finish; The Secrets of Achievement: A Book Designated to Teach That the Highest Achievement is That Which Results in Noble Manhood and Womanhood; Peace Power and Plenty; Architects of Fate Or, Steps to Success and Power: A Book Designated to Inspire Youth to Character Building, Self-Culture and Nobel Achievement; and Optimistic Life. Also see New Thought, Recommended Reading, Self-Help and orisonswettmarden.wwwhubs.com.

Marduk

Babylonian God, King of all Gods, Creator of the Universe and of Humankind, of Light and Life, Marduk is considered the ruler of destinies and he is called the Son of the Sun. He defended the other Gods against the monster Tiamat. He is also called the God of Thunderstorms. Marduk is almost never called by name instead he is known as Bel (Lord). Also see Babylonian Gods and Goddesses.

Margawse

Celtic Goddess, Margawse represents the Mother aspect of the Triple Goddess. Also see Celtic Gods and Goddesses.

Margolis, Char

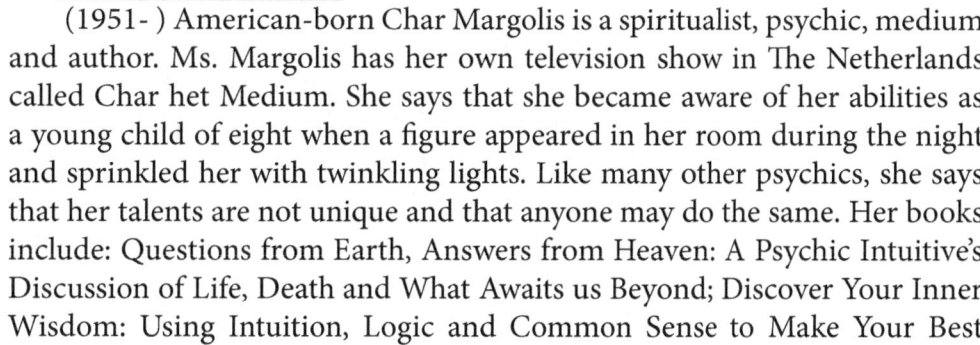

(1951-) American-born Char Margolis is a spiritualist, psychic, medium and author. Ms. Margolis has her own television show in The Netherlands called Char het Medium. She says that she became aware of her abilities as a young child of eight when a figure appeared in her room during the night and sprinkled her with twinkling lights. Like many other psychics, she says that her talents are not unique and that anyone may do the same. Her books include: Questions from Earth, Answers from Heaven: A Psychic Intuitive's Discussion of Life, Death and What Awaits us Beyond; Discover Your Inner Wisdom: Using Intuition, Logic and Common Sense to Make Your Best Choices for Life, Health, Finances and Relationships; Living in Spirit: Why You and Those You Love Will Never Die; and Love Karma Use Your Intuition to Find, Create and Nurture Love in Your Life. Photograph from Kosmos. Also see Mediums, Psychics, Recommended Reading, Spiritualists and char.net.

Markandeya Purana

In Hinduism, Markandeya Purana, which deals with how birds recite the Vedas as well as with the Mother Goddess, Shakti, is one of the texts which explain the myths and rituals of the Gods. Also see Puranas.

Mars

In Occultism, as the celestial body affecting aspects of human life, Mars represents valor, courage, deviation from the norm, protection against physical and spiritual danger, machines, adventure, energy, cars, war and weapons, struggles, and battlefields (domestic battlefields as well), pain, fever, management, ambition, energy or power to overcome obstacles, fighting spirit, sharp words, accidents; particularly fire and cuts or lacerations, personal gain, stubbornness, decision, violence and tantrums. See Planets.

Mars

In Roman mythology, Mars is the God of War and Agriculture, he rules over courage and revenge. He is the son of Jupiter and Juno, the father of Romulus and Remus and the founder of Rome. He is considered the protector of Rome and guardian of the Emperor. Mars is shown here in an 1824 painting by French artist Jacques-Louis David (jacqueslouisdavid.org) called Mars Disarmed by Venus and the Three Graces. Also see Roman Gods and Goddesses.

Martialis

One of three main Flamen (Roman priests specifically assigned to a God or Goddess), Martialis, or Flamen Martialis served Mars. See Flamen.

Martinism

The mystical tradition of the Martinist Order (Ordre Martiniste) is based on Jewish and Christian mysticism and the Qabbalah. It was founded on the teachings of the 18th Century French philosopher Louis Claude de Saint Martin who initiated people into his Society of Friends. After his death the Order was re-founded by the mystic Gerard Encause (aka Papus) and Agustin Chaboseau, who named it the Martinist Order. World wars I and II almost destroyed the Order and its members. The remaining Martinists are closely linked to the Rosicrusians. Also See Occult Orders, Brotherhoods and Secret Societies, Rosicrucian Order and martinism.com.

Martyr

A martyr is a person who dies for their religious faith. Shown here is an 1871 painting entitled The Martyr of the Solway by British artist Sir John Everett Millais.

Maru

From Hindu mythology, Maru is the founder of the human race. Also see Hindu Gods and Goddesses.

Marx-Hubbard, Barbara

(1929-) American-born Barbara Marx-Hubbard is a well known speaker, futurist, social innovator and author. She studied in New York and Paris and holds a B.A. in political science from Bryn Mawr College. She is currently the president of the Foundation for Conscious Evolution which she co-founded. She was considered instrumental in the creation of several future-oriented organizations including: The Association for Global New Thought, the World Future Society and The Foundation for the Future, among others. Her books include: The Hunger of Eve: One Woman's Odyssey Toward the Future; Conscious Evolution: Awakening the Power of Our Social Potential; The Evolutionary

Journey: A Personal Guide to a Positive Future; Emergence: The Shift from Ego to Essence; and Birth2012 & Beyond: Humanity's Great Shift to the Age of Conscious Evolution. Photograph from barbaramarxhubbard-berkeley.evenbrite.com. Also see Futurists, New Thought, Recommended Reading, barbaramarxhubbard.com and evolve.org.

Mary Celeste

The Mary Celeste (originally named Amazon) was a ship found abandoned at sea on December 5th, 1872. Her abandonment is one of the most famous unsolved sea mysteries. When she was found she there was not a soul on board although she was loaded with plenty of water and food and was completely seaworthy. The captain's log registered the last entry on November 25th and no explanation was ever found for her crew's disappearance. Shown here is an 1861 painting of the Mary Celeste while she was still named Amazon. Also see Phantom Ships.

Mary Magdalene

(1st Century C.E.) Disciple (possibly wife) of Jesus of Nazareth, Mary Magdalene is described in Gnostic Literature as She Who Gives Peter the Secret Teachings of Jesus. In the Gospel of Phillip she's called Mother of Angels. The Gospel of Mary Magdalene which survives in two 3rd Century Greek fragments and a longer 5th Century translation into Coptic was never included in the New Testament. The early Church called her the Apostola Apostolarum meaning Apostle of Apostles or the First Apostle. She was labeled as a prostitute, but there is nothing in the New Testament to support this and a lot to dispute it. In some theories she is proposed as the Holy Grail, mother of a child of Jesus. She appears to be depicted here in an 1806 mosaic reproduction of Leonardo da Vinci's painting The Last Supper by Italian artist Giacomo Raffaelli. Also see Holy Grail.

Masleh

In Occult literature, Masleh is considered as the Angel who "actuated the chaos and produced the four elements". In Jewish magical tradition, Masleh is the ruler of the Zodiac. Also see Angels.

Maslow, Abraham

(1908-1970) American-born Abraham Harold Maslow Ph.D. was a psychologist and author, considered the father of humanistic psychology. Son of uneducated Jewish immigrants from. He received his B.A., M.A. and Ph.D. from the University of Wisconsin Madison and continued research at Columbia University. Dr. Maslow taught at the Brooklyn College and co-founded the Journal of Humanistic Psychology. He differed from most psychologists before him in that, while they were studying abnormality and mental illnesses, he was more interested in understanding positive mental health. In Dr. Maslow's later years he was a professor at Brandeis University and a resident fellow of the Laughlin Institute in California. His books include: Toward a Psychology of Being; The Farther Reaches of Human Nature; Religions, Values and Peak-Experiences; The Psychology of Science: A Reconnaissance; and Motivation and Personality. Also see Recommended Reading, abraham-maslow.com and maslow.com.

Mass
Christian principal act of worship also called the Liturgy, Holy Communion and Holy Eucharist. Also see Christianity.

Master Djwhal Khul and Master Koot Humi
Spirit guides said to be channeled by medium Alice Bailey. Also see Channeled Spirit Guides, Channelers, and Alice Bailey.

Masters
Term used in New Age vocabulary, specifically Theosophy to describe highly evolved beings who have attained enlightenment and the need for incarnation but chose to assist humanity in its spiritual evolution. Also see Spiritual Teachers.

Masters, Robert

(1927-2008) American-born Robert E. L. "Papa Bob" Masters Ph.D. was a renowned expert in sexology, poet and author. He co-founded The Foundation for Mind Research and directed it for over 30 years. He traveled all over the world conducting investigations of trance and psychoactive plant induced altered states of consciousness. Dr. Masters was founder and president emeritus of the Association for the Masters Psychophysical Method and author or co-author of over 25 books. Among his books are: Swimming Where Madmen Drown: Traveler's Tales From Inner Space; The Way to Awaken: Exercises to Enliven Body, Self and Soul; The Goddess Sekhmet: Psychospiritual Exercises of the Fifth Way(; Listening to the Body: The Psychophysical Way to Health and Awareness; and Sex Driven People: An Autobiographical Approach to the Problem of the Sex-Dominated Personality. Also see Hallucinogens, Poets, Recommended Reading and robertmasters.org.

Masters, Roy

(1928-) British-born Roy Masters is a Minister, counselor, commentator and author. He began a conservative radio talk show in Los Angeles CA with an "Advice Line". Rev. Masters founded and directed the Foundation of Human Understanding for over 45 years. He also founded the Brighton Academy, an innovative and progressive private school. He is the author of over 16 books on Christianity, health, religion, stress and parenting. His books include: Finding God in Physics: Einstein's Missing Relative; How to Survive Your Parents: And Not Do to Your Children What Your Parents Did to You; The Secret Power of

Words: Why Words Affect You So Deeply; How Your Mind Can Keep You Well; Secrets of a Parallel Universe: Why Our Deepest Problems Hold the Key to Ultimate Personal Success and Happiness; and Beyond the Known. Photograph from the Foundation of Human Understanding. Also see Recommended Reading, Reverends and Ministers, fhu.com and gravitydrivenuniverse.org.

Masvani

Persian mystical poem written in the 13th Century by the Sufi mystic Rumi, the Masvani is divided into six books and 27,000 couplets, it deals with folklores, legends, fables and teachings from the Qur'an. It is considered one of the most important writings of Sufism. Other spellings include Mathnawi and Mesnevi. Also see Sacred Writings.

Matergabia

Slavic Goddess of Housekeeping, Matergabia is offered the first batch of bread. Also see Slavic Gods and Goddesses.

Materialist

A materialist is described as a person who relies exclusively on sensory five senses to define their sense of reality. The materialist has no understanding or belief in superior dimensions and is limited to the physical reality.

Materialization

A term used in Occultism and Theosophy to describe the temporary psychic phenomena of a spirit clothing itself with a material form or using the astral body to solidify temporarily. This can either be done by using the electromagnetic or etheric energy field (ectoplasm) of the medium during a séance, or by act of will, gathering and condensing surrounding etheric energy to produce the materialization. Shown here is a photograph taken in 1920. Also see Apport, and Dematerialization.

Mathematicians

Mathematics is the study of properties, measurements and relationships of sets and quantities, using numbers and symbols. The people who are described herein who are mathematicians include: Ralf Abraham, Roger Bacon, Giordano Bruno, Jerome Cardan, Rene Descartes, Richard Feyman, Rene Guenon, Edward Kelly, Leonardo da Vinci, P.D. Ouspensky, Isaac Newton, Albert Pike, Pythagoras, Peter Russell, Ptolemy, Robert Anton Wilson and Arthur Young. Shown here is part of Italian artist Raphael's (raphaelsanzio.org) 1509 painting called School of Athens.

Mathers, Moira

(1865-1928) Swiss-born Mina Bergson aka Moina Mathers was an artist, occultist and leading member of the Golden Dawn. She was the sister of philosopher Henri Bergson and grew up in London where she studied art at the Slade School of Art. After marrying S.L. MacGregor Mathers she took the name Moina Mathers and became the first initiate in the order. She served as priestess and demonstrated abilities in clairvoyance and scrying by which she is said to have channeled the material that supplied the rituals for the order. After the breakup of the Golden dawn she moved with her husband to Paris where they formed the Isis Temple and later the Alpha et Omega which she took over after his death. Also see Alpha et Omega, Golden Dawn, Occultists and golden-dawn.org.

Mathers, S. L. MacGregor

(1854-1918), born Samuel Liddell Mathers later S. L. MacGregor Mathers was a very influential figure of modern Occultism and one of the key founding members of the Golden Dawn, often described as the Order's leading magician. Many of the rituals used by the Golden Dawn were translated or decoded by Mathers with the help of his wife Moina. He was also a member of the Freemasons where he held the title of Master Mason and the Rosicrusians where he became a member of its Highest Council. His books include: Astral Projection; Ritual Magic and Alchemy; The Secret Knowledge of the Neophyte; Ritual Magic of the Golden Dawn; The Greater Key of Solomon the King: Including a Clear and Precise Exposition of King Solomon's Secret Procedure, Its Mysteries and Magic Rites, Original Plates, Seals, Charms and Talismans; and Sacred Book of the Magic of Abramelin. Also see Astral Projection, Freemasons, Golden Dawn, Occultists, Recommended Reading, Rosicrusians and golden-dawn.org.

Mati Syra Zemlya

Slavic Goddess of the Earth, Mati Syra Zemlya (whose name means Damp Mother Earth or Moist Mother Earth) rules over agriculture, crops, fertility, justice, oaths, oracles, divination, healing and truth. She is also called the Great Mother, Earth Goddess and Moist Mother Earth. Also see Slavic Gods and Goddesses.

Matsya

In Hinduism, Matsya, the fish is the first incarnation or Avatar of the God Vishnu in the Satya Yuga. Shown here is sculpture of Matsya found on the walls of the Kodananda Rama Temple in East Yadavalli Village, West Godavari District in India. See Avatar.

Matsya Purana

In Hinduism, Matsya Purana, which is devoted to the Matysa or fish incarnation of Vishnu and his revelations, is one of the texts which explain the myths and rituals of the Gods. Also see Puranas.

Matthews, Caitlin

(1952-) British-born Caitlin Matthews is a well known author of many books dealing with Druidry, Shamanism and mystery traditions. She is also active teaching divination and meditation in her many lectures and workshops. Both Caitlin and her husband John Matthews have been active in the Druidic community for over 25 years and they served as joint presidents of the Order of Bards Ovates and Druids for several years. She co-founded The Foundation of Inspirational and Oracular Studies (FIOS). She has written over 150 books including: The Elements of the Goddess; The Celtic Book of the Dead: A Guide for Your Voyage to the Celtic Otherworld; King Arthur and the Goddess of the Land; Singing the Soul Back Home: Shamanism in Daily Life; and Psychic Shield: The Personal Handbook of Psychic Protection. Photo by Mark Brome. Also see Druidism, Meditation, Order of Bards Ovates and Druids, Recommended Reading, Shamans and hallowquest.org.uk.

Matthews, John

(1948-) British-born John Matthews is a well known teacher and author of many books dealing with Arthurian, Celtic and Shamanistic traditions. With his wife Caitlin Matthews, and Felicity Wombwell they founded The Foundation of Inspirational and Oracular Studies (FIOS). Matthews has been active in the Druidic community for over 25 years and with his wife joint presidents of the Order of Bards Ovates and Druids for several years. Among his books are: Gawain: Knight of the Goddess: Restoring the Archetype; Book of Arthur: Lost Tales from the Round Table; Quest for the Green Man; Secret Life of Elves and Faeries; The Sidhe: Wisdom from the Celtic Otherworld; and King Arthur: Dark Age Warrior and Mythic Hero. Photo by Mark Brome. Also see Druidism, Order of Bards Ovates and Druids, Recommended Reading, Shamans and hallowquest.org.uk.

Maudy Thursday
See Holy Thursday.

May, Rollo

(1909-1994) American-born Rollo May Ph.D. was one of the leading existential psychologists of his time and internationally renowned author. He received his M.A. at Michigan State College and his B.A. at Oberlin College. He spent some time teaching in Greece before he received his Ph.D. in clinical psychology from Teachers College Columbia University. He was co-founder and faculty member of the Saybrook Graduate School and Research Center in San Francisco, California (now Saybrook University). Among Dr. May's books are: The Meaning of Anxiety; Man's Search for Himself; Love and Will; The Courage to Create; The Discovery of Being: Writings in Existential Psychology; Freedom and Destiny; My Quest for Beauty; Psychology and the Human Dilemma; and The Cry for Myth. Shown here is a 1969 photograph of Dr. May taken by Alfred Eisenstaedt. Also see Recommended Reading and Saybrook University.

Maya

Group of related Native Central American tribes, the Maya lived between the Peninsula of Yucatan in the north and Honduras in the South from 1000 B.C.E. to 1542 C.E. They were ruled by male line hereditary chiefs. They had remarkable architecture, especially their pyramids, some of the greatest ruins are found in Palenque, Uxmal, Mayapan, Copán, Tikal, Uaxactún, and Chichén Itzá. They developed a hieroglyphic language and recorded their mythology, history and rituals. A few of their codices which they used as divinatory almanacs for astronomy, astrology, agriculture and the weather, survived the Spanish conquest. They worshiped many nature Gods and according to their predictions the world will end as we know it in the year 2012. Shown here is one of their codices. Also see Twenty-Twelve.

Maya

From the Sanskrit meaning "illusion" or "wizardry", maya is the term used in Hindu philosophy to define cosmic illusion, referring to mistaking the appearances of things for their intrinsic spiritual nature or on a personal level, of mistaking the real nature of self for something physical and not spiritual. Maya is also described as the cosmic force which produces the phenomena of material existence and allows it to be perceived.

Maya Devi

According to the Buddhists, Maya Devi is the mother of Buddha. The legend says that due to her pure life and spiritual righteousness, she was chosen to be the mother of the coming Buddha. She was sent a dream to deliver the good news in which the new Buddha appeared to her in the form of a white elephant and entered into the right side of her body. She is also called Maya.

Maya Gods and Goddesses

The following Maya Gods and Goddesses are described herein: Acat, Ah Peku, Ah Puch, Bacab, Camazotz, Chac, Chac Xib Chac, Cit Chac Coh, Ek Ahau, Ek Chuah, Ek Xib Chac, Gucumatz, Hacavitz, Hun Pic Tok, Hunab Ku, Hurakan, Itzamna, Ixchel, Ixchup, Kan Xib Chac, Kinich-Ahau, Kisin, Kukulcan, Mayahuel, Nohochayum, Sac Xib Chac, Votan and Xaman Ec and Yum Kaax. Shown here is an ancient Maya vase depicting Gods smoking hallucinogens. Image from mushroomstone.com, photograph by Justin Kerr.

Mayahuel

Maya Goddess of Cacti, Mayahuel rules over the powerful fermented drink called Pulque or Octli made from the Maguey cactus. Mayahuel is depicted here in a 16th Century codex called the Codex Rios. Also see Maya Gods and Goddesses.

Maya Pyramids

The Maya built two types of pyramids, those for sacrificial rituals and sacred pyramids not meant to be touched or climbed. These were built with steps that are too steep to climb. Some of the ritual pyramids had burial chambers for high ranking officials. Photograph by Nicopaz. Also see Aztec Pyramids, Egyptian Pyramids, Toltec Pyramids, and Sacred Sites.

McCannon, Tricia

American-born Tricia McCannon is an internationally renowned clairvoyant, psychic, healer, spiritual teacher, researcher, author and mystic. She is the executive producer of the White Dove World Peace Project and she has spoken all over the United States. She is also the founder of The Phoenix Fire Mystery School, a Priestess in the Fellowship of Isis, a healer of the Seven Ray Healing School and bishop in the Madonna Ministries. Ms. McCannon leads annual spiritual tours to Peru, Egypt, Greece and England and she frequently appears as a guest on radio and television shows including: Sightings, Strange Universe and Unsolved Mysteries. She has written: Dialogues With the Angels; Beings of Light, Worlds in Transition and her latest book Jesus: The Explosive Story of the 30 Lost Years and the Ancient Mystery Religions. Also see Clairvoyants, Healers, Mind-Body Energy Medicine, Mystics, Recommended Reading, Spiritual Teachers, newagespiritualtour.com, trishamccannonspeaks.com, and triciamccannongateway.com.

McCartney, Francesca

American-born Francesca McCartney Ph.D. is a psychic diagnostician (medical intuitive), pastoral counselor, teacher and author. She was the meditation instructor and health intuitive for seven years at the Academy of Eastern Medicine in Walnut Creek, California. Dr. McCartney was a founding member of the USA branch of the Kundalini Research Network while she was a staff writer for the Psychic Life Magazine. She founded the Academy of Intuition Medicine in Mill Valley, California in 1984. She is also a licensed nondenominational Minister and received her Ph.D.'s in Energy Medicine and Intuition Medicine from Greenwich University. Dr. McCartney also studied Eastern mysticism and Western traditions of Theosophy. She has written Intuition Medicine: The Science of Energy, and Body of Health: The Science of Intuition Medicine for Energy and Balance. Photograph from facebook.com. Also see Kundalini Research Network, Meditation, Mind-Body Energy Medicine, Psychic Diagnosticians, Recommended Reading, intuitionmedicine.com, and kundalininet.org.

McGraw, Phillip

(1950-) American-born Phillip "Phil" Calvin McGraw aka Dr. Phil is an award winning psychologist, life strategist, bestselling author and television personality who hosts the popular TV show Dr. Phil. He has an M.A. in experimental psychology and a Ph.D. in clinical psychology from the University of North Texas. His books include: Family First: Your Step-By-Step Plan for Creating a Phenomenal Family; Life Strategies: Doing What Works, Doing What Matters; Fix the One You Got; Self Matters: Creating Your Life From the Inside Out and Real Life: Preparing for the 7 Most Challenging Days of Your Life. Also see Recommended Reading, drphill.com and drphilfoundation.org.

McKenna, Terence

(1946-2000) American-born Terence Kemp McKenna was an ethnobiologist, author and philosopher known for his theories on the use of psychedelic hallucinogens. He studied at the University of California Berkeley and participated in the Tussman Experimental College. He graduated with a B.A. in ecology and conservation. One of his most famous theories was the "Stoned Ape" theory of human evolution. Among McKenna's books are: Food of the Gods: A Radical History of Plants, Drugs, and Human Evolution; The Invisible Landscape: Mind, Hallucinogens, and the I Ching; True Hallucinations: Being an Account of the Author's Extraordinary Adventures in the Devil's Paradise; and Chaos, Creativity, and Cosmic Consciousness. Shown here is a 20th Century painting of Mr. McKenna by American artist Robert Venosa (venosa.com). Also see Hallucinogens, Philosophers and Recommended Reading.

McKibben, William

(1960-) American-born William "Bill" McKibben is an environmentalist, activist educator and author who writes about global warming, alternative energy and genetic engineering. He led one of the largest demonstrations against global warming in American history in 2006. McKibben has received honorary degrees from Green Mountain College, Lebanon Valley College and Unity College. Among his books are: The Comforting Whirlwind: God; Job, and the Scale of Creation; Long Distance: Testing the Limits of Body and Spirit in a Year of Living Strenuously; Deep Economy: The Wealth of Communities and the Durable Future; Maybe One: A Personal and Environmental Argument for Single Child Families; and Enough: Staying Human in an Engineered Age. Photograph from tarsandaction.org. Also see Recommended Reading, billmckibbens.com and 350.org.

McTaggart, Lynne

(1951-) American-born Lynne McTaggart is journalist and author of award-winning books. She is also the founder of the Living in the Field Community where she holds workshops and conferences and with her husband/publisher and is director of the company called "What Doctors Don't Tell You Ltd." Ms. McTaggart has written over 30 books including: The Field: The Quest for the Secret Force of the Universe; What Doctors Don't Tell You; The Truth About the Dangers of Modern Medicine; Guide to the Side Effects of Drugs: A Quick Reference to the Most Common Categories of Drugs; The Cancer Handbook: What's Really Working; The Intention Experiment: Using Your Thoughts to Change Your Life and the World; and The Bond: Connecting Through The Space Between Us. Also see Journalists, Recommended Reading, Self-Help, livingthefield.com and theintentionexperiment.com.

Mead, George Robert

(1863-1933) English-born George Robert Stow Mead aka G.R.S. Mead, was a Theosophist, Gnostic scholar, and writer. He earned his M.A. at St. John's College in Cambridge, MA. Mead was member of the Theosophical Society and private secretary to Helena Blavatsky the last three years of her life where he helped edit The Secret Doctrine. He resigned from the Theosophical Society in 1908 and founded the Quest Society. His books include: Pistis Sophia: A Gnostic Gospel; Fragments of a Faith Forgotten: The Gnostics, A Contribution to the Study of the Origins of Christianity; Doctrine of the Subtle Body in Western Tradition: An Outline of What the Philosophers Thought and Christians Taught on the Subject; and Thrice Greatest Hermes: Studies in Hellenistic Theosophy and Gnosis. Shown here is a 1926 photograph of Mead published in The Quest – Old and New. Also see Gnostics, Recommended Reading and Theosophists.

Mebahiah

According to the Qabbalah, Mebahiah is an Angel who rules over morals and religion and helps those who desire offspring. Also see Angels.

Mecca

Mecca is the most Holy City of Islam, revered even before the revelations of the prophet Muhammad. It is located about 80 Kilometers from the Red Sea in Saudi Arabia. Mecca is where the sacred stone of the Islamic faith called the Ka'aba is found. Photograph taken by Mimin. Also see Islam, Ka-aba, Sacred Sites, sacred-destinations.com and sacredsites.com.

Medical Intuitive
Another term for Psychic Diagnostician. See Psychic Diagnostician.

Medicina Metallorum
See Philosopher's Stone.

Medicine Man
See Shamanism.

Medicine Wheel
To native American Indians a medicine wheel (also called a sacred hoop) is a sacred ceremonial site and or image constructed by laying stones on the ground in a specific pattern. Most follow a basic pattern, having a center of one or more stones, and outer circle and lines with lines radiating from the center to the outer ring. Medicine wheels are constructed for healing, ritual and spiritual purposes. Image from wolf-creekarts.com. Also see medicinewheel.com.

Meditation
Meditation is the mental effort of calming and quieting the mind and relaxing the body to hear the inner voice or higher self. Continued or extended contemplation or spiritual introspection to achieve altered states of consciousness or community with the divine. Edgar Cayce defined meditation as "man listening for God's voice" versus prayer which he said was "man talking to God". There are two main techniques for meditation, heightened concentration where the individual gives their undivided attention to a single thought or idea in a trance like state where the external awareness dims, and the second technique, used mostly in Buddhism, involves a passive examination of all ideas and thoughts taking care to not cling to any idea or thought but to passively letting that idea or thought pass. Shown here is a 20th Century painting by American artist Bruce Harman (harmanvisions.com) called Jesus Meditating.

Meditation
The people described herein who practice and or teach meditation include: Mirra Alfassa, Rudolph Ballentine, Edgar Cayce, Roy Eugene Davis, Anthony de Mello, Shakti Gawain, Joel Goldsmith, Jack Kornfield, Aldous Huxley, Rick Jarow, Jon Kabat-Zinn, Maharishi Mahesh Yogi, Lahiri Mahasaya, Caitlin Matthews, Francesca McCartney, Claudio Naranjo, Osho, Swami Rama, Marjorie L. Rand, Donald Rothberg, Peter Russell, Sharon Salzberg, Susan Shumsky, Swami Sivananda Saraswati, Tara Sutphen, Tulku Thondup, Valentin Tomberg, Irina Tweedie, B. Alan Wallace, Stephen H. Wolinsky and Paramahansa Yogananda. Also see Spiritual Techniques, Transcendental Meditation, americanmeditation.org, how-to-meditate.org, learningmeditation.com, power-of-imagination.com and tm.org.

Medium

According to Occultism a medium is person who has the ability to enter a state of trance and suspend rational consciousness or who is sensitive to vibrations from the spirit plane and may become the conscious or unconscious channel for manifestations of discarnate entities and receive and convey messages from other planes of existence. Mediums are also called Trance Channelers. Also see Channelers, Mediums, Psychics and Psychic Diagnosticians.

Mediums

The people described herein who are said to be mediums include: Rosemary Altea, Ulrica Arfvidsson, Alice A. Bailey, Rita Straus Berkowitz, Sylvia Browne, Florence Cook, Grace Cooke, Margery Crandon, Hester Dowden, Allison DuBois, Helen Duncan, John Edward, William Eglinton, Virginia Essene, Arthur Ford, Agnes Guppy-Volkman, Alexander Harris, Bertha Harris, Daniel Dunglas Home, Gladys Osborne Leonard, Char Margolis, William Stainton Moses, Leonore Piper, Cora Richmond, Jane Roberts, Schneider Brothers, Betty Shine, Gordon Smith, Doris Stokes, Katherine Tingley, James Van Praagh, Neale Donald Walsch, Lisa Williams, Victoria Woodhull and Francisco Candido Xavier. Also see Medium.

Medusa

In Greek mythology, Medusa is the mortal one in the trio of Gorgons. She is originally a beautiful maiden who gives birth to Pegasus and Chrysaor. She had her hair changed into hissing serpents by Minerva and from then on anyone who looks into her eyes was transformed into stone. She is slain by Perseus. Shown here is a 1598 depiction of Medusa by Italian artist Caravaggio (caravaggiogallery.com). Also see Greek Gods and Goddesses, and Gorgons.

Megaera

In Greek mythology, Megaera is the Goddess of Death, Rebirth and Envious Fury, one of the trios of virgin Goddesses known as the Furies. Megaera is shown here in a 1963 painting by Spanish surrealist painter Salvador Dali (dali-gallery.com) called The Furies. See Furies, and Greek Gods and Goddesses.

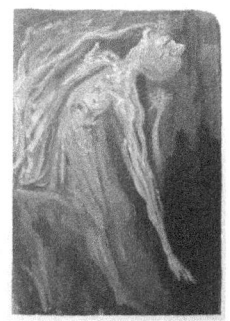

Megalith

From the Greek words mega meaning "great" and lithos "stone", megaliths are giant man-made formations of stones that were erected as sepulchral monuments or as memorials of notable events and are found in various locations around the world. Stonehenge in England has one of the most famous megalithic formations and Carnac in France is the oldest site where megaliths have been found. They are also found around Europe, Africa, the Middle East, and Japan and even on Easter Island. They are reputed to be centers with high concentrations of electromagnetic power that are said to possess magical and healing powers. Megaliths are also said to absorb the energy of the group mind around them. Shown here is the Ballykeel Dolmen near Mullaghbane in South Armagh, Ireland. Also see Dolmen and Group Mind.

Mehen

In Egyptian mythology, Mehen is the divine snake who protects Ra as he journeys through the night on his boat through the Underworld. Shown here is a painting from 1290 B.C.E. from the tomb of Ramses I in the Valley of the Kings in Egypt. Also see Mythological Creatures.

Mehet-Weret

Egyptian Mother Goddess associated with streaming water and the night, Mehet-Weret rules over creation and rebirth and is also known as the Great Tide. She is often depicted as a cow or a woman with the head of a cow. She is also called The Mistress of the Earth. Other spellings include Mehurt, Mehetweret, Mehueret, Mehit-Weret, Meh-Urg, and Mehitweret. Mehet-Weret is shown here from the sarcophagus of Khonsu from around 1180 B.C.E. Also see Egyptian Gods and Goddesses.

Mehiel

In the Qabbalah, Mehiel is an Angel who protects university professors, authors and orators. Also see Angels.

Mehl-Madrona, Lewis

(1954-) American-born (of Cherokee and Lakota heritage) Lewis Mehl-Madrona M.D., Ph.D. is both a traditional and alternative healer. He graduated from Stanford Medical School (at age 21) and began his life as a healer. Dr. Mehl-Madrona is also the author of: Coyote Medicine; Lessons from Native American Healing; Coyote Wisdom: The Power of Story in Healing; Narrative Medicine: The Use of History and Story in the Healing Process; Coyote Healing: Miracles in Native Medicine; and The Healing Power of Story: The Promise of Narrative Psychiatry. Also see Healers, Recommended Reading, healing-arts.org and mehl-madrona.com.

Melekim

Hebrew for "the Kings", Melekim is the group of Angels associated with Tipareth. Also see Angels.

Melpomene
In Greek Mythology, Melpomene, whose name means "songstress", is the Muse of Tragedy. She is one of nine sister Goddesses called the muses. Melpomene is depicted here in an 1891 painting by French artist Gustave Moreau (gustave-moreau.com). Also see Greek Gods and Goddesses, and Muses.

Melusine
In European mythology Melusine is a female elemental or nature spirit found in fresh water rivers and sacred springs. She is different from a mermaid, sometimes she is shown with wings and almost always wearing a crown. Dragons are said to cry when a Melusine dies. Other spellings include Melusina. Shown here in an 1844 painting by German artist Julius Hubner (juliushuebner.de) called Fair Melusine. Also see Cryptids, and Elementals.

Menehune
In Hawaiian mythology, the Menehune are the little people, or Nature Spirits who roam the forests at night and are said to be very mischievous towards humans. They are described as very skilled engineers and architects capable of incredible feats of building during the night building temples, fishponds and roads. The Menehune are also called Nawao. The Menehune are said to be descendants of the Lua-nu'u or Mu People (Lemuria). They are depicted here in a 20th Century rendition by American artist Dietrich Varez (dvarez.com). Also see Lemuria and Nature Spirits.

Menorah
Jewish candelabrum with seven branches used for Hanukkah, the Menorah is one of the oldest symbols of the Jewish faith. According to tradition, during the re-dedication of the Temple the lamps of the Menorah burned for seven days using oil that should have only lasted a day. Also see Hanukkah.

Mental Plane
See Planes of Existence.

Mephistopheles
From the Hebrew mepiz meaning "destroyer" and tophel meaning "liar", Mephistopheles means "He Who Loves not the Light". In Jewish and Christian traditions, although he is not mentioned in The Bible, he is described as one of the fallen Angels, Demon and a familiar spirit of the Devil. Mephistopheles

is also used as an alternative name for the devil. Other spellings include Mephistophiel, Mephistophilus, Mephist and Mephisto. Shown here is the 19th Century work of Russian sculptor Mark Matveevich Antokolsky. Also see Demons.

Mercury

In Occultism, as the celestial body affecting aspects of human life, Venus rules over intellect, spirit, entertainment, skill, writing, manuscripts, language, typewriters, etc.; mental processes and perceptions, communication, mail, newspapers and magazines, telephones, rumors, reports, reporters; acquisition of knowledge, books, documents; brothers, sisters, relatives, direct environment, visits; youth in general; news and messages, professors; gossip; tenants; illnesses. See Planets.

Mercury

Roman Messenger God, Mercury is the God who rules over commerce, magic, science, eloquence, merchandise and merchants, athletes, transportation and travel. He is the son of the Jupiter (or Zeus) and Maia. Other spellings include Mercurius. He is the Greek version of Hermes. Mercury is shown here in an 1855 painting by British artist Evelyn de Morgan (demorgan.org.uk). Also see Roman Gods and Goddesses.

Mercury

In the Qabbalah, Mercury is described as an Angel of Progress. Also see Angels.

Mercy

Mercy is a term to describe compassion shown by one human being to another or a request from one person to another to be shown leniency.

Merfolk

Mermaids and Mermen. Merfolk are depicted here by American artist Lisa Hunt (lisahuntart.com). See Mermaids and Mermen.

Merkaba

From Hebrew meaning "chariot" in the Old Testament the Merkaba is the throne chariot of God. In Wiccan and other traditions Merkaba is an energy or light vehicle used for astral travel or as a conduit for connecting with higher spiritual realms. It is described as star shaped made up of pyramids, a sort of three dimensional Star of David. Other spellings include Mer-Ka-Ba, Mercabah and Merkabah. Also see Astral Bodies and merkaba.org.

Merlin

Legendary Celtic Druid, wise man and magician, Merlin was said to be an expert in shape shifting, herbs, healing, nature, prophecy, counseling, divination, psychic abilities, crystal gazing, magic, spells, incantations and rituals. There are many myths and legends about Merlin, the most famous of which are described in the Arthurian legends where he played the part of counselor and magician to King Arthur. He has also been linked to the Holy Grail legends. Other spellings include Merddin and Myrddin. A young Merlin is depicted here in an 1874 painting by British artist Sir Edward Burne-Jones called The Beguiling of Merlin. Also see Avalon, Holy Grail, arthurian-legend.com and celtic-twilight.com.

Mermaids

In world maritime mythology mermaids are water Elementals described as half woman and half fish that lure sailors to shipwreck while they comb their hair and sing on the rocks at sea in the night. Mermaids are often confused with Sirens. Shown here is a 1905 painting of a Mermaid by British artist John William Waterhouse (jwwaterhouse.com). Also see Elementals, and Sirens.

Mermen

In European folklore mermen are water Elementals described as half man and half fish. Shown here is a 16th Century depiction of a merman by Italian artist Giovanni Andrea Maglioli. Also see Elementals.

Merope

In Greek mythology, Merope is a nymph whose name means "honey-faced". She married a mortal, Sisyphus and became the faintest of the stars. She is one of seven sisters called the Pleiades. Merope is depicted here in an 1884 painting by French artist William-Adolphe Bouguereau called Lost Pleiad. Also see Greek Gods and Goddesses, and Pleiades.

Merovingian Dynasty

The Merovingians were a dynasty of Frankish kings who ruled areas in parts of present-day France and Germany from the 5th to the 8th Century C.E. The descendants of this dynasty were reputed to have powers that included the abilities to heal and to talk telepathically with animals. The Monarchs of this blood line were said to be powerful adepts in Occult Sciences and they were often called Sorcerer Kings. They were also known as the Long Haired Kings or Long Hair Monarchs. The Merovingians are also closely associated with the Prieure de Sion and many are also mentioned in the Dossier Secrets. Also see Dossier Secrets, Prieure de Sion and mergovingiandynasty.com.

Merrows

In Scottish and Irish mythology Merrows are mermaids and mermen. They are described as being affectionate and having gentle dispositions. Shown here is an 1883 painting of Merrows by French artist Charles Edward Boutibonne called The Sirens.

Merry Meet

Wiccan form of greeting.

Merry Part

Wiccan form of parting.

Meskhenet

Egyptian Goddess of Pregnancy, Childbirth and Fate, Meskhenet presides over births and the afterlife. She is personified by the birthing brick. She also reads the destiny of children, guards babies through their infancy and will testify to the character of the newly deceased. Other spellings include Mesenet, Meskhnet, and Meskhent. Image by Jeff Dahl. Also see Egyptian Gods and Goddesses.

Mesmer, Franz

(1734-1815) Austrian-born physician, healer, Freemason and occultist Franz Anton Mesmer proposed that there is an all-pervading magnetic force that links all human beings and which is affected by the gravitational attraction of the planets, he this called Animal Magnetism. He proposed that Animal Magnetism could be activated by any object that was "magnetized" and manipulated by a trained person. Mesmer's therapeutic suggestions lead to the development of hypnotism or at it was called at the time, Mesmerism. Although his ideas and methods were questioned in his time, his Mesmerism has been described as the forerunner of hypnotism although one of his students, the Marquis de Puysegur deserves a lot of that credit too. He published Memoir on the Discovery of Animal Magnetism in 1779. Shown here is an 18th Century portrait of Mesmer by an unknown artist. Also see Animal Magnetism, Freemasons, Healers, Mesmerism, Marquis de Puysegur, Occultists and anton-mesmer.com.

Mesmerism

The healing system proposed by Franz Mesmer, Mesmerism, also called Somnambulism deals with Animal Magnetism and subtle energies which Franz Mesmer said fill the entire universe and forms fields around living bodies. Also see Animal Magnetism, Franz Anton Mesmer, and Therapeutic Systems.

Messiah

From the Hebrew mashiah meaning "anointed" Messiah originally referred to a King or priest in their status as anointed. Currently in Theology and Christianity the concept of the Messiah is equated with Christ, Savior and God. He is described as a guardian Angel of Eden who is armed with a flaming sword and as the Angel of the Great Council. From the Greek translation of the term as Christos, Christianity bestowed the title of Messiah to Jesus of Nazareth. As a broader description, Messiah denotes any redeemer figure. The Messiah is also called the Anointed One. Shown here is a 1655 painting of Jesus Christ by Italian artist Caravaggio (caravaggiogallery.com) called The Head of Christ. Other spellings include Messias. Also see Prophet.

Metagnomy

Divination by visions. Also see Divination.

Metamorphosis

See Shape Shifting.

Metaphysics

From the Greek meta meaning "beyond" and physica meaning "physical", metaphysics is the branch of philosophy that studies questions and concepts that cannot be answered by scientific experiments; such as the fundamental concepts of the nature of reality, existence, substance, space, time, cause, mysticism, religion, soul, etc. Metaphysics is basically divided into three main branches: Ontology, Theology, and Universal Science. Also see metaphysics.com.

Metatron

In Occult literature and Jewish mystical traditions, Metatron is considered the greatest of all the Heavenly hierarchs. He is described as a celestial scribe who records the sins and merits of souls and as the Guardian of Heavenly Secrets. He has been called the King of Angels, the Chancellor of Heaven, Angel of the Covenant, the Prince of Presence and the Chief of the Ministering Angels. Other spellings include Merraton, Metaraon, Metratton and Mittron. Also see Angels.

Metempsychosis

Metempsychosis is defined as the progress or the transmigration of the soul from one level of existence to another. Also see Reincarnation, and Spiritual Evolution. Shown here is a painting by British artist Josephine Wall (josephinewall.com) called Nautilus.

Methetherial
Termed coined by Frederick Meyers meaning "beyond ether" describing the world of spirits.

Methods of Prediction
Of the many, many different methods used to predict future events; this book briefly describes the following: Augury, Clairvoyance, Divination, Intuition, Omen, Oracle, Portent, Precognition, Premonition and Prophesy.

Metis
Greek Goddess of Prudence and Council, Metis is the daughter of Oceanus and Tethys and first wife of Zeus who swallowed her and her unborn child. Shown here is a 1638 painting of Metis by French artist Nicolas Poussin (nicolaspoussin.org) called The Infant Jupiter Nurtured by the Goat Amalthea. Also see Greek Gods and Goddesses.

Metzner, Ralph

(1936-) German-born Ralph Metzner Ph.D. is an American psychologist, researcher and author. He holds a B.A. in philosophy and psychology from Oxford University and a Ph.D. in clinical psychology at Harvard University. He was part of the Harvard Psilocybin Projects (psychedelic hallucinogen research) with Drs. Timothy Leary and Richard Alpert in the 1960's. Dr. Metzner is a psychotherapist and Professor Emeritus of psychology at the California Institute of Integral Studies in San Francisco, and co-founder and former president of the Green Earth Foundation. He conducts workshops on the transformation of consciousness and alchemical divination. Among his books are: Sacred Mushroom of Visions: Teonanacatl; Sacred Vines of Spirits: Ayahuasca; Maps of Consciousness: I Ching, Tantra, Tarot, Alchemy, Astrology, Actualism; Green Psychology – Transforming out Relationship to the Earth; and Birth of a Psychedelic Culture: Conversations about Leary, the Harvard Experiments, Millbrook and the Sixties. Photograph from ciis.edu. Also see Ayahuasca, Hallucinogens, Green Earth Foundation, Recommended Reading, greenearthfound.org and metzneralchemicaldivination.org.

Metztli
In Aztec mythology, Metztli is a Moon Goddess. Shown here is a 16 Century depiction of Metztli from the Codex Rios. Also see Aztec Gods and Goddesses.

Michabo
Algonquin Creator God, Michabo is a shape shifter, trickster and magician. He lives in the house of dawn where he feeds the souls of good men. He is also called Great Hare. Also see Algonquin Gods and Goddesses.

Michael

One of the four main Archangels, Michael is known as the Prince of Splendor and Wisdom. His planet is Mercury, he rules the element of fire and his color is red. Michael is the Angel of truthfulness, knowledge, divination and philosophy. Shown here is a 1636 painting by Italian artist Guido Reni called The Archangel Michael. Also see Angels, and Archangel.

Michael

Michael is Hebrew meaning "The Perfect of God". See Archangel, and Michael.

Michael

Spirit guide allegedly channeled through Alex Sanders. Also see Channeled Spirit Guides, Channelers, and Alex Sanders.

Mictlan

In Aztec Mythology, Mictlan is the lowest of the nine Underworlds, the land of the dead; ruled by Mictlantecihuatl, God of the Underworld and his wife Mictlancihuatl, Goddess of Death. This Underworld is described as the place where the souls of the dead live in a drab existence until it is time to be reborn again. This is the place where the bad souls wait for their next incarnation, the good souls, such as warriors and women who die in childbirth, go to Tlalocan and the enlightened souls go to Tlillan-Tlapllan. Mictlan is also called Mictlancalco. Also see Mythological Places, Tlalocan, Tlillan-Tlapllan and Underworlds.

Mictlantecihuatl

Aztec Goddess of Death and the Underworld, Mictlantecihuatl is the wife of Michlantecuhtli, God of the Underworld. Together they care for the souls of the dead in the Underworld. Shown here is a stone carving depicting Mictlantecihuatl housed in the Museo Nacional de Antropologia in Mexico City, Medico. Also see Aztec Gods and Goddesses and Underworld Gods.

Mictlantecuhtli

Aztec God of the Underworld, Mictlantecuhtli and his wife Mictlantecihuatl care for the souls of the dead in the Underworld. He is also known as the Lord of the Land of the Dead, the Dead Land Lord and the God of the Underworld. Mictlantecuhtli is often depicted with an open mouth, ready to devour the souls of the dead. Shown here is a statue of Mictlantecuhtli housed in the British Museum in England. Other spellings include Mictlanteculi. Also see Aztec Gods and Goddesses, and Underworld Gods.

Midgard

In Norse mythology, Midgard, meaning "middle earth or physical plane is the home of humankind is one the nine worlds make up the universe and are guarded by Odhin. Midgard is surrounded by the Ocean, the abode of the world serpent Jormungand. Other spellings include Mithgard. Also see Mythological Places, and Nine Worlds.

Midgard Serpent

In Norse mythology, the Midgard Serpent or Jormungand is a giant snake which lives in the ocean surrounding Midgard. Shown here is a 1790 painting by British artist Henry Fuseli called Thor Battering the Midgard Serpent. Also see Jormungand, Mythological Creatures, and Nine Worlds.

Milam Bardo

In Tibetan Yoga and Buddhist traditions Milam Bardo is the plane of the dream state. See Bardo.

Millay, Jean

American-born Jean Millay Ph.D. is an artist, biofeedback researcher, artist and author, who taught parapsychology for 8 years and served as president of the Parapsychology Research Group. She received her B.A. from the University of California in Berkeley and her Ph.D. in human science from the Saybrook Institute. She teaches college classes in parapsychology and biofeedback. Dr. Millay is a co-inventor of the stereo brain wave biofeedback light sculpture, device that compares brain waves and shows the information in patterns of light and sound. Her movie The Psychedelic Experience won a film festival prize in 1965. She is the author of Multidimensional Mind: Remote Viewing in Hyperspace; and Radiant Minds: Scientists Explore The Dimensions of Consciousness. Also see Parapsychologists and Psychic Researchers, Recommended Reading and Remote Viewing.

Miller, Zachary James

American-born Zachary James Miller Ph.D. is a therapist, parapsychologist, researcher, magus, shaman, counselor and independent filmmaker. He is considered one of the international authorities on consciousness and its relation to ancient sacred teachings. Dr. Miller was also the founder and director of The Enigma Group. He is also a former member of the Ordo Templi Orientis and longtime student of the occult, alternative medicine, parapsychology, quantum physics, parallel lives, astral projection, remove viewing, tantric yoga, comparative religions, consciousness expansion and more. Dr. Miller has released a DVD called Intention, Belief, Emotion and Will: Consciousness and The Scientific Basis for Magick. Photograph from theenigmagroup.com. Also see Astral Projection, Consciousness Researchers, Ordo Templi Orientalis, Parapsychologists and Psychic Researchers,

Quantum Physics and Quantum Mechanics, Remote Viewing, Shamans, theenigmagroup.com and zacharyjamesmiller.com.

Millman, Dan

(1946-) American-born Dan Millman is a former world champion athlete, Stanford Gymnastics coach, martial arts instructor and Oberlin college professor and current spiritual and motivational speaker and author. He has written more than a dozen books that have been translated into 30 languages including: Way of the Peaceful Warrior: A Book That Changes Lives, Sacred Journey of the Peaceful Warrior; The Life You Were Born to Live: A Guide to Finding Your Life Purpose; The Laws of Spirit, Powerful Truths for Making Life Work; Divine Interventions: True Stories of Mysteries and Miracles That Change Lives; The Journeys of Socrates; Bridge Between Worlds: Extraordinary Experiences That Change Lives; and Peaceful Warrior: The Graphic Novel. Also see Recommended Reading, thepeacefulwarriormovie.com and danmillman.com.

Mimamsa

From Sanskrit mimasa meaning "reflection" is one of the six darshans of the Hindu philosophy. Mimamsa derives from the earlier parts of the Vedas and its purpose is to give rules for the interpretation of the same and also to explain the philosophical reasons for the observance of the Vedic rituals. As with all other Darshans, the goal of Mimasa is that of spiritual enlightenment. Also see Darshan, and Spiritual Goals.

Mimir

Norse God of Wisdom and Knowledge, the Wisest of the Gods, Mimir is the uncle of Odhin. He rules over pools, lakes, springs, peace, the arts and teaching. Mimir is the Keeper of the Magic Cauldron and Guardian of the Spring of Wisdom (called Mimisbrunnr). He has also been described as a water spirit. Other spellings include Mimi and Mimr. Shown here is a 1903 depiction by German artist Robert Engels called Odin Drinks from Mímisbrunnr While Mímir Watches. Also see Norse Gods and Goddesses.

Min

Ancient Egyptian God of Fertility, Min rules over male sexual potency. He is especially worshiped by miners and travelers. He is Chief of Heaven, Lord of the Foreign Lands, Lord of the Eastern Desert, Protector of the Moon and the Noble One. Min bestows sexual powers and orgiastic festivals are held in his honor and offerings are made to him at harvest and before journeys. Other spellings include Amsu, Menew, Menu and Minu. Min is shown here from a relief on the Karnak Temple near Luxor in Egypt. Also see Egyptian Gods and Goddesses, and Gods of Heaven.

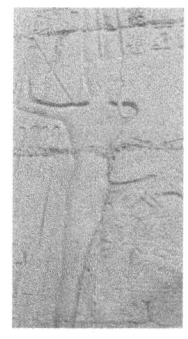

Mind

In occult philosophy, the mind is an immortal part of the personality and soul, not part of the brain but rather which uses the brain for some of its functions.

Mind-Body Energy Medicine

Mind-Body Energy Medicine is a New Age concept, as with Holistic Healing that we are more than just our bodies when dealing with disease and illnesses. The people described herein who deal with Mind-Body Energy Medicine include: Jeanne Achterberg, Ted Andrews, Elizabeth Barrett, Fadel Behman, Daniel Benor, Harvey Bigelsen, Deepak Chopra, Kenneth "Bear Hawk" Cohen, Donna Eden, Marcia Emery, David Feinstein, Richard Gerber, Sylvia Haskvitz, William James, Jon Kabat-Zinn, Shelley Kaehr, Deborah King, Leonard Laskow, Elizabeth Lipski, Tricia McCannon, Francesca McCartney, Daniel Monti, Nancy Mramor, James L. Oschman, Christine Page, Paul Pearsall, Kenneth Pelletier, Joseph Pizzorno, Martin L. Rossman, Beverly Rubik, Peter Russell, Halé Sofia Schatz, Norman Shealy, John Upledger, Mikao Usui and Andrew Weil. Also see Alternative Healing, Holistic Healing and Therapeutic Systems.

Mind Altering Drugs

See Hallucinogens.

Mind Reading

See Telepathy.

Mind's Eye

See Third Eye.

Mindell, Arnold

(1940-) American-born Arnold "Arny" Mindell Ph.D. is a renowned physicist, psychotherapist, Jungian analyst, theorist and author. He received his M.A. in physics from MIT and his Ph.D. in psychology from the Union Institute. He founded the Center for Process Oriented Psychology in Zurich, Switzerland and Portland, Oregon. Dr. Mindell has written 19 books (which have been translated into 20 languages). His books include: The Quantum Mind and Healing: How to Listen and Respond to Your Body's Symptoms; Coma: Key to Awakening; Quantum Mind: The Edge Between Physics and Psychology; Your Body Speaks Its Dream; Earth Based Psychology: Path Awareness from the Teachings of Don Juan, Richard Feynman and Lao Tse and Process Mind: A User's Guide To  Connecting With The Mind of God. Photograph from mysacredjourney.wordpress.com. Also see Jungian Analysts, Physicists, Quantum Physics and Quantum Mechanics, Recommended Reading and aamindell.net.

Mindfulness
Mindfulness is described in Gnosticism as a state of being fully present, of continuous consciousness without judgment of oneself or others.

Minerva
Roman Virgin Warrior Goddess, Minerva is the Goddess of Women's Rights and Freedom, she rules over protection, intelligence, creativity, writing, music, handicrafts, wisdom, prudence, wise council, peace, horses, oxen, snakes, trees, medicine, schools and war. She is the daughter of Jupiter and legend has it that she sprang from the head of Jupiter, fully grown and in full armor. Minerva is also known as the Maiden Goddess and the Patron of Warriors. The Greek version of Minerva is Athene. Shown here is a 1488 painting by Italian artist Sandro Botticelli (sandrobotticelli.net) called Minerva and the Centaur. Also see Roman Gods and Goddesses.

Ministers
In Christianity, Ministers are clergymen and spiritual teachers of the Christian Church. Also see Clergymen, Christianity, Religious Teachers and Reverends and Ministers.

Minotaur
In Greek mythology, the Minotaur is a monster with a bull's head and a man's body, offspring of Queen Pasiphae of Crete and a bull. Minos, the King of Crete and husband to Pasiphae confined the Minotaur to the labyrinth of Cnossus and every nine years seven maidens and seven young men were sent as sacrifices to be devoured by the Minotaur. Shown here is an 1826 statue by French sculptor Etienne-Jules Ramey called Theseus Fighting the Minotaur. Also see Mythological Creatures.

Miracle
An event such as an exception to the laws of nature or a physical healing that contradicts or is unexplainable by modern science and the natural laws as we currently understand them. A miracle is also described as astonishing event that is attributed to the action of a Divine power.

Mishlove, Jeffrey
(194?-) American-born Jeffrey "Jeff" Mishlove Ph.D. is the president of the Intuition Network and well known author. Dr. Mishlove holds a B.A. in psychology from the University of Wisconsin, an M.A. in criminology and Ph.D. in parapsychology, both from the University of California, Berkeley. He was the host and producer of the weekly, national, public television series Thinking Allowed from 1986 until 2002. Dr. Mishlove is currently dean of programs for the University of Philosophical Research. Among his books are: The Roots of Consciousness: Psychic Exploration Through History, Science

and Experience; The PK Man: A True Story of Mind Over Matter; PSI Development Systems; The Spiritual Universe; and Thinking Allowed: Conversations on the Leading Edge of Knowledge. Photograph from 123people.com. Also see Parapsychologists and Psychic Researchers, Recommended Reading.thinkingallowed.com, jeff.gaia.com, intuition.org and mishlove.com.

Mishnah

The Mishnah is a collection of Jewish traditions, part of the Talmud. See Talmud.

Missal

In the Catholic Church the missal is a liturgical book containing the instructions for the celebration of Masses throughout the year. Missals were originally written only in Latin. Shown here is a 1902 painting by British artist John William Waterhouse (jwwaterhouse.com) called The Missal. Also see Sacred Writings.

Mitchell, Edgar

(1930-) American-born Edgar "Ed" Dean Mitchell, Sc.D. is a scientist, astronaut, Freemason and founder of the Institute of Noetic Sciences. He was the 6th man to walk on the Moon on the Apollo 14 mission in 1971. He earned two Bachelor of Science degrees from the U.S. Naval Postgraduate School and Carnegie Mellon University, his Doctor of Science degree in Astronautics and Aeronautics at MIT and he has been awarded honorary doctorates from four other Universities. Returning to Earth Dr. Mitchell had a spiritual experience in which he felt that we all participate in a universe of consciousness which lead him to found the Institute of Noetic Sciences in 1973. He currently serves on the Institute's board of directors as well as being advisory board chairman of the Institute for Cooperation in Space which he co- founded. Also see Consciousness Researchers, Freemasons, Institute of Noetic Sciences and Scientists, edmitchell-apollo14.com, noetic.org and quantrek.com. Photograph from asia.edu.tw.

Mithra

In Persian mythology, Mithra is the God of Life and Fertility. He is the advisor of Ahura Mazda and messenger between the Gods and men. Shown here is a statue of Mithra housed in the Vatican from an unknown artist. Other spellings include Mithras. Also see Persian Gods and Goddesses.

Mixcoatl

Aztec God of Thunder and the Hunt, Mixcoatl is one of the Gods who created the world. He is also called the Lord of the Chase. He is depicted as having black eyes, his nose pierced with a berry pit and his body covered in vertical white stripes. Other spellings include

Yoamaxtli and Yemaxtli. Shown here is a depiction of Mixcoatl from the 16th Century Codex Terleliano-Resemnis. Also see Aztec Gods and Goddesses.

MMS
See Motivation Management Service Institute.

Mnemosyne
Greek Goddess of Memory who guards the Waters of Remembering and Forgetting, Mnemosyne is a Titan who together with Zeus parented the nine Muses. Shown here in an 1881 painting by British artist Dante Gabriel Rossetti (rossettiarchive.org) called Mnemosyne (or The Lamp of Memory). Also see Greek Gods and Goddesses, and Titans.

Moai
Huge stone carved monoliths, in different sizes and shapes, carved out of rock by ancestors of the people of Rapa Nui (also known as Easter Island). There are hundreds of Moai around the Island. As with many other religious structures found of the Island, one of the sanctuaries, Ahu Akivi, with seven Moai (the only ones that face the ocean rather than inland, they measure 16 feet tall and weigh around 18 tons each) are situated such that the Sun sets between them during the equinox. Photograph from wondermondo.com. Also see Rapa Nui.

Mohenjo Daro
The ruins of Mohenjo Daro in the Indus Valley of Pakistan are one of the twelve areas known as the Vile Vortices which are described as areas around the world said to have the same qualities as the famous Bermuda Triangle. In these areas strange phenomena are reported such as compasses and other instruments going crazy and ships and planes disappearing. Photograph by Frederick M. Asher. See Vile Vortices.

Moirae
See Fates.

Mojo
From the African magical religious tradition of Hoodoo, a mojo, also called a mojo bag, is an amulet consisting of a small sack filled with herbs, coins, roots and other magically empowered objects. Also see Gris-Gris, Hoodoo, and Magical Amulets.

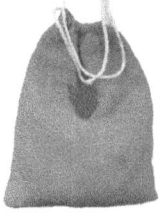

Mojo
In modern terminology, a mojo has come to mean spell or hex.

Mokosh
Slavic Goddess of Fertility, Mokosh presides over water, fertility, rain and animals. Mokosh is depicted here in a 1991 painting by Russian artist Alex Fantalov (fantalov.narod.ru). Also see Slavic Gods and Goddesses.

Moksha
From the Sanskrit moksa, meaning to "release", Moksha is a Buddhist and Hindu term used to describe the ultimate spiritual goal, the state of freedom or enlightenment that frees the soul from the need of reincarnation and liberates it from earthly bondage. Another term for Moksha is Nirvana. Other spellings include Moksa and Mukti. Also see Enlightenment, Illumination and Spiritual Goals.

Monad
From the Greek monas, meaning "alone" or "single", monad is described as an individual substance that reflects the order of the material world. Metaphysics defines monads as basic substances that make up the universe but are immaterial since they lack spatial extension and at the same time are perfectly synchronized with each other by God in a pre- established harmony. In the Qabbalah, Monad is sometimes used to describe Kether. Giordano Bruno called the monad a microscopic embodiment of the Divine, essence which constitutes and pervades the universe.

Monasticism
From the Greek monachos meaning "solitary person" monasticism is the religious practice of renouncing worldly affairs to devote one's life to religious and or spiritual work. Shown here is a 1480 painting by Domenico Ghirlandaio called St. Jerome in his Study housed in the church of Ognissanti in Florence, Italy. Also see Spiritual Techniques.

Monism
In Occultism and Theosophy, monism is the cosmic doctrine which explains cosmic phenomena as being derived of one Godhead or Principle of Being.

Monition
Monition is a form of supernatural warning or revelation of a past or present event. This ranges from superficial events to warnings of danger or even death. Also see Augury, Clairvoyance, Omen, and Precognition.

Monkey

In Chinese astrology, the monkey is one of the 12 animals of the zodiac. People born in the year of the monkey are described as intelligent, enthusiastic and stubborn. Also see Chinese Zodiac.

Monolith

A very large single block of stone, monoliths are usually erected or placed as a shrine or monument. Also see Megalith.

Monroe, Robert

(1915-1995) American-born Robert "Bob" Allan Monroe was a businessman who experienced astral projections. He studied pre-med, arts and sciences, and engineering at Ohio State University. He worked as a writer and director for radio stations in Cleveland and Cincinnati and later moved to New York City where he wrote and produced his first network program. He later began a more spiritual quest and founded The Monroe Institute to research and educate on the exploration of human consciousness with a method he developed called Hemi-Synch (hemispherical synchronization). He also wrote three books: Journeys Out of the Body; Far Journeys; and Ultimate Journey. Also see Astral Projection, Consciousness Researchers, Recommended Reading and monroeinstitute.com.

Montgomery, Ruth

(1913-2001) American-born Ruth Shick Montgomery was a journalist in Washington DC and president of the National Press Club. She was best known however for her channeling of automatic writing. She said that she was able to communicate with several discarnate entities including her friend the late Arthur Ford. She wrote a series of books about these communications, including: A World Beyond: A Startling Message From the Eminent Psychic Arthur Ford From Beyond the Grave; The World to Come: The Guides' Long-Awaited Predictions for the Dawning Age; The World Before; Companions Along the Way; Herald of the New Age; Born to Heal: The Astonishing Story of Mr. A and the Ancient Art of Healing With Life Energies; and Strangers Among Us: Enlightened . Beings From a World. to Come. She also wrote a book about psychic Jeanne Dixon called The Gift of Prophesy. Also see Automatic Writing Channelers, Channeled Spirit Guides, Journalists and Recommended Reading.

Monti, Daniel

American-born Daniel A. Monti M.D. is a well known researcher and expert of mind-body medicine. He received his M.D., summa cum laude from The State University of New York at Buffalo School of Medicine and did his post-doctoral work in the Research Scholars Program, Department of Psychiatry and Human Behavior, at Jefferson Medical College, Philadelphia, PA. He is currently executive and medical director of the Jefferson-Myrna Brind Center of Integrative Medicine at Thomas Jefferson University Hospital. He was awarded the NeuroEmotional Technique Doctor of the Year Award for his research. Dr. Monti is currently writing on energy systems and mental and physical health. He has written: The Great Life Makeover: A Couples Guide to Weight, Mood and Sex for the Best Years of Your Life – and Your Relationship; and Integrative Psychiatry. Also see Mind-Body Energy Medicine and Recommended Reading.

Moody, Raymond

(1944-) American-born Raymond A. Moody M.D., Ph.D. is a well known bestselling author, and world's leading authority on Near Death Experiences. He wrote the international best seller Life After Life. Dr. Moody received his Ph.D. in philosophy from the University of Virginia, where he did all his undergraduate work. He then earned an M.D. from the Medical College of Georgia, with a specialty in psychiatry. Dr. Moody, known as the father of the Near Death Experience, also coined the phrase. He has also researched past life regression using an ancient Greek technique from the Oracles of the Dead. Dr. Moody's best selling books include: Life after Life: The Investigation of a Phenomenon  – Survival of Bodily Death; Reunions: Visionary Encounters With Departed Loved Ones; Coming Back: A Psychiatrist Explores Past-Life Journeys; Reflections on Life after Life; The Light Beyond; The Last Laugh; and Glimpses of Eternity: Sharing a Loved One's Passage From This Life to The Next. Photograph from rozhlas.cz. Also see Near Death Experience, Recommended Reading, Re-incarnation (Life After Life) and lifeafterlife.com.

Moon

The Moon is one of the 22 major arcana of the tarot deck of cards. Its number is XVIII, its Qabbalistic title is Child of the Sons of the Mighty and Ruler of Flux and Reflux and its meaning is: dissatisfaction, error, deception, and voluntary change. Also see Tarot.

Moon

In Occultism, as the celestial body affecting aspects of human life, the Moon represents femininity, maternity, procreation and fertility, psychic abilities, sensibility, change, rhythms, indecision, family, intimacy in the home, mother, maternity, babies and children, care, seeds, feeding, food, stomach, chest and emotions, tides, water, sea, ships and crews, home, all that holds and protects, lost objects and candles. See Planets.

Moore, Marcia

(1929-1979) American-born Marcia Moore was a metaphysical teacher, yogi and noted astrologer who placed much emphasis on reincarnation and even developed a technique called hypersentience to enable people to recall previous incarnations. She became a well-known leader in the astrological world in the 1970's. Ms. Moore later became interested in expanding consciousness and experimented with psychedelic hallucinogens using the mine-altering drugs LSD and ketamine. She wrote and co-authored several books including Diet, Sex and Yoga; Astrology Today – A Socio-Psychological Survey; Astrology in Action; Diet, Sex and Yoga; and Journeys into the Bright World. At the height of her career, in 1979 she disappeared. Two years later a portion of her skull was found in the woods nearby and it is surmised that she went into the forest and froze to death after injecting herself with ketamine. Also see Astrologers, Hallucinogens, Recommended Reading, Reincarnation (Life After Life), and Yogis.

Moore, Mary-Margaret

American-born Mary-Margaret Moore is a person who, while under hypnosis dialoging with the doctor about the existence of God began channeling information from a spirit calling himself Bartholomew. This "dialogue" continued for 18 years. She grew up in Hawaii and received two degrees from Stanford University in California. She has studied the teachings of Ramana Maharishi as well as the I Ching, Zen, Christian Saints and the Sufis. She has co-authored five books with the information channeled from Bartholomew: I Come As a Brother: A Remembrance of Illusions; From the Heart of a Gentle Brother; Planetary Brother; Reflections of an Elder Brother: Awakening From the Dream; and Journeys with a Brother: From Japan to India. Photograph from marymargaretmoore.com. Also see I Ching, Channelers, Channeled Spirit Guides, Recommended Reading, Zen and marymargaretmoore.com.

Moore, Robert

(1942-) American-born Robert L. Moore Ph.D. is a consultant and internationally known Jungian psychoanalyst and author. He is Director of Research for the Institute for Science of Psychoanalysis, a Training Analyst at the C.F. Jung Institute of Chicago and professor of psychology, psychoanalysis and spirituality of the Chicago Theological Seminary. He lectures internationally on psychotherapy and psychoanalysis. Among his books are: King, Warrior, Magician, Lover: Rediscovering the Archetypes of the Mature Masculine; Facing the Dragon: Confronting Personal and Spiritual Grandiosity; The Archetype of Initiation: Sacred Space, Ritual Process and Personal Transformation; The Cult Experience: Responding to the New Religious; and The Magician and the Analyst: The Archetype of the Magus in Occult Spirituality and Jungian Analysis. Also see Jungian Analysts, Recommended Reading, Spiritual Teachers and robertmoore-phd.com.

Moran, Victoria

American-born Victoria Moran, the "Charmed Life Lady", is an international motivational speaker, spiritual-life coach, yogi, radio host, blogger, and bestselling author. She grew up in New Thought, studied Theosophy and yoga from an early age, and earned a degree in comparative religions. Her signature book is Creating a Charmed Life: Sensible, Spiritual Secrets Every Busy Woman Should Know, translated into 27 languages, followed by the sequel, The Charmed Life Handbook. Her other titles include: The Love-Powered Diet: When Willpower is Not Enough: A Revolutionary Approach to Health Eating and Recovery from Food Addition; Shelter for the Spirit: Create Your Own Haven in a Hectic World; Lit from Within: A Simple Guide to the Art of Inner Beauty; Fat, Broke and Lonely No More: Your Personal Solution to Overeating, Overspending and Looking for Love in All the Wrong Places; and Living The Charmed Life: Your Guide to Finding Magic in Every Moment and Meaning in Every Day. Also see New Thought, Recommended Reading, Spiritual Teachers, Yogis, and victoriamoran.com.

Morgawr

The Morgawr is a mythical cryptid that has be sighted and allegedly photographed in the area of Falmouth, Cornwall, England. This Loch Ness type mythological creature was sighted several times and supposedly photographed by David Clarke in 1977 as shown here. Also see Cryptids and Mythological Creatures.

Mormonism

Also known as the Church of Jesus Christ of Latter Day Saints (or LDS), more commonly known as the Mormons. This Christian based religion was founded by its own prophet Joseph Smith in 1830. According to Smith, an Angel named Moroni led him to the discovery and understanding of gold tablets which form of the Book of Mormon first published in 1830. The Mormons originally practiced polygamy, practice which was later officially banned by the church although a few renegades still practice it. This Church is very active in collecting genealogical information and is based out of Salt Lake City, Utah. Image from mormonhaven.com. Also see Moroni, Religions, Joseph Smith, lds.org, mormon.org, mormonhaven.com, scriptures.lds.org and religioustolerance.com.

Morning Star

In Pawnee mythology, the Morning Star is a soldier God who leads the Sun into the sky. Morning Star is sent by Tirawa to guard the East. He is a benevolent God who protects humans. Also see Pawnee Gods and Goddesses, and Tirawa.

Moroni

According to Joseph Smith, founder of the Mormons, Moroni is the Angel who appeared to him on many occasions and who helped him discover and decipher the gold tablets that form the Book of Mormon. Shown here is a statue of Moroni on the Birmingham Alabama Temple, in Gardendale Alabama. Photograph taken by Matthew Brown. Also see Angels, Book of Mormons, Mormons, and John Smith.

Morpheus
Greek God of Dreams, Morpheus is the son of Somnus, God of Sleep. He has the ability to appear to humans in their dreams and to shape their dreams. He sleeps in a cave surrounded by poppy flowers. Shown here is an 1811 painting by French artist Pierre-Narcisse Guerin called Morpheus and Iris. Also see Greek Gods and Goddesses.

Morrigan, The

Celtic Goddess of Witches, The Morrigan rules over magic, war and love, prophesy, lust, revenge, rivers, lakes and the night. She is the wife of the Dagda and is also known as the Great Queen, Queen of Phantoms and Demons, Patroness of Priestess, Moon Goddess, Great Mother, Great White Goddess, Taker of the Slain and Queen of the Fairies. Other spellings include Morgan, Morrigu, and Morrighan. The Morrigan is depicted here by American artist Jessica Galbreth (enchanted-art.com). Also see Celtic Gods and Goddesses.

Morrissey, Dianne

American-born Dianne Morrissey Ph.D. is a hypnotherapist and researcher in the field of Near Death Experiences and related paranormal phenomena. She interest began due to a Near Death Experience when she was electrocuted at age 28 (and declared dead for 45 minutes) where she had a profound experience that transformed her entire life. She is currently the president of the SFS Friends of IANDS (International Association for Near-Death Studies) has lectured in over 23 Colleges and Universities with over 35,000 people have attended her workshops. She says of death "If I lived a billion years more, in my body or yours, there's not a single experience on Earth that could ever be as good as being dead. Nothing." Dr. Morrissey has written: Anyone Can See The Light How You Can Touch Eternity – And Return Safely; and You Can See the Light: How You Can Touch Eternity – And Return Safely. Also see Near Death Experience and Recommended Reading.

Morse, Melvin

American-born Melvin Morse M.D. is a pediatrician and neuroscientist with over 15 years of research on children's Near Death Experiences. He received his medical degree from George Washington University School of Medicine; he interned in Pediatrics at the University of California at San Francisco then completed a residency in Pediatrics at Seattle Children's Hospital. Dr. Morse is also a Clinical Associate Professor of Pediatrics at University of Washington. He has written four books on the subject of Near Death Experiences: Closer To The Light: Learning from Near Death Experiences of Children; Transformed By The Light: The Powerful Effect of Near-Death Experiences on People's

Lives, Parting Visions: Uses and Meanings of Pre-Death, Psychic, and Spiritual Experiences; and Where God Lives: The Science of the Paranormal and How Out Brains are Linked to the Universe. Also see Near Death Experience, Recommended Reading, Scientists, melvinmorse.com and spiritualscientific.com.

Mortuary Magic

Magic rituals performed to assure that a deceased will have a good life in the spirit world. The Egyptians made an elaborate science in their mortuary magic and rituals. Shown here is part of the Papyrus of Ani or the Egyptian Book of the Dead. Also see Coffin Texts, Pyramid Texts, Egyptian Book of the Dead, and Sacred Writings.

Moses, Harry Morgan

American-born Harry Morgan Moses Ph.D., D.D. is a nationally renowned motivational speaker, author and corporate trainer. He received his Ph.D. from the Emerson Institute. In 1976 he was told by a team of doctors that he would never walk again. Today he is an avid skier and sportsman. He founded the New Thought Center in San Diego, California, co-founded the Affiliated New Thought Network and the New Thought Ministries of Oregon. Reverend Dr. Moses currently serves as the senior advisor of the Emerson Institute and spiritual director of SpiritWorks Center for Spiritual Living in Burbank, California. His has written: It's So Easy When You Know How. Also see New Thought, Recommended Reading, Reverends and Ministers, Spiritual Teachers, newthought.com and spiritworkcenter.com.

Moses, William Stainton

(1839-1892) British-born William Stainton Moses D.D. (pen name M. A. Oxon) was a well known minister, religious teacher, Spiritualist and medium. He studied at Bedford School, University College School, London and Exeter College, Oxford. He co-founded the Society for Psychical Research and was a founding member of the London Spiritualist Alliance (later called the College of Psychic Studies). During his life he encountered serious illnesses that interfered with his studies and his ministry. Although showed no signs of psychic abilities when he has young after five months from his introduction to Spiritualism he was supposedly able to levitate tables, constantly produce apports, strange lights, music and scents in abundance. It is also claimed that on a few instances there were also faint materializations. He wrote: Spirit Teachings, Psychography; Spirit Identity; and Higher Aspects of Spiritualism. Also see Apport, Mediums, Reverends and Ministers, Spiritualists and meilach.com.

Moss, Richard

American-born Richard Barry Moss M.D. is an internationally known spiritual teacher, visionary thinker and author of books on transformation and self-healing. He has taught for more than 30 years, presenting conferences in institutions and universities such as Harvard, Stanford, Georgetown and U.C. Berkeley. Dr. Moss currently organizes and coordinates conferences, seminars and talks as well as producing audio and video material. His books include: The I that is We; The Second Miracle; The Black Butterfly; How Shall I Live: Transforming Surgery or Any Health Crisis Into Greater Aliveness; The Black Butterfly: An Invitation to Radical Aliveness; and The Mandala of Being: Discovering the Power of Awareness. Photo from harmonyfarmonline.com. Also see Philosophers, Recommended Reading, Self-Healing, Shamans, Spiritual Teachers and richardmoss.com.

Moss, Robert

(1946-) Australian-born Robert Moss is a historian, philosopher, journalist, dream researcher, shamanistic counselor and best selling novelist. He survived three near death experiences while he was a child and describes himself as having "successfully reincarnated himself several times within one lifetime". Moss is a former lecturer in ancient history at the Australian National University and the creator of Active Dreaming, an original synthesis of modern dreamwork and shamanic techniques for shifting consciousness and soul recovery healing.. His books include: Conscious Dreaming; Dreamgates: Exploring the Worlds of Soul, Imagination and Life Beyond Death; Dreaming True; Dreamways of the Iroquois; The Dreamer's Book of the Dead; The Three "Only" Things: Tapping the Power of Dreams, Coincidence and Imagination; The Secret History of Dreaming; and Active Dreaming. Also see Dream Analysts, Historians, Journalists, Near Death Experience, Recommended Reading, Shamans; mossdreams.com and Moss' beliefnet blog http://blog.beliefnet.com/dreamgates/.

Most Haunted

All over the world there are haunted places where people report sightings, strange sounds and smells. The most haunted places described herein are: Alcatraz, Avebury, Borley Rectory, Enfield Poltergeist, Gettysburg Battlefield, Lincoln Theatre, the Queen Mary, the Tower of London and the Winchester Mansion. Shown here is one of the most famous ghost photographs ever taken, the ghost is said to be Lady Dorothy Townshend who lived in the 1700's in Raynham Hall in Norfolk, England. Shown here is a 1936 photograph taken by Captain Provand. Also see Ghosts, Haunting, Spirit Photography, ghosthuntingsecrets.com, hauntedamericatours.com, prairieghosts.com, and headlesshorseman.co.uk.

Mother

Celtic Mother is one of the aspects of the Triple Goddess along with Maiden and Crone. Mother represents fertility, ripeness, stability, full Moon, energy, power and life. Image from etsy.com. Also see Celtic Gods and Goddesses, Margawse, and Triple Goddess.

Mother Church
See Christian Science.

Mother Earth
See Mother Nature.

Mother Meera
(1960-) Indian-born Kamala Reddy aka Mother Meera is a spiritual leader, believed by her followers to be the incarnation of the Divine Mother Shakti. She is said to have experienced her first Samadhi at the age of six which lasted a day. Her spiritual teachings relate mainly to Bhakti which is devotion to God. Her darshan consists of her own ritual where she will touch someone's head and then look deeply into their eyes; she reportedly permeates them with light and energy to assist them on their spiritual quests. She receives thousands of people from all religions but refuses to give lectures. Other spellings include Mera. She has written: Bringing Down the Light: Journey of a Soul After Death. Also see Recommended Reading, Spiritual Leaders, mmdarshanamerica.com, mothermeerashram.org and mothermeera-india.com.

Mother Nature
Also called Mother Earth, Mother Nature is the metaphorical expression of the Earth as life-giving and nurturing as well as sustainer of life embodied in the form of the Mother. Shown here is a painting called Gaia or Mother Earth by British artist Josephine Wall (josephinewall.com). Also see Gaea, Gaia, World Soul, 4qf.org, algore.com, arlingtoninstitute.org, bluediamondpachamama.com, experiencefestival.com, terrapsych.com, and thevisionandthevoice.com.

Mother Teresa
(1910-1997) Albanian-born Agnes Gonxha Bojaxhiu aka Mother Teresa was a Roman Catholic nun who founded the Missionaries of Charity and won the Nobel Peace Prize in 1979 for her continuous humanitarian work for the sick, orphaned and dying of Calcutta, India. She was beatified as Blessed Teresa of Calcutta by Pope John Paul II in 2003. The Missionaries of Charity is run by over 4,000 nuns in centers all over the world. Mother Teresa also

received the Balzan Prize, the Albert Schweitzer International Prize, the Kennedy Prize the United States Presidential Medal of Freedom and the Congressional Gold Metal. When awarded the Nobel Peace Prize she was asked "What can we do to promote world peace?" she replied "Go home and love your family". Also see Nobel Prize Laureates, Spiritual Leaders, motherteresa.org and nobel-prizes.com.

Motivation Management Service Institute

The Motivation Management Service Institute (or MMS) (in their own words) was founded in 1974 by Chérie Carter-Scott Ph.D. who designed a series of Executive Business Coaching, Business Skills Training and Life Skill Coaching courses offered for personal growth and professional training. MMS LLC is a human development institute whose purpose is to develop, produce, and promote courses in personal development, empowerment, professional training, educational programs, and related product lines. Motivation Management Service Institute LLC is a motivational training and corporate training institute that caters to the training needs of organizations while keeping in mind today's industry challenges. MMS Institute facilitates initiative-driven corporate programs, motivation management services, workshops, seminars, and courses customized to achieve an organization's business objectives, mission statements and goals. We do this through Corporate Consulting, Skill Based Training, Stress Management Courses, Change Management and a various other courses. Also see Cherie Carter-Scott, New Age Associations and Societies and themms.com.

Motto
See Magical Name.

Mount Etna
Mount Etna is a volcano on the Island of Sicily. In Greek and Roman mythology it is where Zeus confined the Giants. Mount Etna is depicted here in an 1842 painting by British-American artist Thomas Cole (explorethomascole.org). Also see Sacred Sites, sacred-destinations.com and sacredsites.com.

Mount Fuji
Considered the home of the Gods, in Japan Mount Fuji has a long tradition of mythical legends surrounding it. Photograph taken by Taoy. Also see Sacred Sites, sacred-destinations.com and sacredsites.com.

Mount Kailash

In Buddhist and Hindu mythology, Mount Kailash, in the Himalayas, is considered the mountain at the center of the Earth and regarded as the spiritual center of the universe and the most mystical mountain of the Himalayan range. Mount Kailash is also known as axis mundi is considered the Heaven of Indra and home of the celestial spirits and Gods. It is also said to have its slopes covered with glittering gemstones and trees full of delicious fruit. Mount Kailash is also known and Mount Meru. Image from digital-dharma.net. Also see Sacred Sites, sacred-destinations.com and sacredsites.com.

Mount Olympus

Mount Olympus, considered a Sacred Site, is a mountain in Greece, between Thessaly and Macedonia. In Greek mythology it is the Pantheon of the Gods and Goddesses with a palace on the summit built by Hephaestus. Zeus rules and has his throne in Mount Olympus and it is here that the Gods and Goddess listen to the songs of the Muses and feast on nectar and ambrosia. Mount Olympus is depicted here by American artist Andy Park (andyparkart.com) in 2005. Also see Mythological Places, Olympian Gods, Sacred Sites, sacred-destinations.com and sacredsites.com.

Mount Parnassus

In Greek history and mythology, Mount Parnassus is a mountain near Delphi that is sacred to Apollo, Dionysus and the Muses and is the site of the Oracle of Apollo. Mount Parnassus and the Gods are shown here in a 1625 painting by French artist Nicolas Poussin (nicolaspoussin.org) called Apollo and the Muses (Parnassus). Also see Sacred Sites, sacred-destinations.com and sacredsites.com.

Mount Shasta

Mount Shasta is volcanic peak in northern California and a mythical place for several occult traditions. Native tribes in the area describe seeing fairy like creatures and giants beings (such as Sasquatch). Theosophical and Rosicrucian orders describe a hidden city within Mount Shasta that house Atlantean and Lemurian Masters. As a result of these beliefs, the area around Mount Shasta is considered a Sacred Site and has been the center of attention of various Occultist groups and many such groups over the last decades have made it their home. Photograph taken by Caia Cupito. Also see Sacred Sites, sacred-destinations.com and sacredsites.com.

Mountain Fairies

Mountain fairies are fairies found around mountains. Shown here is a depiction of a fairy by American artist Mary Baxter St. Clair (enchantedislandstudio.com) called Garden of Dreams. Also see Fairies.

Mramor, Nancy

American-born Nancy Mramor Ph.D. is a professional speaker, award winning author and educational, health, clinical and holistic psychologist and psychotherapist. After being diagnosed with leukemia she used her 25 years of experience in teaching mind-body medicine including visualization techniques and prayer to heal herself. Dr. Mramor teaches spiritual fitness techniques at hospitals, universities and conferences internationally. She has been featured on over 250 radio and television stations. Dr. Mramor's private practice includes mind/body psychotherapy and spiritual fitness coaching and her Mastering Relaxation curriculum has been internationally acclaimed. She has written: Spiritual Fitness: Embrace Your Soul, Transform Your Life. Photograph from drmramor.com. Also see Holistic Healing, Mind-Body Energy Medicine, Recommended Reading, Self-Healing and drmramor.com and inspiredhealth.info.

Mu

See Lemuria.

Mudra

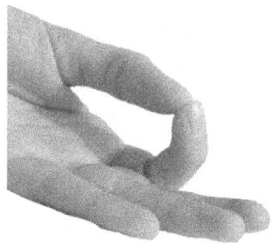

From Sanskrit meaning "seal" or "gesture", in Theosophy, Buddhism and Hinduism, mudras are a series of signs made with the hands and fingers for magical purposes. In Hindu mythology, Gods and Goddesses are depicted with many arms and each hand holding a different mudra. In Buddhist ceremonies the mudras act as a visual seal to affirm mystical or magical incantations or utterances. Theosophy describes mudras as symbols of power over evil influences. Mudras are often used together with the mantras, or other spiritual utterances. Also see Magical Amulets.

Mueler

In Araucanian (Chile) mythology, Mueler is the Storm God. Also see Araucanian Gods and Goddesses.

Muhammad

(570-632 B.C.E.) Born in Mecca Abu al-Qasim Muhammad ibn 'Abd Allah ibn 'Abd al-Muttalib ibn Hashim, (Muhammad's full name), was the prophet who founded the Muslim religion of Islam. He was the son of a wealthy merchant of the Banu Sashim (Hashimites), a branch of the Quraish (or Quraysh) tribe in Mecca but lost both parents at age six. Muhammad rejected the materialistic society and found solace in spiritual retreats in mountain caves. Legend says that Muhammad was forty years old when he dreamed that the Archangel Gabriel (Jabril) came to him and took him to Jerusalem where he prayed with Abraham, and Moses he then traversed the seven celestial spheres and approached God. He described his visions as "the breaking of the light of dawn". Muhammad took as his mission to spread the message of Islam (meaning surrendering oneself to the will of God). Other spellings include Mahomet and Mohhamed. Image from top-10-list.org. Also see Islam, Spiritual Leaders and Prophets.

Muladhara

From Sanskrit meaning "basic" or root chakra, Muladhara is the chakra located as the base of the spine and corresponding to the adrenal glands. It governs kundalini. It is associated with survival instincts and the connection to mother earth, its color is red and its element is earth. This chakra is also called the center of security. See Chakras.

Muldoon, Sylvan

(1903-1969) American-born Sylvan Joseph Muldoon was a practitioner, investigator and writer on astral projection. He says that he had his first astral projection experience spontaneously when he was 12 years old awakening to see himself floating on top of his body with a silver cord attached, thinking that he had died he tried to awaken family members with no success. He eventually returned to his body and he says that these continued throughout his life, often in a state of catalepsy. Later, with the collaboration of Hereward Carrington he wrote The Projection of the Astral Body in 1929 which is still regarded as a classic in the field. He also wrote: The Case for Astral Projection; The Phenomena of Astral Projection; and Sensational Psychical Experiences. Also see Astral Projection and Recommended Reading.

Mullahs

In Islam, Mullahs are religious and spiritual leaders. Also see Islam, Religious Teachers and Mullahs.

Muller, Wayne

American-born Wayne Muller D.D. is a bestselling author, spiritual teacher and therapist. He graduated from Harvard Divinity School and for the last 25 years has worked with some of the most disadvantaged people in society. He is the founder of Bread for the Journey and the Institute for Engaged Spirituality. Reverend Muller is on the faculty of the Institute of Noetic Sciences the Omega Institute and a senior scholar with the Fetzer Institute. He also gives lectures and hosts spiritual retreats worldwide. His books include: Legacy of the Heart: The Spiritual Advantage of a Painful Childhood; Sabbath: Finding Rest, Renewal and Delight in Our Busy Lives; Living the Generous Life: Reflections on Giving and

Receiving; Learning to Pray: How We Find Heaven on Earth; and A Life of Being, Having, and Doing Enough. Photo taken by Robert Vente (ventephoto.com). Also see Bread for the Journey, Recommended Reading, Reverends and Ministers, Spiritual Retreats, Spiritual Teachers, breadforthejourney.org and waynemuller.com.

Multiverse
See Parallel Universes.

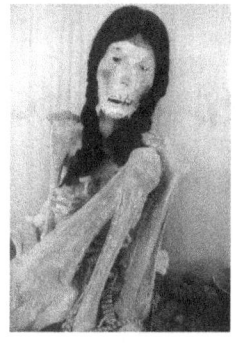

Mummy
A mummy is the remains of a dead person whose dried skin and flesh have been preserved intentionally or unintentionally. The most famous mummies known are the Egyptians who used long and elaborate (70 days) processes to preserve their dead for the afterlife. The oldest known mummies (from five to eight thousand years old) are from the Chinchorro and Aymara Indians found in southern Peru and northern Chile. Shown here is a Chilean 3,000 year old mummy dubbed Miss Chile housed in the Gustavo Paige museum in San Pedro de Atacama, Chile. Photograph from alovelyworld.com. Also see mummiesfilm.com and mummytombs.com.

Munda
See Upanishads.

Muninn
In Norse mythology, Muninn is one of the two (the other being Huginn) ravens of the God Odhin. Munnin is the raven who represents "memory" while Huginn represents "thought". Muninn and Huginn travel the world from dawn to dusk and then perch on Odhin's shoulders and whisper the news in his ear. Other spellings include Munin. Shown here is a 1919 painting by British artist Arthur Rackham (rackham.artpassions.net) called The Twa Corgies. Also see Mythological Creatures and Odhin.

Murphy, Bridey
One of the most widely publicized studies of reincarnation in the mid 20th Century is the book written by Morey Bernstein entitled The Search for Bridey Murphy. The book was based on the past life descriptions made by an American housewife from Colorado named Virginia Tighe who, under hypnosis recalled a past life under the name of Bridey Murphy. Murphy said that she had lived in County Cork, Ireland in the late 17th and early 18th Century. Her descriptions of life in Ireland in the 17th Century, which included physical places, local customs and way of life, were considered very accurate, even by the standards of those who set out to disprove her story. Also see Recommended Reading.

Murphy Joseph

(1898-1981) Irish-born Joseph Murphy Ph.D. DRS, LL.D. was a well known Divine Science Minister, author, counselor and lecturer of New Thought for almost 50 years. He was raised a Roman Catholic and studied for the priesthood and joined the Jesuits. Dr. Murphy later moved to the United States and eventually moved to Los Angeles, CA where he was ordained into Religious Science by Ernest Holmes. A few years later he became the Minister Director of the Church of Divine Science, building one of the largest New Thought congregations. He was director for the next 28 years. Dr. Murphy wrote over 30 books, including: The Power of Your Subconscious Mind; The Amazing Laws of Cosmic Mind; Secrets of the I Ching; The Cosmic Energizer: Miracle Power of the Universe; The Subconscious Mind: A Source of Unlimited Power; The Cosmic Power Within You; Prayer is the Answer and Psychic Perception: The Magic of Extrasensory Power. Also see New Thought, Recommended Reading, Reverends and Ministers, dsschool.org and josephmurphy.wwwhubs.com.

Murray, Margaret

(1863-1963) Indian-born Margaret Alice Murray was a prominent British anthropologist, Egyptologist, scholar of Wicca and pioneer campaigner for women's rights. She studied anthropology and linguistics at the University College of London. She was the first female Egyptologist employed at the Manchester Museum and she participated in several archeological excavations in Egypt and Palestine. She later became Assistant Professor of Egyptology at the University College of London for the next 11 years. Her books include: God of Witches; The Splendor That Was Egypt: A General Survey of Egyptian Culture; Legends of Ancient Egypt; Egyptian Temples; The Genesis of Religion; The Witch-Cult in Western Europe; and her autobiography My First Hundred Years. Also see Anthropologists, Egyptologists, Recommended Reading and Wicca.

Muses

Greek sister Goddesses, companions of Apollo and daughters of Zeus and Mnemosyne, the Muses rule over spring, music, poetry, memory, and the arts and sciences. They are said to inspire artists, especially writers, poets, musicians and philosophers. Their music is composed of a seven tone scale which comes from the music of the seven spheres of planets. The Muses are also described as the companions of the Graces and are also called the Mountain Goddesses. The nine Muses are: Calliope, (She of the Beautiful Voice), Muse of Epic or Heroic Poetry; Clio, (Proclaimer), Muse of History; Erato, (Lovely), Muse of Lyric and Love Poetry; Euterpe, (Well Pleasing), Muse of Flute Playing and Music; Melpomene, (Songstress), Muse of Tragedy; Polyhymnia, (She of the Many Hymns), Muse of Mimes and Sacred

Poetry; Terpsichore, (Whirler of the Dance), Muse of Lyric Poetry and Dancing; Thalia, (Blooming or Luxuriant), Muse of Comedy; and Urania, (Heavenly), Muse of Astronomy and Astrology. Other spellings include Mousa, Moisa and Musa. The muses are shown here in a 1615 painting by Flemish artist Hendrik van Balen called Minerva Among the Muses. Also see Greek Gods and Goddesses.

Music Therapy
See Sound Therapy.

Muspelheim
In Norse mythology, Muspelheim is one of the lowest realms of the Nine Worlds; the world of the fire giants. Also see Mythological Places, and Nine Worlds.

Mut
Egyptian Sky Goddess and Great Divine Mother, Mut is known as the Lady of Thebes, The Great Sorceress and the Mistress of Heaven. Mut is depicted as a woman with a vulture headdress, a woman with wings or as a vulture. She is the consort of Amon, daughter of Ra and adopted mother of Khonsu. Mut is also the Goddess of Marriage and Creation. Other spellings include Maut. Image from etsy.com. Also see Egyptian Gods and Goddesses, and Gods of Heaven.

Mut
In Egyptian mythology, the Mut are the restless spirits of the dead condemned by Osiris who prowl the Underworld. Also see Supernatural and Spiritual Beings.

Muta
Roman Goddess of Silence. She is also known as Dea Tacita and Tacita. Also see Roman Gods and Goddesses.

Myers, Frederick
(1843-1901) British-born Frederick William Henry Myers was a well known poet, essayist and paranormal researcher. He studied at Cheltenham and at Trinity University College in Cambridge. He worked for a time as teacher and then as school inspector while he wrote. He was one of the founding members of the Society for Psychical Research where he was involved in research of life after death, and he was also a member of the Theosophical Society. Myers coined the terms telepathy (which replaced "thought transference") and methetherial, meaning "beyond the ether", to describe the world in which the spirits exist. He wrote extensively but is best known for Human Personality and its Survival of Bodily Death, published posthumously. Myers in shown here in a 20th Century portrait painted by English artist William Clarke Wontner. Also see Parapsychologists and Psychic Researchers, Poets, Recommended Reading, Reincarnation (Life After Life), Society for Psychical Research and Theosophists.

Myomancy

Divination with rats and mice, myomancy studies the behavior and appearance of rodents. Also see Divination.

Myss, Caroline

(1952-) American-born Caroline Myss Ph.D. is a well known psychic diagnostician (medical intuitive) and mystic as well as author of several New Age books and speaker on spirituality on international tours. She has a B.A. in Journalism, an M.A. in Theology and a Ph.D. in Energy Medicine. Dr. Myss worked for several years as a medical intuitive with Dr. Norman Shealy. Among her books are: Anatomy of the Spirit: The Seven Stages of Power and Healing; Invisible Acts of Power: Personal Choices that Create Miracles; Entering the Castle: An Inner Path to God and Your Soul; The Creation of Health: The Emotional, Psychological and Spiritual Responses that Promote Health and Healing; Invisible Acts of Power: Channeling Grace into Your Everyday Life; and Sacred Contracts: Awakening Your Divine Potential. Photograph by PIMS Photographic Inc. Also see Mystics, Psychic Diagnosticians, Recommended Reading, store.myss.com and myss.com.

Mystery

From the Greek word mystos meaning "keep silent", mystery is used to describe the doctrine of the schools of magic. Mystery has also been defined as a religious truth beyond human comprehension that can only be understood by divine revelation. Shown here is a painting by Canadian artist Mario Duguay (marioduguay.com) called Initiation.

Mystery Religions

A mystery religion is any religion with an inner core of beliefs and practices that are revealed only to those who have been initiated. Shown here is a 1624 depiction of Hermes Trismegistus by German artist Daniel Stolcius von Stolcenberg. Also see Mystery Schools, and Religions.

Mystery Schools

The mystery schools refer to ancient mysterious religions and schools where the inner core of the practices and beliefs were known only to a few select initiates. These initiates were sworn to secrecy. Shown here is a 1509 painting of Aristotle's School of Athens by Italian artist Raphael (raphaelsanzio.org). Also see Ancient Mysteries, and Mystery Religions.

Mystic

From the Greek word mystikos, meaning "initiated person", mystic is the term applied to a person initiated into the religious mysteries. The way of the mystic is of devotion and meditation, deriving his/her knowledge and insight through direct spiritual communion with his/her higher self and God. Mystics are also described as those who have spiritual awareness of other planes of being or inner and more evolved worlds. Also see Ascended Masters, Mystics and Spiritual Teachers.

Mysticism

Mysticism is a system of beliefs in intuitive spiritual revelations for the purpose of union with the divine. This mystical union is achieved through intuition, faith, insight and spiritual awareness. It is also described as a spiritual search for inner truth and wisdom for the purpose of union with the Divine. Mysticism is any doctrine, philosophy or belief system that relates to the spiritual side of the world. The basis of mysticism is that the world is a spiritual place and this is the only reality. Also see Philosophical and Mystical Movements.

Mystics

The mystics described herein include: Lynn Andrews, Sri Aurobindo, William Blake, Helena Blavatsky, Jacob Bohme, Paul Brunton, Kuda Bux, Emma Curtis-Hopkins, Stanislas de Guaita, Meister Eckhart, Robert Fludd, Neville Goddard, Joel Goldsmith, Madame Jeanne Guyon, Manly Palmer Hall, Andrew Harvey, Iamblichus, Ibn al-'Arabi, Muhyi Ad-Din, William Quan Judge, Harvey Spencer Lewis, Guido von List, Isaac Luria, Mahatma Gandhi, Tricia McCannon, Caroline Myss, Martines de Pasqually, Pythagoras, Rabi'a, Sri Ramakrishna, George William Russell, Mouni Sadhu, Saint John of the Cross, Saint Teresa of Avila, Count Saint-Germain, Agnes Mary Sanford, Sankara Saranam, Sai Baba Sathya, Francis Schlatter, Jesse Francis Sheppard, Sai Baba Shirdi, Huston Cummings Smith, David Spangler, Emmanuel Swedenborg, Eckhart Tolle, Valentin Tomberg, Louis Claude de Saint-Martin, Evelyn Underhill, Swami Vivekananda, Arthur Edward Waite, Hank Wesselman, Stuart Wilde and Francis Younghusband. Also see Mystic.

Myth

A traditional or legendary story usually passed down by word of mouth, that ostensibly relates actual events to explain some practice, belief, or natural phenomenon, and which is especially associated with religious and magical rites and beliefs.

Mythology

From Greek meaning "to relate myths", mythology literally means the retelling of myths. It usually refers to a collection of myths belonging to a specific people and their deities, history, ancestors and beliefs. The people described herein who study and write about mythology include: Sir E.A. Wallis Budge, Joseph Campbell, Phil Cousineau, Manly Palmer Hall, Andrew Lang and Caroline Pearson. Shown here is a drawing of a Chryselephantine statue of the Greek God Zeus on Mount Olympus. Image from karenswhimsy.com. Also see bulfinch.englishatheist.org, egyptianculture.net, egyptianmyths.net, goddessaday.com, gods-heros-myth.com, jameswbell.com, mother- god.com, mythinglinks.org, paleothea.com, pantheon.org, shee-eire.com, sisterhoodofavalon.org, theoi.com and timelessmyths.com.

Mythological Creatures

Of the hundreds of mythological creatures, the following are described herein: Alma, Ammut, Barghest, Benu, Camahueto, Centaur, Cerberus, Chupacabras, Cryptids, Cyclops, Dragon, Elemental, Fachan, Fairy, Fenrir Wolf, Firebird, Freki, Geri, Gremlin, Griffin, Guirivilo, Gullimbursti, Gullinkambi, Harpies, Hippocampus, Hippogriff, Huallepen, Huginn, Hydra, Kaliya, Kelpie, Kraken, Lock Ness Monster, Makara, Managarm, Mehen, Melusine, Midgard Serpent, Minotaur, Morgawr, Muninn, Nature Spirits, Ngurvilu, Nidhogg, Nuckelavee, Nymphs, Oannes, Pegasus, Phoenix, Phooka, Ratatosk, Sasquatch, Sleipnir, Sphinx, Unicorn, Werewolf, Winged Horses, Wyvern and Yeti. Shown here is an 1806 depiction of mythological creatures by German artist Friedrich Justine Bertuch. Also see Cryptids, hafepea.org and unknown-creatures.com.

Mythological Places

Of the mythological places from ancient mythology and religious and mystical traditions, this book deals with the following: Aztec: Mictlan, Omeyocan, Tlalocan, Tlillan-Tlapallan and Ubshukina; Babylonian: Aralu and Ubshukina; Christian: Eden, Hell and Limbo; Egyptian: Duat and Hall of Maat; Greek: Elysian Fields, Hades, Mount Olympus, Styx and Tartarus; Inca: Hanan Pacha, Kay Pacha and Uku Pacha; Jewish: Abbadon and Gehenna; Maya: Xibalba; Norse: Alfeim, Asgard, Hel, Jotunheim, Midgard, Muspelheim, Nifelheim, Svartalfaheim, Valhalla, Vanaheim and Yggdrasil; Rosicrucian: Abiegnus; Tibetan: Shambhala and Shangri-La; and work of art by an unknown artist. Also see Underworlds. Universal: Agartha and hell. Shown here is a 16th Century.

N

Naadame
In The Greater Key of Solomon, Naadame is described as the Prince of all the Angels and Caesars. Also see Angels.

Nabi
A Jewish seer, prophet, interpreter of oracles; one who relays messages from the dead. Shown here is a 1630 painting by Dutch artist Rembrandt (rembrandtpainting.net) called the Prophet Jeremiah Lamenting the Destruction of Jerusalem.

Nabia
Seership, soothsaying; Nabia is the oldest and most respected of Hebrew mystic phenomena, and which includes divination, clairvoyance, visions, trance states and oracles.

Nabu
In Babylonian mythology, Nabu is the God Wisdom and Speech, son of Marduk. He is also the God of Agriculture and Commerce. Nabu is also called Patron of the Scribes and the Keeper of the Tablets of Destiny, which the Gods use to record their decisions. Shown here is a 1939 relief of Nabu by American sculptor Lee Lawrie found on the Library of Congress John Adams Building in Washington, D.C. Also see Babylonian Gods and Goddesses.

Nachash

In Genesis in the Old Testament Nachash is the serpent of the Tree of Knowledge. Nachash is depicted here in part of the 1508 Sistine Chapel painting by Italian artist Michelangelo (michelangelo.com) called The Temptation and Fall of Adam and Eve.

Nadis

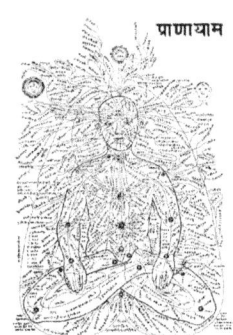

From the Sanskrit nad meaning "channel" or "vein", in traditional Indian philosophy the Nadis are channels though which energy or prana flows. They connect at the Chakras and the main channels of nadi include Ida, Pingala and Shushumna. There are believed to be around 72,000 nadis. Shown here is an 18th Century depiction of Nadis by an unknown artist. Also see Chakras, Ida, Pingala, and Shushumna.

Naenia

Roman Goddess of who presides over funerals. Shown here is a 1902 painting by Evelyn de Morgan (demorgan.org.uk) called Our Lady of Peace. Also see Roman Gods and Goddesses.

Nag Hammadi Scrolls

The Nag Hammadi Scrolls, also called the Gnostic Gospels are a collection of Biblical texts discovered on the west bank of the Nile in upper Egypt in 1945. They are a collection of 13 codices of Gnostic scriptures and commentaries written in the 2nd or the 3rd Century, although the codices are 4th Century copies. Included in the texts is the Gospel of Thomas which was written before any of the other Gospels. Two years after the discovery of the Nag Hammadi Scrolls the Dead Sea Scrolls were found in the Qumran Caves. Also see Dead Sea Scrolls, Sacred Writings, gnosis.org and nag-hammadi.com.

Nagas

In Indian mythology Nagas are serpentine beings and minor deities. Varuna is their King and they are often depicted with seven or more heads wearing hoods. They are described as being extraordinarily beautiful. In Buddhism they are considered guardian deities of doors. Shown here is a Naga guarding the Royal Palace in Phnom Penh, Cambodia. Photograph from sricaitanyadas.multiply.com. Also see Supernatural and Spiritual Beings.

Nagomancy

See Necromancy.

Nagua

In Aztec mythology, the Nagua are tutelary spirits in the shape of an animal or plant. Every God and mortal has their personal Nagual with whom they share their fate until they die. The singular of Nagua is Nagual. Also see Supernatural and Spiritual Beings.

Naiads

In Greek and Roman mythology, Naiads are nymphs or water Elementals of brooks, springs, lakes, ponds, wells and fountains. They are gifted in social graces such as music and dancing. They are also described as having prophetic and healing powers. Other spellings include Naiades. Naiades are depicted here in an 1896 painting by British artist John William Waterhouse (jwwaterhouse.com) called Hylas and the Nymphs. Also see Elementals, and Nymphs.

Namaste

In Nepal and India namaste is a form of greeting as well as a parting phrase and gesture. From Sanskrit namas meaning "to bow", namaste literally means "I bow to you" although it also said to mean "I honor the divinity you are". When spoken to another person the gesture of a slight bow is made with hands pressed together, fingers pointed upwards, in front of the chest. This gesture can also be made without words and it carries the same meaning. Other spellings include Namaskar.

Namburbi Rituals

In Babylonia and Assyria, the Namburbi rituals are sets of rituals performed for reversing and dispelling the predicted results of evil oracles.

Nammu

In Sumerian mythology, Nammu is the Sea Goddess who gave birth to Heaven and Earth. She is the mother of Enki and pushes him to create human mortals. She is also the mother of all Deities. Also see Gods of Heaven, and Sumerian Gods and Goddesses.

Nanay

Sumerian Love Goddess closely associated with Inanna. Also see Sumerian Gods and Goddesses.

Nanna

The name used by Sin during the Full Moon phase. See Sin.

Nanna

Norse Goddess of Love and Gentleness, Nanna is known as the Great Mother and Earth Goddess. She is the Mother of Forsetti and the wife of Baldur. Nanna is of the Vanir Gods that lives in Vanaheim. Other spellings include Anna, Ianna and Nana. Shown here is a painting by French painter Sophie Anderson called Love in a Mist. Also see Norse Gods and Goddesses, and Vanir.

Nanta

Enochian term for "Spirit of the Earth".

Nanta

See Tablet of Union.

Napaeas

In Greek mythology, Napaeas are Valley Nymphs. They are shown here with a Satyr in an 1873 painting by French artist William-Adolphe Bouguereau (bouguereau.org) called Nymphs and Satyr. Also see Nymphs.

Naqshbandiyah

See Fakir.

Narada Purana

In Hinduism, Narada Purana, which deals with the description of man's duties to society according to the sage Narada, is one of the texts which explain the myths and rituals of the Gods. Also see Puranas.

Naranjo, Claudio

(1932-) Chilean-born Claudio Naranjo M.D., Ph.D. is a psychiatrist, anthropologist and author known for his work with mind-altering substances (psychedelic hallucinogens). He studied medicine, music and philosophy in the Universidad de Chile and taught psychology at the Universidad Catolica de Chile. After moving to the United States, he worked with the founder of the Gestalt Therapy, Fritz Perls and was among the staff of the Esalen Institute. He taught comparative religion at the California Institute of Asian Studies, meditation at Nyingma Institute in Berkeley and humanistic psychology ant the University of California Santa Cruz. He is considered today an important figure in the Human Potential Movement in Berkeley, California. Dr. Naranjo is also the founder of the EduSAT Program. Among his books are: The Healing Journey: New Approaches to Consciousness; How to Be: Meditation in Spirit and Practice; The One Quest; and The Way of Silence and the Talking Cure: On Meditation and Psychotherapy. Photograph from revistanamaste.com. Also see Anthropologists, Hallucinogens, Meditation, Recommended Reading, claudionaranjo.net and fundacionclaudionaranjo.com.

Narasimha

In Hinduism, Narasimha, the half-man half-lion is the forth incarnation or Avatar of the God Vishnu appearing in the Satya Yuga. Narasimha is shown here on a relief on the Chennakesava Temple in Belur, India. See Avatar.

Narby, Jeremy

(1959-) Swiss-Canadian Jeremy Narby, Ph.D. is an anthropologist and author. He grew up in Canada and Switzerland studying history at the University of Canterbury and receiving his Ph.D. in anthropology from Stanford University. He spent several years living in the Peruvian Amazon with the Ashaninca researching the rainforest resources and cataloging indigenous plants, particularly Ayahuasca, an indigenous psychedelic hallucinogen. Since 1989, Dr. Narby has been the Amazonian projects director for the Swiss NGO, Nouvelle Planete. He has written: The Cosmic Serpent: DNA and the Origins of Knowledge; Shamans Through Time: 500 Years on the Path to Knowledge; Intelligence in Nature; and The Psychotropic Mind: The World According to Ayahuasca, Iboga, and Shamanism. Photograph taken by Isabelle Meister. Also see Anthropologists, Ayahuasca, Hallucinogens, Recommended Reading, Shamans and nouvelle-planete.ch.

Narcissus

In Greek mythology, Narcissus is the God in love with his own reflection due to punishment of the Gods. Other spellings include Narkissos. Shown here is a 1903 painting by British artist John William Waterhouse (jwwaterhouse.com) called Echo and Narcissus. Also see Greek Gods and Goddesses.

Narudi

In Chaldean magic, Narudi is an Akkadian spirit, Lord of the Greatest Gods, whose image is placed in houses to ward off wicked people. Also see Supernatural and Spiritual Beings.

Nash, Carroll B.

(1914-1998) American-born Carroll Blue Nash Ph.D. was professor of biology and director of the parapsychology laboratory at St. Joseph's College in Pennsylvania. He was also a founding member and president of the Parapsychological Association. He studied at the George Washington University in Washington, D.C. and the University of Maryland. Dr. Nash was the first American to receive the William McDougall Award for Distinguished Work in Parapsychology. Nash studied personality variables in psi, precognition and developed dice tests for psychokinesis. He wrote several articles on parapsychology but he is best known for his books Parapsychology: The Science of Psiology; Science of PSI: ESP and PK; Comparison of Responses to ESP and Subliminal Targets; and Medical Implications of Parapsychology. Photograph from williamjames.com. Also see Parapsychological Association, Parapsychologists and Psychic Researchers, Psychokinesis and Recommended Reading.

Natal Chart
See Birth Chart and Astrology.

Natural Magic
Natural magic is magic that deals with the occult virtues or magical energies and spiritual powers of herbs, plants, gems, metals and others. In Western magical traditions natural magic is one of two types of magic, the other being ceremonial magic. Shown here is a 1997 painting by American artist Thomas Kinkade (thomaskinkade.com) called the Garden of Prayer. Also see Ceremonial Magic, Occult Virtues and Magical Methods.

Nature Spirits
Nature Spirits are described as mythological creatures or Lesser Deities usually attached to a place such as a mountain, river, lake, forest, grove or tree. Some Nature Spirits are described as having a human form while others are described as half human, half animal. The Nature Spirits described herein are: Bannick, Banshee, Bean-Nighe, Domovoi, Fauns, Gandharvas, Glaistig, Green Ladies, Green Men, Hags, Huacas, Kachinas, Kikimora, Lares, Menehune, Penates, Rusalkas, Salvani, Satyrs, Seleni, Silenus, Skritek, Urisk, Vodyanik, Yakshas and Yakshis. Shown here a painting by American artist Meredith Miller (meredithmillerart.com) called Bringers of the Night Rainbow. Also see Elementals, Fairies, Mythological Creatures, and Nymphs.

Nature Worship
The expression of human feelings of awe, gratitude and dependence in the powers of nature. In most ancient cultures, Gods where related to powers of nature. Shown here is a 1900 painting called the Gates of Dawn by British artist James Herbert Draper. Also see Magical Methods.

Naturopathy
As a natural holistic system of medicine, naturopathy, also called naturopathic medicine recognizes the integrity of the whole person (mind and body) and emphasizes the importance of assisting the body in resisting disease rather than attacking the disease itself. Naturopathy as well as Christian Science believes that disease is caused by mental and emotional problems which develop into physical problems. The methods used in Naturopathy may include acupuncture, aromatherapy, exercise, fasting, massage, meditation, special diets and psychological therapy. Also see Disease, Holistic, Therapeutic Systems and naturopathic.org.

Nauthiz

As the 7th symbol of the runes, Nauthiz represents constraint. Also see Runes.

Navagrahas
In Hinduism Navagrahas, from Nava meaning "nine" and Graha meaning "planet" or "realm" are the nine Deities or Gods who personify the celestial bodies. They are: Surya, ruling the Sun; Chandra, ruling the Moon; Mangala, ruling Mars; Buddha, ruling Mercury; Brihaspati, ruling Jupiter; Shukra, ruling Venus; Shani, ruling Saturn; Rahu, ruling the North Lunar Node; and Ketu, ruling the South Lunar Node. The Navagrahas are shown here on a stone carving from Eastern India housed in the Ashmolean museum in Oxford, England. Photograph by David Eferro. Also see Hindu Gods and Goddesses.

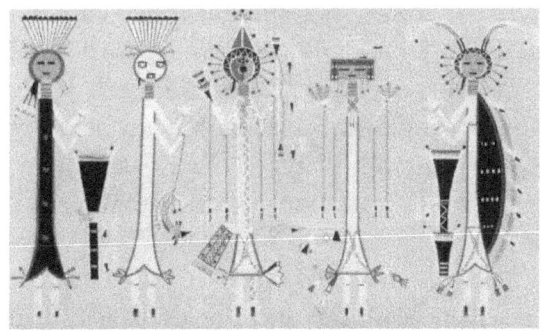

Navajo Gods and Goddesses
The following Navajo Gods and Goddesses are described herein: Ahsonnutli, Changing Woman, Estanatlehi, Hastsehogan, Hastsezini, Spider Woman, Tonelili and Yolkai Estasan. Shown here is a sand painting depicting Navajo Gods. Image from navajopeople.org.

Nawao
See Menehune.

Nazca Lines
The Nazca lines are giant lines or roads, carved in the ground, that form geometric figures and plant and animal drawings in the southern Peruvian desert. These lines extend over 500 km2 and were constructed over 2,000 years ago and depict about 70 different images of plants and animals. What makes the Nazca Lines so mysterious is the fact that from ground level the figures are virtually indecipherable but instead they are plainly visible from the air and they were only discovered in the 1920's when commercial airplanes began flying over the area. Their original significance or purpose has yet to be explained. Other spellings include Nasca lines. Also see sacred-destinations.com.

NDE
See Near Death Experience.

Ndmh

In Jewish magical tradition, Ndmh is described as an Angel of the summer equinox invoked as protection against the evil eye. Also see Angels.

Near Death Experience

A Near Death Experience is basically explained as being clinically dead and returning with the memory of what happened. Accounts of Near Death Experience or NDE's have been recorded for hundreds of years but have only been studied recently. According to Raymond Moody, author of Life After Life, there are nine stages to the experience including the "tunnel" sensation (where the person feels drawn through a tunnel with a bright light at the end) and meeting deceased relatives and loved ones, sometimes participating in their own "life review" and being reluctant to go back. The people described herein who claim to have had Near Death Experiences include: Phyllis M. H. Atwater, William Barrett, Hal Zina Bennet, Dannion Brinkley, Sylvia Browne, John DeMartini, Betty J. Eadie, Joyce Hawkes, Carl Jung, Denise Linn, Raymond Moody, Dianne Morrissey, Melvin Morse, Robert Moss, Kenneth Ring, Miguel Angel Ruiz, Agnes Mary Sanford, Kimberly Clark Sharp and Tara Sutphen. Shown here is a painting by Canadian artist Mario Duguay (marioduguay.com) called My Steps Towards the Light. Also see Afterlife, Greeters, Life Review, litesofheaven.com, near-death.com, neardeathsite.com, nderf.org, spiritualscientific.com and towardthelight.org.

Nebo

Babylonian God of Wisdom, Nebo rules over literature and science, writing and speech. He is the speaker of the Gods and he speaks for humans when they die producing a record of their deeds on Earth. Also see Babylonian Gods and Goddesses.

Nechtan

Celtic God of Water whose sacred well is the Source of All Knowledge. Nechtan later became Saint Nectan in Wales. Other spellings include Nectan. Also see Celtic Gods and Goddesses.

Necromancer

A Necromancer is a practitioner of Necromancy. See Necromancy and Divination.

Necromancy

From the Greek words nekros and manteia meaning "dead" and "divination" and also known as nagomancy and psychomancy, necromancy is the ancient practice of communicating with spirits of the dead, usually for the purpose of obtaining insights into the future. Some define necromancy as raising images of the dead and relate it to evil and black magic. Shown here is an 1806 depiction of John Dee and Edward Kelly practicing necromancy by an unknown artist. Also see Divination, and Spiritualism.

Necromanteion

The Necromanteion, meaning "oracle of death" was an ancient temple in Greece dedicated to Hades and Persephone. It was located on the Acheron river near the ancient city of Ephyra, site believed to be the door to Hades. Elaborate fasting and cleansing ceremonies were performed before priests would deliver their oracles. Other spellings include Nekromanteion. Photograph from worldisround.com. Also see Oracle and Psychomanteum.

Needleman, Jacob

(1934-) American-born Jacob Needleman is a professor of philosophy, consultant and author of numerous books dealing with spiritual ideas and philosophy. He currently is professor emeritus of philosophy at San Francisco State University and consultant in a wide variety of disciplines. Among Prof. Needleman's books are: Time and the Soul; The Wisdom of Love: Why Can't We Be Good?; Lost Christianity; A Sense of the Cosmos; The Way of the Physician; The American Soul; and What Is God?. Photograph from afradvice.com. Also see Philosophers, Recommended Reading and jacobneedleman.com.

Nefertem

Egyptian God of the Lotus. Nefertem is said to have been born without mother or father but coming into being from a lotus blossom. He is the God of Sunrise who helps bring the Sun into the sky. Although he has no formal temple or cult people carry small statues or images of him for protection. Also see Egyptian Gods and Goddesses.

Nehalennia

Norse Goddess of Seafaring, Fishing and Fruitfulness, Nehalennia is also known as the Goddess of Plenty. She is associated with vegetation, dogs and the sea and is invoked by sailors before crossing the North Sea. Nehalennia is usually depicted with a basket of apples. Shown here is a photograph of an altar of Nehalennia from the Rijksmuseum van oudheden in Leiden, Netherlands. Also see Norse Gods and Goddesses.

Nehebkau

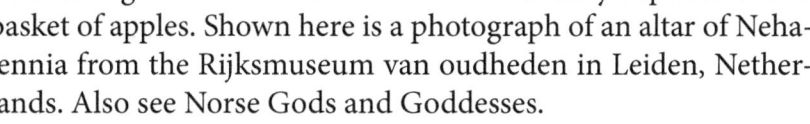

Egyptian serpent God of the Underworld, dangerous to both humans and Gods, Nehebkau is the God of Death, and Vengeance. Although he is considered dangerous he will often give food to the dead. Other spellings include Nehebu Kau. Shown here is a statue of Nehebkau housed in the Kelsey museum or archaeology at the University of Michigan. Also see Egyptian Gods and Goddesses and Underworld Gods.

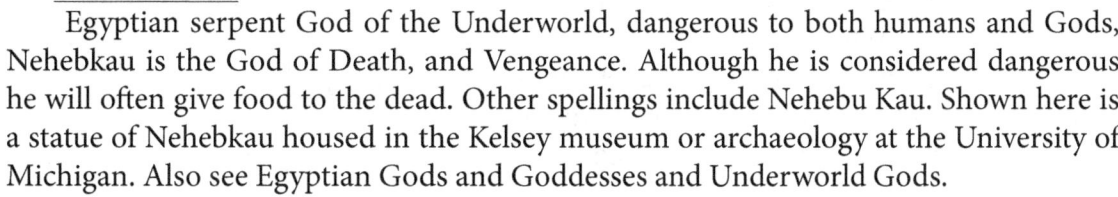

Nehushtan

From the Old Testament of The Bible the Nehushtan, also called the Brazen Serpent and the Bronze Serpent, was a sacred object in the form of a bronze serpent on a pole. It was used by Moses to save the Israelites from snake bites. The Nehushtan is depicted here from Italian artist Michelangelo's (michelangelo.com) 1508 Sistine Chapel.

Neihardt, John G.

(1881-1973) American-born Jonathan "John" Gneisenau Neihardt was a philosopher, historian, poet and author. He founded the Society for Research on Rapport and Telekinesis (or SORRAT). He held the title of State's poet laureate awarded to him by the Nebraska Legislature for over fifty years and he also received the Poetry Society of America Prize for the best verses in 1919, the Gold Scroll Medal of Honor of National Poetry Center and the Writers Foundation award for Poetry. He is best known for his book Black Elk Speaks: Being the Life Story of a Holy Man of the Oglala Sioux. Among his other books are: The Divine Enchantment: A Mystical Poem, and, Poetic Values: Their Reality and Our Need of; A Bundle of Myrrh; The Quest; When the Tree Flowered: The Fictional Biography of Eagle Voice, a Sioux Indian and Patterns and Coincidences: A Sequel to All is But a Beginning. Also see Historians, Parapsychologists and Psychic Researchers, Philosophers, Poets, Recommended Reading and neihardtcenter.org.

Neith

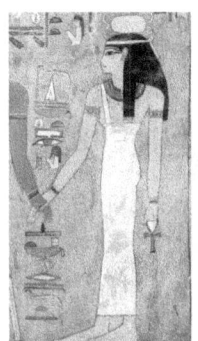

Egyptian Goddess of War and the Hunt, Neith is also called Opener of the Ways, Great Goddess, Mother of the Gods, Guardian of Hidden Mysteries and Lady of the West. She is the mother of Ra and Sobek and is described as a mystical Goddess who deals with herbs, magic, mystical knowledge, rituals, meditation and healing. Neith is said to be a very wise Goddess to whom the other Gods seek for help in resolving their disputes and problems. There is an inscription on one of her temples that says "I am all that has been, that is, and that shall be. No mortal has yet been able to lift the veil which covers me". Other spellings include Net, Neit and Nit. Here Neith is shown with Hathor. Image from maatkara.extra.hu. Also see Egyptian Gods and Goddesses.

Nekhebet

Egyptian Guardian Goddess, referred to as The Lady of the South, the White Crown and the Vulture Goddess, Nekhebet is the protector of Upper Egypt and is considered Goddess of Motherhood and Childbirth. She is often depicted wearing the crown of Upper Egypt and was considered the Pharaoh's personal Goddess from the time he was born until the time he died. Other spellings include Nechbet, Nekhbet, and Nekhebet. Shown here is a painting of Nekhebet from a wall on the Mortuary Temple of Hatshepsut, in Deir el Bahri, near Thebes, Egypt. Also see Egyptian Gods and Goddesses.

Nemamiah

Qabbalistic Angel, Nemamiah means "lovable". Nemamiah is also described as an Archangel who presides as guardian of admirals, generals and all those who engage in just causes. Also see Angels.

Nemesis

Greek Goddess of Destiny, Nemesis rules over divine retribution and divine anger, and she is the personification of divine justice and the vengeance of the Gods. Nemesis is also known as Adasteia and is also called the Daughter of Night. Shown here is an 1882 painting by French artist William-Adolphe Bouguereau (bouguereau.org) called Evening Mood. Also see Greek Gods and Goddesses.

Nemeth, Maria

American-born Maria Nemeth Ph.D., MCC is an internationally recognized licensed clinical psychologist, master certified coach and motivational speaker and author. She was an associate clinical professor in the Department of Psychiatry at the University of California Davis School of Medicine. Dr. Nemeth founded the Academy for Coaching Excellence and her seminar Mastering Life's Energies. For than 20 years, Dr. Nemeth has trained ministers, clinicians, executives, teachers, coaches and private individuals and her courses and workshops have been taken by thousands of people. She has written The Energy of Money: A Spiritual Guide to Financial and Personal Fulfillment (which won the 1999 Audie Award for best Personal Development Series); You and Money: Would it be All Right with You if Your Life Got Easier?; and Mastering Life's Energies Mastering Life's Energies: Simple Steps to a Luminous Life at Work and Play. Also see Recommended Reading, Self-Help and academyforcoachingexcellence.com

Nemhain

Celtic Goddess of War and Battle. Shown here is a 20th Century depiction of a Celtic Goddess by Spanish artist Luis Royo (luisroyo.com) in his work called The Wind From Hastings. Also see Celtic Gods and Goddesses.

Nenechen

In Araucanian (Chile) mythology, Nenechen is the Supreme God and Creator. Also see Araucanian Gods and Goddesses.

Neopaganism

Neopaganism is the religious movement that attempts to revive pre-Christian European religious practices and the term used to describe such movements. The most well known branches of Neopaganism are Wicca and Druidry. Other spellings include Neo-Paganism. Also see Religions and religioustolerance.org.

Neoplatonism

The philosophy developed by Plotinus, Iamblichus and Porphyry in the 3rd Century, which combines Oriental Mysticism, Gnosticism and the doctrines of Plato. Neoplatonism holds that all manifestation, spiritual and material, emanates from a single Godhead through the action of Divine will. It also states that reason alone can not satisfy the spiritual longings of the human soul. Other spellings include Neo-Platonism. Also See Philosophical and Mystical Movements.

Neophyte

From the Greek neophytos meaning "newly planted", a neophyte is a student of Occultism or Theosophy who may or may not have been formally initiated into an Order, Brotherhood, Occult Society or Fraternity. A neophyte is also described as a candidate for initiation into the Mysteries. Shown here is an 1877 sketch of a neophyte by French artist Gustave Dore (gustavedoreart.com). Also see Spiritual Seekers.

Nephelomancy

Divination by observing the clouds and interpreting their shapes, nephelomancy is a form of Aeromancy. Also see Aeromancy, and Divination.

Nephesh

From Hebrew meaning "soul", in the Qabbalah the Nephesh is the animal soul in man as opposed to the Neshamah which is the divine soul in humans. Also see Neshamah.

Nephilim

In Wiccan, Pagan and Occult traditions the Nephilim are the half-human half-Angels born from the Grigori. They learned the arts of divination, astrology, healing and herbal magic from the Grigori. Also see Grigori. Also see Supernatural and Spiritual Beings. Shown here is a 1923 sculpture by American Daniel Chester French called The Sons of God saw the Daughters of Men that they were Fair.

Nephthys

Egyptian Goddess of the Underworld who represents life and death. Nephthys is also known as the Mistress of the Palace, Mistress of the Gods and the Lady of Life. She is the daughter of Nuit and Geb and the dark sister of Isis and her other siblings; Osiris and Seth. Nephthys is wife/sister of Seth and the mother of Anubis and is described as being fair skinned with green eyes. Nephthys is the funerary Goddess of Death and guardian of hidden things. She rules over dark magic, mystical things, invisibility, intuition and dreams. She offers guidance to the newly dead and helps with the birth of children. Other spellings include Neb Hut, Nebhet and Nebthe. Nephthys is shown here in a depiction from the Egyptian Book of the Dead. Also see Egyptian Gods and Goddesses, and Underworld Gods.

Neptune

Roman God of the Sea, Neptune rules over horses, bulls, fishermen, springs, streams, lakes, rivers, storms, earthquakes, ships and he protects from droughts. He is the son of Saturn and brother of Jupiter and Pluto. Other spellings include Neptunus. Neptune is Poseidon to the Greeks. Neptune is depicted here in a 1754 painting by American artist John Singleton Copley (johnsingletoncopley.org) called The Return of Neptune. Also see Roman Gods and Goddesses.

Neptune

In Occultism, as the planet or celestial body affecting aspects of human life, Neptune represents the sea, clairvoyance, mediums, astral reality, crystal balls, mysterious secrets, the unknown and inexplicable, prophets and prophecies, inspiration, idealism, addictions, that which is artificial or synthetic, illusions, ambushes, meetings, businesses and illegal activities, hermits, informants, sacrifices, banishments, incarcerations, hospitals, asylums and jails, bribery and corruption, worries and hidden sorrows, and suicide. Also see Planets.

Nereids

In Greek mythology, the Nereids are 50 Nymphs who live at the bottom of the Mediterranean Sea. They often come to the surface to aid sailors and other travelers riding dolphins and other sea animals such as the hippocampus. The Nereids are the daughters of Nereus and Doris and they are the attendants to Poseidon. Other spellings include Neriedes. The Nereids are shown here in a painting by 1903 painting by British artist Sir Edward John Poynter called the Cave of the Storm Nymphs. Also see Nymphs.

Nereus

Greek God of the Mediterranean Sea, Nereus is the son of Pontus and Gaea, the husband of Doris and the father of the Nereids. He is described as the Wise Old Man of the Sea. Nereus is a shape-shifter and he is often depicted with a fish tail. Shown here is an image of Nereus from a 520 B.C.E. cup housed in the J. Paul Getty Museum in Malibu, California. Also see Greek Gods and Goddesses.

Nergal

In Babylonian and Assyrian mythology, Nergal is the God of Death and King of the Underworld who rules over the spirits of the dead. He also rules over hunting and war and is described as having the body of a lion with wings with a human head. Nergal is the son of Enlil and the husband of Ereshkigal. Also see Assyrian Gods and Goddesses, Babylonian Gods and Goddesses, and Underworld Gods.

Nerthus

Norse Goddess of Witchcraft, Nerthus rules over peace, fertility, springs, wealth, purification and the Earth and the Sea. She is also called Terra Mater or Mother Earth and the Fertility Goddess. Other spellings include Erce. Nerthus is depicted here by American artist Lisa Hunt (lisahuntart.com). Also see Norse Gods and Goddesses.

Neshamah

From the Qabbalah, Neshamah is the divine soul in humans as opposed to the Nephesh which is the animal soul in humans. Also see Nephesh.

Netzach

The seventh sephirah on the Qabbalistic Tree of Life whose symbols are candles, lamps, roses and seven pointed stars and represents victory. See Tree of Life.

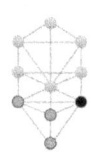

New Age

Term that was popularized in the 1980's that relates to a wide range of a renewed interest ranging everywhere from Behavioral Medicine and Quantum Physics to Holistic Medicine, Yoga, Philosophy, Religion, Spiritualism, Spirituality, Astrology, Shamanism, Channeling, Occultism, Psychic Healing, Parapsychology, Reincarnation and Mysticism many among others. New Age has also been described as a movement which is characterized by an eclectic approach to healing and spiritual exploration. Also see Magical Methods, Spiritual Goals, Spiritual Techniques, acceleratedlearningmethods.com, age-of-the-sage.org, bizspirit.com, cosmicconnections.com, crystalinks.com, dimensionconnection.com, duversity.org, earthtransitions.com, empoweringmessages.com, enchantedspirit.org, eq.org, esotericscience.org, fmbr.org, galactic-server.com, gravitycontrol.org, insightjourneys.com, integrallife.com, intent.com, iups.edu, mediums-spiritguides.com, mysteriousbritain.co.uk, mysteriouspeople.com, namastecafe.com, nautis.com, new-age-spirituality.com, paralumun.com, peaceinspace.com, peacexpeace.org, perceivingreality.com, sacredscience.com, shockinstitute.com, spiritofmaat.com, theorderoftime.com, thespiritseekers.org, think-aboutit.com, truthseekingsouls.com, unexplained-mysteries.com and world-mysteries.com.

New Age Associations and Societies

Of the thousands of Associations and Societies dealing with New Age issues the following are described herein: Academy of Parapsychology and Medicine, American Association for the Advancement of Science, American Association of Electronic Voice Phenomena, American Board of Integrative Holistic Medicine, American Federation of Astrologers, American Federation of Astrologers, American Holistic Medical Association, American Society for Psychic Research, Anthroposophical Society, Arthur Findlay College, Association for Humanistic Psychology, Association for Research and Enlightenment, Association for Scientific Study of Consciousness, Association for the Masters Psychophysical Method, Association for Transpersonal Psychology, Association for Treatment and Training in the Attachment of Children, Association TransCommunication, Ayurvedic Institute, Bread for the Journey, Brotherhood of Light, Builders of the Adytum, California Institute for Human Science, California Institute of Integral Studies, Center for Creativity and Inquiry, Center for Ecoliteracy, Center for Frontier Sciences, Center for Mindfulness in Medicine, Health Care and Society, Center for Spirituality and the Mind, Chopra Center, Circle Sanctuary, Dallas Institute of Humanities and Culture, Dianetics, Doctor-Healer Network, Elisabeth Kübler-Ross Foundation, Enigma Group, Enneagram Worldwide, Esalen Institute, Fearless Living Institute, Findhorn Foundation, Foundation for Shamanic Studies, General Evolution Research Group, Gesundheit Institute, Gnostic Society, Goddess Network, Green Earth Foundation, Halexandria Foundation, Holos University Graduate Seminary, Holotropic Breathwork, Inner Visions, Institute for the Study of Human Knowledge, Institute of Core Energetics, Institute of Noetic Sciences, Institute of Transpersonal Psychology, International Association for Near-Death Studies, International Association for the Study of Dreams, International Association of Rubenfeld Synergists, International Holistic Health Energy Institute, Inward Bound, Kundalini Research Network, Lucidity Institute, Motivation Management Service Institute, New Energy Movement, Newton Institute, Omega Institute for Holistic Studies, Parapsychological Association, Quantum Touch, Ramtha's School of Enlightenment, Reverse Speech, Rosemary Altea Association of Healers, Rosemary Altea Healing and Educational Foundation, Rosicrucian Egyptian Museum, Salugenecists, Saybrook University, School for Self-Healing, School of Spiritual Psychology, Self-Realization Fellowship, Shamanic Journeys, Society for Chaos Theory in Psychology and Life Sciences, Society for Psychical Research, Spirit Rock Meditation Center, Spiritual Alliance to Stop Intimate Violence, Therapeutic Touch, Tree of Life Rejuvenation Center, Twilight Brigade, United States Association of Body Psychotherapy, US Psi Squad, Walking Stick Foundation, White Eagle Lodge, World Commission on Global Consciousness and Spirituality, World Wisdom Council and Worldwide Indigenous Science Network.

New Energy Movement

Co-founded by Dr. Brian O'Leary, the New Energy Movement is (in its own words) dedicated to the study and promotion of advanced, clean, and sustainable energy sources for our imperiled planet. We recognize that the single most highly-leveraged opportunity for advancement towards solving our complex global problems lies in a transformation of the way human civilization generates and utilizes energy. We intend to lead humanity toward an enhanced economy and society made possible by exciting scientific advances in New Energy research and development. Our primary task is to encourage intelligent public debate and action on how best to accelerate these advances, making a rapid transition away from our dangerous dependence on fossil fuels and nuclear power. Our priority is to educate the general public, investors, journalists and energy policy-makers about the necessity to support the development of advanced energy technologies now emerging from the laboratories and work spaces of scientists and inventors all over the world. These powerful New Energy sources include zero-point energy devices, magnetic generators, and advanced hydrogen processes. Coupled with wind, solar, geo-thermal and other conventional alternative technologies, these advanced energy processes must be employed if we are to accomplish the Herculean task of shifting rapidly from our dangerous dependence on polluting technologies to clean, sustainable energy sources. Also see Brian O'Leary, New Age Associations and Societies and newenergymovement.org.

New Physics
See Quantum Physics.

New Thought
Movement started by Phineas Quimby in 1908 that practices spiritual and mental healing. Its purpose is "To teach the infinitude of the Supreme One, the Divinity of man and his infinite possibilities through the creative power of constructive thinking and obedience to the voice of the Indwelling Presence which is our source of inspiration, power, health and prosperity". The people described herein who are related to the New Thought Movement include: William Walker Atkinson, Raymond Charles Barker, Deepak Chopra, Robert Collier, Melinda Cramer, Emma Curtis-Hopkins, Horatio Dresser, Emmet Fox, Edwene Gaines, Neville Goddard, Joel Sol Goldsmith, Stuart Grayson, Ernest Holmes, Orison Swett Marden, Barbara Marx-Hubbard, Victoria Moran, Harry Morgan Moses, Joseph Murphy, Phineas Parkhurst Quimby, Elizabeth Towne, Iyanla Vanzant, Paul Von Ward and Wallace Wattles. Also see Therapeutic Systems and newthoughtalliance.org.

Newberg, Andrew

(1966-) American-born Andrew "Andy" B. Newberg M.D. is assistant professor in the Department of Radiology at the Hospital of the University of Pennsylvania with secondary appointments in the Department of Religious Studies and the Department of Psychiatry. He is board-certified in Internal Medicine, Nuclear Medicine and Nuclear Cardiology. Dr. Newberg is also co-founder and director of the Center for Spirituality and the Neurosciences at the University of Pennsylvania. His current research focuses on the relationship between brain function and mystical or religious experiences. He has written: Why God Won't Go Away: Brain Science and the Biology of Belief, Why We Believe What We Believe: Uncovering Our Biological Need for Meaning, Spirituality and Truth; Born to Believe: God, Science and the Origin of Ordinary and Extraordinary Beliefs How God Changes Your Brain: Breakthrough Findings From a Leading Neuroscientist; and

Words Can Change Your Brain: 12 Conversation Strategies to Build Trust, Resolve Conflict, and Increase Intimacy. Photograph from newswise.com. Also see Recommended Reading, Scientists, andrewnewberg.com and uphs.upenn.edu/ radiology/research/labs/csm.

Newbrough, John

(1828-1891) American-born John Ballou Newbrough M.D., D.D.S. was a physician, dentist, clairvoyant and psychic. He attended the Cincinnati Medical College. He was a trustee of the New York Spiritualist Association and was well known for his psychic gifts. He could paint in total darkness, channel automatic writing and read pages from any book in a library without seeing the book. He established a community to care for orphans called Faithists of the Seed of Abraham but a year later an outbreak of influenza devastated the area and killed Newbrough himself. He wrote books on religious philosophy and is best known for: Oahspe: A Kosmon Bible in the Words of Jehovah and his Angel Ambassadors: A Sacred History of the Dominions of the Higher and Lower Heavens on Earth for the Past Twenty Four Thousand Years and The Book of Light: A Religion for Today: Being Seven Books, Containing Essential Spiritual Wisdom From Oashspe. Also see Automatic Writing, Clairvoyants and Spiritualists.

Newton, Isaac

(1642-1727) British-born Sir Isaac Newton was a mathematician, physicist, astronomer, alchemist, Hermeticist, natural philosopher and theologian. He is considered one of the most influential men in history. Sir Newton was a member of Parliament for the University of Cambridge to the Convention Parliament and served as Warden of the Royal Mint and later as Master of the Mint. He was knighted in Cambridge in 1705. He is considered the founder of modern physical science. He is mentioned in the Dossier Secrets as the Grand Master of the Prieure de Sion. Sir Newton is depicted here in a 1702 painting by German-born British artist Sir Godfrey Kneller. Also see Alchemists, Dossier Secrets, Hermeticists, Philosophers, Physicists, Prieure de Sion, Theologians and newton.ac.uk.

Newton, Michael

American-born Michael Newton Ph.D. is a certified master hypnotherapist with a Ph.D. in counseling psychology, member of the American Counseling Association, and founder of the Society for Spiritual Regression, now The Newton Institute for Life Between Lives Hypnotherapy. He has worked as a behavioral counselor and group therapy director for spiritual renewal organizations and metal health centers and is considered a pioneer in discovering the mysteries about life after death through Spiritual Regression. Dr. Newton received the National Association of Transpersonal Hypnotherapists annual award of "Most unique contribution by a hypnotherapist" in 1998 for his work on soul memory research and mapping the cosmology of the afterlife. He has written three best

selling books (that have been translated into 25 languages): Journey of Souls: Case Studies of Life Between Lives; Life Between Lives: Hypnotherapy for Spiritual Regression and Destiny of Souls: New Case Studies of Life Between Lives. Photograph from eastonhypnosis.com. Also see Newton Institute for Life Between Lives Hypnotherapy, Recommended Reading, Regression Therapy, Reincarnation (Life After Life), netwoninstitute.org and spiritualregression.org.

Newton Institute, The

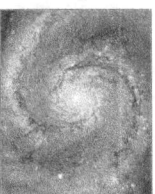

The Newton Institute for Life Between Lives Hypnotherapy (or TNI) began as The Society for Spiritual Regression but changed its name to honor its founder. The Institute is (in their own words) the home of certified practitioners who provide the experience of Life Between Lives Hypnotherapy to individuals throughout the world who wish to find out more about their immortal identity. Life Between Lives Hypnotherapy is a method, pioneered by Michael Newton, using a deep state of hypnosis, whereby individuals can access soul memories. For hidden within are memories of your life as a soul, between incarnations, your life with soul friends and family, planning your future lives on earth. This technique offers you an opportunity to experience a trance-induced "superconscious" state of awareness that brings a deep sense of love, compassion and an understanding of your life purpose. Everyone's experience is unique and personal so you can be confident of a spiritual journey that will fulfill your own needs and wishes. Also see New Age Associations and Societies, newtoninstitute.org and spiritualregression.org.

Nguruvilu

In Araucanian Mapuche (Chile) mythology, Nguruvilu, from nguru meaning "fox" and filu meaning "snake" is a water creature found in rivers and lakes. It is said to prowls in the waters creating whirlpools to drown unwary victims. Other spellings include Guirivilo, Guruvilu, Ñuruvilu, Ñirivilu, and Nirivilo. Image by Amiacon. Also see Mythological Creatures.

Niamh

Celtic Goddess of Beauty and Brightness, daughter of Manannan, Niamh, which means "radiance or brightness", is also called Niamh of the Golden Hair. She is usually depicted as a beautiful woman with long golden hair riding her white horse. Shown here is a painting by Serbian artist Bojana Dimitrovski (bojanadimitrovski.com) called Oisin and Niamh. Also see Celtic Gods and Goddesses.

Nichols, Ross

(1902-1975) English-born Philip Peter Ross Nichols aka Nuinn (magical name) was a poet, artist, historian, occultist, author and Cambridge academic who founded the Order of Bards, Ovates and Druids. He received his M.A. in History at Oxford University and was a member and chairman of the Ancient Druid Order, when the order divided in 1964 he became the chief of the Order of Bards, Ovates and Druids. Friend of Gerald Gardner he chose to revive Druidry and Celtic spirituality while Gardner revived Wicca. He traveled all over the world studying and sketching archeological remains and ancient monuments. His best known books are: Prose Chant Proems, The Cosmic Shape: An Interpretation of Myth and Legend, With Three Poems and Lyrics; Sassenach Stray: A Set of Eight Variations and Tailpiece; Seasons at War: A Cycle of Rhythms; and The Book of Druidry published posthumously. Also see Druidism, Historians, Occultists, Order of Bards, Ovates and Druids, Poets, and druidry.org.

Nicksa

Elemental King, Nicksa rules over the element of Water and the Water Elementals, which are: Mermaids, Mermen, and Undines. He is usually depicted with a crown of shells carrying a trident. Other spellings include Necksa and Niksa. Also see Elemental Kings and Elementals.

Nictalopes

Name given to people who can see in the dark.

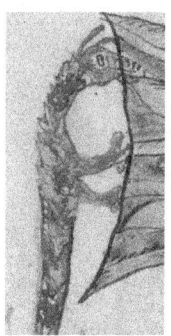

Nidhogg

In Norse mythology, Nidhogg meaning "tearer of corpses" is a monstrous serpent or dragon that gnaws almost perpetually at the deepest root of the world tree Yggdrasil. Nidhogg is depicted here in a 17th Century Icelandic manuscript. Also see Mythological Creatures, and Yggdrasil.

Nidra

In Hindu mythology, Nidra is the Goddess and personification of sleep. Also see Hindu Gods and Goddesses.

Nifelheim

In Norse mythology, Nifelheim or land of the mist, wet and cold, is one the Nine Worlds make up the universe and are guarded by Odhin. Nifelheim which is also known as the World Beneath the Worlds, (one of the underworlds) is the abode of Hel. Other spellings include Niflheim. Also see Mythological Places, and Nine Worlds.

Nightingale, Earl

(1921-1989) American-born Earl Nightingale was a famous radio motivational speaker and later TV host as well as entrepreneur, author and one of the greatest philosophers of his time. His radio program Our Changing World was the most highly syndicated radio program ever. In his lifetime Nightingale recorded over 7,000 radio programs, 250 audio programs as well as others. The most famous of his audio programs was called The Strangest Secret. In 1985 he was inducted into the Association of National Broadcasters Radio Hall of Fame. His book Earl Nightingale's Greatest Discovery: The Strangest Secret - Revisited won the Napoleon Hill Gold Metal for Literary Excellency. He also wrote This Is Earl Nightingale and The Earl Nightingale Program: Our Changing World. Shown here is a photograph taken in1986. Also see Philosophers, Recommended Reading, Self-Help and earlnightingale.com.

Nike

Greek Goddess of Victory, Nike represented success in all undertakings especially in athletics, music and battle. She is worshiped by the Romans under the name Victoria. Nike assumed the role of the Zeus' personal charioteer. Also see Greek Gods and Goddesses. Shown here is a statue of Nike discovered in Samothrace by an unknown artist from 220-190 B.C.E.

Niliahah

In the Qabbalah, Niliahah is described as a poet Angel who is in charge of occult sciences, he delivers prophesies in rhymes and rules over wise men who love peace and solitude. Also see Angels.

Nimbus

The Nimbus is described as a circle of luminosity that surrounds the bodies of Saints, Deities and Angels. The Nimbus is depicted here in a 1660 painting by Spanish artist Bartolomeo Esteban Murillo called The Immaculate Conception. Also see Aura, Celestial Light, and Halo.

Nine Worlds

In Norse cosmology, the Nine Worlds, also called Yggdrasil, are the planes of existence of the universe. These Nine Worlds are guarded by Odhin and the Valkyries, they are: In the Upper Realm: Asgard, the abode of the Aesir, ruled by Odhin, Chief of the Norse Gods; Vanaheim, home of the Vanir Gods; and Alfheim, home of the Elves and Dwarfs, ruled by Freyr. Below, connected to the Upper Realm by Bifrost, the Rainbow Bridge are: Jotunheim, home of the Giants; Midgard, meaning "middle earth," and referring to the physical plane or abode of man (Midgard is surrounded by the ocean, the world of the serpent Jormungand); and Svartalfaheim, home of the Dark Dwarfs and Elves. The

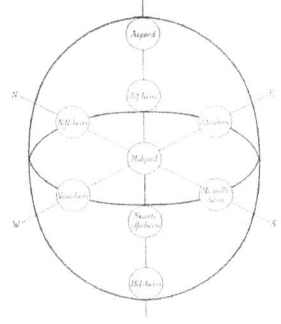

lowest level, Land of the Dead or Underworld, also has three Realms: Nifelheim, land of the Dark, Mist, Wet and Cold, ruled by Hel; Muspelheim, realm of the fire giants; and Hel, abode of the dead. Also see Mythological Places, Odhin, Valkyries, and Yggdrasil.

Ningal

In Sumerian mythology, Ningal, whose name means "Great Lady", is the daughter of Enki, the wife of Sin and mother of Inanna, Ereshkigal and Shamash. Shown here is a 2004 painting by Russian artist Yuri Yudaev of an ancient relief of Ur in front of the Goddess Ningal, housed in the Philadelphia University Museum in Philadelphia, PA. Also see Sumerian Gods and Goddesses.

Ninhursag

In Babylonian Mythology, Ninhursag is the Mother of the Gods. She is the daughter of Anu and lover of Enki. Ninhursag is also called Queen of the Mountainhead. Other spellings include Nerig and Nirig. Shown here is a statue of brick terracotta from the 12th Century BCE found at the Tell of the Apadana in Susa in Iran and housed in the Louvre Museum in Paris, France. Also see Babylonian Gods and Goddesses.

Ninib

In Babylonian Mythology, Ninib is the God of Spring and Vegetation. He is also the God who opposed Marduk. Other spellings include Nirig and Nerig. Also see Babylonian Gods and Goddesses.

Ninurta

In Assyrian, Sumerian and Babylonian Mythology, Ninurta is the God of War and the Weather, especially thunderstorms. He is also the God of Hunting and the husband of Gula. He is also known as the Patron of the Physicians. Also see Assyrian Mythology, Babylonian Gods and Goddesses, and Sumerian Gods and Goddesses.

Nirmana-Kaya

See Trikaya.

Nirvana

From the Hinduism, Nirvana is the blissful state of union with the Divine, the ultimate goal to discharge karmic debt and the need to reincarnate and the obliteration of the ego and self. A Buddhist Abbot named Sumangala described Nirvana as "a condition of peace and blessedness so high above our present state that it is impossible for us to understand it". Nirvana has been described by Occultists and Theosophists as a state of peace in omniscience achieved with the final extinction of individuality without loss of consciousness. Shown here is a painting by Canadian artist Mario Duguay called The Door to the Heart. Also see Enlightenment, Illumination, Moksha, Satori and Spiritual Goals.

Njord

Norse God of the Sea, Njord has dominion over fishing, sailors, navigation, livestock, prosperity, lands, sea, fire, wind, wisdom and stubbornness. He is the husband of Skadi and the father of Freyr and Freyja. He gives good fortune to sailors and hunters and is invoked for prosperity. Njord is one of the Aesir (Gods) of Odhin. Njord is depicted here from the 1893 Poetic Edda by Swedish artist Carl Frederick von Stalza. Other spellings include Njor and Njoror. Also see Aesir, and Norse Gods and Goddesses.

Nobel Prize Laureates

The people included herein who are Nobel Prize Laureates include: the Dalai Lama, Richard, Phillips Feynman, Thich Nhat Hanh, Mother Teresa, Charles Richet and William Butler Yeats. Also see nobelprizes.com.

Noetic

From the Greek nous meaning "mind" the term noetic refers to intellectual activity of the inner mind; or the process from intuitive consciousness or psychic knowing. Also see noetic.org.

Nohochacyum

Maya Creation God he defends humans from evil. Also see Maya Gods and Goddesses.

Nokomis

Algonquin Earth Goddess who nurtures all living things, Nokomis is also called the Grandmother, Sacred Earth Mother and Earth Goddess. Also see Algonquin Gods and Goddesses.

Norns

In Norse mythology, the Norns are Triple Goddesses, three sisters described as old crones who spin destiny and control the past, present and future. They are also called the Weird Sisters. They are: Skuld, meaning "Should"; Urd, meaning "That Which has Become"; and Verdandi, meaning "That Which is Becoming". Shown here in an 1865 rendition painting by German artist Ludwig Pietsch called The Norns. Also see Fates, Norse Gods and Goddesses, and Triple Goddesses.

Norse Gods and Goddesses

The following Norse Gods and Goddesses are described herein: Aegir, Angerboda, Atla, Audhumla, Augeia, Aurgiafa, Balder, Baugi, Bergelmir, Bil, Boda, Bragi, Egia, Eir, Fimila, Fjorgyn, Forseti, Freyja, Freyr, Frigga, Frimla, Fulla, Gefion, Gerda, Gialp, Gna, Greip, Gullveig, Heimdal, Hel, Hermod, Hnossa, Hoder, Hoenir, Holda, Horn, Idunn, Jarsaxa, Jord, Loki, Mimir, Nanna, Nehallennia, Nerthus, Njord, Odhin, Ran, Saga, Sif, Sigyn, Sindur, Skadi, Skud, Syn, Thor, Tyr, Ulfrun, Ull, Urd, Vali, Valkyries, Verdandi, Vidar, Vilur and Wayland. Shown here is a painting an 1800 painting of Norse Gods by French artist Francois Gerard called Ossian Awakening the Spirits.

North Pole

The North Pole one of the twelve areas known as the Vile Vortices which is described as areas around the world said to have the same qualities as the famous Bermuda Triangle. In these areas strange phenomena are reported such as compasses and other instruments going crazy and ships and planes disappearing. Image from dailyplanetmedia.com. See Vile Vortices.

North Star

In Pawnee mythology, North Star is a benevolent creator God. His opposite is South Star. Also see Pawnee Gods and Goddesses.

Northrup, Christiane

American-born Christiane Northrup M.D. is a gynecologist, obstetrician, author and lecturer. She is internationally known and described as a visionary in women's holistic health issues. Dr. Northrup maintains an e-community known as The Women's Wisdom Circle. She says that she spent the first half of her life studying what can go wrong with the female body and how to fix it and the second half of her life to illuminating everything that can go right. She has written several best selling books including: Women's Bodies, Women's Wisdom: Creating Physical and Emotional Health and Healing (which has been translated into 15 languages); Mother Daughter Wisdom: Creating A Legacy of Physical and Emotional Health; A Healthy Woman's Life: Dr. Christiane Northrup's Seven-Step Program to Creating Health Daily and The Secret Pleasures of Menopause. Also see Holistic Healing Recommended Reading, Self-Help and for audio and video programs see drnorthrup.com.

Nostradamus

(1503-1566) French-born Michel de Nostredame aka Nostradamus was a physician, astrologer, magician, and prophet. Born to a Jewish family who converted to Catholicism, he was first known for his innovative medical treatments during the plague of 1546-47 where he lost his first wife and two children. He married again later and had six children. Legend says that as a young man traveling in Italy he met a group of Franciscan friars whom he greeted by kneeling in front of the youngest monk, Felice Perreti. When asked why; he said he had to kneel before His Holiness. Years later, after his own death, in 1585, Felice Perreti became Pope Sixtus the Fifth. Nostradamus was also physician to Kings Henry II, Francis II and Charles IX. He is mostly known for writing a series of verses that he published under the title of Centuries and Presages aka The Prophesies of Nostradamus, which among some other 1,500 prophesies, predicted the French Revolution and World War II. Shown here is an 1842 portrait of Nostradamus. Also see Astrologers, Prophets, Recommended Reading and nostradamus.org.

Notarikon

In ancient Hebrew mysticism, Notarikon is one of three ancient methods used by Qabbalists to derive more spiritual and esoteric meanings from The Bible by rearranging words and sentences. The other two methods are Gematria and Temurah. Image from hebrew4christians.com. Also see Divination, Gematria and Temurah.

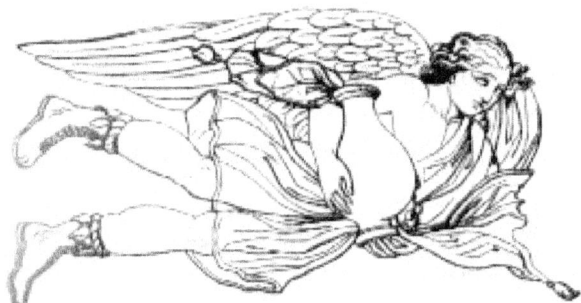

Notus

Greek God of the South Wind who brings the storms of late summer and autumn and rules over change, passion, happiness and rain. Notus is one of the four Anemoi or Gods of the Winds. He is the son of Aeolus and Eos. Other spellings include Notos. Shown here is an 1874 depiction of Notus from Dr. Vollmer's book on Mythology. Also see Anemoi, and Greek Gods and Goddesses.

Nous

The Rosicrucians define Nous as "that energy, power and force emanating from the source of all life, possessing positive and negative polarities, manifesting it in vibrations of various rates of speed, which, under certain conditions and obeying the dictates of natural law, establish the world of form, be that form visible or invisible". Also see Psychic Energies.

Nous

In Occult Philosophy nous is the spirit or mind, the first and most sublime of emanations from the Godhead.

Nox

In Roman mythology, Nox is the Goddess of the Night. She is the Mother of the Day and the Light and of Dreams and Death. She is the daughter of Chaos, the

sister of Erebus and the mother of Aether and Hemera. Nox is depicted here is an 1883 painting by French artist William-Adolphe Bouguereau (bouguereau.org) called La Nuit. Also see Roman Gods and Goddesses.

Nuada

Celtic God of Magic, Nuada rules over historians, harpers, poets, writing, healing and warfare. He is also known as a Sea God and King of the Tuatha de Dannan. Other spellings include Nodens and Nudd. Nuada is also called the Silver Arm. Shown here is a 1978 depiction of Nuada by Irish artist Jim Fitzpatrick (jimfizpatrick.ie) called Nuada the High King. Also see Celtic Gods and Goddesses, and Tuatha de Danaan.

Nucklavee

In Scottish mythology, Nuckelavees are sea creatures described as monstrous sea horses with flippers for feet and a single red eye in the middle of the forehead. Also see Cryptids, Hippocampus, and Mythological Creatures.

Nuit

Egyptian Goddess of the Sky, specifically the Night Sky, Nuit represents the fullness of the cosmos. She is the daughter of Tefnut and Shu, sister of Geb and mother of Osiris, Isis, Seth and Nephthys. She swallows the sun every evening and gives birth to it every morning. Nuit is depicted stretching from horizon to horizon with only her fingertips and feet touching the ground. She is also called the Brilliant, the Great, the Great Protectress and She of Long Hair. Other spellings include Nathor, Nuith, Nut, and Nwt. Also see Egyptian Gods and Goddesses.

Numen

In ancient Rome the Numen is a divine spirit or power whose presence is perceived as occult power. Also see Supernatural and Spiritual Beings.

Numerology

Also called numeromancy, numerology is an occult divination system based on the idea that the universe is constructed mathematically and that all things can be expressed in numbers. Numerology was described by Pythagoras who believed that all relations could be reduced to number relations or as he said "all things are numbers". The Buddhist, Hindu and Chinese, among others have elaborate divination systems based on mystical numerological correspondences. Also see Divination, Gematria, astrology-numerology.com and starlightnumerology.com.

Numeromancy

See Numerology.

Numina

From Latin numen meaning "presence", numina refers to the manifestation of power or will of a God or spirit that affects places and objects and is observable by the occurrence of natural phenomena. One of the most recognizable examples of numina is the biblical story of Moses. Shown here is an 19th Century painting by English poet and artist William Blake (william-blake.org) called Moses and the Burning Bush.

Numinous

Supernatural, divine, spiritual, sacred and mysterious, numinous refers to a sense or feeling of awe-inspiring wonder of the presence of the divinity or spiritual beings.

Nushu

In China up until last Century, only men learned to read and write, or so they thought. Nushu was a language invented by women and known only to women for hundreds of years. This language is basically the same as Chinese writing but with fewer characters. Women communicated by sending each other embroidered fans, napkins, shawls and other cloth objects with secret messages embedded.

Nyaya

From the Sanskrit meaning "rule" or "method", Nyaya is one of the six Darshans from Hindu philosophy. Nyaya is considered both a philosophy and religion. Its principal text is the Nyaya-sutras which is attributed to Prince Gautama. Nyaya's ultimate goal is to free man from the bondages of matter which came about due to ignorance and illusion, by means of the right knowledge. The modern Nyaya schools teach that there are four ways to obtain the right knowledge: perception, inference, comparison and testimony. As with all other Darshans, the goal of Nyaya is that of spiritual enlightenment. Also see Darshan, and Spiritual Goals.

Nyingpo

Tibetan name for the World Soul. Also see Gaia.

Nymphaeum

In ancient Greece and Rome a nymphaeum was a monument consecrated and dedicated to the nymphs. Many of the nymphaeums were natural grottoes believed to be inhabited by local nymphs. Most nymphaeums furnished fresh water, either from natural springs or by man-made supply. Shown here is the Jerash Nymphaeum constructed in 191 B.C.E. in Joerash, Jordan. Photograph taken by Frederick Questier in 2005.

Nymphs

In Greek and Roman mythology, Nymphs are lesser female Deities, who live in and around groves and fountains, forests, streams, meadows and the sea. They are described as young and beautiful, amorous and gentle maidens, fond of music and dancing. The Nymphs are depicted here in an 1878 painting by French artist William-Adolphe Bouguereau (bouguereau.org) called Nymphaneum. The Nymphs described herein are:

Earth Nymphs: Dryads, Forests; Hamadryads, Trees; Napaeae, Mountains and Valleys; and Oreads, Mountains and Grottoes. Shown here is a 1660 painting by Dutch artist Caesar van Everdingen called Bacchus with Nymphs and Cupid.

Water Nymphs: Naiads, Freshwater Streams and Ponds; Nereids, Mediterranean Sea; Oceanids, Oceans; and Potameides, Rivers. Shown here is a 19th Century painting by French artist Paul Albert Laurens called Catching Waves. Also see Elementals, Fairies, Mythological Creatures, and Nature Spirits.

Oannes

In ancient Chaldean mythology Oannes were fish-headed beings from another world. They were considered Sea Gods and lived with men by day teaching them art, science and religion and building the great Sumerian civilization and by night returning to the Persian Gulf and swimming into the sunset. Shown here is a depiction of Oannes from I. P. Cory's 1832 book called Ancient Fragments. Also see Cryptids, and Mythological Creatures.

Oates, David John

Australian-born David John Oates is a certified hypnotherapist and trainer and the founder of Reverse Speech. In the twenty odd year studies on reverse speech he has designed therapeutic and training techniques and has published several books, including: Reverse Speech: Voices From The Unconscious; Its Only A Metaphor; Reverse Speech: Hidden Messages in Human Communication; and Beyond Backward Masking: Reverse Speech and the Voice of the Inner Mind. Oates lectures around the world and has hosted his own show The David John Oates Reverse Speech Show. Photograph from reversespeech.com.au. Also see Electronic Voice Phenomena, Recommended Reading, Reverse Speech, davidoates.com and reversespeech.com.

OBE

Out of Body Experience. See Astral Projection.

Obeah

Also called Obi, Obeah refers to the religious practices and folk magic in the West Indies and many Caribbean countries. It is based on both white and black magic. Obeah is similar to Santeria, and Voodoo. Also see Religions.

OBOD

See Order of Bards, Ovates and Druids.

Obsession

According to Occultists, obsession is described as a cutting off of the higher will from the lower or conscious will, which is induced by evil thoughts or extreme fear from the spiritual consciousness. This in turn ends up in the withdrawal of a soul from its sphere of sensation and its replacement or complete domination by another soul, human or other. When this is done on purpose the method employed is to flatter the lower will until access to the sphere of sensation is established and then applying strain on the lower will until it is weakened allowing the passage of the force behind the obsession.

Occult

From the Latin occulere, occult means "to hide" or "to cover up". Occult wisdom means secret wisdom or knowledge that should be kept hidden, not be revealed to the non-initiated. Occult knowledge has also been defined as divine wisdom that can only be communicated or acknowledged from within.

Occult Orders

Also known as Fraternities, Societies, Schools, Orders, Organizations or Brotherhoods, Occult Orders are schools wherein a secret knowledge unknown to the common man may be learned. Admission to these orders requires initiation where tests and rituals take place as a general rule and where oaths of secrecy and silence are made. Shown here is Eliphas Levi's Great Symbol of Solomon from his 1855 book Transcendental Magic. Also see Occult Orders, Brotherhoods and Secret Societies and knowledgefiles.com.

Occult Orders, Brotherhoods and Secret Societies

Of the many Occult Orders, Brotherhoods and Secret Societies, the following are described herein: Alpha et Omega, Benandanti, Cathars, Church of the Light, Fraternity of the Inner Light, Freemasonry, Germaeorden, Golden Dawn, Hermetic Brotherhood of Luxor, Illuminati, Knights Templar, Martinism, Order of Bards, Ovates and Druids, Order of Skull and Bones, Ordo Templi Orientis, Prieure de Sion, Rosicrucian Order, Servants of the Light, Society of Friends, Society of the Inner Light, Stella Matutina, Temple of Ara, Thelema and Theosophical Society. Shown here is a 1659 drawing by Basilius

Valentinus from the book Azoth of the Philosophers called Visita Interiora Terra Rectificanto Inveniens Occultum Lapidem, meaning "Visit the interior of the earth and rectifying you will find the hidden stone". Also see knowledgefiles.com.

Occult Powers
See Psychic Abilities.

Occult Virtues
The occult virtues relate to the magical properties found in herbs, gemstones, metals and other objects. Also see and Natural Magic.

Occultism

Defined as an extension of psychology and science, the study of the occult has, throughout human history occurred in all societies. It is the study and practice of that which is hidden or secret, pertaining to magic, esoteric studies, the higher powers of the mind and the manipulation of energies which are invisible and normally imperceptible. It has also described as a branch of knowledge which is hidden from the many and reserved for the few, a wisdom that is kept secret so as to be kept pure. Shown here is the 1855 Occultist and Magician's Pentagram by French occultist Eliphas Levi. Also see Esoterism and Occultists.

Occultists
An Occultist is a student, practitioner or adept of the Occult sciences; one who practices Occultism. The people described herein include the following Occultists: Heinrich Cornelius Agrippa, Apollonius of Tyana, Dolores Ashcroft-Nowicki, Mary Ann Atwood, Samael Aun Weor, Guy Warren Ballard, Franz Bardon, Francis Barrett, Annie Besant, Algernon Blackwood, Helena Blavatsky, Jacob Bohme, Robert Boyle, Giordano Bruno, Walter Ernest Butler, Count Alessandro di Cagliostro, Paul Foster Case, Pietro d'Abano, Arthur Conan Doyle, James Churchward, Pamela Colman-Smith, D. J. Conway, Antoine Court de Gebelin, Stanislas de Guaita, Louis de Nevers, John Dee, Florence Farr, Robert Felkin, Simon Forman, Dion Fortune, Gerald Gardner, Francesco Giorgi, William G. Gray, John Michael Greer, Rene Guenon, George Gurdjieff, Manly Palmer Hall, Annie Horniman, William Quan Judge, King Solomon, Carl Jung, Gareth Knight, Arnoldo Krumm-Heller, Charles Leadbeater, Sybil Leek, Eliphas Levi, Harvey Spencer Lewis, William Lilly, Guido von List, Arthur Machen, Moina Mathers, S.L. MacGregor Mathers, Franz Mesmer, Ross Nichols, Henry Olcott, Papus, Israel Regardie, Dane Rudhyar, Mouni Sadhu, Count Saint-Germain, Joseph-Alexandre Saint-Yves, Cyril Scott, Charles Richard Seymour, Idries Shah, Alfred Percy Sinnett, Austin Osman Spare, Thomas Spence, Rudolf Steiner, Max Theon, Valentin Tomberg, Johannes Trithemius, Arthur Edward Waite, Johann Weyer, Charles Williams, John Yarker, William Butler Yeats and C. C. Zain. Also see Occultism.

Oceanids

In Greek and Roman mythology, the Oceanids are Nymphs of the Ocean, daughters of Oceanus and Tethys. There are over 3,000 Oceanids. Shown here is an 1860 painting of Oceanids by French artist Gustave Dore (gustavedoreart.com) called Las Oceanides. Also see Nymphs.

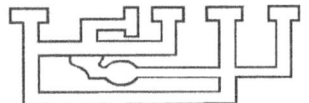

Oceanus

Greek God of the Sea; one of the Titans, Oceanus is the eldest son of Uranus and Gaea, and the father of the Oceanids. Together with his sister-wife Tethys, he rules over the ocean. He is the inventor of the arts and magic and his powers are later passed on to Poseidon. Oceanus is also known as He who Belongs to the Swift Queen. He is depicted as having the upper body of a muscular man with horns and a long beard and the lower body of a serpent. Oceanus is shown here from the Trevi Fountain in Rome, Italy. Other spellings include Oceanos and Okeanos. Also see Greek Gods and Goddesses, and Titans.

Och

Olympian Spirit who governs the Sun and other provinces of the Universe. See Olympian Spirits.

Oculomancy

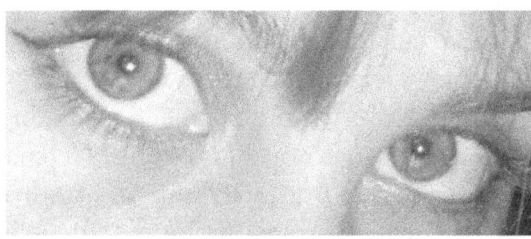

Divination by the eyes, oculomancy, which is also a form of scrying, studies the reflections and shadows of the eyes. Photograph taken by Arleen Fernandez. Also see Divination, and Scrying.

Odhin

Nordic God of War and Wisdom, Odhin rules Heaven and Earth, storms, rain, harvest, runes, poetry, magic, words of power, divination, initiation, music, prophesy, wisdom, war, inspiration, horses, medicine, fate, and death. He is one of the triad of Deities together with Thor and Freyr. He rules over the Aesir and presides over banquets of those slain in battle. On his shoulders perch two ravens, Hugin, meaning "thought" and Munin, meaning "memory" that can fly about all the worlds to bring him knowledge. He is also known as Protector of Heroes, Patron of Poets, God of the Wild Hunt, Father of the Gods and King of Gods. Odhin has a magical horse named Sleipnir who has eight legs and teeth inscribed with runes with the special ability to gallop through the air and over the sea. Other spellings include Odin, Odhinn, Odinn, Othinn, Voden, Wodin, Woden, Wodan, and Wotan. Odhin is depicted here with his two ravens (Huginn and Muninn) and his two wolves (Geri and Freki) in an 1888 depiction by German artist Johannes Gehrts. Also see Aesir, Gods of Heaven, and Norse Gods and Goddesses.

Odic Force

Term introduced by Carl Reichenback for an all-penetrating energy or force that he said emanates from everything from humans (where he said the strongest emanations came from the mouth, hands and forehead) to crystals and magnets. He stated that this force emanates from every object in the universe including the Sun and the Moon and that its outer rim on the aura protects humans from the assaults of evil spirits. The Odic Force has also been called the Odic Light, Odic Shield and Odyllic Force. Also see Psychic Energies and Carl Reichenback.

Odin

As the 25th symbol of the runes, Odin represents the unknowable. Also see Runes.

O'Donnell, Michele

American-born Michele O'Donnell, R.N. is a holistic health care provider, author, spiritual counselor and Minister. After training as a registered nurse she completed two years of undergraduate work at Case Western University in Cleveland, Ohio and spent several years in the pediatric intensive care, emergency room and coronary care units. She later attended a three year Bible college and was ordained a non-denominational charismatic faith. She founded the Holistic Health Care Center in San Antonio, Texas where she currently provides physical, spiritual and emotional healing treatment for degenerative diseases and well as speaking internationally. She has written Of Monkeys and Dragons: Freedom from the Tyranny of Disease; The God That We've Created: The Basic Cause of All Disease; and When the Wolf is At the Door: The Simplicity of Healing. Also see Holistic Healing, Recommended Reading, Spiritual Teachers, livingbeyonddisease.com and micheleodonnell.com.

Offering

An offering is a ritual gift or sacrifice to a God, spirit or supernatural being. Offerings have been made for religious and magical purposes in most cultures throughout the history of the world. Shown here is a 1912 painting by British artist John William Godward (johnwilliamgodward.org) called An Offering to Venus. Also see Libation, Magical Methods and Sacrifice.

Offshore Rio de Janeiro

Offshore Rio de Janeiro in Brazil in an area called the Rio Grande Rise there is one of the twelve areas known as the Vile Vortices which is described as areas with the same qualities as the famous Bermuda Triangle, where strange phenomena are reported such as compasses and other instruments going crazy, strange lights on the ocean and in the sky and ships and planes disappearing. Image from orangesmile.com. See Vile Vortices.

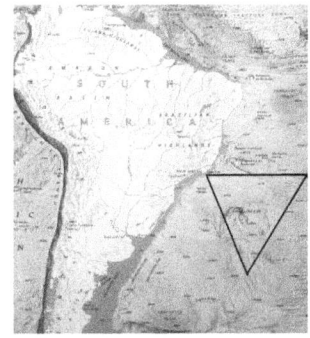

Ogdoas

In Gnosticism, Ogdoas are described as a group of the highest heavenly powers. Also see Supernatural and Spiritual Beings.

Ogham

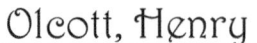

Celtic alphabet, Ogham consists of twenty letters, each letter consisting of one to five strokes or lines in a certain position and each letter also representing a tree. Pieces of wood with Ogham writing were used for divination and secret communications. Ogham has been found on stone monuments in Scotland, Ireland and Wales, attributed to the Druids. Other spellings include Ogam and Ogun. Ogham is also called the Magical Fairy Alphabet. Also see ogham.lyberty.com.

Ogma

Celtic God of Poets and War, Ogma rules over writers, eloquence, literature, language, inspiration, magic, spells, arts, music and reincarnation. He is also known as the Sun Face. Ogma is also called Grianainech and Cermait. Other spellings include Ogham, Oghma and Ogmios. Also see Celtic Gods and Goddesses.

Ogre

In Occult lore an Ogre is described as an evil Earth Elemental large and hideous in appearance. An Ogre is shown here in a 1624 painting by Italian artist Giovanni Lanfranco called Norandino and Lucina Discovered by the Ogre. Also see Elementals.

Oimelc

See Imbolc.

Olcott, Henry

(1832-1907) American-born Colonel Henry Steel Olcott was an attorney and philosopher, one of the founding members of the Theosophical Society and closest collaborator to Madame Helena Blavatsky. Olcott also worked with fellow occultist Annie Besant in establishing the Central Hindu College at Varanasi in India where he taught Theosophy. Among the curiosities of his life was the occasion is which he participated together with two other men in the investigation of the murder of Abraham Lincoln. Olcott was also well known in India and Ceylon (Sri Lanka) where he performed magnetic healing and was described by a Prime Minister as "one of the heroes in the struggle for independence". He was co-founder and president of the Theosophical Society and after Madame Blavatsky's death, close collaborator of Annie Besant. He spent much of his life traveling, lecturing and establishing new branches of the Theosophical Society. He wrote: A Collection of Lectures on Theosophy and Archaic Religions. Also see Occultists, Philosophers, Recommended Reading, Theosophical Society, Theosophists and theosophical.org.

Old Souls

Old souls refers to persons who are more spiritually advanced than many, those who have incarnated many times on the Earth. Also see Spiritual Teachers.

O'Leary, Brian

(1940-2011) American-born Brian O'Leary Ph.D. was a scientist-astronaut, author and philosopher who described himself as a passionate environmentalist and practical visionary open to innovative solutions. He worked for NASA and was assistant professor of astronomy at Cornel University. He received his Ph.D. in astronomy from the University of California Berkeley. He was special consultant to the U.S. House of Representatives Subcommittee on Energy and the Environment. Dr. O'Leary researched, lectured and written about the new paradigms of science and global transformation; his most recent teaching post was a course Science, Ecology, Ethics and Consciousness at the University of Philosophical Research in Los Angeles. He moved to Ecuador in 2004 where he co-founded with his artist wife Meredith Miller the Montesuenos Conference and Bed & Breakfast center dedicated to peace, sustainability, the arts and new science. He wrote over ten books including: The Second Coming of Science: An Intimate Report of the New Science; Miracle in the Void; The Energy Solution Revolution; and his latest book Re-Inheriting the Earth: Awakening to Sustainable Solutions and Greater Truths. Also see New Energy Movement, Recommended Reading, Scientists, montesuenos.org and brianoleary.info.

Olga

Spirit guide said to be channeled through medium Rudi Schneider of the Schneider Brothers. Also see Channeled Spirit Guides, Channelers, and Schneider Brothers.

Oliver, John J.

American-born John J. Oliver is a renowned psychic. He has participated as a psychic consultant in hundreds of police investigations, has been giving personal readings (over 13,000) and helped in ghost investigations for many years. He taught psychic development at the University Union at the University of Virginia and at J. Sergeant Renolds College's Continuing Education Department in Richmond Virginia for seven years. He has also presented thousands of seminars throughout the United States and Europe. Oliver has also stared in the television shows Haunting Evidence and FBI Psychic Investigators. Also see Psychics, Readings and johnjoliver.com.

Olympian Gods

In Greek mythology, the Olympian Gods are the thirteen major Gods who live on Mount Olympus in Greece. They are:

Aphrodite, Goddess of Sexual Love and Beauty; Apollo, God of Prophesy and Punishment; Ares, God of War; Artemis, Goddess of Magic; Athene, Goddess of War; Demeter, Goddess of Harvest and Crops; Hades, God of the Underworld; Hephaestus, God of the Fire; Hera, Goddess of Heaven; Hermes, God of Magic and Philosophy; Hestia, Goddess of the Hearth and Fire; Poseidon, God of the Sea, and Zeus, Supreme God and Chief of the Olympian Gods. Shown above is a 1624 painting called The Council of the Gods by Flemish artist Peter Paul Rubens (peterpaulrubens.org). Also see Greek Gods and Goddesses, and Mount Olympus.

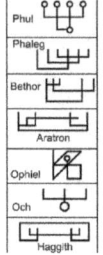

Olympian Spirits

According to the Arbatel, the Olympian Spirits are spirits who dwell in air and space and govern provinces into which the universe is divided. The Olympian Spirits are also called the Stewards of Heaven. There are seven Olympian Spirits:

Arathron, who governs Saturn;

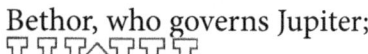

Bethor, who governs Jupiter;

Hagith, who governs Venus;

Och, who governs the Sun;

Ophiel, who governs Mercury;

Phaleg, who governs Mars; and

Phul, who governs the Moon.

Also see Supernatural and Spiritual Beings.

O'More, Malachy
See Malachy Prophesies.

Om

From Sanskrit meaning God, Om is a sacred word to Hindi and Occultists believed to have mystical and magical powers. Om is commonly used in prayer and meditation and it symbolizes the cosmic cycle. It is considered the greatest of all mantras, embodying the essence of the entire universe. Other spellings include Aum. Also see mantra and om-sweet-om.net.

Om

Gnostic name for Father God.

Om Mani Padme Hum

From Lamaism, the most famous of the mantras. Buddhists believe that saying the mantra out loud or silently invokes the powerful benevolent attention and blessings of Avalokitesvara, the Patron Saint of Tibet and embodiment of compassion. See Mantras. Also see om-sweet-om.net.

Omacatl

In Aztec mythology, Omacatl is the God of Happiness. He is the brother of Quetzalcoatl and he rules over joy and festivity and is worshiped by the rich and sick. Shown here is a depiction of Omacatl from the 16th Century Codex Florentine. Also see Aztec Gods and Goddesses.

Omega Institute for Holistic Studies

The Omega Institute for Holistic Studies headquartered in Rhinebeck, New York and also called simply Omega, was founded in 1977 and, as a healing center and through retreats and workshops has been a pioneer teaching, exploring and learning about spiritual growth, self- awareness, health and well being. Also see New Age Associations and Societies, and eomega.org.

Omen

Something (such as an event, phenomenon or sign) perceived or interpreted to be a portent of a good or evil that will influence an event or circumstances in the future. Ancient cultures observed the flight of birds, eclipses, meteors, comets, the movement of clouds and storms and the paths or actions of certain sacred animals as Omens. Photograph taken by Heather Eaton. Also see Methods of Prediction.

Ometecuhtli

In Aztec mythology, Ometecuhtli is the Supreme God who is the source of all life. He lives outside space and time. Ometecuhtli is the husband of Omecihuatl and the father of Huitzilopochtli, Quetzalcoatl, Tezcatlipoca and Xipe-Totec. He is depicted here with his wife in the pre-Hispanic Codex Fejervary-Mayer. Other spellings include Ometecutli. Also see Aztec Gods and Goddesses.

Ometeotl

Aztec God who embodies positive and negative, male and female, light and dark dualistic sides of life. Ometeotl lives in Omeyocan, the highest of the thirteen heavens. He is also called the God of the Near and Close and He Who Is at the Center. Ometeotl is shown here from the pre-Spanish conquest Codex Borgia. Also see Aztec Gods and Goddesses, and Gods of Heaven.

Omeyocan

Aztec Heaven, Omeyocan is the highest of the thirteen heavens, ruled by Ometeotl. Also see Mythological Places.

Omni

In all ways, in all places, of all things.

Omnipotence

Absolute and unlimited universal power over all things, Omnipotence is the power to do absolutely anything and is attributed to God alone. Omnipotence is also called the Principle of Power.

Omnipresence

Property or power of God to be in all places and all things at all times. Omnipresence is also called the Principle of Substance.

Omniscience

The total and perfect knowledge of God, Omniscience includes all actual things and beings, including the past, present and future. Omniscience is also called the Principle of Mind.

Onatha

Iroquois Goddess of Harvest and Wheat. Other spellings include Onatah. Also see Iroquois Gods and Goddesses.

Oneiromancy
From Greek, oneiros, "dream" and mantis, "diviner", oneiromancy is divination by the interpretation of dreams. It is also called Oniromancy. Shown here is a painting by British artist Josephine Wall (josephinewall.com) called Psyche's Dream. Also see Divination.

Ontology
From the Latin meaning "study of being", ontology is the study of the nature of being and the nature of reality.

OOBE
Out of Body Experience. See Astral Projection.

Oomancy
Divination by eggs, oomancy interprets size, shape and color of eggs, inside and out. Also see Divination.

Ophanim
See Thrones.

Ophians
See Ophites.

Ophiel
Olympian Spirit who governs Mercury and other provinces in the Universe. See Olympian Spirits.

Ophites
From the Greek meaning snake, the Ophites (also called Serpentinians and Ophians) were members of several Gnostics sects in Egypt and Syria around 100 C.E. who existed for several centuries. The word Ophites derives from the Greek ophis meaning "serpent" and relates to the belief that the serpent of the Garden of Eden described in Genesis was a symbol of gnosis (or knowledge) and was revered as such. Shown here is a 14th Century drawing of by French alchemist Nicolas Flamel called Serpent on the Cross. Also see Gnosticism.

Opiel
In Aramaic Incantation Texts from Nippur, Opiel is an Angel invoked in love charms. Also see Angels.

Opochtli

In Aztec mythology, Opochtli is the God of Fishing and Bird Catching. He is depicted as a man painted in black with wild bird feathers on his head. Opochtli is also known as He Who Divides the Waters and the Left Handed One. Opochtli is depicted here in the 16th Century Florentine Codex. Also see Aztec Gods and Goddesses.

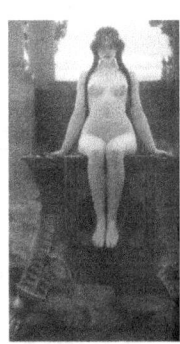

Ops

Roman Goddess of the Harvest, Ops is the wife of Saturn and mother of Jupiter. She is also known as the Goddess of Wealth and Success. Shown here is a 1618 painting called The Union of Earth and Water by Flemish artist Peter Paul Rubens (peterpaulrubens.org). Also see Roman Gods and Goddesses.

Oracle

From the Latin orare meaning "to speak" or "to pray", an oracle is divine communication or divination obtained through a medium or prophet who was associated with a specific place. The Greeks and Romans dedicated shrines to oracles where people went to consult priests/priestesses or prophets/prophetesses. Some of the most famous sites are the Oracle of Zeus at Olympia, the Oracle of Apollo at Delphi and the Oracle of Zeus at Donona although there are dozens of others. The Egyptians and Hebrews understood oracles from different perspectives, the Egyptians by observing motion of images and the Hebrews by reviewing dreams and observing sacred objects. Shown here is an 1899 painting by British artist John William Godward (johnwilliamgodward.org) called The Delphic Oracle. Also see Delphi, Methods of Prediction, Omen and Pythias.

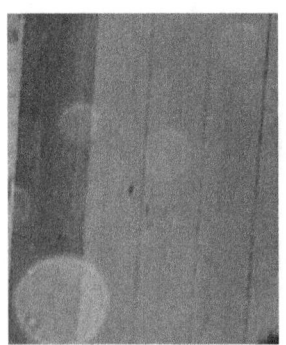

Orbs

Orbs, or Orbs of Light as they are also called, are described as spheres of light that are floating in the air. Orbs can be seen by sensitive people and sometimes appear in photographs. They are believed to be the spiritual energy or the soul of a discarnate entity, or in other cases Devas, Spirits or other Spirits of Nature. Photograph taken by Heather Eaton. Also see Devas and Supernatural and Spiritual Beings.

Orbs of Light

See Orbs.

Orcus

In Roman mythology, Orcus is a God of the Underworld; he is the punisher of broken oaths. Orcus is known as Hades to the Greeks. Orcus is shown here on an ancient Etruscan mural. Also see Roman Gods and Goddesses, and Underworld Gods.

Ordeals

In Mysticism, Gnosticism and Occultism, ordeals refer to the challenges presented to the consciousness on the astral, mental and causal planes of the students and initiates.

Order

An Order is a brotherhood, society or fraternity of like-minded people. Also see Occult Orders, Brotherhoods, and Secret Societies.

Order of Bards, Ovates and Druids

Also known as OBOD, the Order of Bards, Ovates and Druids, is a Druidic Spiritual Brotherhood founded in 1964 in England by Ross Nichols and others. It traces its origins back to 1717 to the Ancient Order of Druids. There are over 90 groups with over 7,000 members and the Order has branches in England, Europe, North America and Australia. Also see Awen, Caitlin Matthews, John Matthews, Ross Nichols, Occult Orders, Brotherhoods and Secret Societies, and duidry.org.

Order of The Stella Matutina

See Stella Matutina.

Order of Skull and Bones

Also known as Skull and Bones and Brotherhood of Death, the Order of Skull and Bones is an Order based at Yale University in New Haven, Connecticut. This brotherhood has existed for more than 175 years and has maintained a very select membership and Masonic type rituals. Also see Occult Orders, Brotherhoods and Secret Societies.

Ordo Stella Matutina

See Stella Matutina.

Ordo Templi Orientis

Also known as OTO, the Ordo Templi Orientis (Order of the Oriental Templars) is an Esoteric Order founded in 1895 by Carl Kellner. It is a Masonic Academy of Esoteric studies although its philosophy also revolves around sex magic. The Ordo Templi Orientis became well known when Aliester Crowley joined in 1910 and was named Grand Master in England two years later, after the death of Kellner, Crowley tried to reform the Order more to his taste and rewrote many of the ceremonial rituals based on his Thelema. The people described herein who were members of the Ordo Templi Orientis include: Aliester Crowley, Gerald Gardner, Arnoldo Krumm Heller, Zachary Miller and John Yarker. Also see Occult Orders, Brotherhoods and Secret Societies, Thelema, oto.org, oto-usa.org org and the-equinox.

Oreads

In Greek and Roman mythology, the Oreads are Nymphs that inhabit grottoes and mountains. They are called the Nymphs of the Mountains. Other spellings include Oreades. Nymphs depicted here in an 1852 painting by German artist Franz Xaver Winterhalter (franzxaverwinterhalter.org) called Florinda. Also see Nymphs.

Oriah "Mountain Dreamer"

American-born Oriah Mountain Dreamer is an international bestselling author, facilitator of spiritual retreats and speaker. She has spent years studying and training in inter-tribal shamanic medicine and ceremonies where she received the spiritual name "Mountain Dreamer". She is the author of the internationally known book The Invitation based on her poem of the same name and translated into 15 languages, as well as the books: The Dance: Moving to the Rhythms of Your True Self; The Call: Discovering Why You Are Here; Confessions of a Spiritual Thrillseeker: Medicine Teachings From the Grandmothers; What We Ache For: Creativity and the Unfolding of Your Soul; and The Dance: Moving to The Deep Rhythms of Your Life. Also see Recommended Reading, Shamans, Spiritual Retreats, Spiritual Teachers, oriah.org and oriahmountaindreamer.com.

Orloff, Judith

(1951-) American-born Judith Orloff, M.D. is an internationally renowned psychiatrist, author and practicing psychic diagnostician (medical intuitive). She graduated from the University of Southern California School of Medicine and completed a four year psychiatric residency program at the University of California Los Angeles. She is Assistant Clinical Professor of Psychiatry at the University of California Los Angeles and lectures and presents workshops throughout the world. She has written: Positive Energy: 10 Extraordinary Prescriptions for Transforming Fatigue, Stress and Fear into Vibrance, Strength and Love; Dr. Judith Orloff's Guide to Intuitive Healing: Five Steps to Physical, Emotional and Sexual Wellness; Second Sight; and her latest book Emotional Freedom: Liberate Yourself From Negative Emotions and Transform Your Life. Also see Psychic Diagnosticians, Recommended Reading, drjudithorloff.com and visit her Intuition Channel on YouTube with free video classes at youtube.com/judithorloffmd.

Ormazd

In Zoroastrian literature Ormazd, an aspect of Ahura Mazda, is the Prince of Light and the Supreme Power of Goodness. His twin brother Ahriman is described as the Prince of Evil and Darkness. Other spellings include Ormuzd. Also see Zoroastrian Gods and Goddesses.

Ornithomancy

Divination by birds, ornithomancy is the interpretation of the flight of birds. It was commonly practiced by the Romans among others. Also see Divination.

Ornstein, Robert

(1942-) American-born Robert Evans Ornstein Ph.D. is a psychologist, writer and professor. He received his Ph.D. in psychology from Stanford University and currently works there as a professor. He is also chairman of the Institute for the Study of Human Knowledge. His doctoral thesis was published as a book, On the Experience of Time after winning the American Institutes for Research Creative Talent Award. Dr. Ornstein has won awards from more than a dozen organizations and has written many books on the nature of the human mind and brain. Among his books are: The Psychology of Consciousness; The Evolution of Consciousness: Of Darwin, Freud, and Cranial Fire: The Origins of the Way We Think; The Healing Brain: Breakthrough Discoveries About How the Brain Keeps Us Healthy; MindReal: How the Mind Creates Its Own Virtual Reality; and Humanity on a Tightrope: Thoughts on Empathy, Family, and Big Changes for a Viable Future. Photograph from ishk.net. Also see Consciousness Researchers, Institute for the Study of Human Knowledge, Recommended Reading, ishk.com and robertornstein.com.

Orpheus

Legendary Greek mystical figure, Orpheus is said be the author of sacred poems from which Orphism is derived. Shown here is a 1901 painting by British artist Henry Ryland called The Young Orpheus. Also see Orphism.

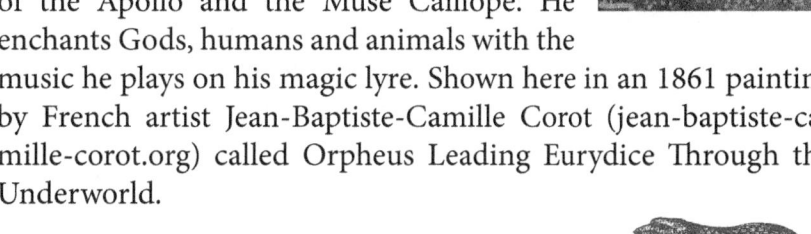

Orpheus

In Greek mythology, Orpheus is the son of the Apollo and the Muse Calliope. He enchants Gods, humans and animals with the music he plays on his magic lyre. Shown here in an 1861 painting by French artist Jean-Baptiste-Camille Corot (jean-baptiste-camille-corot.org) called Orpheus Leading Eurydice Through the Underworld.

Orphic Mysteries

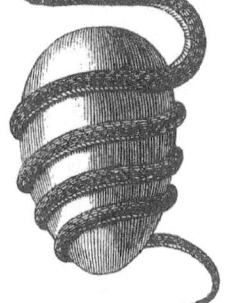

Also known as Orphism, the Orphic Mysteries was a religious and philosophical cult of ancient Greece that was attributed to the writings of Orpheus. They believed in the divine origin of the soul but they also believed in the dual aspects of good and evil in human nature. They also believed in reincarnation and karma and professed that through the process of transmigration of the soul by initiation into the mysteries would lead the soul to be freed from evil and attain spiritual blessedness. The ancient symbol of the Orphic Mysteries was the snake-entwined egg, representing the Cosmos as encircled by the fiery Creative Spirit. The Orphic symbol is depicted here from Jacob Bryant's An Analysis of Ancient Mythology. Shown here is the Orphic Egg from the 1774 edition of J. Bryant's An Analysis of Ancient Mythology. Also see Philosophical and Mystical Movements.

Oschman, James

American-born James "Jim" L. Oschman Ph.D. is a research scientist, lecturer and award winning author. He received his B.A. in biophysics and his Ph.D. in biology from the University of Pittsburgh, Pennsylvania. Dr. Oschman is considered a leading authority on energetic and bodywork therapies in alternative medicine. He is the president of Nature's Own Research Association and member of the Scientific Advisory Board for the National Foundation for Alternative Medicine. He has worked in major research laboratories around the world and has had many scientific papers published in the world's leading journals. Dr. Oschman is the author of Energy Medicine: The Scientific Basis and Energy Medicine in Therapeutics and Human Performance, which are considered as a theoretical basis for scientists in the exploration of biophysics and physiology of energy medicine. Also see Mind- Body Energy Medicine, Recommended Reading, Scientists and energyresearch.bizland.com.

Osho

(1931-1990) Indian-born Rajneesh Chandra Mohan Jain aka Bhagwan Shree Rajneesh aka Osho was a spiritual teacher who inspired the Osho Movement. He became well known in the west in the 1960's and 1970's and spoke of many spiritual traditions and teachers including: Krishna, Jesus, Buddha and Zen masters. Osho said that the most important things in life are love, laughter, awareness and meditation. His books include: Emotional Wellness: Transforming Fear, Anger, and Jealousy into Creative Energy; Being in Love: How to Love with Awareness and Relate Without Fear; Essence of Spiritualism: Based on Discourses of Osho and His Three Enlightened Disciples: Osho Siddhartha, Osho Shailendra and Osho Priya; and Awareness: The Key to Living in Balance: Insights for A New Way of Living. Photograph from shradhanjali.com. Also see Meditation, Recommended Reading, Spiritual Teachers and osho.com.

Osiris

Egyptian God of the Underworld, Osiris is one of the main Egyptian Gods; he not only is the Ruler of the Dead but he has the power that grants all life from the Underworld. He rules over harvest, initiation, death, reincarnation, judgment, justice, religion, civilization, law, and power. Osiris is also called the Lord of Life after Death, God of the Underworld, King of the Dead, Nature God, Universal Lord, Lord of Lords and God of Gods. He is mentioned in the Egyptian Book of the Dead by over 200 different titles. He the son of Geb and Nuit, the husband/brother of Isis, brother of Seth, Isis and Nephthys, and father of the Anubis and Horus. Osiris ruled the upper world before he was murdered by his brother Seth and became the God of the Underworld. Other spellings include Usire and Usiri. Osiris is shown here on a wall painting from the tomb of Sennedjem (an 18th Dynasty Necropolis official) in the Tombs of Nobles in Luxor – Thebes, Egypt. Also see Egyptian Gods and Goddesses, and Underworld Gods.

Ostara
Wiccan festival celebrated on the Spring Equinox to honor the beginning of spring. See Wicca.

Osteen, Joel
(1963-) American-born Joel Scott Hayley Osteen is a television evangelist, best selling author and senior pastor of Lakewood Church in Houston, whose weekly broadcasts are viewed by millions around the world. He worked side by side with his father Pastor John Osteen in Houston Texas for the Lakewood Church for seventeen years before taking over the Church's leadership at the death of his father. Pastor Osteen's television broadcast is one of the most watched inspirational programs in the United States. His books include Become a Better You: 7 Keys to Improving Your Life; Your Best Life Now: 7 Steps to Living at Your Full Potential; Starting Your Best Life Now: A Guide for New Adventures and Stages on Your Journey; Your Best Life Now For Moms; Daily Readings From Become a Better You: 90 Devotions for Improving Your Life Every Day; and The Christmas Spirit: Memories of Family, Friends, and Faith. Pastor Osteen currently travels around the country presenting programs in large stadiums. Also see Evangelists, Recommended Reading, Spiritual Teachers and joelosteen.com.

Otheos
According to the Qabbalah, Otheos is a spirit of Earth whose name is invoked for discovering treasures. Also see Supernatural and Spiritual Beings.

Othila
As the 4th symbol of the runes, Othila represents separation. Other spellings include Othala. Also see Runes.

OTO
See Ordo Templi Orientis.

Ouija Board
An oracle or instrument for communication with spirits and discarnate entities, the ouija board is usually a rectangular piece of polished wood inscribed with the letters of the alphabet and the words yes, no, and goodbye on which a small triangle of wood is placed where the operator(s) place their hands and ask questions. The triangle

then moves to the letters or words of its own volition. The ouija board is considered one of the most controversial methods of spirit communication because no special abilities are required to use it. Shown here is a 20th Century version of the Ouija board by William Flud. Also see Divination Tools.

Ouroboros

In magic and alchemy, the image of the serpent, dragon or lizard biting its own tail, the Ouroboros represents the spirit of Mercury and its circle symbolizes the endless successions of incarnations or transmutations. The Ouroboros dates back to the ancient Egyptians and appears on the tomb furnishings of Tutankhamen. Depictions of Ouroboros have also been found in the ancient Mayan and Aztec civilizations. Other spellings include Uroboros.

Ouspensky, P. D.

(1878-1948) Russian-born Pyotr (or Peter) Demianovich Ouspensky aka P. D. Ouspensky was a mathematician and philosopher. He studied mathematics, geometry, psychology and science as well as philosophy, mysticism and religion. Sometime student of the mystic G.I. Gurdjieff, he published several books, among them are: In Search of the Miraculous; Fragments of an Unknown Teaching; A New Model of the Universe: Principles of the Psychological Method in Its Application to Problems of Science, Religion and Art; and, The Psychology of Man's Possible Evolution and The Cosmology of Man's Possible Evolution; Tertium Organum: The Third Canon of Thought, A Key to the Enigmas of the World; and The Fourth Way: A Record of Talks and Answers to Questions Based on the Teaching of G. I. Gurdjieff. Other spellings of his name are Uspenskii and Uspensky. Also see Mathematicians, Philosophers, Recommended Reading and ouspensky.org.uk.

Out of Body Experience

See Astral Projection.

Ovates

Druid prophets and philosophers who wore green robes, one of the three divisions of the Order, along with the Bards and the Priests. Shown here is a 1782 painting by Dutch painter Nicolai Abraham Abildgaard called Ossian. See Druidism.

Oversoul

The "I Am" portion of the soul.

Ovinnik

Slavic God of the Barns, Ovinnik is described as a black cat with burning eyes. He is worshiped to protect the barns and animals from burning. Photograph by Laveol. Also see Slavic Gods and Goddesses.

Owen, Robert Dale

(1801-1877) Scottish-born, Robert Dale Owen was a well known intellectual and spiritualist. He moved to the United States in 1825 and helped his father found the Utopian community of New Harmony in Indiana. He later lived in Europe and then New York City where he was the editor of the Free Enquirer, served in the House of Representatives, drafted the bill for the founding of the Smithsonian Institution and served as a United States Minister at Naples. Owen was described as an educator, labor leader, diplomat, senator, legislator and champion of new religious faith. He wrote two well known books on Spiritualism: Footfalls on the Boundary of Another World and The Debatable Land Between this World and the Next. Owen is shown here in a 19th Century portrait by William Henry Brooke. Also see Recommended Reading and Spiritualists.

Ox

In Chinese Astrology, the Ox is one of the 12 animals of the Zodiac. People born in the year of the Ox are described as bright, patient and inspiring. Also see Chinese Zodiac.

P

PA
See Parapsychological Association.

Pabid
In Brazilian mythology, when a person dies and the energy leaves them through their eyes, a Pabid is formed. This spirit of the dead, roams the in afterlife. Also see Supernatural and Spiritual Beings.

Pacha Mama
Inca and Araucanian Earth Goddess, Pacha Mama ensures the fertility of the soil and rules over nature, healing and agriculture. Pacha Mama is still revered in Chile, Peru, Bolivia, Paraguay, Uruguay, Ecuador and Argentina. Other spellings include Pachakama, Mama Pacha and Pachamama. Also see Araucanian Gods and Goddesses, and Inca Gods and Goddesses.

Pachacamac
Incan Supreme God, son of Inti, Pachacamac rules over earthquakes, arts, occupations and oracles, he is also known as the Lord of the Earth. He is described as a happy God. Also see Inca Gods and Goddesses.

Pacifica
See Lemuria.

Paddy
Spirit guide said to be channeled through medium Jack Webber. Also see Channeled Spirit Guides, Channelers, and Jack Webber.

Padma
In Hinduism, Padma means "lotus" and it is a feminine symbol of purity and beauty. It is associated with Gods and the chakras, especially with Sahasrara.

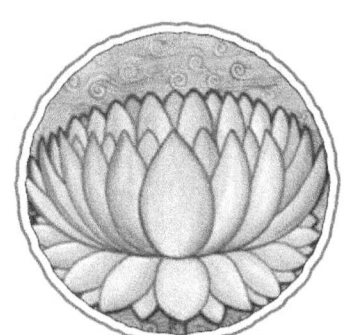

Padma Purana
In Hinduism, Padma Purana which is devoted to creation of the world and Patala or lower part of the Underworld, is one of the texts which explain the myths and rituals of the Gods. Also see Puranas.

Pagan
Originally pagan was used as a derogatory term to describe those who did not profess Christian, Islamic or Jewish faiths. The term Pagan has been recently adopted by New Age terminology and followers of the Wiccan religion, Shamanism and other western spiritual or nature based Deity groups. Also see Paganism, Shamanism, Wicca, avalontraditions.com and weavings.co.uk.

Paganism
From Latin paganus, meaning "civilian" or "country dweller", Paganism is a blanket term currently used to connote a broad set of western spiritual or religious beliefs and practices of natural or polytheistic religions such as Wicca and Shamanism. Also see Neopaganism, Religions, Shamanism, Wicca, avalontraditions.com, a- rainbow-of-spirituality.org, outofthedark.com, paganpresence.com, pagannews.com, paganmystics.ning.com, and weavings.co.uk.

Page, Christine
British-born Christine R. Page M.D. is a known as a mystical physician as well as homeopath, international speaker and author of seven books. She received her M.D. from London University and specializes in pediatrics, obstetrics and general practice. With over 30 years of experience in the caring profession and her knowledge of complementary medicine, she has contributed to its widespread acceptance within the British health system. Dr. Page is the past president of ISSSEEM, organization devoted to the study of subtle energy and president of Holos University, encouraging research into energy medicine and the interactions between mind, body and spirit. Among her books are Beyond the Obvious: Bringing Intuition Into Our Awakening Consciousness; Mind Body Spirit Workbook: A Handbook of Health; The Mirror of Existence: Stepping into Wholeness; Spiritual Alchemy: How To Transform Your Life; and The Mystery of 2012: Predictions, Prophecies and Possibilities. Also see Homeopathy, Mind-Body Energy Medicine, Recommended Reading and christinepage.com.

Pah
In Pawnee mythology, Pah is the Moon God, sent by Tirawa to provide night. Also see Pawnee Gods and Goddesses, and Tirawa.

Palaspas
See Palm Sunday.

Pallas
In Greek mythology Pallas was a Naiad, daughter of Triton. She was also a childhood friend of the Goddess Athena and is sometimes confused with her. The girls were raised together and learned to fight together. Shown here is a 1637 painting called Pallas and Arachne by Flemish artist Peter Paul Rubens (peterpaulrubens.org).

Pallomancy
Divination by pendulum, pallomancy interprets the movements of the pendulum. Also see Divination, and Pendulum.

Palm Sunday
Also called Palaspas, Palm Sunday is the Christian Holy day that celebrates the entrance of Jesus Christ into Jerusalem. Shown here is a 1306 painting by Italian artist Giotto (giotto.com) called Entry into Jerusalem. See Christianity, and Holy Week.

Palma
Palma is the spirit guide said to be channeled thorough Stella Cranshaw. Also see Channeled Spirit Guides, Channelers, and Stella Cranshaw.

Palmer, Helen
American-born Helen Palmer is an internationally recognized spiritual teacher, lecturer and bestselling author. She is the founding director of the International Enneagram Association, co-founder of Enneagram Worldwide and the Enneagram Professional Training Program. She has taught at the California School of Professional Psychology, California Institute of Integral Studies, the Esalen Institute and the John F. Kennedy University, among others. She is also a Fellow of the Noetic Sciences Institute. Ms. Palmer's books are: The Enneagram in Love and Work: Understanding Your Intimate and Business Relationships; The Enneagram: Understanding Yourself and the Others in Your Life; Inner Knowing: Consciousness, Creativity, Insight and

Intuition The Enneagram Advantage: Putting the Nine Personality Types to Work in the Office; and The Enneagram in Love and Work: Understanding Your Intimate and Business Relationships. Photograph from we.got.net. Also see Enneagram Worldwide, Recommended Reading, Spiritual Teachers, ennea.com, enneagram.com, enneagramworldwide.com, and internationalenneagram.org.

Palmistry

Also known as chiromancy, palmistry is character interpretation based on the study of the palm of a person's hands by interpreting the characteristics of the skin texture, creases, pads, shapes and colors, and the lines and undulations. There are three main lines which are interpreted: the life line, the head line and the heart line. The distinction is made between the dominant hand (the hand the person uses) and the passive hand (the other hand). The art of palmistry art was known in ancient China, Tibet, Persia, Syria and Egypt, and it was further developed in ancient Greece, where it was recognized as legitimate  by such philosophers as Aristotle and Plato. The people mentioned herein who practice palmistry include: Ghanshyam Singh Birla, Cheiro, Beverly Jaegers, Marie-Anne Lenormand and Tara Sutphen. Shown here is a 1777 painting by British artist Sir Joshua Reynolds called The Fortune Teller. Also see Divination, handresearch.com and palmistry.com.

Pan

Greek God of Nature, Pan rules over male sexuality, animals, forests, pastures, nature, fertility, plants, healing, orchards, gardens, fishing, agriculture, flocks and shepherds. He is described as a small ugly bearded man with the horns, hoofs and ears of a goat, who is a great musician and plays a magical pipe of reeds as he chases after wood Nymphs. Pan is the son of Hermes and is also known as the Little God, the Horned God and the Horned One of Nature. Pan is depicted here in a 1980 painting by Dutch artist Johfra Bosschart (johfra.no.sapo.pt). Also see Greek Gods and Goddesses.

Pandora

In Greek mythology, Pandora was the first woman; she was given a box with all the evils of the world and told not to open it. Curiosity gets the best of Pandora and when she hears whispers from the box, she opens it and releases all the evils, sorrows, and vices of humanity that had been placed in the box by Jupiter. The only thing left in Pandora's Box is hope which she lets out to help humanity. She is depicted here in an 1878 painting by Dante Gabriel Rossetti (rossettiarchive.org).

Panpsychism

The doctrine that states that the entire universe is animated and has consciousness. Also see Animism.

Pantheism

From the Greek words pan meaning "all" and theos meaning "God", Pantheism is the doctrine that describes the universe as being conceived of as a whole and where God, conversely is conceived of as the laws, forces and substances of the universe. In Hindu and Buddhist doctrines, Pantheism is found in the sacred writings of the Vedas, Upanishads and Bhagavad-Gita. Orthodox Christian theologians reject Pantheism on the basis that it makes God impersonal and excludes human and divine freedom. As Samuel Johnson stated, the doctrine "confounds God with the universe". Also see Philosophical and Mystical Movements, and pantheism.net.

Pantheon

A collective term to describe all the Gods of a race, nation, religion or time, or a temple or place dedicated to the same Gods, such as Mount Olympus. Shown here is the Roman Pantheon, an incredible engineering feat including a concrete dome structure which is still standing 19 Centuries after it was built.

Pantheon of the Gods
See Mount Olympus.

Papus

(1865-1916) Spanish-born French Gerard Anaclet Vincent Encausse, pen name Papus, was a physician, hypnotist, author and occultist. Initiated into Martinism he founded two Occult Orders: the Martinist Order and the Group for Esoteric Studies. He was a member of Madame Blavatsky's French Theosophical Society for a time, the Gnostic Church of France where he was elected Grand Hierophant, and he was the last chief of the Kabbalistic Order of the Rose-Croix. Papus is most remembered as an author of books on Occultism, magic, the Tarot and the Qabbalah. He was introduced to Occultism by Joseph Alexandre Saint-Yves and was both physician and occult consultant to Tsar Nicholas II and Tsarina Alexandra. Some his books include: Systematic Treatise on Occult Science; Systematic Treatise of Practical Magic; Tarot of the Bohemians: The Most Ancient Book in the World for the Use of Initiates; The Qabalah: Secret Tradition of the West and Astrology for Initiates: Astrological Secrets of the Western Mystery Tradition. Also see Gnostics, Occultists, Qabbalists, Recommended Reading and Theosophists.

Papyrus of Ani
See Egyptian Book of the Dead.

Paraatman
A Sanskrit word meaning "Supreme Spirit" or "Universal Spirit".

Paracelsus

(1493-1541) Swiss-born Aureolus Phillipus Theophrastus Bombast von Hohenheim, (he renamed himself Paracelsus to show that he was "beyond Celsus" -famous Roman physician-), was a physician, surgeon, chemist, alchemist and astrologer. He spent much of his life traveling in Europe, Russia, Asia and Egypt. Since many of his remedies were based on the belief that "like cures like" and "the dose makes the poison" he is considered the father of modern homoeopathy, spagyrics and toxicology. Paracelsus maintained that human life is inseparable from that of the universal mind and that there is a force which he called munia which radiated from within and around the human body. He was also the first writer to classify the Elementals. Among his books are: The Hermetic and Alchemical Writings of Paracelsus; The Aurora of the Philosophers; and The Prophecies of Paracelsus: Occult Symbols and Magic Figures with Esoteric Explanations; Concerning the Spirits of the Planets. Paracelsus is depicted here in a 1617 painting by Flemish artist Peter Paul Rubens (peterpaulrubens.org). Also see Alchemists, Astrologers, Elementals and Homeopathy.

Paraclete
From Greek meaning "One Who Consoles", Paraclete is used as another term to describe the Holy Ghost. Also see Holy Ghost and Shekinah.

Paradise

From the old Persian pairedaeza, meaning "enclosure" originally referred to an enclosed garden or a park. Currently the term is used as a synonym for Eden or Heaven. Shown here is a 20th Century painting by American artist Dale Terbush (masterlight.com) called A Place for Us in Paradise.

Paradox
A paradox is a statement, group of statements or proposition which sounds self-contradictory or against common logic and leads to a contradiction where the premises themselves are not all really true or cannot all be true together.

Paraiso
One of three Canticas that compose Dante Alighieri's Divine Comedy. See Divine Comedy.

Paralda
Elemental King, Paralda rules over the element of Air and the Air Elementals, which are: Sylphs and Zephyrs. He is described as a huge sylph with flowing beard and cape. Also see Elemental Kings, and Elementals.

Parallel Lives
Theory that proposes that we may incarnate in more than one person at one time and that we may be living simultaneously in parallel lives.

Parallel Universes
Quantum physics states that there may be many parallel universes or "multiverse" coexisting with ours and that we may be in constant interaction with them.

Paramahamsa
From Hinduism Paramahamsa is a term used to describe an adept, master and teacher of Occultism or Esoteric Science. Also see Spiritual Teachers.

Paranormal
Paranormal is a term that is used to describe any phenomenon which does not have a logical explanation according to the laws of science and nature as we currently understand them. Also see Preternatural, Supernatural, paranormalplus.com, paranormalawarenesssociety.org, paranormal-encyclopedia.com, paranormalhelp.com, and paranormality.com.

Parapsychological Association

The Parapsychological Association. (or PA) is, in their own words the international professional organization of scientists and scholars engaged in the study of 'psi' (or 'psychic') experiences, such as telepathy, clairvoyance, remote viewing, psychokinesis, psychic healing, and precognition. Such experiences seem to challenge contemporary conceptions of human nature and of the physical world. They appear to involve the transfer of information and the influence of physical systems independently of time and space, via mechanisms we cannot currently explain. The primary objective of the Association is to achieve a scientific understanding of these experiences. Also see New Age Associations and Societies and parapsych.org.

Parapsychology
The investigation and study of paranormal phenomenon that relates to the human mind, such as psychic abilities which include: extrasensory perception, clairvoyance, precognition, psychokinesis, telepathy as well as other psychic phenomena. Also see Parapsychologists and Psychic Researchers, parapsych.com, parapsycology.org, parapsychologylab.com, pflyceum.org and rhine.org.

Parapsychologists and Psychic Researchers
The people mentioned herein who deal with parapsychology and psychic research are: William Barrett, Hal Zina Bennet, Susan Jane Blackmore, Gerard Croiset, Sir William Crookes, Georges Devereux, Curt John Ducasse, Arthur Findlay, Hans Holzer, James Hervey Hyslop, William James, Stanley Krippner, Cesare Lombroso, Jean Millay, Zachary Miller, Jeffrey Mishlove, Frederick Myers, Carroll Nash, John Neihardt, Harry Price, Henry Habberley Price, Harold E. Puthoff, Dean Radin,

Konstantin Raudive, Joseph Banks Rhine, Charles Richet, David Scott Rogo, Kevin Ryerson, Minot Judson Savage, Gary Schwartz, Harold Morrow Sherman, Jose Silva, Charles Tart, Charles Drayton Thomas, William A. Tiller, Montague Ullman, Peter Underwood, Alan Vaughan, Paul Von Ward, Alfred Russel Wallace and Carl August Wickland. Also see Parapsychology.

Parashurama

In Hinduism, Parashurama, is the sixth incarnation or Avatar of the God Vishnu appearing in the Treta Yuga. Parashurama is depicted here in a 20th Century painting by Indian artist B. G. Sharma (bgsharmaart.com). See Avatar.

Parasite

In Occultism a parasite is any entity or being that lives on the psychic or spiritual energy of another entity or being. Also see Psychic Vampire.

Pariacaca

In Inca mythology, Pariacaca is the God of Water, who specifically rules over the rainstorms. Legend says that he was born as a falcon but turned into a human being later. Also see Inca Gods and Goddesses.

Parthenope

In Greek mythology, Parthenope is a Sea Goddess, one of the three sirens along with Ligeia and Leucosia. Parthenope is shown here in a mosaic unearthed in the 1990's in the ancient city of Zeugma in Belkis Village in Turkey. Also see Greek Gods and Goddesses, and Sirens.

Paruksti

In Pawnee mythology, Paruksti is the Force of Nature, manifested as storms and thunder and personifying the powers of self-renewal and life on earth. Also see Pawnee Gods and Goddesses.

Parvati

Hindu Goddess of Power and Strength, representing the Virgin aspect of the Goddess Kali, one of the Triad of Goddesses that included Uma and Durga. Parvati means "Daughter of the Mountain" and she represents the union of man and woman, of God and Goddesses and of desire and ecstasy. She is also known as the Goddess of the Himalayas, the Wife of Shiva and the Mother Goddess. She is described as a gentle and beautiful Goddess. Parvati has also been called Haimavati and Mena. Also see Hindu Gods and Goddesses.

Pasqually, Martinez de

(1727-1774) French-born Jacques de Livron Joachim de la Tour de la Casa Martinez de Pasqually was a qabbalist, freemason, mystic and founder of the Order of Knight Masons, Elect Priests of the Universe (Odre des Chevelier Macons Elus Cohen de L'Universe)" also known as the Order of Elect Cohens. He spent most of his life on the spiritual mission traveling extensively and initiating students. After his death his disciple Louis Claude de Saint Martin carried his mystic work later known as Martinism. Other spellings of his name include Martines and Pascualle. His books include: Treatise on the Reintegration of Beings Into Their Original Estate, Virtues and Powers Both Spiritual and Divine; Of Errors and Truth and Natural Table of the Correspondences Between God, Man and the Universe. Shown here is an 18th Century portrait of Pasqually by an unknown artist. Also see Freemasons, Mystics and Qabbalists.

Passing Over

Passing over refers to the death of the physical body. Shown here is an 18th Century depiction of the soul leaving the body at death by English artist William Blake (william-blake.org). Also see Transition.

Passion Sunday

See Palm Sunday.

Passover

See Pesach and Judaism.

Past Life Regression

See Regression Therapy.

Patecatl

In Aztec mythology, Patecatl is the God of Medicine. He is the husband of Mayahuel and he rules over healing and fertility and is accredited with the discovery of Peyote. Shown here is a 16th Century depiction of Patecatl from the Codex Telleriano-Remensis. Also see Aztec Gods and Goddesses.

Patha

In Jewish magical tradition, Patha is an Angel invoked in the closing of the Sabbath. Also see Angels.

Pathworking

Derived from the Qabbalah, Pathworking is an esoteric technique of guided meditation. Dolores Ashcroft-Nowicki described pathworking as "A journey between this side of the mental worlds and the other side". This is done by using mental doorways between the physical and known to the astral and unknown. Also see Creative Visualization, Magical Methods and Positive Thinking.

Paul, Margaret

American-born Margaret Paul Ph.D. is an international best selling author, relationship workshop leader, noted public speaker, chaplain, humanitarian and consultant. She is considered an expert on relationships and marriage and is the co-creator of Inner Bonding a six step spiritual healing process. She has led groups, taught classes and workshops as well as working with individuals and companies for over forty years. Dr. Paul has written: Inner Bonding: Becoming a Loving Adult to Your Inner Child; and Do I Have to Give Up Me To Be Loved by God? Also see Recommended Reading, Reverends and Ministers, Spiritual Teachers and innerbonding.com.

Paulicians
See Bogomils.

Pauline Arts
A text that lists the Angels of day and night and deals with the zodiac. Pauline Arts is one of four texts that are known as the Lemegeton or Lesser Key of Solomon. See Lemegeton.

Pawnee Gods and Goddesses
The following Pawnee Gods and Goddesses are described herein: Chahuru, Evening Star, Hoturu, Morning Star, North Star, Pah, Paruksti, Shakura, South Star and Tirawa.

Pax
In Roman mythology, Pax is the Goddess of Peace. She is known to the Greeks as Eirene. Pax is shown here in a 1629 painting called War and Peace where Minerva is saving Pax from Mars by Peter Paul Rubens (peterpaulrubens.org). Also see Roman Gods and Goddesses.

Pazuzu
Assyrian Wind Demon God, Pazuzu is considered a benevolent God who protects women in childbirth against Lamashtu, a she-demon. Amulets made of Pazuzu's head are used by women for protection. Shown here is a 1,000 BCE bronze statue, around 15 cms. high, housed in the Louvre Museum in Paris, France. Also see Assyrian Gods and Goddesses, and Demons.

Peale, Norman Vincent

(1898-1993) American-born Norman Vincent Peale D.D. was one of the most influential clergymen in the United States in the 20th Century as well as bestselling author and champion of self-help and positive thinking. He studied at Ohio Wesleyan University and Boston University and worked as a reporter before entering the ministry. Ordained in the Methodist Episcopal Church in 1922 he later changed his affiliation to the Dutch Reformed Church where he became famous for his sermons. Among his more than 40 books are: The Art of Living; The Power of Positive Thinking; You Can If You Think You Can; Norman Vincent Peale's Treasure of Courage and Confidence; Positive Imaging: The Powerful Way to Change Your Life; The True Joy of Positive Living: An Autobiography; Have a Great Day; and Enthusiasm Makes the Difference. Photograph from icollector.com. Also see Positive Thinking, Recommended Reading, Reverends and Ministers, Self-Help and normanvincentpeale.wwwhubs.com.

Pearce, Joseph Chilton

(1926-) American-born Joseph "Joe" Chilton Pearce is an internationally renowned thinker, bestselling author and advocate of evolutionary child-rearing practices. He was a faculty member on child development at the Jung Institute in Switzerland and is currently a member of the Scientific Advisory Board of the Institute of HeartMath and faculty member of the Omega Institute. Among his books are: Magical Child: Rediscovering Nature's Plan for Our Children; The Biology of Transcendence: A Blueprint of the Human Spirit; The Crack in the Cosmic Egg: Challenging Constructs of Mind and Reality; Spiritual Initiation and the Breakthrough of Consciousness; Spiritual Initiation and the Breakthrough of Consciousness: The Bond of Power; Evolution's End: Claiming the Potential of Our Intelligence; and The Death of Religion and the Rebirth of Spirit: A Return to the Intelligence of the Heart: The Bond of Power. Photograph from pamragland.com. Also see Jungian Analysts, Recommended Reading and heartmath.org.

Pearl, Eric

(1955-) American-born Eric Pearl D.C. is an internationally recognized healer and bestselling author. He worked for 12 years as a chiropractor before reportedly discovering and developing the ability to heal serious illnesses. His healings have been reported and documented in six books including his international best seller: The Reconnection: Heal Others; Heal Yourself which has been translated into 30 languages. Dr. Pearl travels extensively teaching and lecturing on Reconnective Healing and has taught healing techniques to more than 45,000 people in over 60 countries. Pearl's healings have elicited great interest from some of the world's top medical researchers, including several hospitals in the United States. Also see Healers, Recommended Reading and thereconnection.com.

Pearsall, Paul

(1942-2007) American-born Paul Pearsall M.D. was a clinical neuropsychologist, self-help author, and professor at the University of Hawaii, CEO of Ho'ala Hou in Hawaii, as well as senior research advisor for the Human Energy Systems Laboratory at the University of Arizona and member and advisor to several other health centers. He graduated with awards from Wayne State University and did his post graduate studies at Harvard and Albert Einstein Schools of Medicine. He was professor for the Department of Psychiatry and Behavioral Neuroscience at Wayne State University School of Medicine as well as several other positions. Dr. Pearsall published 18 best selling books, among them: The Last Self-Help Book You'll Ever Need: Think Negatively; Be a Good Blamer and Throttle Your Inner Child; The Heart's Code: Tapping the Wisdom and Power of Our Heart Energy and Awe: The Delights and Dangers of Our Eleventh Emotion. Also see Mind-Body Energy Medicine, Recommended Reading, Self-Help and paulpearsall.com.

Pearson, Carol

American-born Carol Sue Pearson Ph.D. is the Executive Vice President and Provost of Pacifica Graduate Institute in Santa Barbara, CA. She leads seminars and workshops all over the world. Dr Pearson received her B.A., M.A. and Ph.D. in English from Rice University and an honorary Doctorate in Humane Letters from Norwich University. She is also certified in Personal Mythology Methods by the Midway Center of the D.C. Psychiatric Institute Foundation. Her books include: The Hero Within: Six Archetypes We Live By; Awakening the Heroes Within: Twelve Archetypes to Help Us Find Ourselves and Transform our World; Magic at Work: Camelot; Creative Leadership and Everyday Miracles; The Hero and the Outlaw: Building Extraordinary Brands Through the Power of Archetypes, Mapping the Organizational Culture, and The Transforming Leader: New Approaches to Leadership for the Twenty-First Century. Also see Mythology, Recommended Reading and herowithin.com.

Peck, M. Scott

(1936-2005) American-born Morgan Scott Peck M.D. was a psychiatrist and best selling author. He received his B.A. from Harvard University, did premed studies at Columbia University in New York and received his M.D. from Case Western Reserve University, in Cleveland, Ohio. Hi served in the U.S. Army as lieutenant colonel in Japan and Washington. Among Dr. Peck's books are: The Road Less Traveled: A New Psychology of Love, Traditional Values and Spiritual Growth; Denial of the Soul: Spiritual and Medical Perspectives in Euthanasia and Mortality; The Road Less Traveled and Beyond: Spiritual Growth in the Age of Anxiety; In Heaven As On Earth: A Vision of the Afterlife; and Glimpses of the Devil: A Psychiatrist's Personal Accounts of Possession, Exorcism and Redemption. Also see Recommended Reading and mscottpeck.com.

Pedra da Gavea

At 842 meters above sea level and close to Rio de Janeiro in Brazil, the Pedra da Gavea is a mysterious rock formation with a huge carving of a face and inscriptions in a mysterious language that remain unexplained. One theory is that the rock is the burial place of a Phoenician king.

Peg Leg Jack
See Fachen.

Pegasus

In Greek mythology, Pegasus is a winged horse who sprang from the blood of the Gorgon, Medusa when Perseus cut off her head. Pegasus was tamed by Athene who presented the winged steed to the Muses. Pegasus is shown here from a 1622 painting called Perseus freeing Andromeda by Flemish artist Peter Paul Rubens (peterpaulrubens.org). Also see Mythological Creatures, and Winged Horses.

Pegomancy

Divination by observing water, Pegomancy interprets the images on the surface of the water. Pegomancy is a form of scrying. Also see Divination, and Scrying.

Pele

In Hawaiian mythology, Pele is the Goddess of Volcanoes. She lives in the volcano Kilauea on Hawaii and she rules over fire, lightning, violence and dance. She is also called Ka wahine 'ai honua, meaning "Woman Who Devours the Land". Pele can be gentle and visit common people to whom she is said to appear as a tall beautiful woman or an ugly old lady. She is described as a jealous Goddess who receives the souls of the dead. Pele is depicted here in a painting by American artist Herb Kawainui Kane (herbkanestudio.com). Also see Hawaiian Gods and Goddesses.

Pelletier, Kenneth

(1946-) American-born Kenneth R. Pelletier, Ph.D. M.D. (hc) is a Clinical Professor of Medicine Family & Community Medicine, and Public Health at the University of Arizona School of Medicine and the Department of Medicine and Department of Psychiatry at the University of California School of Medicine in San Francisco, among many other professional activities. He has published over 300 professional journal articles and more than 10 books in alternative/integrative medicine, behavioral medicine and disease management. Dr. Pelletier's books include: Mind as a Healer, Mind as a Slayer: A Holistic Approach to Preventing Stress Disorders; Holistic Medicine: From Stress to Optimum Health; Sound Mind – Sound Body: A New Model for Lifelong Health; Healthy People in Unhealthy Places; Stress and Fitness at Work; Toward a Science of Consciousness; Longevity: Fulfilling Our Biological Potential; The Best Alternative Medicine: What Works? What Does Not? and New Medicine: Complete Family Health Guide – Integrating Complementary, Alternative and Conventional Medicine for the Safest and Most Effective Treatment. Photograph from gurutube.net. Also see Holistic Healing, Mind-Body Energy Medicine, Recommended Reading and drpelletier.com.

Pemphredo

In Greek mythology, Pemphredo is one of the Graeae. Her name means "Alarm" or "Wasp". Other spellings include Pephredo. Also see Graeae, and Greek Gods and Goddesses.

Penates

In Roman mythology, the Penates are the Nature Spirits or Lesser Deities of the storeroom and protectors of the house. Offerings of incense, wine, flowers and fruit are frequently made to their images. They are often depicted dancing and holding a drinking horn. They are frequently invoked together with the Lares. Shown here is a Roman relief from the West façade of the Ara Pacis (Altar of Augustan Peace) from 9 B.C.E. showing Aenaes sacrificing to the Penates. Also see Lares, Nature Spirits, and Roman Gods and Goddesses.

Penczak, Christopher

(1973-) American-born Christopher Penczak is an eclectic witch, author and spiritual teacher drawing upon both modern and traditional sources. He is a priest at the Cabot Tradition of Witchcraft, an ordained Minister in the Universal Brotherhood Movement and part time faculty member of the North Eastern Institute of Whole Health. Christopher travels extensively teaching a wide variety of topics including witchcraft, Wicca, magic, healing, shamanism, Theosophy and psychic development. Among his books are City Magick: Urban Rituals, Spells, and Shamanism; The Inner Temple of Witchcraft: Magick, Meditation and Psychic Development; The Outer Temple of Witchcraft: Circles, Spells and Rituals; The Mystic Foundation: Understanding and Exploring the Magical Universe; Sons of the Goddess: A Young Man's Guide to Wicca; and The Temple of High Witchcraft: Ceremonies, Spheres, and the Witches' Qabbalah. Photograph from themagicalbuffet.com. Also see Recommended Reading, Shamans, Spiritual Teachers, Wicca, Wiccans and christopherpenczak.com.

Pendulum

A weight suspended from a chain or string used for dowsing, radiesthesia and divination. The material for the pendulum itself may include crystals, metals and even roots of herbs or wood. The interpretation of the movements of the pendulum is called pallomancy or radiesthesia. Also see Divination Tools, Pallomancy, and Radiesthesia.

Pentacle
A magic diagram of a five pointed star, or pentagram surrounded by a circle, pentacles can be inscribed on metal, wood or other material used to create a talisman. The pentacle is also a symbol that refers to the element Earth and the initiates understanding of the Universe. Wiccans consider the pentacle to be a prime magical symbol and use it as a talisman for protection and power.

Pentagram
Considered divine and magical, the pentagram is a geometric figure and powerful symbol with five lines and five points, in the shape of a star. It is used by Occultists to invoke spirits; the star pointed upwards for benevolent spirits. Frequently referred to in Occultism and Wicca, the pentagram is attributed to the five elements of fire, water, air, earth and spirit (or akasha). It is a symbol for perfection  and beauty, associated with the Goddess and symbolic of the sacred feminine. The pentagram is also called the Star of the Magi, the Blazing Star and the Wizard's Foot. Other spellings include pentacle and pentalpha.

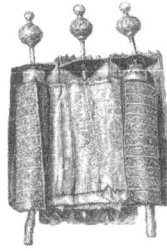
Pentateuch
From Greek words penta, meaning "five" and teukhos, meaning "vessel" or "scroll", the Pentateuch is another term for Torah or the first of five books of the Hebrew Scriptures. Shown here is an 1881 rendition of the Torah from the 1881 book Picturesque Palestine, Sinai and Egypt by British cartographer Sir Charles William Wilson. See Torah.

Pentecost
Christian festival when Christians celebrate the gift of the Holy Spirit. It is regarded as the birthday of the Christian church. Depicted here is a 1545 painting by Italian artist Titian called Pentecost or The Descent of the Holy Ghost. Also see Christianity.

Pentecost
See Judaism, and Shavout.

Perception
The mental faculty of recognition, perception means to understand or perceive something by rationalizing the thought with the mind. Our perception of the physical world begins with the senses and leads us to generate empirical concepts of the world around us as relates to our preexisting concepts. Do you see the goblet or the faces?

Percipient

A percipient is a person who receives and or perceives telepathic messages.

Perennial Philosophy

From the Latin philosophis perenis, perennial philosophy refers to the existence of a universal set of truths and values that are common to all cultures. This means that while all religions may be different, the essence is the same in each.

Persephone

Greek Goddess of the Underworld, Persephone rules over the seasons, corn, winter and overcoming obstacles and she is the personification of the revival of nature in spring. She is the daughter of Zeus and Demeter and is also known as the Corn Maiden, the Queen of the Underworld and the Destroyer. She was abducted by Hades and made his wife and Queen of the Underworld. Through Zeus' intervention she is allowed to spend eight months of the year with her mother. Other spellings include Proserpina and Proserpine. Persephone and Demeter are depicted here in 1891 painting by British artist Lord Frederick Leighton (frederic-leighton.org) called The Return of Persephone. Also see Greek Gods and Goddesses, and Underworld Gods.

Persephone

Roman Goddess of Rest, Winter, Survival and Overcoming Obstacles, Persephone is also Goddess the Seasons and the Underworld. She is the consort of Pluto and called the Grain Goddess and the Goddess of Corn. Other spellings include Proserpina. She is depicted here in an 1877 painting by British artist Dante Gabriel Rossetti (rossettiarchive.org). Persephone is also called Libitina. Also see Roman Gods and Goddesses, and Underworld Gods.

Persian Gods and Goddesses

The following Persian Gods and Goddesses are described herein: Ahurani, Anahita, Daena, Mah, Mithra, Vourukasha and Zurvan. Shown here is an ancient relief of the Investiture of Narseh at Naqsh-e Rostam in Iran.

Personality

According to occult philosophy, the personality is the mortal, personal ego of man or the "self" built up during the incarnation. This personality is a product of heredity and environment and is the embodiment of personal traits such as: consciousness, memory, manners, habits, tastes, personal beliefs, expectations, desires and moral character.

Personology

Personology is the study and interpretation of a person's predictable behavior based on the observation of facial features and other physical attributes. It was developed in the 1930's by Los Angeles Circuit Court judge Edward Vincent Jones who later abandoned his judicial career for full time researching of personology. He is said to have compiled a list of 200 identifiable facial features, list that was later narrowed to 68. Examples of personology correlations include traits such as fine hair indicating a sensitive person versus coarse hair would indicate a less sensitive person, or wild and unruly hair would indicate someone who "thinks outside the box". Also see personology.com and million.net.

Pert, Candace

(1946-) American-born Candace Beebe Pert Ph.D. is an internationally known neuroscientist pharmacologist, investigator and author. She received her Ph.D. in pharmacology from Johns Hopkins University of School of Medicine. Dr. Pert did research at the National Institute of Mental Health from 1975 to 1987 serving as Chief of the Section on Brain Biochemistry of the Clinical Neuroscience Branch. She has published over 250 articles on peptides and the immune system. Dr. Pert is the holder of a number of patents for modified peptides and is currently Chief Scientific Officer for RAPID Laboratories, Inc. She discovered the opiate receptor or cellular bonding site for endorphins in the brain. She has written two books: Molecules of Emotion: the Science Behind Mindbody Medicine, and Everything You Need to Know to Feel Go(o)d and three CD's: Psychosomatic Wellness, Your Body is Your Subconscious Mind and To Feel Good. Also see Recommended Reading, Scientists and candacepert.com.

Perth

As the 6th symbol of the runes, Perth represents initiation. Other spellings include Perthro. Also see Runes.

Perun

Slavic Supreme God, Perun rules over lightning, thunder, storms, fire, fertility, war, warriors, weapons, victory, peace, crops, forests, purification and oracles. He is also known as the Lord of the Universe, the Supreme God and the Creator God. Perun is depicted here in a painting by Russian artist Andrei Klimenko. Other spellings include Piorun, Per___ P_____ ___ P_____ Also see Slavic Gods and Goddesses.

Pesach

In Judaism, the festival of Pesach or Passover takes place around March/April, and commemorates Moses freeing the Israelites from their enslavement under the Pharaoh in Egypt. This festival lasts for eight days and during that time no 'leavened' food may be consumed.

Shown here is a 20th Century depiction of Pesach by Russian artist Elena Flerova (flerova.com). Other spellings include Pesah. Also see Judaism.

Pet Psychic
See Animal Communication Specialist.

Pethel
In Jewish magical tradition, Pethel is a Most Holy Angel invoked in magical rituals at the closing of the Sabbath. Also see Angels.

Peter
Spirit guide said to be channeled through medium Hester Dowden. Also see Channeled Spirit Guides, Channelers, and Hester Dowden.

Petitioning
See Supplication.

Phaistos Disk
The Phaistos disk is a 2.000 B.C.E. clay disk from the Minoan palace of Phaistos in Greece, stamped with a spiral of symbols whose purpose and meaning remain disputed. It is considered one of the most famous mysteries of archeology. It was discovered by Luigi Pernier in 1908 and is currently housed in the Heraklion Archeological Museum in Crete, Greece. Also see Unsolved Mysteries.

Phaleg
Olympian Spirit who governs Mars and other provinces of the Universe. See Olympian Spirits.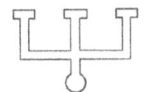

Phantasmata
According to occult terminology, the phantasmata are thought forms purposely created by the imagination that are able to communicate with their creator. Also see Astral Bodies, Etheric Projection, Thought Forms, and Tulpas.

Phantom Ships
Around the world and since there have been ships there have also been phantom ships. Phantom ships which are also called ghost ships are ghostly images of ships that have sunk or been shipwrecked that appear to sailors passing the place where the ship met her fate. A few of the most famous of the phantom ships are the Flying Dutchman, the Caleuche and the Lady Lovibond, and one of the most famous places to see phantom ships is the

Goodwin sands in Kent, England. Shown here is a 1980 painting of a phantom ship by American artist Lafayette Claud Eaton Jr. Also see Caleuche, Flying Dutchman Lady Lovibond and Mary Celeste.

Pharaoh

Meaning "Great House" Pharaoh was the title given to the Kings of Egypt in ancient Egypt. They were considered incarnations of Horus, son of Osiris. Pharaohs were considered God-Kings who became Gods when they died and their spirits became one with Osiris. They were also known as The Two Lords in reference to Horus and Seth. Although most of the Pharaohs were men two great women held that title, Hatshepsut and Cleopatra. Shown here is the mask of Tutankhamen. Also see ancientegypt.co.uk.

Phenomenology

Phenomenology is the study of structures of consciousness or psychism as experienced from the first-person point of view and in relation to the mind. Also see phenomenology.org, spep.org, and phenomenologycenter.org.

Philology

From Greek meaning "love of words", philology is the study of language and human communication. It is also defined as the study of names or words and their vibrations.

Philosopher's Stone

Also known as medicina metallorum, meaning "medicine of metals", from the alchemical point of view, the philosopher's stone was the original substance from which all metals derived and so could be used in the transformation of lead and other base materials into gold. It was also said to make the elixir of life which would grant eternal life and cure all illnesses. According to occultists the philosopher's stone is a symbol of transmutation from lower natures of materialism to higher more spiritual natures. It is also called the Stone of the Wise. Shown here is a 1771 painting called The Alchemist in Search of the Philosophers Stone by British artist Joseph Wright of Derby. Also see Alchemy.

Philosophers

The people described herein who are considered philosophers include: David Abram, Apollonius of Tyana, Aristotle, Sri Aurobindo, Marcus Bach, Roger Bacon, Leonardo Boff, Robert Boyle, Giordano Bruno, Paul Brunton, Eric Butterworth, Chaeremon of Alexandria, Confucius, Pietro d'Abano, Andrew Jackson Davis, John DeMartini, Rene Descartes, Curt John Ducasse, Empedocles, Marsilio Ficino, Geber, Kahlil Gibran, Johann Wolfgang von Goethe, Gerald Heard, Vernon Howard, Iamblichus, Heinrich Khunrath,

Athanasius Kircher, Lao Tzu, Michael Maier, Maimonides, Terence McKenna, Robert Moss, Jacob Needleman, John Neihardt, Isaac Newton, Earl Nightingale, Henry Steel Olcott, P. D. Ouspensky, Plato, Pliny the Elder, Plotinus, Posidonius, Henry Habberley Price, Proclus, Ptolemy, Pythagoras, Phineas Quimby, Peter Russell, Count Saint-Germain, Louis Claude de Saint-Martin, William Samuel, Sankara Saranam, Sai Baba Sathya, John Rogers Searle, Michel Sendivogius, Henry Sidgwick, Socrates, David Spangler, Rudolf Steiner, Emmanuel Swedenborg, Thomas Taylor, Basilius Valentinius, Carl von Reichenbach, Alan Wilson Watts, Ken Wilber, Robert Anton Wilson and Arthur Young. Shown here is a 1612 called The Four Philosophers by Flemish artist Peter Paul Rubens (peterpaulrubens.org). Also see Philosophy.

Philosophical and Mystical Movements

Of the thousands of philosophical and mystical movements, the following are described herein: Aesthetics, Ascension Movement, Bhakti, Carpocratians, Chaos Magic, Confucianism, Cosmic Movement, Deism, Druidry, Existentialism, Feng Shui, Gnosticism, Hasidism, Hermeticism, I Ching, Mysticism, Neo-Platonism, Orphism, Pantheism, Qabbalah, Quietism, Sacred Geometry, Shamanism, Spiritism, Spiritualism, Stoicism, Sufism, Taoism, Teleology, Thanatology, Thaumaturgy, Theology, Theosophy, Theurgy, Transcendentalism, Unanimism, and Zen. Also see Spiritual Goals, and Spiritual Teachers.

Philosophical Furnace
See Athanor.

Philosophy
From Greek philos meaning "lover" and sophia meaning "wisdom", philosophy is the pursuit of and the love for knowledge and its application, seeking out the hidden meaning of things. It is now used to describe the pursuit of knowledge in fundamental abstract matters such as life and death, truth, reality, mind, matter, proof, etc. Shown here is a 19th Century statue by French sculptor Auguste Rodin (auguste-rodin.com) called The Thinker housed in the Legion of Honor Museum in San Francisco, California. Also see allaboutphilosophy.org, philosophyarchive.com and philosophyprofessor.com.

Philtre
Philtre is a magical love potion. Philtre was usually made of wine or tea with herbs and or drugs, although the recipes and ingredients varied from place to place. Shown here is a 1903 painting by British artist Evelyn de Morgan (demorgan.org.uk) called The Love Potion. Also see Magical Methods.

Phinuit
Spirit guide said to be channeled through medium Leonore Piper. Also see Channeled Spirit Guides, Channelers, and Leonore Piper.

Phobia

From Greek meaning "fear" a phobia is an unreasonable, irrational and persistent fear of persons, activities, situations or objects.

Phoebe

In Greek mythology, Phoebe is one of the Titans, daughter of Gaea and Uranus. She is Apollo's grandmother and she gave him Oracle of Delphi. Phoebe is depicted here in a 19th Century painting by an unknown artist. Also see Greek Gods and Goddesses, and Titans.

Phoenix

In Russian, Chinese, Japanese, Egyptian, Arabian, Greek, Roman and Native American mythology, the phoenix is a fire bird which burns itself with flames and is resurrected from its own ashes. The Phoenix represents virtue, grace, prosperity, immortality, resurrection and life after death. The Chinese describe the phoenix as a mythical bird that never dies. Also see Mythological Creatures.

Phooka

In Irish mythology, the phooka is a very mischievous mythological creature that appears as different beasts. Legend says that when the phooka appears as a friendly black horse he will let the unwary traveler mount it and will then take them on a wild and sometimes deadly ride. Phookas are said to appear most frequently on Samhain (Halloween). Shown here is a depiction of a Phooka by British artist Brian Froud (worldoffroud.com). Other spellings include pooka and puca. Also see Kelpies, and Mythological Creatures.

Phosphorus

See Lucifer.

Phronesis

According to Gnostic literature, Phronesis, which means "prudence", is one of four luminaries that emanates from the divine will. Also see Supernatural and Spiritual Beings.

Phul

Olympian Spirit who governs the Moon and other provinces of the Universe. See Olympian Spirits.

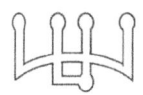

Phylactery

From the Greek term for the Hebrew tefillin which means either of two leather boxes worn on the arm or head which contain scrolls with specific Biblical verses and scriptural passages used especially by observant Orthodox Jewish men during morning weekday prayers. Shown here is a 1500 painting by Italian artist Raphael (raphaelsanzio.org) called Angel with Phylactery.

Phylactery

In Pagan and Druidry practices, the phylactery is an amulet or talisman used to protect from harm. The phylactery is composed of magical texts and or herbs.

Phyllorhodomancy

Divination by rose petals or rose leaves. Also see Divination.

Phyltotherapy

See Herbalism.

Physicists

A physicist is a person who studies the science of matter and energy and the interaction between the two. There are many fields in physics such as, mechanics, thermodynamics, electromagnetism, atomic, nuclear, quantum, etc. The physicists described in include: Fritjof Capra, William Crookes, Richard Feynman, Geber, John Samuel Hagelin, Michio Kaku, Sir Oliver Lodge, Arnold Mindell, Sir Isaac Newton, Harold Puthoff, Jack Sarfatti, Asoka Selvarajah, Russell Targ, Evan Walker, Daniel Sewell Ward and Fred Alan Wolf.

Picucci, Michael

American-born Michael Picucci Ph.D. is a scholar, lecturer, author, psychotherapist, sexologist, somatic experiencing practitioner master addictions counselor, and originator of the Authentic Process Therapy. He co-founded the Institute for Staged Recovery and the Institute for Authentic Process Healing and has received state and national awards for Outstanding Leadership in Research and Applications for reducing human suffering. He has written: The Journey Toward Complete Recovery: Reclaiming Your Emotional, Spiritual and Sexual Wholeness, Ritual and Resource: Energy for Vibrant Living; Complete Recovery: An Expanded Model of Community Healing; and An Introduction to Focalizing: Organic Solutions to Real Time Challenges. Photograph taken by Chris Kreussling. Also see Healers, Recommended Reading, focalizing.com, stagedrecovery.com and theinstitute.org.

Pierrakos, Eva

(1915-1979) Austrian-born Eva Broch Wassermann later Eva Pierrakos was well known for her mediumistic abilities in automatic writing, channeling and developed a system called Pathwork. She presented hundreds of lectures called The Pathwork Guide Lectures and private consultations though a channeled entity known as The Guide. She married John Pierrakos, creator of Core Energetics and they established themselves in a secluded valley in New York where they continued their work. Her books include: Guide Lectures for Self-Transformation; Fear No Evil: The Pathwork Method of Transforming the Lower Self; Creating Union: The Pathwork of Relationship; Surrender to God Within: Pathwork at the Soul Level; Complete Lectures of the Pathwork; and The Pathwork of Self-Transformation. Also see Automatic Writing, Channeled Spirit Guides, Channelers, Psychics, Recommended Reading, awakentruth.org and pathwork.org.

Pierrakos, John

(1921-2001) Greek-born John C. Pierrakos was a psychiatrist, pioneer in holistic medicine and psychology, and co-creator of Core Energetics and the Institute of Core Energetics which is a holistic healing approach that emphases the integration of emotions as well as mind as part of the physical healing process. Dr. Pierrakos said that he was able to see and perceive the aura and the chakras. Among his books are: The Energy Field in Man and Nature; Observations of Group Phenomena and Group Therapy; Creative Aspects of the Ego in the Core-Energetic Process; Human Energy Systems Theory: History and New Growth Perspectives; Core Energetics: Developing the Capacity to Love and Heal; and Eros, Love and Sexuality: The Forces that Unify Man and Woman.

Photograph from biodinamicamexico.com. Also see Core Energetics, Holistic Healing, Institute of Core Energetics, Recommended Reading and coreenergetics.org.

Pietas

In Roman mythology, Pietas is the Goddess of Piety who rules over respect for ancestors and nations and duty toward the Gods. Shown here is a 1498 statue of Pietas by Italian artist and sculptor Michelangelo (michelangelo.com). Also see Roman Gods and Goddesses.

Pike, Albert

(1809-1891) American-born Albert Pike was an attorney, mathematician, poet, writer and one of the most influential Freemasons of all times. After passing the entrance exams at Harvard University he chose not to attend and instead self-educated himself and became a schoolteacher for a time. He married and became owner of the Little Rock Arkansas Advocate newspaper. He later studied law, sold the newspaper, passed the bar and wrote several guidebooks for lawyers as well as poetry highly regarded in his time. In 1859 he received an honorary Ph.D. from Harvard which he declined. He joined Freemasons in 1840, becoming very active in the organization. He was elected the Sovereign Grand Commander of the Scottish Rite's Southern Jurisdiction in 1959; he remained Sovereign Grand Commander for the next 32years until his death. He revised the rituals of the order and published Morals and Dogma of the Ancient and Accepted Scottish Rite of Freemasonry in 1871. Photograph taken by Mathew Brady. Also see Freemasons, Mathematicians, Poets, and Recommended Reading.

Pilgrimage

Pilgrimage is used to describe a search or journey of a great spiritual significance. Pilgrimages may be journeys to places such as a sacred site or shrine. Shown here is an 1862 depiction of a pilgrimage by British artist John Dawson Watson. Also see Sacred Sites, sacred-destinations.com and sacredsites.com.

Pillan

Araucanian (Chile) mythology Pillan is the Chief of Gods. He rules over fire, thunder and war and, aided by evil spirits, causes earthquakes, storms and volcanic eruptions. Also see Araucanian Gods and Goddesses.

Pinga

Inuit Goddess of Game and Hunt, Protector of Medicine Men, Pinga is also called The One on High. She watches how men treat animals. Also see Inuit Gods and Goddesses.

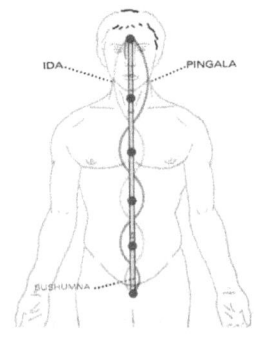

Pingala

In Buddhism and Hinduism, pingala is the right hand nadi or channel of energy in each being that, when awaken, moves kundalini energy outwards through the chakras. Pingala is also called the Sun Current. The left hand channel is called ida and the central channel is called the shushumna. Image from alquimistadeconsciencias.blogspot.com. Also see Chakras, Ida, Kundalini, Nadis, and Sushumna

Piper, Leonore

(1859-1950) American-born Leonore Evelina Simmonds aka Leonore Piper was considered one of the foremost trance mediums and channelers of her time. She said she was clairvoyant from childhood although she began entering a state of trance when she was un adult. She claimed to have several spirit guides or Channeled Spirit Guides but her main control was a spirit named Phinuit and later another entity called Imperator. She was studied by several psychic researchers, including Sir Oliver Lodge. William James and James Hyslop who were convinced of her authenticity. Mrs. Piper was described as an honest hard working woman. Photograph from Also see Channeled Spirit Guides, Channelers, Clairvoyants and Mediums.

Pisces

One of the twelve signs of the zodiac, Pisces is ruled by Neptune and symbolized by the fish. Also see Astrology, and Zodiac.

Pistis Sophia

In Gnostic literature, Pistis Sophia, which means "faith and wisdom", is a female Aeon, said to have procreated "the Superior Angels". She is known as the one of the greatest of the Aeons and supposedly sent the snake to entice Adam and Eve. Shown here in a 1921 painting by British artist Lord Frederick Leighton (frederic-leighton.org) called Invocation.

Pitris

Hindu word used to describe the spirits of our direct ancestors and discarnate entities. or as the legendary progenitor of any family. Also see Supernatural and Spiritual Beings.

Pitris

In Occultism Pitris are the progenitors of humans, who assist human evolution by influencing minds and providing vital energy. Also see Supernatural and Spiritual Beings.

Pixies

In Scottish and Irish mythology, Pixies are Earth Elementals. Other spellings include Piskies, Pisgies and Pigsies. It is said that they like to dance and ring bells, as well as throw pots and pans at young girls. Pixies are depicted here in an 1847 painting by Scottish artist Sir Joseph Noel Patton called The Reconciliation of Oberon and Titania. Also see Elementals.

Pizzorno, Joseph

American-born Joseph "Joe" E. Pizzorno Jr., N.D. (Naturopathic physician) is an author, physician, researcher, educator, spokesperson and one of the world's leading authorities on scientifically based natural medicine. He was appointed a member of the White House Commission of Complementary and Alternative Medicine Policy by President Clinton and to the Medicare Coverage Advisory Committee by President Bush's administration. Dr. Pizzorno is also the founding president of the Bastyr University and Salugenecists, Inc. Dr. Pizzorno has received many awards and honors including Naturopathic Physician of the Year by the American Association of Naturopathic Physicians and Humanitarian of the Year by the cancer Treatment Centers of America. His books include: Total Wellness Systems: Improve Your Health by Understanding the Body's Healing; Textbook of Natural Medicine; The Wellness Revolution: How Understanding the Six Roots of Illness Can Change Your Life; and The Clinician's Handbook of Natural

Medicine. Photograph from ncns.info. Also see Mind-Body Energy Medicine, Recommended Reading, Salugenecists, drpizzorno.com and salugenecists.com.

Place Memory
See Imprinting.

Planchette
A planchette is a heart shaped or triangular board supported by castors on two sides and a pencil on the point, which when held by one or more person, moves to spell answers to questions or to deliver messages from the spirits. Shown here is an 1885 depiction of the planchette from The Scientific American magazine. The planchette predates the ouija board. Also see Ouija Board.

Plane
In Occultism a plane is a realm or range in a given state of consciousness. Also see Planes of Existence.

Planes of Existence
The Planes of Existence, also called Planes of Manifestation, are explained as the seven spiritual planes through which we, as divine sparks of God evolve. The planes have different levels or layers of vibrations, the higher up the more pure vibrations and proximity to Angelic or Divine realms, and the lower planes closer to the physical or manifest plane of existence. The planes are described by Occultists as the following: Physical or Material Plane (starting with the smallest and darkest), is the physical world and what we perceive through our "normal physical" senses. There is an "in between" plane called the Etheric Plane which lies between the Physical and the Astral Plane; Lower Astral, Psychic Plane or Plane of Illusion, is described as an intermediate level of reality beyond the visible material and physical. The world of dreams, psychic manifestations and thought forms; Upper Astral is the plane of emotions; Lower Mental is the plane of concrete thought and memory; Upper Mental is the plane of abstract mind; Lower Spiritual is the plane of concrete spirit; and Upper Spiritual is the plane of pure spirit or Abstract Spirit, the first phase of manifestation drawing its substance and energy directly from the Great Unmanifest. Upon this plane All are One and One is All. Image from kheper.net.

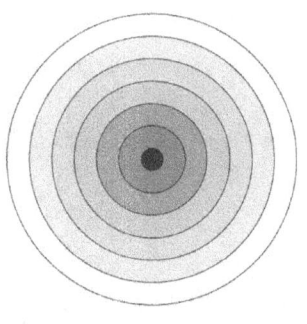

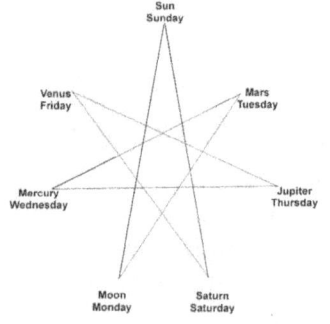

Planes of Manifestation
See Planes of Existence.

Planetary Days
An ancient system using the seven traditional planets (including the Moon and the Sun) in which every day of the week is ruled by one of the planets. Also see Planetary Hours.

Planetary Grids
See Earth's Grids

Planetary Hours
An ancient system using the seven traditional planets (including the Moon and the Sun as shown here) in which every hour of the day is ruled by one of the planets. Also see Planetary Days.

Planetary Hours

Sunrise	Sunday	Monday	Tuesday	Wednesday	Thursday	Friday	Saturday
1	Sun	Moon	Mars	Mercury	Jupiter	Venus	Saturn
2	Venus	Saturn	Sun	Moon	Mars	Mercury	Jupiter
3	Mercury	Jupiter	Venus	Saturn	Sun	Moon	Mars
4	Moon	Mars	Mercury	Jupiter	Venus	Saturn	Sun
5	Saturn	Sun	Moon	Mars	Mercury	Jupiter	Venus
6	Jupiter	Venus	Saturn	Sun	Moon	Mars	Mercury
7	Mars	Mercury	Jupiter	Venus	Saturn	Sun	Moon
8	Sun	Moon	Mars	Mercury	Jupiter	Venus	Saturn
9	Venus	Saturn	Sun	Moon	Mars	Mercury	Jupiter
10	Mercury	Jupiter	Venus	Saturn	Sun	Moon	Mars
11	Moon	Mars	Mercury	Jupiter	Venus	Saturn	Sun
12	Saturn	Sun	Moon	Mars	Mercury	Jupiter	Venus
13	Jupiter	Venus	Saturn	Sun	Moon	Mars	Mercury
14	Mars	Mercury	Jupiter	Venus	Saturn	Sun	Moon
15	Sun	Moon	Mars	Mercury	Jupiter	Venus	Saturn
16	Venus	Saturn	Sun	Moon	Mars	Mercury	Jupiter
17	Mercury	Jupiter	Venus	Saturn	Sun	Moon	Mars
18	Moon	Mars	Mercury	Jupiter	Venus	Saturn	Sun
19	Saturn	Sun	Moon	Mars	Mercury	Jupiter	Venus
20	Jupiter	Venus	Saturn	Sun	Moon	Mars	Mercury
21	Mars	Mercury	Jupiter	Venus	Saturn	Sun	Moon
22	Sun	Moon	Mars	Mercury	Jupiter	Venus	Saturn
23	Venus	Saturn	Sun	Moon	Mars	Mercury	Jupiter
24	Mercury	Jupiter	Venus	Saturn	Sun	Moon	Mars

Planetary Seals and Magical Squares
Also called Planetary Sigils, in Astrology and Occultism, each planet (including the Moon and the Sun) has its own Planetary Seal based on the planet's Magical Square, where theoretically the seal touches every number within the square, although in the practice this is not the case. They are:

Planetary Seal	Planet	Magical Square
(seal)	Saturn	4 9 2 / 3 5 7 / 8 1 6
(seal)	Jupiter	4 14 15 1 / 9 7 6 12 / 5 11 10 8 / 16 2 3 13
(seal)	Mars	11 24 7 20 3 / 4 12 25 8 16 / 17 5 13 21 9 / 10 18 1 14 22 / 23 6 19 2 15
(seal)	Sun	6 32 3 34 35 1 / 7 11 27 28 8 30 / 19 14 16 15 23 24 / 18 20 22 21 17 13 / 25 29 10 9 26 12 / 36 5 33 4 2 31

Planetary Seal	Planet	Magical Square
	Venus	
	Mercury	
	Moon	

Planetary Sigils
See Planetary Seals and Magical Squares.

Planetary Spirits
In Occult and Qabbalistic literature, the Planetary Spirits are one of seven spiritual beings or personal Gods who govern each the seven traditional planets and the signs of the zodiac. They are:

Astaroth The Spirit of Mercury who rules over Gemini and Virgo.

Bartzabel The Spirit of the Mars who rules over Aries and Scorpio.

Chasmodai The Spirit of Luna (Moon) who rules over Cancer.

Hismael The Spirit of Jupiter and Venus who rules over Sagittarius and Pisces.

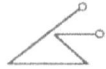

Kedemel The Spirit of Venus and Jupiter who rules over Taurus and Libra.

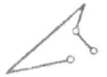

Sorath The Spirit of the Sun and rules over Leo.

Zazel The Spirit of Saturn who rules over Capricorn and Aquarius. Also see Supernatural and Spiritual Beings

Planets

In Astrology, the traditional Planets (which also are referred to as the celestial bodies, because they include the Sun and the Moon), affect all aspects of human life with their particular influences. Also see Astrology. Shown here is a montage of planets prepared and photographed by NASA. Also see astrology.com. The following influences are described or each of the Planets:

Sun
Rules over masculinity; ambition, career, honor, patrimony, fame, luck, gold and wealth; rank and high position, royalty (together with Jupiter), sovereign, father or captain of a group or organization. The human body as a whole, health and healing, children, diamonds, lovers, entertainers, entertainment, theater and stage, movie and theater actors, amusement parks, authority, tyrant, pride and fall from pride, arrogance and the law.

Moon
Represents femininity and maternity, procreation and fertility, development of psychic abilities, sensibility, public and relations, change, rhythms, indecision, family, intimacy in the home, mother, maternity, babies and children, care, maturity of seeds, feeding, food, stomach, chest, emotions and weakness, the tides, water, the sea, ships and crews, home, all that holds and protects, lost objects and candles.

Mars
Represents valor, courage, deviation from the norm, protection against physical and spiritual danger, machines, adventure, energy, cars, war and weapons, struggles, battlefields (domestic battlefields as well), pain, fever, management, ambition, energy or power to overcome obstacles, fighting spirit, sharp words, accidents, particularly fire and cuts or lacerations, personal gain, stubbornness, decision, violence and tantrums.

Mercury
Rules over intellect, spirit, entertainment, skill, writing, manuscripts, language, typewriters, mental processes and perceptions, communication, mail, newspapers and magazines, telecommunication, telephone, rumors, reports, reporters, acquisition of

knowledge, books, documents, brothers, sisters, relatives, direct environment, visits, youth in general, news and messages, professors, gossip, tenants and illnesses.

Jupiter
Represents finances, banks, bankers, prestige and reputation, wagers, horses and horse races, luck in general, religions and philosophies, lawyers and judges, the law, universities, benefits and expansion, riches, royal courts, wisdom, editorials, authors, foreigners and foreign relations, discovery voyages, insurances, small children, dreams, ceremonies, rituals and parades, liver, blood and all that relates to them.

Venus
Represents and rules over love, marriage, personal relations, beauty, art, artists, artistic spirit, music, social events, sociability, romances and courtships, wedding celebrations, elegance, harmony, pleasure, peace, unbalance, money, investors and investments, property, furniture, contracts, agreements, nieces and nephews.

Saturn
Represents or rules over houses, property and buildings, old people and old things, stability, wisdom through age, antiques, karma, mines, time, watches, patience, decision, self-discipline, promises, responsibilities, depression, loneliness, economy, savings; routine, history, sadness, melancholy, all that impairs or impedes, sarcasm, career, fame, reputation (name or fame), destiny, managers, workers and the government.

Uranus
Represents or rules over magical powers, the new and modern, liberty, paradoxes, space and nuclear technology; chaos and crisis, divorce, science, nonconformity, rebellion, unpredictability, insurrections, anarchy, desires and expectations, humanitarian endeavors, friends, club members, fraternities, associations, daughters and sons, abortions and deaths in the family.

Pluto
Represents the sub world, life after death, hidden or buried treasures (oil, gems or minerals).

Plant Alchemy
See Spagyrics.

Plant Rhys Dwfen
In Welsh, Scottish and Irish mythology, the Plant Rhys Dwfen, also called the Children of the Deep Rhys are described as Fairies who inhabit an area which is invisible to human eyes because of a certain herb that grows

there. They are said to take on human form and visit the markets. Shown here is a 1908 painting by British artist Arthur Rackham (rackham.artpassions.net) called A Fairy. Also see Fairies.

Plato

(427-347 B.C.E.) Originally Aristocles of Athens, Plato was a Greek philosopher and disciple of Socrates, considered one of the all time geniuses. Deeply affected by Socrates' execution, Plato spent much time traveling in Egypt and Italy and studied with Pythagoras in Greece. He taught and wrote most of his life creating a profound philosophy concerning humankind's social and personal conduct. Plato believed that the material world was an inferior reflection of a higher truth and that knowledge had no practical use but existed for the abstract good of the soul. He wrote in his work, Phaedrus that not one person who decided in his youth to hold the opinion that there were no Gods ever came to end his life with that conviction and that deep down within the soul, humankind "knows" there is a Supreme Creator. One of his best known writings is The Republic. Plato is shown here in a 1509 painting by Italian artist Raphael (raphaelsanzio.org) called The School of Athens. Also see Mystics, Philosophers and plato.stanford.edu.

Pleiades

Also called the Seven Sisters, in Greek mythology the Pleiades (originally called Atlantides) are seven sister Goddesses. They are the daughters of Atlas (daughter of Oceanos – later Atlas is described as the son-in-law of Poseidon) and were turned into stars by Zeus. The Pleiades are: Alcyone, Goddess of the Sea and the Moon, (also called Queen Who Wards Off Evil); Celaeno, married to Prometheus; Electra, mother of the Harpies; Maia, Goddess of Fertility, the eldest and most beautiful of the Pleiades and mother of Hermes by Zeus; Merope, whose name means "honey-faced", married a mortal, Sisyphus (she is the faintest of the stars); Sterope, wife of Ares, and Taygete. The Pleiades are depicted here in an1885 painting by American artist Elihu Vedder (elihuvedder.org). Also see Greek Gods and Goddesses.

Plerona

From Greek meaning "fullness" and in Gnostic cosmology, pleroma refers to the totality of the powers of God and the place of dwelling of the spirit. The term plerona is used in Christian theological contexts.

Plesithea

In Gnostic literature, and The Secret Books of the Egyptian Gnostics, Plesithea is the mother of Angels, described as a virgin with four breasts. Also see Angels.

Pliny the Elder

(23-79 C.E.) Roman-born Gaius Plinius Secundus known as Pliny the Elder was a philosopher, naturalist scholar, author and naval and military commander. He was educated in Rome and did his military service in Germania. Although wrote extensively, the one surviving book of his is an encyclopedia of natural science called Historia Naturalis. It is divided into 37 books that deal with geography, anthropology, botany, mineralogy, zoology and the nature of the physical universe. His chapter on botany includes the medicinal uses of plants. Pliny is quoted as saying "True glory consists of doing what deserves to be written and writing what deserves to be read". He died during the 79 AD eruption of Mount Vesuvius that destroyed both Pompeii and Herculaneum. Shown here is a contemporary portrait of Pliny the Elder signed by Bollinger Jr. Also see Philosophers and Recommended Reading.

Plonka, Lavinia

American-born Lavinia Plonka is a motivational speaker, teacher, yogi, author and expert on body language. She uses physical movement as a tool for health improvement and personal development. As a mime/choreographer, Ms. Plonka was an artist in residence for the Guggenheim Museum and movement consultant for theater and television companies. She is currently director of Asheville Movement Center in Asheville, North Carolina. She studied and taught yoga and martial arts Aikido, and was a mime as well as and is a master teacher of the Feldenkrais Method®. She has written: What Are You Afraid Of: A Body / Mind Guide to Courageous Living and Walking Your Talk: Changing Your Life Through the Magic of Body Language. Also see Recommended Reading, Self-Help, Yogis, and laviniaplonka.com.

Plotinus

(205-270 C.E.) Roman-born Neo-Platonist philosopher and center of an influential circle of intellectuals Rome, Plotinus is also regarded as the founder of the Neo-Platonic School of Philosophy. He is considered the most influential philosopher after Plato and Aristotle. Plotinus taught Pythagorean and Platonic wisdom and his works include 54 treatises in Greek, called the Enneads which are distributed in six groups of nine books each, an arrangement probably made by his student Porphyry who edited his writings. His writings inspired mystics, occultists, religious and Gnostics throughout the centuries. Plotinus is shown here from a 1509 painting by Italian artist Raphael (raphaelsanzio.org) called The School of Athens. Also see Philosophers and plato.stanford.edu.

Ploughing Festival

One of the most important of the Buddhist festivals, this festival is to celebrate the Buddha's first moment of enlightenment, said to have happened when the Buddha was seven years old and had gone with his father to watch the ploughing. See Buddhism.

Plummer, George Winslow

(1876-1944) American-born George Winslow Plummer best known as co-founder of the Societas Rosicruciana in America. He studied art at Brown University, moved to New York and joined the Freemasons. He assumed leadership of the Societas Rosicruciana in 1909 and remained its sole leader until his death. Plummer also founded the First Rosicrucian Church in the United States and was ordained bishop in 1918. In 1924 he co-founded the Anglican Universal Church of Christ in the U.S.A. Bishop Plummer also wrote many books including: Principles and Practice for Rosicrucians; Master's Word: A Short Treatise on the Word, the Light and the Self; The Art of Rosicrucian Healing; Rosicrucian Fundamentals: An Exposition of the Rosicrucian Synthesis of Religion, Science and Philosophy, in Fourteen Complete Instructions; Consciously Creating Circumstances and The Science of Death. Photograph from sria.org. Also see Freemasons, Recommended Reading and Rosicrucians.

Pluto

In Astrology, as the celestial body affecting aspects of human life, Pluto represents the sub world, life after death, the hidden or buried (oil, gems or minerals). See Planets.

Pluto

Greek God of Death and the Underworld, Pluto is also the God of Riches and as such he rules over the treasures of the earth, such as crops and minerals. As God of Death he rules over death and the dead, illumination, metamorphosis, evolution and revolution; funerary professions; taxes and inheritances, debts and creditors, wills and legacies; and bankrupts and losses. He is the son of Cronus and Rhea and the brother of Zeus and Poseidon. Pluto is also called Dis Pater and Orcus. Shown here is a 1778 statue of Pluto by German artist and sculptor Dominik Auliczek found in the Gardens of Nymphenburg Palace in Munich, Germany. Photograph by Rufus46. Also see Greek Gods and Goddesses, and Underworld Gods.

Pneuma

From Greek meaning "breath" or "spirit", and according to Stoicism, Pneuma is the spirit or vital energy, as opposed to the psyche or soul that exists in all living things. Also see Stoicism.

Pneumatics

In Gnostic traditions, pneumatics are the highest order of humans as opposed to the somatics (or hylics). The penumatics are defined as spiritually initiated or enlightened, escaping the material world via secret knowledge while the somatics are too attached to the material world and ignorant of the spiritual side. Also see Hylics, and Somatics.

Pneumatographers
New age term for automatic writing mediums. Also see Automatic Writing, and Mediums.

Poets
The poets described herein include: Dante Alighieri, William Blake, Giordano Bruno, Stanislas de Guaita, Stuart Grayson, Thich Nhat Hann, Victor Hugo, Aldous Huxley, Kahil Gibran, Johann Wolfgang von Goethe, Andrew Lang, Stephen Levine, Robert E. Masters, Frederick Myers, John G. Neihardt, Ross Nichols, Albert Pike, George William Russell, Sankara Saranam, Cyril Scott, Evelyn Underhill, Charles Williams and William Butler Yeats.

Polerian
In Theosophy Polerian refers to one of humanities Root Races, described by Helena Blavatsky, said to have originated 130 to 150 million years ago in the Etheric plane and marking the beginning of denser physical states toward the physical evolution of humankind. See Root Races.

Polerity
Polarity refers to positive and negative aspects of all things. Also see Yin/Yang.

Poltergeist
Poltergeist comes from German and means "noisy ghost". Poltergeists are said to be annoying discarnate entities who manifest their presence by rapping on walls, hiding or breaking objects, and in general being a nuisance. There are also said to be cases in which poltergeists attach themselves to people rather than places. And there are cases, originally attributed to poltergeists in which the psychic disturbances are due to externalization of psychic energy from emotionally distressed children or adolescents, excluding the presence of poltergeists. The people and places mentioned herein that are said to have been haunted by poltergeists include: Borley Rectory, Enfield, Daniel Dunglass Home, Michael Talbot and Eleonore Zugun. Also see Apparition, Ghosts and Most Haunted.

Polyhymnia
In Greek mythology Polyhymnia, meaning "She of Many Hymns" is the Muse of Mimes and Sacred Poetry. She is one of nine sister Goddesses called the Muses. Shown here is a 1460 painting of Polyhymnia by Italian artist Francesco del Cossa. Also see Greek Gods and Goddesses, and Muses.

Polytheist
One who believes in many Gods.

Pomona
In Roman mythology, Pomona is the Goddess of the Blooming Fruit Trees. She rules over orchards and gardens. She scorned the love of Silvanus

and married Vertumnus after he tricked her. Pomona had a special priest in Rome called the Flamen Pomonalis and a sacred grove near Ostia called the Pomonal. She is usually depicted as a beautiful maiden holding fruits. Shown here is a 1522 painting by Italian artist Francesco Melzi called Pomona and Vertumnus. Also see Roman Gods and Goddesses.

Ponder, Catherine

(1927-) American-born Catherine Ponder is a Unitarian Minister, lecturer and bestselling author of inspirational books. Known as a pioneer of positive thinking she is described as "the Normal Vincent Peal among lady ministers". She has served in Unity Churches since the mid 1950's and given lectures in most of the major cities in the United States. Reverend Ponder currently heads a global ministry in Palm Desert. California. Among her books are: The Dynamic Laws of Prosperity; How to Live a Prosperous Life; Dynamic Laws of Healing; Healing Secrets of the Ages; The Millionaire from Nazareth: His Prosperity Secrets For You!, Dare to Prosper; The Prosperity Secrets of the Ages: How to Channel a Golden River of Riches Into Your Life; The Dynamic Laws of Prayer and The Dynamic Laws of Prosperity: Giving Makes Your Rich. Also see Positive Thinking, Recommended Reading, Reverends and Ministers, Self-Help Spiritual Teachers and catherineponder.wwwhubs.com.

Pono

From Hawaiian religion Huna, Pono is one of its seven philosophical principles and it means "effectiveness is the measure of truth". Also see Huna.

Popol Vuh

From the Maya civilization the Popol Vuh, meaning "council book" or "book of the community" is one of the most important surviving sacred books. It describes the creation of Earth and its inhabitants, followed by the stories of the lives of the Hero Twins (Xblanque and Hunahpu) and then describes the Mayan dynasties. Other spellings include Popol Wu'uj. Also see Sacred Writings.

Poppet

In western European folk magic and Wicca a poppet is a doll constructed of wax, wood, corn or cloth meant to represent a specific person in sympathetic magic, sometimes these poppets may include hair or nail clippings from the person. Other spellings include poppit, pippy and puppet. Also see Sympathetic Magic and Voodoo Dolls.

Populus

As a Qabbalistic geomantic figure, Populus is ruled by the Moon and represents movement and change, sometimes good and sometimes bad and is used in the ancient art of Geomancy. Also see Divination, and Geomancy.

Portals

Portals are described as inter-dimensional doorways, wormholes or openings that can transport entities, physically or mentally, into other dimensions or realities. Shown here is a painting by Canadian artist Mario Duguay (marioduguay.com) called Openness.

Portent

A portent is an event, object or phenomenon that is perceived as an omen or warning to a future event. Also see Methods of Prediction and Omen.

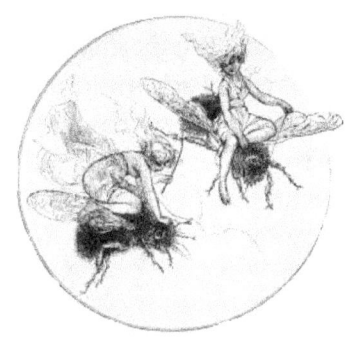

Portunes

In Scottish and Irish mythology, Portunes are described as tiny Fairies who help humans with farm work. Shown here is an 1870 depiction of fairies by Irish artist Thomas Keightley. Also see Fairies.

Portunus

In Roman mythology, Portunus is the God of Keys and Doors. He rules over livestock and he protects warehouses where grain is stored, harbors and gates. Other spellings include Portumnes and Portunes. Also see Roman Gods and Goddesses.

Poseidon

Greek God of the Sea, son of Cronus and Rhea, brother of Zeus, Hera, Hades, Hestia and Demeter, husband of Amphitrite and father of Triton. Poseidon rules over marine life, sea storms, earthquakes, human emotions, intuition, sailors and ships, hurricanes, earthquakes, rain and revenge. He is also called Earthshaker, Supreme Lord of the Inner and Outer Seas and Overlord of Lakes and Rivers. He had numerous love affairs with Nymphs and Goddesses. He is known to the Romans as Neptune and is one of the Olympian Gods. Shown here is a 1757 painting by French artist Carle van Loo called Neptune and Amymone. Also see Greek Gods and Goddesses, and Olympian Gods.

Poseidonis

Described by occultists and psychics as the last of the three main islands the lost continent of Atlantis, Poseidonis is said to have sunk around 10.000 B.C.E. Poseidonis is depicted here in a 1904 rendition by British theosophist William Scott-Elliot. Also see Atlantis.

Posidonius

(135-51 B.C.E.) Posidonio de Apamea aka Posidonius was Greek philosopher, historian, astronomer, politician and teacher, considered the most learned man of his time. Posidonius is nicknamed "The Athlete". Through his writings and his personal relations, Posidonius spread Stoicism in the Roman world. His ethical doctrine differed from contemporary Stoicism, in that he viewed human passions as inherent qualities not faulty judgments. He believed that all things in the Universe are united by a vital force that emanates from the Sun. His writings on the history of the time, between 146 to 88 B.C.E., filled 52 volumes. Posidonius spent many years traveling through Greece, Spain, Italy, Africa and Gaul among other places. Other spellings include Poseidonius. Also see Historians, Philosophers and Stoicism.

Positive Thinking

In this Quantum New Age reality, positive thinking is a way of re-conditioning the mind and re-wiring the brain towards positive spiritual and physical goals, self-improvement and health. Also see Affirmation, Autosuggestion, Creative Visualization, Law of Attraction, Norman Vincent Peale, Catherine Ponder, Spiritual Techniques, academyforguidedimagery.com, creativethinkingwith.com and power-of-imagination.com. Shown here is an image called What matters most is how you see yourself.

Possession

In Occultism, possession is a state in which the personality of a living individual is stolen and his body is controlled by another soul or entity.

Potameides

Greek and Roman Nymphs of rivers. Potameides are shown here in an 1859 painting by British artist Henrietta Rae called Hylas and the Water Nymphs. Also see Nymphs.

Potter, Beverly

American-born Beverly A. "Doc" Potter Ph.D. is a motivational speaker, corporate trainer and author. She received her Ph.D. in counseling psychology from Stanford University (where she was a member of the Staff Development Program) and a Masters in vocational rehabilitation from San Francisco State University. Dr. Potter currently works with corporations, government agencies, colleges and universities. Among her books are: Overcoming Job Burnout: How to Renew Enthusiasm for Work; The Worrywart's Companion: Twenty-One Ways to Soothe Yourself and Worry Smart; Brain Boosters: Food and Drugs That Make You Smarter; High Performance Goal Setting: Using Intuition to Conceive and Achieve Your Dreams; The Healing Magic of Cannabis; Get Peak Performance Every Day: How to Manage Like a Coach; The Way of the Ronin: Riding the Waves of Changes at Work; Managing Yourself for Excellence: How to Be a Can-Do Person; and Question Authority and Think for Yourself. Photograph from amazon.com. Also see Recommended Reading, Self-Help and docpotter.com.

Poughkeepsie Seer
See Andrew Jackson Davis.

Power Spots
See Sacred Sites.

Powers
Powers refer to psychic abilities, such as clairvoyance, astral travel and the ability to recall past lives. Also see Psychic Abilities.

Powers
In Christianity, Powers are a class of Angels in the celestial hierarchy. Their principle task is to see that there is order on the celestial pathways between Heaven and Earth. They are also called Potentates, Dynamis and Spirits in Form. Powers are one of the nine choirs of Angels in Heaven. Shown here is a 1508 painting by Italian artist Michelangelo (michelangelo.com) called The Last Judgement from the Sistine Chapel. Also see Angels.

Practical Qabbalah
The portion of the Qabbalah which deals with the fabrication of talismans for use in ceremonial magic. Shown here is a symbolic sunflower with the name of God inscribed upon its petals in seventy two languages. Above the circle are the seventy two powers of God. Below are two trees, the one on the left bearing the symbols of the planets and the one on the right the signs of the zodiac and the names of the tribes of Israel. Image from metaphysics-for-life.com.

Prana
From Sanskrit, meaning "breath", in mystic and occult philosophies prana is the vital life force or universal energy that courses through the human body and sustains life. It is considered the vital link between the spiritual-self and the physical-self. This universal energy is generated by the Sun and occurs naturally in the atmosphere where it is absorbed by the body's energy centers or chakras. In Hinduism, prana is the energizing power behind occult phenomena and the power or animating force of the Universe. Prana is also called the Breath of Life. Also see Psychic Energies.

Pranayama

Yoga breath control system, pranayama is used to produce an altered state of consciousness. Also see Altered States of Consciousness, and Yoga.

Prayer

An appeal, petition, confession, contrition, supplication, thanksgiving or a loving thought aimed at a specific Deity. A prayer may be a feeling or sensation of devout spiritual communion with God. They may be formal or spontaneous, spoken or silent, based on religious texts or inspired by heart and mind, and may be practiced individually or in groups. Prayers also describe a formula or sequence of words used for praying. Shown here is an 1865 painting by French artist William-Adolphe Bouguereau (bouguereau.org) called The Prayer. Also see Spiritual Techniques.

Prayer Wheel

In Tibetan Buddhist spiritual traditions a prayer wheel, also called a Mani wheel is a wheel on a spindle made from leather, metal or wood inscribed with prayers or mantras. According to the tradition spinning the wheel has the same effect as orally reciting the prayers. Image from buddhagroove.com.

Pre-Existence

Belief that the soul exists prior to incarnating in this life. Also see Reincarnation.

Preachers

A preacher is one who preaches, usually religion. In Christianity, Preachers are clergymen and spiritual teachers of the Christian Church. Also see Clergymen, Christianity, Religious Teachers and Reverends and Ministers.

Precept

From the Latin precipere meaning "to teach", a precept is a principle that defines a certain standard of moral conduct.

Precognition

Precognition is the present perception of future events through extrasensory or psychic means. It has been described as the ability to "for-sense" rather than "for-see" events. Image from devine-light-healing.com. Also see Methods of Prediction, and Psychic Abilities.

Prediction

To foretell future events by previous knowledge or shrewd inference from facts of experience, or the ability to foretell, forecast or see future events without the implication of underlying knowledge. Also see Magical Methods and Methods of Prediction.

Predictions of Death

The people described herein who predicted their own deaths include: Evangeline Adams, Simon Forman and Emanuel Swedenborg.

Premonition

Intuitive feelings such as a sense of dread, warning of future events, usually negative in nature such as accidents and natural disasters. Premonition is also called Presentiment. Also see Methods of Prediction, Omen and Psychic Abilities.

Presence

Presence is the perception or feeling that the soul or essence of a person, animal, spirit or discarnate entity is in the vicinity, but is not physically there. Also see Clairvoyance.

Presentiment

See Premonition.

Pretas

Hindu ghosts of the dead that are not yet at rest.

Preternatural

Preternatural is a term that is used to describe any natural phenomenon which does not have a logical explanation according to the laws of science and nature as we currently understand them. Also see Paranormal, and Supernatural.

Priapus

Greek God of Fertility and Sex, Priapus rules over procreative power in humans and animals and is the protector of gardens and herbs. He is the son of Dionysus and Aphrodite. Priapus is called Mutinus and Lutinus by the Romans.

This depiction of Priapus weighing his phallus was uncovered in a building in Pompeii, Italy. Also see Greek Gods and Goddesses.

Price, Harry

(1881-1948) British-born Harry Price was a well known parapsychologist, psychic researcher and author. He became an expert amateur conjurer on stage magic and this knowledge would assist him in the investigation of paranormal phenomena. Price set up the National Laboratory of Psychical Research and was appointed foreign research officer for the American Society for Psychical Research. He researched and tested the medium Helen Duncan and testified against at her famous witchcraft trial. Price also investigated England's most haunted houses. His books include: The Most Haunted House in England: Ten Years' Investigation of Borley Rectory; Poltergeist Over England Three Centuries of Mischievous Ghosts; Fifty Years of Psychical Research: A Critical Survey Longmans; Cold Light on Spiritualistic "Phenomena" - An Experiment with the Crewe Circle; and The End of Borley Rectory. Also see Parapsychologists and Psychic Researchers, Recommended Reading and harryprice.co.uk.

Price, Henry H.

(1899-1984) British-born Henry Habberley Price a philosopher, professor of logic and author who became a well known figure in parapsychology. He studied at Winchester College and New College in Oxford and taught logic at the University of Oxford. Price was the president of the Society for Psychical Research in London for three years and then council member. He lectured for many years and wrote many articles and books. Some of his best known books are: Essays in the Philosophy of Religion; Hume's Theory of the External World, Thinking and Experience and Some Aspects of the Conflict between Science and Religion; Thinking and Representation; Truth and Corrigibility; and Personal Survival and the Idea of Another World. Also see Parapsychologists and Psychic Researchers, Philosophers and Recommended Reading.

Priest

A Priest is a male religious practitioner devoted to the service of his chosen Deity who receives his authority from a religious organization.

Priestess

A Priestess is a female religious practitioner devoted to the service of her chosen Deity, who receives authority from a religious organization. Shown here is a 1902 painting by French artist William-Adolphe Bouguereau (bouguereau.org) called Young Priestess.

Priests

In Christianity, Priests are clergymen and spiritual teachers of the Christian Church. Also see Christianity, Clergymen, Religious Teachers and Reverends and Ministers.

Prieure de Sion

Also known as the Priory of Sion (or Zion) and Sionis Prioratus, the Prieure de Sion is an mythical secret order supposedly operating behind the Knights Templar which it was said to have created as an administrative and military arm. Its earliest roots are traced to a Gnostic society in 1099 headed by Godefroi de Bouillion. This Secret Society was said to have been founded to protect the Holy blood line of the descendants of Jesus and Mary Magdalene's child in Rennes-le- Château in southern France down through the Merovingian Dynasty. According to the Dossiers Secrets,

among the Grandmasters of the order were people such as Nicolas Flamel, Leonardo da Vinci and Isaac Newton. Also see Dossiers Secrets, Knights Templar, Merovingian Dynasty, Occult Orders, Brotherhoods and Secret Societies, and Rennes-le-Chateau.

Prince of Darkness
In Jewish and Occult traditions, the Prince of Darkness is the Angel of Death, or Satan.

Prince of Peace
The title Prince of Peace or Angel of Peace is usually in reference to Jesus Christ.

Prince Siddhartha Gautama
(563-483 B.C.E.) Prince Siddhartha Gautama was the person to be conferred with the title of Buddha. He is considered the founder of Buddhism as well as an Enlightened One, due to his spiritual enlightenment, wisdom, supreme knowledge, self-realization, healing and compassion. He was also known as Shakyamuni, Butsi and Gautama Buddha. Also see Buddha, Buddhas and Buddhism.

Principle of Mind
See Omniscience.

Principle of Power
See Omnipotence.

Principle of Substance
See Omnipresence.

Principalities
The Principalities are a class of Angels in the celestial hierarchy. They are the protectors of Religion and watch over the leaders of nations and people, inspiring them to make the right choices and decisions. The Principalities are also called Princedoms. They are one of the nine choirs of Angels in Heaven. Shown here is a 1476 painting by Italian artist Francesco Botticini showing the nine choirs of angels called The Assumption of the Virgin. Also see Angels.

Prithivi
One of the five main tattwas, Prithivi is associated with the element of earth, its symbol is a yellow or gold square and it represents anything in a solid tangible or physical state. See Tattwa.

Proclus

(412-485 C.E.) Greek philosopher who was very influential in the development of Neo-Platonic ideas. He studied philosophy under Olympiodorus the Elder at Alexandria and under Plutarch and Syrianus at Athens. Proclus is most known for his collaboration in the refinement of the Neo-Platonic views of Iamblichus, who, like himself, opposed Christianity and defended Paganism. He believed that thoughts were reality and concrete "things" were mere appearances and illusions and that the ultimate reality is God. Also see Neo-Platonism and Philosophers.

Proctor, Charlene

(1959-) American-born Charlene M. Proctor D.D., Ph.D. is a spiritual teacher and educator in the field of women's empowerment and the founder of the Goddess Network, Inc. an on-line educational resource for topics on spirituality and relationships. Reverend Dr. Proctor is a Minister of Spiritual Peacemaking and a certified Oneness Blessing facilitator, helping to awaken individuals from all walks of life to the magnificence of their own Divine gifts. She currently facilitates the PATH to Empowerment program for Lighthouse Path in Michigan, a residential women's shelter for homeless mothers, teaching them how to live with confidence and grace. Rev. Dr. Proctor has written: Let Your Goddess Grow!: Seven Spiritual Lessons on Female Power and Positive Thinking!; The Women's Book of Empowerment: 323 Affirmations That Change Everyday Problems into Moments of Potential; and The Oneness Gospel: Birthing the Christ Consciousness and Divine Human in You. Also see Recommended Reading, Reverends and Ministers, Spiritual Teachers, charleneproctor.com and thegoddessnetwork.net.

Project Blue Book

As the only official study conducted by the United States Air Force of unidentified flying objects (UFOs), Project Blue Book (also called Blue Book Project) started in 1952 and officially ended in 1970. Its goal was to determine if UFO's were a potential threat to National security. Over 12,600 sightings and reports were studied. Most of the cases were concluded to be natural phenomena or hoaxes, but about 700 of the reports were classified as unknown. Due to the Freedom of Information act, the records of Project Blue Book are now declassified and are available for reviewing. Also see Area 51 and bluebookarchive.com.

Project Star Gate

The Project Star Gate, also called the Stargate Project was the code name for one of several projects undertaken by the United States Government to investigate psychic phenomena, especially remote viewing for potential military and domestic applications. Also see remoteviewed.com.

Projective Hand

The projective hand is the dominant hand; so a left handed person's projective and is the left hand and a likewise with a right handed person. Also see Receptive Hand.

Prometheus

Greek God of Fire, Prometheus is a Titan, who stole fire from Olympus to give to humans and also, shaped humans out of clay and endowed them with the divine spark of life. He is said to have invented: architecture, writing, astronomy, navigation and medicine. He is also known as He Who Foresees. Prometheus is depicted here in an 1868 painting by French artist Gustav Moreau (gustave-moreau.com). Also see Greek Gods and Goddesses.

Prophecy

A prophesy is described as a vision or revelation of events that will happen in the future and the act of divining or foretelling future events. Prophecies may be achieved through personal insights or visions, by Divine inspiration or by using exterior divination methods such as astrology, oracles or scrying. Also see Methods of Prediction, Prophet and Prophets.

Prophet

A person who predicts future events though divine inspiration, psychic perception, divination or other means. In religion a prophet relates specifically to a person who interprets or speaks for God. Shown here is a 1628 painting called The Prophet Elijah Receiving Bread and Water from an Angel by Flemish artist Peter Paul Rubens (peterpaulrubens.org). Also see Messiah, Oracle, Prophecy, Prophets and Soothsayer.

Prophets

The prophets that are mentioned herein include: Buddha (Prince Siddhartha Gautama), Muhyi Al-Din Ibn al-'Arabi, Jesus of Nazareth, Malachy Prophesies (Malachy O'More), Mani, Muhammad (Abu al-Qasim Muhammad ibn 'Abd Allah ibn 'Abd al-Muttalib ibn Hashim), Nostradamus and Zoroaster. Shown here is a 1512 painting by Italian artist Raphael (raphaelsanzio.org) called The Prophet Isaiah. Also see Prophecy and Prophet.

Prophetic Kabbalah

See Abraham Abulafia.

Protean Soul

In Occultism a protean soul is a thought form or astral body which can be manipulated by an adept to assume any shape. Also see Astral Bodies, Phantasmata and Tulpa.

Proteus

In Greek mythology, Proteus is a God of the Sea, son of Oceanus and Tethys. He is also called The Old Man of the Sea. He is said to be a shape shifter and has the gift of prophesy. Proteus is shown here in a 16th Century depiction by Italian writer Andrea Alciato. Also see Greek Gods and Goddesses.

Prudence

See Virtues.

Pryse, James Morgan Jr.

(1859-1942) American-born James Morgan Pryse Jr. was a journalist, writer and founder of the Gnostic Society. He joined the Theosophical Society in Los Angeles and moved to New York to work for the society's press. A few years later he moved to London because of a request from Madame Helena Blavatsky. After Blavatsky's death he lived in Ireland and later returned to the United States to work with William Quan Judge in the American Theosophical Society. In 1925 he founded the Gnostic Society. Among his books are: Reincarnation in the New Testament; The Sermon on the Mount: and Other Extracts From the New Testament; A Verbatim Translation From the Greek with Notes on the Mystical or Arcane Sense and The Restored New Testament: the Hellenic Fragments, Freed From the Pseudo-Jewish Interpolations, Harmonized, and don into English Verse and Prose. Also see Gnostic Society, Gnostics, Journalists, Recommended Reading, Reincarnation (Life After Life), Theosophists and gnosis.org.

Pseudopod

A pseudopod is described as a false limb that appears on a medium's body during a séance formed by ectoplasm. Also see Ectoplasm, and Elongation.

Psionics

Psionics is the practice of using a variety of psychic abilities. Also see Psychic Abilities.

Psyche

In Greek mythology Psyche is a nymph who personifies the human soul. She is the wife of Eros and the mother of Voluptas. Shown here is an 1882 painting by French artist Francois Gerard called Cupid and Psyche.

Psyche
From Greek meaning "soul", the psyche is the mind; the center of thought, emotion and behavior, the portion of the mind that relates to the social and physical environment.

Psyche
In Roman mythology, the Goddess Psyche is described as a beautiful princess loved by Cupid and who is made immortal by the God Jupiter. Psyche is depicted here in a 1904 painting by British artist John William Waterhouse (jwwaterhouse.com) called Psyche Entering Cupid's Garden. Also see Roman Gods and Goddesses.

Psychic
A psychic is a person who is sensitive to non-physical influences and spiritual energies and may also possess abilities such as clairvoyance, intuition, precognition, premonition, psychometry, second sight, telepathy and other paranormal abilities. Also see Psychic Abilities, Psychics, Sensitive, psychicchildren.co.uk, psychic-experiences.com, psychicinvestigators.net, psychics.co.uk, psychicscience.org and psychicvista.com.

Psychic Abilities
Term used to describe the ability to receive information without the use of the physical five senses. Also see Clairvoyance Intuition, Precognition, Premonition, Second Sight, Telepathy, divineanswers.com, extrasensory-perceptions-guide.com, psychicchildren.co.uk, psychics.co.uk, psychicinvestigators.net, psychicscience.org and psychicvista.com.

Psychic Attack
A psychic attack is a form of malicious action against someone done by a person or persons with occult knowledge. Psychic attacks take place on the lower Astral Plane and come through to the Physical Plane by means of suggestion aimed at the victim. These types or attacks are very rare due to the mental effort involved required to produce results at this level.

Psychic Centers
See Chakras.

Psychic Cord
See Silver Cord.

Psychic Diagnostician
A psychic diagnostician, also called a medical intuitive is a psychic or intuitive person who has the ability to perceive information concerning the human body and to diagnose and recommend treatment for physical problems or illnesses. Although there have been and are many effective psychic diagnosticians, the two most famous, documented and researched people in this field were Andrew Davis Jackson aka the Poughkeepsie Seer and Edgar Cayce aka the Sleeping Prophet. Also

see Psychic Diagnosticians.

Psychic Diagnosticians
The people mentioned herein who are described as psychic diagnosticians include: Rosalyn Bruyere, Edgar Cayce, Andrew Jackson Davis, Donna Eden, Dora Kunz, Francesca McCartney, Caroline Myss and Judith Orloff. Also see Psychic Diagnostician.

Psychic Energy

Psychic energy is the energy created in the atmosphere surrounding us by the emotions and feelings of people. Positive psychic energy or good vibrations are generated by feelings of love, sympathy, happiness, laughter and other positive emotions, while negative psychic energy or negative vibrations are generated by feelings of hatred, jealousy, greed and other harmful emotions. Also see Psychic Energies. Shown here is a 20th Century painting by American artist Daniel B. Holeman (awakenvisions.com) called Psychic Energy System. Also see Psychic Energy.

Psychic Energies
Of the different terms, forms and definitions for psychic energies, this book describes with the following: Akasha, Animal Magnetism, Astral, Astral Light, Aura, Ch'i, Ether, Nous, Odic Force, Prana, Rhabdic Force, Rupa, Shabd, Telesma, Vasanas, Vibrations and Wakan.

Psychic Healing
Psychic healing is an esoteric technique which involves the channeling of spiritual energy or psychic power through a healer into a patient. The religious aspect of psychic healings involves personal or group prayer. Also see Absent Healing, Energy Medicine, Faith Healing, Spiritual Techniques, Quantum Touch, and Reike.

Psychic Shield
See Shield.

Psychic Vampire
Also called an astral vampire, a psychic vampire is an entity who preys on the life force or spiritual energy of another, knowingly or not. These psychic vampires can be incarnate or discarnate.

Psychics
The psychics described in herein include: Rosemary Altea, Ulrica Arfvidsson, Dolores Ashcroft-Nowicki, Chrissie Blaze, Helena Blavatsky, Sylvia Browne, Kuda Bux, Jerome Cardan, Edgar Cayce, Sonia Choquette, Stella Cranshaw, Gerard Croiset, Jeanne Dixon, Allison DuBois, John Edward, William Eglinton, Arthur Ford, Dion Fortune, Eileen Garrett, Agnes Guppy-Volkman, Bertha Harris, Beverly Jaegers, Elizabeth Joyce-Swaim, Nina Kulagina, Dora Kunz, Charles Lead-

beater, Char Margolis, John J. Oliver, Eva Pierrakos, Noreen Renier, Jane Roberts, Linda Salvin, Schneider Brothers, Jesse Francis Sheppard, Gordon Smith, William Thomas Stead, Doris Stokes, Tara Sutphen, Michael Talbot, James Van Praagh, Alan Vaughan and Victoria Lynn Weston.

Psychogeist
A term used to describe the astral body. See Astral Body, and Astral Bodies.

Psychokinesis
Also called telekinesis, psychokinesis is the ability to influence or move physical matter through the use of mental energy; as in mind over matter. A famous Russian psychic Nelya Mikhailova who had this ability was photographed using Kirlian photography while she moved objects and the photographs taken revealed a rhythmic pulsing of her energy field. Psychokinesis is also called telekinesis and levitation. The people mentioned herein who display psychokinetic abilities include: Stella Cranshaw, Nina Kulagina, Matthew Manning, Carroll Nash, and Joseph Banks Rhine. Also see Kirlian Photography and Spiritual Techniques.

Psychomancy
See Necromancy.

Psychomanteum

In ancient Greece the psychomanteums were oracles of the dead. Seekers fasted and partook in certain rituals before gazing into a pool of water where they consulted with the spirits of the dead. An alternative method used in the psychomanteums was divination by dream interpretation. Shown here is the Temple of Hephaestus in Athens, Greece. Photograph by Yair Haklai. Also see Necromanteion and Oracle.

Psychometry
The ability to receive knowledge or intuitive impressions from persons or events connected with an object or a place upon handling the object or sensing the place, a form of retrocognition. Occultists call also call psychometry reading or seeing. Also see Spiritual Techniques, and Retrocognition.

Psychotherapy
Psychotherapy is the treatment of emotional of psychological problems in a relationship and a one on one communication with a trained therapist. The term was coined by the English psychiatrist Walter Cooper Dendy in 1853 as "psycho-therapeia". Two of the first, foremost and most famous psychotherapists of modern times were Sigmund Freud and Carl Jung. Also see, Carl Jung, wholenesstherapy.com, psychotherapy.net and psychcentral.com.

Ptah

Egyptian Creator God, Ptah rules over regeneration, science, arts and miracles. He is also known as the Principle of Life and Light, the Creator of Earth, the Divine Artificer, the Father of Beginnings and The Opener. He is the consort of Sekmet and their son is considered as the ruling Pharaoh. He is the symbol of the creative power of the God behind the Gods, of the elements of primary forces. Ptah is also described as a powerful healer and patron of artisans, stonecutters, blacksmiths, architects, boat builders and metalworkers. He is depicted as a man with a punt beard wrapped like a mummy but with his hands and head free of bandages. Shown here is a wood statue of Ptah with a bronze scepter, inlayed with gold, inscribed Ptah, Lord of Ma'at, housed in the Cairo Museum in Cairo, Egypt. Also see Egyptian Gods and Goddesses.

Ptolemy

Egyptian-born (85-165 C.E.) Claudius Ptolemaeus aka Ptolemy, was a Greek-speaking (possibly Egyptian-born) philosopher, geographer, astronomer and astrologer who lived in Roman Egypt. He was the author of several scientific treatises, three of which have been of continuing importance to modern Islamic and European science. They are: Almagest "The Great Treatise", (an astronomical treatise), Harmonics; and Tetrabiblos "Four books", in which he attempted to adapt astrology to the Aristotelian natural philosophy of his day. Shown here is a 1584 depiction of Ptolemy attributed to French artist Andre Thevet. Also see Astrologers, Philosophers, Tetrabiblos and houseofptolemy.org.

Puchan

Hindu God who takes souls to the afterlife and protected travelers from wild animals and bandits. Puchan rules over marriage, journeys, roads, prosperity, cattle and meetings, he is also known as The Nourisher. Other spellings include Pushan. Also see Hindu Gods and Goddesses.

Puck

In Welsh and English lore, Puck is described as mischievous shape shifting Earth Elementals who takes great pleasure in provoking embarrassing situations. Other spellings include, Pucke, Puckle, Puok, and Pukis. Puck is depicted here in 1785 rendition by English poet and artist William Blake (william-blake.org) called Oberon, Titania and Puck with Fairies Dancing from Shakespeare's a Midsummer Night's Dream. Also see Elementals.

Puella

As a Qabbalistic geomantic figure ruled by Venus, puella represents peace, love and art, good in all related to women and is used in the ancient art of Geomancy. Also see Divination, and Geomancy.

Puer

As a Qabbalistic geomantic figure ruled by Mars, it represents activity and energy but is evil in most demands except when related to War or Love and it is used in the ancient art of Geomancy. Also see Divination, and Geomancy.

Puranas

In Hinduism, the Puranas are documents or texts which explain the myths and rituals of the Gods. There are eighteen main Puranas: Agni Purana, which relates the teachings that the Fire God Agni gave to the sage Vasishtha; Bhagavata Purana, devoted to Vishnu; Bhavishya Purana, dealing with rituals; Brahma Purana, devoted to the Sun God Surya; Brahma Vaivasvata Purana, dealing with the worship of Krishna and Radha; Brahamanda Purana, devoted to the God Brahma; Garuda Purana, dealing with death and its rituals; Kurma Parana, dealing with the Kurma or tortoise incarnation of Vishnu and his revelations; Lingam Paruna, devoted to the worship of the lingam of Shiva; Markandeya Purana, dealing with how birds recite the Vedas as well as with the Mother Goddess, Shakti; Matsya Purana, devoted to the Matsya or fish incarnation of Vishnu and his revelations; Narada Purana, dealing with the description of man's duties to society according to the sage Narada; Padma Paurna devoted to creation of the world and Patala or lower part of the Underworld; Skanda Purana, devoted to the God of War Skanda; Vamana Purana, dealing with the Vamana or dwarf incarnation of the God Vishnu; Varaha Purana, dealing with the Varaha or boar incarnation of Vishnu and his revelations; Vayu Purana, devoted to the God Shiva; and Vishnu Purana, dealing with the God Vishnu. Shown here is an image of Vyasa, said to be the compiler of the Puranas, Vedas and Bagahavad Gita. Also see Hinduism and Sacred Writings.

Purce, Jill

(1947-) British-born Jill Purce is a teacher, lecturer, editor, author and international pioneer on mystical aspects of the human voice, sound vibrations, sacred geometry and the labyrinth, science and religion. She studied at Reading University, Chelsea College of Art, Biophysics Department and Kings College in London. She studied music in Germany with composer Karlheinz Stockhausen, with whom she worked for some years, Mongolian and Tibetan chanting in the Indian Himalayas and shamanism amongst American Indians and Shamans from various traditions. Her workshops and lectures are in much demand in Europe and North America on The Healing Voice, the Voice of Shamanism, Ritual and Resonance – Healing the Family and Ancestors. She lives in London with her husband Rupert Sheldrake. She has produced recordings: Overtone Chanting Meditations and The Healing Voice and written The Mystic Spiral: Journey of the Soul. Photograph from hollyhock.ca. Also see Recommended Reading, Shamans, Sound Therapy, jillpurce.com and healingvoice.com.

Purgatorio
One of three Canticas that compose Dante Alighieri's The Divine Comedy. See Divine Comedy.

Purification
To rid a person, place or object from undesired vibrations, sticky thought forms or disrupting psychic energy. To make pure, clean and free from physical or spiritual contaminants or pollutants or to purge of sin or guilt. Shown here is a 1600 painting by Greek artist El Greco (Domenikos Theotodopoulos). Also see Spiritual Techniques.

Purim
In Judaism, the festival of Purim, also called the Festival of Lots and the Feast of Ester is a one-day festival takes place four weeks before Passover and usually falls in late February or early March. It recalls the story of Esther, a Queen who foiled a plot by one of her advisors, Haman, to kill all the Jews. Shown here is a 1625 painting of Purim by Dutch artist Jan Lievens called Feast of Ester. Also see Judaism.

Putana
In Hindu mythology, Putana is a female demon or witch who tried to kill Krishna when he was a baby by suckling him to death with the poison in her breasts. She is regarded even today as a female demon that causes illness in children. Shown here is baby Krishna killing Putana. Also see Demons.

Puthoff, Harold

(1936-) American-born Harold E. "Hal" Puthoff Ph.D. is a physicist and parapsychologist. He was a U.S. Naval officer assigned to the National Security Agency (NSA) for a time. He earned his Ph.D. from Stanford University and developed a tunable Raman laser, but is mostly known for his research on remote viewing at the Stanford Research Institute. During the 1970's and the 1980's he directed a program at SRI International funded by the CIA/DIA to study the abilities of psychics. He is currently the Director of the Institute for Advanced Studies at Austin and he regularly serves corporations, government agencies, the Executive Branch and Congress as consultant. He has numerous patents and has published many papers and several books with his colleague Russel Targ and others, including: A Perceptual Channel for Information Transfer Over Kilometer Distances: Historical Perspective and Recent Research. He is also the co-author of Fundamentals of Quantum Electronics by Richard H. Pantell. Photograph from newrealitiestv.com. Also see Parapsychologists and Psychic Researchers, Physicists, Recommended Reading, Remote Viewing and earthtech.org.

Puysegur, Marquis de

(1751-1825) French-born Armand Marie Jacques de Chastenet aka Marquis de Puysegur was one of the founders of hypnotism, known then as Mesmerism and Somnambulism. He was one of Franz Mesmer's disciples for a time but rejected the magnetic fluid theory, believing that the hypnosis (or magnetism) was the result of interaction between the patient and the hypnotizer. He was a highly successful hypnotherapist and founded the Société Harmonique des Amis Réunis where he trained hypnotherapists. Puysegur used the term "artificial somnambulism" to describe the sleeping trance that he induced in his patients. Although Puysegur always gave credit to his teacher Franz Anton Mesmer, he is credited with many discoveries and applications of the field of hypnotherapy. Image from hypnose-clinique.com. Also see Franz Anton Mesmer, and Mesmerism.

Pwyll

Celtic God who rules the Underworld. Pwyll is also called Pwyll Pen Annwn. Shown here is a depiction of Pwyll from the 11 Century Welsh Magibinion. Also see Celtic Gods and Goddesses and Underworld Gods.

Pyramid Texts

Ancient Egyptian funerary texts engraved on the walls of Egyptian pyramids of the 5th and 6th dynasty. The Pyramid Texts consist of magic formulae, prayers and spells for the deceased to be safe on his journey through the underworld. Image from arthistory.about.com. Also see Amduat, Egyptian Book of the Dead, and Sacred Writings.

Pyramids

See Aztec Pyramids, Egyptian Pyramids, Mayan Pyramids, and Toltec Pyramids.

Pyromancy

Divination by fire, pyromancy is basically the observation of flames (sometimes assisted with burning herbs or substances) although there are several other forms, including: alomancy, botanomancy, capnomancy, lampadomancy and sideromancy. Also see Divination.

Pythagoras

(582-500 B.C.E.) Greek philosopher, mathematician, geometrician, religious reformer and mystic, Pythagoras of Samos (Pythagoras the Samian) was the founder of the religious movement called Pythagoreanism. Born on the Greek Island of Samos he later studied in Egypt and Phoenicia. He preached the importance of meditation and the philosophy of reincarnation, although he is best remembered for his Pythagorean theorem. It was said that he claimed that he had been Euphorbus, a warrior in the Trojan War a previous incarnation. Pythagoras called the Supreme Mind the power within all things, the cause of all things, and he described the body of God as being completely composed of light. He founded a secret society called the Pythagorean Brotherhood and is considered by some modern occultists as the founder of Occultism. He was described by Bertrand Russell in a History of Western Philosophy as the "most influential of all western philosophers". Pythagoras is depicted here in Italian artist Rafael's 1509 painting The School of Athens. Also see Mathematicians, Mystics, Philosophers, Recommended Reading, Reincarnation (Life After Life) and plato.stanford.edu.

Pythagoreanism

Religious movement founded by Pythagoras. See Pythagoras.

Pythias

Also known as Pythoness, Pythias is the Greek term used to describe sensitive or psychic women who delivered oracles of Apollo at the Temple of Delphi. These women were chosen young and pure and lived the rest of their life secluded in the temple where they ritually went into altered state of consciousness and delivered oracles. A Pythia is depicted here in an 1891 painting by British artist John Maler Collier (john-collier.org) called The Priestess of Delphi. Also see Bagoe, Divination, and Oracles.

Recommended Reading

H

Hagelin, Dr. John (1954-)
Manual for a Perfect Government: How to Harness the Laws of Nature to Bring Maximum Success to Governmental Administration (1998)

Haich, Elisabeth (1897-1994)
Initiation (1965)
Self Healing, Yoga and Destiny (with Selvarajan Yesudian) (1966)
Sexual Energy and Yoga (1972)
The Wisdom of the Tarot (1975)
The Day With Yoga: A Spiritual Yoga Path for Thinking People (1977)

Hale, Susan
Song and Silence: Voicing the Soul and Sacred Space– Sacred Sound: The Acoustic Mysteries of Holy Places (2007)

Hall, Manly Palmer (1901-1990)
Initiates of the Flame (1922)
Secret Teachings of All Ages: An Encyclopedic Outline of Masonic, Hermetic, Qabbalistic and Rosicrucian Symbolical Philosophy (1928)
Lectures on Ancient Philosophy—An Introduction to the Study and Application of Rational Procedure (1929)
The Secret Destiny of America (1944)
Healing: The Divine Art (1944)
Meditation Symbols In Eastern and Western Mysticism-Mysteries of the Mandala

Hamblin, Henry Thomas (1873-1958)
The Message of a Flower: The Divine Immanence in Nature (1921)

Dynamic Thought: Harmony, Health, Success, Achievement, Self Mastery, Optimism, Prosperity, Peace of Mind, Through the Power of … (1922)
Look Within and Find All You Need (1924)
The Life of the Spirit (1925)
Within You Is the Power (1925)
The Open Door (1932)
Life Without Strain: The Strifeless Way to Harmony, Peace and Joy (1941)
The Story of My Life: Henry Thomas Hamblin (1947)
My Search for Truth (1951)

Hameroff, Stuart (1947-)
Ultimate Computing: Biomolecular Consciousness and Nanotechnology (1987)
Toward a Science of Consciousness: The First Tucson Discussions and Debates (with Alfred Kaszniak and Alwyn Scott) (1996)

Hanh, Thich Nhat (1926-)
Being Peace (1987)
Old Path White Clouds: Walking in the Footsteps of the Buddha (1991)
Peace Is Every Step: The Path of Mindfulness in Everyday Life (1992)
Zen Keys: A Guide to Zen Practice (1994)
True Love: A Practice for Awakening the Heart (1997)
Living Buddha, Living Christ (1997)
The Heart of the Buddha's Teachings (1999)
Interbeing: Fourteen Guidelines for Engaged Buddhism (1999)
Going Home: Jesus and Buddha as Brothers (1999)
No Death, No Fear (2003)
Touching the Earth: Intimate Conversations with the Buddha (2004)
The Art of Power (2007)
Mindful Movements: Mindfulness Exercises Developed by Thich Nhat Hanh and the Plum Village Sangha (with Wietske Vriezen) (2008)
You Are Here: Discovering the Magic of the Present Moment (2009)
Reconciliation: Healing the Inner Child (2010)

Harman, Willis (1909-1997)
Incomplete Guide to the Future (1976)
Higher Creativity: Liberating the Unconscious for Breakthrough Insights (with Howard Rheingold) (1984)
Global Mind Change: The Promise of the Last Years of the Twentieth Century (1988)
Insight into the New Age: Scientific Techniques to Unlock Your Creative Potential (1988)
New Metaphysical Foundations of Modern Science (1994)

Harris, Alexander (1897-1974) (book about)
They Walked Among Us (by Louie Harris) (1980)

Hartmann, Dr. Franz (1838-1912)
An Adventure Among the Rosicrucians (1887)
The Principles of Astrological Geomancy: The Art of Divining by Punctuation, According to Cornelius Agrippa and Others (1889)
The Life and Doctrines of Jacob Boehme, The God-Taught Philosopher an Introduction to the Study of His Works (1891)
Incarnation and the Configuration of the Person of the Redeemer (1891)
The Life and Doctrines of Philippus Theophrastus Bombast of Hohenheim Known as Paracelsus (1891)
Occult Science in Medicine (1893)
Correlation of Spiritual Forces (1897)
With the Adepts: Adventure Among the Rosicrucians (1910)
Magic, White and Black: Or, The Science of Finite and Infinite Life, Containing Practical Knowledge, Instruction and Hints for … (1910)
The Life of Jehoshua, the Prophet of Nazareth: An Occult Study and a Key to The Bible, Containing the History of an Initiate (1912)

Harvey, Andrew (1952-)
Hidden Journey: A Spiritual Awakening (1991)
The Return of the Mother (1995)
The Mystic Vision: Daily Encounters With the Divine (with Anne Baring) (1995)
The Essential Mystics: The Soul's Journey into Truth (1996)
The Divine Feminine: Exploring the Feminine Face of God Throughout the World (with Anne Baring) (1996)
The Essential Mystics: Selections from the World's Great Wisdom Traditions (1997)
The Essential Gay Mystics (1997)
Teachings of the Christian Mystics (1998)
Son of Man: The Mystical Path to Christ (1998)
Perfume of the Desert, Inspirations from Sufi Wisdom (with Eryk Hanut) (1999)
Teachings of the Hindu Mystics (2001)
Sun At Midnight: A Memoir of the Dark Night (2002)
The Direct Path: Creating a Journey to the Divine Through the World's Great Mystical Traditions (2003)
A Walk with Four Spiritual Guides: Krishna Buddha, Jesus and Ramakrishna (2003)
The Direct Path: Creating a Journey for the Divine Using the World's Mystical Traditions (2009)

Haskvitz, Sylvia
Eat by Choice, Not by Habit: Practical Skills for Creating a Healthy Relationship with Your

Body and Food (2005)

Hawkes, Dr. Joyce
Cell-Level Healing: The Bridge from Soul to Cell (2006)
Resonance: Nine Practices for Harmonious Health and Vitality (2012)

Heard, Gerald (1889-1971)
Narcissus: An Anatomy of Clothes (1924)
Ascent of Humanity: An Essay on Evolution of Civilization from Group Consciousness Through Individuality and Super-Consciousness (1929)
The Emergence of Man (1932)
The Source of Civilization (1935)
The Third Morality (1937)
Pain, Sex and Time: A New Outlook on Evolution and the Future of Man (1939)
The Creed of Christ: An Interpretation of the Lord's Prayer (1940)
Man The Master (1942)
Training for the Life of the Spirit (1942)
The Eternal Gospel (1946)
Is God Evident? An Essay Toward a Natural Theology (1948)
Prayers and Meditations (1949)
Is Another World Watching? The Riddle of the Flying Saucers (1950)
Gabriel and the Creatures (1952)
The Five Ages of Man: The Psychology of Human History (1963)

Hill, Napoleon (1883-1970)
The Magic Ladder to Success (1930)
Think and Grow Rich (1937)
How to Sell Your Way through Life (1939)
Law of Success in 16 Lessons: Teaching, for the 1st Time in the History of the World, True Philosophy Upon Which All Personal Success is Built (1941)
Success Through a Positive Mental Attitude (with W. Clement Stone) (1960)
Master Key to Riches (1965)
Grow Rich!: With Peace of Mind (1967)
You can Work Your Own Miracles (1970)
Succeed and Grow Rich Through Persuasion (with E. Harold Keown) (1970)

Holmes, Ernest (1887-1960)
Creative Mind: Tapping the Power Within (1919)
The Science of Mind (1926)
Can We Talk to God? (1934)
Questions and Answers on the Science of Mind (with Alberta Smith) (1935)

Your Invisible Power (1940)
Mind Remakes Your World: How to Think Yourself Into Better Health, Greater Happiness, and More … (with Maude Allison Latham) (1941)
New Thought Terms and Their Meanings: A Dictionary of Terms and Phrases Commonly Used in Metaphysical and Psychological Study (1942)
This Thing Called Life (1943)
This Thing Called You (1948)
How to Use the Science of Mind (1950)
How to Change Your Life (1957)
Words That Heal Today (1958)

Holzer, Hans (1920-2009)
Ghosts I've Met (1965)
The Truth about Witchcraft (1969)
Window to the Past: Exploring History Through ESP (1969)
The Aquarian Age: Is There Intelligent Life on Earth? (1971)
The Psychic Side of Dreams (1976)
Where the Ghosts Are: The Ultimate Guide to Haunted Houses (1984)
Love Beyond the Grave (1992)
Life Beyond: Compelling Evidence for Past Lives and Existence After Death (1994)
The Directory of Psychics: How to Find, Evaluate, and Communicate with Professional Psychics and Mediums (1995)
The Secret of Healing: The Healing Powers of Ze'Ev Kolman (1996)
Are You Psychic: Unlocking the Power Within (1997)
Ghosts: True Encounters with the World Beyond (1997)
Hans Holzer's Psychic Yellow Pages: The Very Best Psychics, Card Readers, Mediums, Astrologers and Numerologists (2001)
Beyond Death (with Phillip Solomon) (2001)
Hans Holzer's The Supernatural: Explaining The Unexplained (2003)

Howard, Vernon (1918-1992)
Psycho-Pictography: The New Way Use the Miracle Power of Your Mind (1965)
The Mystic Path to Cosmic Power (1967)
Pathways to Perfect Living (1969)
Esoteric Mind Power: Secrets for New Success and Happiness (1973)
The Power of Your Supermind (1973)
The Mystic Masters Speak!: A Treasure of Cosmic Wisdom (1974)
Esoteric Encyclopedia of Eternal Knowledge (1974)
Inspire Yourself (1975)
Treasury of Positive Answers (1977)
Cosmic Command (1979)

Hubbard, L. Ron (1911-1986)
Dianetics: The Modern Science of Mental Health (1950)
Child Dianetics. Dianetic Processing for Children (1951)
Dianetics: The Evolution of a Science (1955)
The Creation of Human Ability (1955)
Scientology: The Fundamentals of Thought (1956)
Have You Lived Before This Life? (1960)
Scientology: A New Slant on Life (1965)
The Volunteer Minister's Handbook (1976)
The Way to Happiness (1981)

Huxley, Aldous (1894-1963)
On the Margin (1923)
Do What You Will (1929)
Music at Night (1931)
Words and their Meanings (1940)
The Art of Seeing (1942)
The Perennial Philosophy (1945)
Science, Liberty and Peace (1946)
Themes and Variations (1950)
Tomorrow and Tomorrow and Tomorrow (1952)
The Doors of Perception (1954)
Brave New World Revisited (1958)
Heaven and Hell (1956)

Hyslop, Dr. James Hervey (1854-1920)
Science and a Future Life (1905)
Enigmas of Psychical Research (1906)
Borderland of Psychical Research (1906)
Psychical Research and the Resurrection (1908)
Psychical Research and Survival (1913)
Life After Death: Problems of the Future Life and Its Nature (1918)
Contact with the Other World: The Latest Evidence as to Communication With the Dead (1919)

I

Ingerman, Sandra
Soul Retrieval: Mending the Fragmented Self (1991)
Welcome Home: Following Your Soul's Journey Home (1993)
Medicine for the Earth: How to Transform Personal and Environmental Toxins (2000)
Shamanic Journeying: A Beginner's Guide (2004)
How to Heal Toxic Thoughts (2007)
Awakening to The Spirit World: The Shamanic Path of Direct Revelation (with Henry Barnard Wesselman) (2010)
How to Thrive in Changing Times: Simple Tools to Create True Health, Wealth, Peace, and Joy for Yourself and the Earth (2010)

J

Jaegers, Beverly (1935-2001)
The Human Aura: How I Teach My Students to See It (1971)
Precognition: Learning to Predict the Future! (1973)
Practical ESP and Clairvoyance - Fascinating, Workable New Methods to Develop Telepathy, Psychometry and Clairvoyance (1974)
    Secrets of the Aura (1978)
    The Magic Power of Healing: Learn to Heal Yourself (1979)
    Psychometry: The Science of Touch (1985)
    Beyond Palmistry: The Art and Science of Modern Hand Analysis (1992)
    The Psychic Paradigm (1998)

James, William (1842-1910)
The Will to Believe and Other Essays in Popular Philosophy (1897)
The Principles of Psychology (1890)
Talks to Teachers on Psychology: and to Students on Some of Life's Ideals (1899)
Varieties of Religious Experience: A Study in Human Nature (1902)
Pragmatism: A New Name for Some Old Ways of Thinking (1907)
A Pluralistic Universe (1909)
The Meaning of Truth: A Sequel to "Pragmatism" (1909)
Some Problems of Philosophy: A Beginning of an Introduction to Philosophy (1911)
Memories and Studies (1911)
Essays in Radical Empiricism (1912)

Jarow, Dr. Rick
In Search of the Sacred: A Pilgrimage to Holy Places (1986)
Creating the Work You Love: Courage, Commitment and Career (1995)
Opening to Shakti: Practices for Creativity, Self-Expression and Freedom (2000)
The Ultimate Anti-Career Guide: The Inner Path to Finding Your Work in the World (with Ani

DiFranco) (2001)
Tales for the Dying: The Death Narrative of the Bhagavata-Purana (2003)
Alchemy of Abundance: Using the Energy of Desire to Manifest Your Highest Vision, Power and Purpose (2005)

Jenkins, John Major (1964-)
The Mirror in the Sky: Maya Cosmogenesis 2012: The True Meaning of the Maya Calendar End-Date (1985)
Journey to the Mayan Underworld (1987)
Tzolkin: Visionary Perspectives and Calendar (1994)
Joloj Kexoj and PHI-64: Dual Principle Core Paradigm of Mayan Time Philosophy and its Conceptual Parallel in Old World Thought (1994)
Mysteries of Mayan Time Philosophy (1995)
A Long, Long Time Ago: The Tree of Life Cosmology (1995)
The Guile of a Plumed Serpent (1996)
The Reasons Behind the Mayan End Date (1996)
Maya Cosmogenesis 2012: The True Meaning of the Maya Calendar End-Date (1998)
Galactic Alignment: The Transformation of Consciousness According to Mayan, Egyptian and Vedic Traditions (2002)
Pyramid of Fire: The Lost Aztec Codex: Spiritual Ascent at the End of Time (with Martin Matz) (2007)
The 2012 Story: The Myths, Fallacies, and Truth Behind the Most Intriguing Date in History (2009)

Johnson Robert A. (1921-)
We: Understanding the Psychology of Romantic Love (1983)
Inner Work: Using Dreams and Active Imagination for Personal Growth (1986)
Ecstasy: Understanding the Psychology of Joy (1987)
She: Understanding Feminine Psychology (1989)
He: Understanding Masculine Psychology (1989)
Femininity Lost and Regained (1990)
Owning Your Own Shadow: Understanding the Dark Side of the Psyche (1991)
Transformation: Understanding the Three Levels of Masculine Consciousness (1991)
The Fisher King and the Handless Maiden: Understanding the Wounded Feeling Function in Masculine and Feminine Psychology (1993)
Lying with the Heavenly Woman: Understanding and Integrating the Feminine Archetypes in Men's Lives (1994)
Balancing Heaven and Earth: A Memoir (with Jerry M. Ruhl) (1998)
Contentment: A Way to True Happiness (with Jerry M. Ruhl) (1999)
Living Your Unlived Life: Coping with Unrealized Dreams and Fulfilling Your Purpose in the Second Half of Life (with Jerry Ruhl) (2007)

Jones, Dr. Marc Edmund (1888-1980)
The Ritual of Living: An Occult Manual (1930)
The Guide To Horoscope Interpretation (1941)
How To Learn Astrology: The Guide to Horoscope Interpretation, Problem-Solving by Horary Astrology (1943)
Occult Philosophy: An Introduction, the Major Concepts and a Glossary – Key Truths of Occult Philosophy Expanded (1948)
Essentials of Astrological Analysis: Illustrated in the Horoscopes of One Hundred and Seventy-Four Well-Known People (1960)
The Sabian Symbols in Astrology (1969)
Scope of Astrological Prediction: An Introduction to the Dynamic Horoscopy (1969)
Astrology: How and Why It Works, An Introduction to Basic Horoscopy (1969)
The Sabian Book Of Letters To Aspirants (with Helen Rentsch and Helen Hill) (1973)
Mundane Perspectives In Astrology: The Expanded Dynamic Horoscopy (1975)
How To Live With The Stars: Simple Personal Astrology (1976)
Fundamentals Of Number Significance: An Autobiographical Account of Accomplishment (1978)
Man, Magic And Fantasy: The Domestication of Imagination (1978)

Joyce-Swaim, Elizabeth
Psychic Attack – Are You A Victim? (2007)
Ascension—Accessing The Fifth Dimension: The Truth About 2012 (2010)

Judge, William Quan (1851-1896)
Bhagavad-Gita Combined with Essays on the Gita
The Bhagavad-Gita: The Book of Devotion, Dialogue Between Krishna, Lord of Devotion, and Arjuna, Prince of India
Echoes from the Orient: A Broad Outline of Theosophical Doctrines
An Epitome of Theosophy and Theosophy Generally Stated
Letters That Have Helped Me
The Ocean of Theosophy
Practical Occultism: From the Private Letters of W.Q. Judge

Jung, Dr. Carl Gustav (1875-1961)
Modern Man in Search of a Soul (1933)
The Integration of the Personality (1939)
Memories, Dreams, Reflections (with Aniela Jaffe, et al) (1953)
The Psychology of the Transference (1954)
The Interpretation of Nature and the Psyche - Synchronicity: An Acausal Connecting Principle (with Wolfgang Pauli) (1955)
The Archetypes and The Collective Unconscious (with R.F.C. Hull) (1959)
On the Nature of the Psyche (1960)

Kabat-Zinn, Dr. Jon (1944-)
Full Catastrophe Living: Using the Wisdom of Your Body and Mind to Face Stress, Pain and Illness (1990)
Wherever You Go, There You Are: Mindfulness Meditation in Everyday Life (1994)
Coming to Our Senses: Healing Ourselves and the World Through Mindfulness (2005)
Arriving at Your Own Door: 108 Lessons in Mindfulness (2007)
Letting Everything Become Your Teacher: 100 Lessons in Mindfulness (with Hor Tuck Loon) (2009)

Kaehr, Dr. Shelley (1967-)
Origins of Huna: Secret Behind the Sacred Science (2002)
Gemstone Journeys (2002)
Lifestream: Journey into Past and Future Lives (2003)
Beyond Reality: Evidence of Parallel Universes (2004)
Gemstone Journeys (2004)
Divination of God: The Obscure Ancient Tool of Prophecy Revealed (2005)
Edgar Cayce Guide to Gemstones, Minerals, Metals and More (2005)
Just Write It: Step By Step Guide to Writing and Publishing Your First Book (2006)
Lemurian Seeds: Hope for Humanity (2006)
Explorations Beyond Reality: Living Evolution Through Genetic Memory (2006)
Crystal Skull Consciousness (2007)
Beyond Physical Reality: Expanding Awareness (2007)
Damned: True Tales of the Cursed, Hexed and Bewitched (2009)

Kaku, Dr. Michio (1947-)

Nuclear Power: Both Sides: The Best Arguments For and Against the Most Controversial Technology (with Jennifer Thompson) (1982)

Quantum Field Theory: A Modern Introduction (1993)

Hyperspace: A Scientific Odyssey through Parallel Universes, Time Warps and the Tenth Dimension (1994)

Visions: How Science Will Revolutionize the 21st Century (1997)

Beyond Einstein: Superstrings and the Quest for the Final Theory (with Jennifer T. Thompson) (1997)

Introduction to Superstrings and M-Theory (1999)

Strings, Conformal Fields, and M-Theory (2000)

The Super Power Issue – A User's Guide to Time Travel – All it Takes is a Grasp of Theoretical Physics, Control of the Space-Time Continuum, and Maybe a Ball of Cosmic String (2003)

Einstein's Cosmos: How Albert Einstein's Vision Transformed Our Understanding of Space and Time (2004)

Parallel Worlds: The Science of Alternative Universes and Our Future in the Cosmos (2005)

Physics of the Impossible: A Scientific Exploration Into the World of Phasers, Force Fields, Teleportation, and Time Travel (2008)

Physics of the Future: How Science Will Change Daily Life by 2100 (2010)

Kardec, Allan (1804-1969)

Book on Mediums: or, Guide for Mediums and Invocators (1874)

Gospel According to Spiritism: Contains Explanations of the Moral Maxims of Christ in Accordance With Spiritism and Their Application in Various Circumstances of Life

Kasl, Dr. Charlotte

Women, Sex and Addiction: A Search for Love and Power (1989)

Many Roads, One Journey: Moving Beyond the Twelve Steps (1992)

Finding Joy: 101 Ways to Free Your Spirit and Dance With Life (1994)

Yes You Can!: A Guide to Empowerment Groups (1995)

A Home for the Heart: A Practical Guide to Intimate and Social Relationships (1998)

If the Buddha Dated: Handbook for Find Love on a Spiritual Path (1999)

If the Buddha Married: Creating Enduring Relationships on a Spiritual Path (2001)

Zen and the Art of Falling in Love: A Handbook for Finding Love on a Spiritual Path (2003)

If the Buddha Got Stuck: A Handbook for Change on a Spiritual Path (2005)

Zen and the Art of a Happier Life: A Handbook for Change on a Spiritual Path (2010)

Kharitidi, Olga

Entering the Circle: Ancient Secrets of a Siberian Wisdom Discovered by a Russian Psychiatrist (1996)

The Master of Lucid Dreams: In the Heart of Asia a Russian Psychiatrist Learns How to Heal the Spirits of Trauma (2001)

King, Deborah
Truth Heals – What You Hide Can Hurt You (2009)
Be Your Own Shaman: Heal Yourself and Others with 21st Century Energy Medicine (2011)

Kingma, Daphne Rose
True Love: How to Make Your Relationship, Sweeter, Deeper, and More Passionate (1991)
The Men We Never Knew: Women's Role in the Evolution of a Gender (1993)
Weddings from the Heart: Contemporary and Traditional Ceremonies for an Unforgettable Wedding (1995)
Finding True Love: The Four Essential Keys to Discovering the Love of Your Life (1996)
A Lifetime of Love: How to Bring More Depth, Meaning and Intimacy Into Your Relationship (1998)
Coming Apart: Why Relationships End and How to Live Through the Ending of Yours (2000)
The Book of Love (2001)
The Future of Love: The Power of Soul in Intimate Relationships (2001)
Attitudes of Gratitude in Love: Creating More Joy in Your Relationship (2002)
Loving Yourself: Four Steps to a Happier You (2004)
101 Ways to Have True Love in Your Life (2006)
The Ten Things to Do When Your Life Falls Apart: An Emotional and Spiritual Handbook (2010)

Kingston, Karen
Creating Sacred Space with Feng Shui and Clearing Your Clutter with Feng Shui (1997)
Clear Your Clutter with Feng Shui (1999)
Clutter Free in Seven Days (2002)

Kircher, Athanasius (1602-1680) (books about)
Athanasius Kircher and the Progress of Medicine (by Harry Beal Torrey) (1938)
Athanasius Kircher S.J.: Master of a Hundred Arts (by Coner Reilly) (1974)
Athanasius Kircher: A Renaissance Man and the Quest for Lost Knowledge (by Joscelyn Godwin) (1979)
Athanasius Kircher (1602-1680) (by Fred Brauen) (1982)
Athanasius Kircher: A Man Under Pressure (by John Fletcher) (1988)
The Ecstatic Journey: Athanasius Kircher in Baroque Rome (by Ingrid D. Rowland) (2000)
The Great Art of Knowing: The Baroque Encyclopedia of Athanasius Kircher (by Daniel Stozenberg) (2001)
Athanasius Kircher: The Last Man Who Knew Everything (by Paula Findlen) (2004)

Knight, Christopher

The Hiram Key: Pharoahs, Freemasons and the Discovery of the Secret Scrools of Jesus (with Robert Lomas) (1996)

The Second Messiah: Templars, The Turin Shroud, and the Great Secret of Freemasonry (with Robert Lomas) (1997)

The Holy Grail, Part of Mysteries of the Ancient World: The Mysteries of the Ancient World Explored and Explained (with Robert Lomas) (1998)

Uriel's Machine: The Ancient Origins of Science (with Robert Lomas) (1999)

The Book of Hiram: Freemasonry, Venus and the Secret Key to the Life of Jesus (with Robert Lomas) (2003)

Civilization One: The World is Not as You Thought it Was (with Alan Butler) (2004)

Who Built the Moon? (with Alan Butler) (2005)

Solomon's Power Brokers: The Secrets of the Freemasons, the Church and the Illuminati (with Alan Butler) (2007)

Before the Pyramids: Cracking Archeology's Greatest Mystery (with Alan Butler) (2009)

Knight, Gareth (1930-)

A Practical Guide to Qabbalistic Symbolism (1965)

Occult Exercises and Practices: Gateways to the Four 'Worlds' of Occultism (1969)

Experience of the Inner Worlds: A Course in Christian Qabbalistic Magic (1975)

A History of White Magic (1978)

Magic and the Western Mind: Ancient Knowledge and the Transformation of Consciousness (1978)

The Secret Tradition in Arthurian Legends (1983)

The Rose Cross and the Goddess: The Quest for the Eternal Feminine Principle (1985)

Dion Fortune's the Magical Battle of Britain (1993)

Magical Images and Magical Imagination: A Practical Handbook for Self Transformation Using the Techniques of Creative Visualization and Meditation (1998)

Dion Fortune and the Inner Light (2000)

The Occult Fiction of Dion Fortune (2007)

Magic and the Power of the Goddess: Initiation, Worship, and Ritual in the Western Mystery Tradition (2008)

The Faery Gates of Avalon (2008)

Yours Very Truly – Gareth Knight Selected Leters (2010)

Knight, JZ (1946-)

The Plane of Bliss: On Earth as It Is In Heaven (by Debbie Christie, et.al) (1985)

JZ Knight: A State of Mind – My Story: The Ramtha Adventure Begins (1987)

Destination Freedom: A Time Travel Adventure (1989)

UFOs and the Nature of Reality: Understanding Alien Consciousness and Interdimensional Mind (with Judi Pope Koteen) (1991)

Finding Enlightenment Through Ramtha: the Emergence of Gnosticism in the West (by J. Gordon Melton) (1996)

Finding Enlightenment: Ramtha's School of Ancient Wisdom (by J. Gordon Melton) (1998)
A Beginner's Guide to Creating Reality (2000)
Changing the Timeline of Our Destiny (2001)
Making Contact: Our Soul's Journey and Purpose Through Life (2002)
A Master's Reflection on the History of Humanity (2002)
A Masters Key for Manipulating Time (2002)
Prophets of Our Destiny (2003)
That Elixir Called Love: the Truth About Sexual Attraction, Secret Fantasies, and the Magic of True Love (2003)
When Fairy Tales Do Come True (2003)
Ramtha, The White Book (2004)

Kornfield, Dr. Jack (1945-)
Living Buddhist Masters (1977)
Seeking the Heart of Wisdom: The Path of Insight Meditation (with Joseph Goldstein) (1987)
Stories of the Spirit, Stories of the Heart: Parables of the Spiritual Path From Around the World (with Christina Feldman) (1991)
A Path with Heart: A Guide Through the Perils and Promises of Spiritual Life (1993)
Soul Food: Stories to Nourish the Spirit and the Heart (with Christina Feldman) (1996)
Teachings of the Buddha (with Gil Fronsdal) (1996)
Living Dharma: Teachings of Twelve Buddhist Masters (1996)
After the Ecstasy, The Laundry: How the Heart Grows Wise on the Spiritual Path (2000)
The Art of Forgiveness, Lovingkindness and Peace (2002)
Buddha's Little Instruction Book (2004)
The Wise Heart: A Guide to the Universal Teaching of Buddhist Psychology (2008)

Korotkov, Dr. Konstantin
Aura and Consciousness: New Stage of Scientific Understanding (with P. Ratman) (1998)
Light After Life: A Scientific Journey Into the Spiritual World (with Leonid Tunik and A.L. Kouznetsov) (1998)
Human Energy Field: Study with GDV Bioelectography (2002)
Measuring Energy Fields: State of the Science (2004)
Energy Fields Electrophotonic Analysis in Humans and Nature (2011)
The Energy of Consciousness (2012)

Kovelman, Dr. Joyce
Namaste: Initiation and Transformation: A How to for Those Who Wish to Embrace ASOUL (1998)
One Upon a Soul: The Story Continues… Science, Psychology and the Realms of Spirit (1998)

Koven, Jean-Claude

Going Deeper: How to Make Sense of Your Life When Your Life Makes No Sense (2004)

Kowalski, Rev. Gary (1953-)
The Souls of Animals (1991)
Goodbye Friend: Healing Wisdom For Anyone Who Has Ever Lost a Pet (1997)
Understanding the World's Religions: A Story Guide to Huston Smith's The World's Religions (1997)
Green Mountain Spring and Other Leaps of Faith (1997)
The Bible According To Noah: Theology As If Animals Mattered (2001)
Science and the Search for God (2003)
Revolutionary Spirits: The Enlightened Faith of America's Founding Fathers (2008)
Jesus for The Non-Religious (2008)
Questions You Might Ask (2009)

Krieger, Dolores (1935-)
The Therapeutic Touch: How to Use Your Hands to Help and Heal (1979)
Foundations for Holistic Health Nursing Practices: The Renaissance Nurse (1981)
Spiritual Aspects of the Healing Arts (1985)
Living the Therapeutic Touch: Healing As a Lifestyle (1987)
Accepting Your Power To Heal: The Personal Practice of Therapeutic Touch (1993)
Spiritual Healing (1995)
Therapeutic Touch Inner Workbook: Ventures in Transpersonal Healing (with Jeanne Achtenberg) (1997)
Therapeutic Touch As Transpersonal Healing (2002)
The Spiritual Dimension of Therapeutic Touch (2004)

Krippner, Dr. Stanley (1932-)
Dream Studies and Telepathy (with Montague Ullman) (1970)
Shamlet: The Tragical History of Hamlet, Prince of Denmark (1971)
Song of the Siren: A Parapsychological Odyssey (1976)
Human Possibilities: Mind Research in the USSR and Eastern Europe (1980)
The Realms of Healing (with Alberto Villoldo) (1986)
Healing States: A Journey Into the World of Spiritual Healing and Shamanism (with Alberto Villoldo) (1987)
Dreamworking: How to Use Your Dreams for Creative Problem Solving (with Joseph Dillard) (1988)
Personal Mythology: The Psychology of Your Evolving Self (with David Feinstein) (1988)
Dream Telepathy: Experiments in Nocturnal ESP (with Montague Ullman and Alan Vaughan) (1989)
Spiritual Dimensions of Healing: From Native Shamanism to Contemporary Health Care (with Patrick Welch) (1992)

A Psychiatrist in Paradise: Treating Mental Illness in Bali (with Denny Thong and Bruce Carpenter) (1993)

The Mythic Path: Discovering the Guiding Stories of Your Past (with David Feinstein) (1997)

Extraordinary Dreams and How to Work with Them (with Fariba Bogzaran and Andre Percia de Carvalho) (2002)

Becoming Psychic: Spiritual Lessons for Focusing Your Hidden Abilities (2004)

Mysterious Minds: The Neurobiology of Psychics, Mediums and Other Extraordinary People (with Harris L. Friedman) (2010)

Krishnamurti, Jiddu (1895-1986)
The Immortal Friend (1928)
The First and Last Freedom (1954)
Commentaries on Living (1967)
Beyond Violence (1973)
At the Feet of the Master (1970)
The Only Revolution (1970)
The Flight of the Eagle (1971)
The Impossible Question (1972)
You Are the World (1972)
The Awakening of Intelligence (1973)
Truth and Actuality (with David Bohm) (1978)
Meditations (1979)
The Wholeness of Life (1979)
Exploration into Insight (1980)
The Way of Intelligence (1985)

Kubler-Ross, Dr. Elizabeth (1926-2004)
On Death and Dying (1969)
Questions and Answers on Death and Dying (1972)
Death: The Final Stage of Growth (1974)
To Live Until We Say Good-Bye (with Mal Warshaw) (1978)
Living With Death and Dying (1981)
Remember the Secret (with Heather Preston) (1981)
Working it Through (1982)
On Children and Death (1985)
On Life After Death (1991)
The Tunnel and the Light: Essential Insights on Living and Dying (1995)
The Wheel of Life: A Memoir of Living and Dying (1997)
Why Are We Here (1999)
Life Lessons: Two Experts of Death and Dying Teach Us About the Mysteries of Life and Living

(with David Kessler) (2001)
On Grief and Grieving: Finding the Meaning of Grief Through the Five Stages of Loss (with David Kessler) (2005)

Kuhlman, Kathryn (1907-1976) (books about)
Kathryn Kuhlman: The Woman Who Believes In Miracles (by Allen Spraggett) (1970)
Daughter of Destiny: Kathryn Kuhlman, Her Story (by Jaime Buckingham) (1976)
Kathryn Kuhlman: The Life She Led, The Legacy She Left (by Helen Kooiman Hosier) (1976)
Kathryn Kuhlman: A Spiritual Biography of God's Miracle Working Power (by Robert Liardon) (1990)
Kathryn Kuhlman: The Woman Behind the Miracles (by Wayne E. Warner) (1993)
The Kathryn Kuhlman I Knew (by James McDonald) (1996)
Kathryn Kuhlman: Her Spiritual Legacy and Its Impact on My Life (by Benny Hinn) (1999)

Kunz, Dora (1904-1999)
Spiritual Aspects of the Healing Arts (1985)
Spiritual Healing (1995)
The Real World of Fairies: A First-Person Account (1999)
The Spiritual Dimension of Therapeutic Touch (2004)

Kushner, Rabbi Lawrence (1943-)
The River of Light: Spirituality, Judaism, and the Evolution of Consciousness (1981)
The Book of Letters: A Mystical Alef-Bait (1990)
The Books of Words: Talking Spiritual Life, Living Spiritual Talk (1993)
The Book of Miracles: A Young Person's Guide to Jewish Spiritual Awareness (1997)
Invisible Lines of Connection: Sacred Stories of the Ordinary (1996)
Eyes Remade for Wonder: A Lawrence Kushner Reader (1998)
Kabbalah: The Way of Light (1999)
Because Nothing Looks Like God (with Karen Kushner and Dawn Majewski) (2000)
The River of Light: Jewish Mystical Awareness (2000)
The Way Into Jewish Mystical Tradition (2001)
Jewish Spirituality: A Brief Introduction for Christians (2001)
Filling Words with Light: Hasidic and Spiritual Refractions of Jewish Prayer (2004)
In God's Hands (with Gary Schmidt and Matthew Baek) (2005)
Kabbalah: A Love Store (2006)
I'm God, Your Not: Observations on Organized Religion and Other Disguises of The Ego (2010)

L

LaBerge, Dr. Stephen (1947-)
Lucid Dreaming (1985)
Exploring the World of Lucid Dreaming (with Howard Rheingold) (1990)
Lucid Dreaming: A Concise Guide to Awakening in Your Dreams and in Your Life (2004)

Lad, Dr. Vasant
Ayurveda: The Science of Self-Healing: A Practical Guide (1985)
The Yoga of Herbs: An Ayurvedic Guide to Herbal Medicine (with David Frawley) (1986)
Ayurvedic Cooking for Self-Healing (1997)
The Complete Book of Ayurvedic Home Remedies (1998)
Texbook of Ayurveda: Fundamental Principles of Ayurveda (2002)
Strands of Eternity (2004)
Ayurvedic Perspectives on Selected Pathologies (2005)
Secrets of the Pulse: The Ancient Art of Ayurvedic Pulse Diagnosis (2006)
Ayurvedic Perspectives on Selected Pathologies: An Anthology of Essential Reading from Ayurveda Today (with Glen Crowther) (2005)
Marma Points of Ayurveda: The Energy Pathways for Healing Body, Mind and Consciousness with a Comparison to Traditional Chinese Medicine (with Anisha Durve) (2008)

Lane, Dr. Belden C.
Storytelling, The Enchantment of Theology (1982)
Spirituality in Time and Place (et al) (1992)
The Solace of Fierce Landscapes: Exploring Desert and Mountain Spirituality (1998)
Landscapes of the Sacred: Geography and Narrative in American Spirituality (2002)

Merton's Hermitage and the Desconstruction of the Self: A Topoanalysis Using Gaston Bachelard's The Poetics of Space (2003)

Merton's Hermitage: Bachelard, Domestic Space, and Spiritual Transformation (2004)

Lang, Andrew (1844-1912)
The Red Fairy Book (1890)
The Green Fairy Book (1892)
The Pink Fairy Book (1897)
The Book of Dreams and Ghosts (1897)
Custom and Myth (1898)
Myth, Ritual and Religion (1899)
The Blue Fairy Book (1889)
The Yellow Fairy Book (1894)
The Grey Fairy Book (1900)
The Violet Fairy Book (1901)
Magic and Religion (1901)
The Crimson Fairy Book (1903)
The Brown Fairy Book (1904)
The Orange Fairy Book (1906)
The Olive Fairy Book (1907)
The Lilac Fairy Book (1910)

Laskow, Dr. Leonard (1954-)
Healing With Love: A Physician's Breakthrough Mind/Body Medical Guide for Healing Yourself and Others: The Art of Holoenergetic Healing (1992)

Lattin, Don
The Harvard Psychedelic Club: How Timothy Leary, Ram Dass, Huston Smith &Andrew Weil Killed in the Fifties & Ushered In a New Age for America (2010)

Leadbeater, Rev. Charles (1854-1934)
Dreams: What They Are and How They are Caused (1903)
Clairvoyance (1903)
The Real Astral Plane (1905)
The Inner Life (1910)
Life after Death, and How Theosophy Unveils It (with Annie Besant) (1912)
The Hidden Side of Things (1913)
Man Visible and Invisible: Examples of Different Types of Men as Seen by Means of Trained Clairvoyance (1920)
The Science of the Sacraments (1920)
Invisible Helpers (1922)

The Masters and The Path (1925)
Glimpses of Masonic History (1926)
The Hidden Life in Freemasonry (1926)
The Chakras: A Monograph (1927)
How Theosophy Came to Me (1930)

Leek, Sybil (1917-1983)
The Jackdaw and The Witch: A True Fable (1966)
Diary of a Witch: The Private Life of One of the World's Most Famous and Colorful Psychics (1969)
The Sybil Leek Book of Fortune Telling (1969)
How to Be Your Own Astrologer (1970)
Cast Your Own Spell (1970)
The Complete Art of Witchcraft (1971)
Telepathy: The Respectable Phenomenon (1971)
My Life in Astrology (1972)
Sybil Leek's Book of Herbs (1973)
Tomorrow's Headlines Today (1974)
Reincarnation: The Second Chance (1974)
The Night Voyagers: You and Your Dreams (1975)
Sybil Leek's Book of the Curious and the Occult (1976)
Moon Signs Lunar Astrology (1977)
Astrology and Love (1977)

Lemuria (Mu) (books about)
The Riddle of the Pacific (by John Macmillan Brown) (1924)
The Lost Continent of Mu Motherland of Man (James Churchward) (1926)
The Children of Mu (James Churchward) (1931)
The Problem of Lemuria: The Sunken Continent of the Pacific (Lewis Spence) (1932)
Lemuria, The Lost Continent of the Pacific (by Eishnar Spenie Cerve – pen name of Lewis Spence) (1932)
The Sacred Symbols of Mu (James Churchward) (1933)
Cosmic Forces as They Were Taught in Mu: The Ancient Tale That Religion and Science are Twin Sisters (James Churchward) (1934)
Second Book of Cosmic Forces of Mu (James Churchward) (1935)
The Pulse of the Earth (by Johannes Herman Frederik Umbgrove) (1942)
Lemurian Seeds: Hope for Humanity (Shelley Kaehr) (2006)

Leonard, R. Cedric (1934-)
Flying Saucers, Ancient Writings and the Bible (1969)
Quest for Atlantis: New Evidence Concerning the Legendary Lost Continent (1979)

Quest for Atlantis II: A Scientific Inquiry (2005)

Levi, Eliphas (1810-1875)
The Mother of God (1844)
The Testament of Liberty (1848)
Transcendental Magic, Its Doctrine and Ritual (with Arthur Edward Waite) (1855)
Magic: A History of its Rites, Rituals and Mysteries (with Arthur Edward Waite) (1860)
The History of Magic: Including a Clear and Precise Exposition of Its Procedure, Its Rites and Its Mysteries (1861)
The Key to the Great Mysteries (1861)
Stories and Images (1862)
The Science of Spirits (1865)
The Great Secret or Occultism Unveiled (1868)

Levine, Stephen (1937-)
A Gradual Awakening (1979)
Who Dies? An Investigation of Conscious Living and Conscious Dying (1982)
Meetings at the Edge: Dialogues with the Grieving and the Dying, the Healing and the Healed (1984)
Healing into Life and Death (1987)
Embracing the Beloved: Relationship as a Path of Awakening (with Ondrea Levine) (1995)
A Year to Live: How to Live This Year as if It Were Your Last (1997)
To Love and Be Loved: The Difficult Yoga of Relationship (with Ondrea Levine) (1997)
Turning Toward the Mystery: A Seeker's Journey (2003)
Unattended Sorrow: Recovering from Loss and Reviving the Heart (2005)
The Grief Process: Meditations for Healing (with Ondrea Levine) (2006)
Breaking the Drought: Visions of Grace (2007)

Lewis, Dr. Harvey Spencer (1883-1939)
Rosicrucian Manual (1918)
A Thousand Years of Yesterdays: A Strange Story of Mystic Revelations (1920)
The Mystical Life of Jesus (1929)
Rosicrucian Principles for the Home and Business (1929)
Rosicrucian Questions and Answers with Complete History of the Order (1929)
Self Mastery and Fate: with the Cycles of Life (1929)
Mansions of the Soul: The Cosmic Conception (1930)
Lemuria, The Lost Continent of the Pacific (written under the pen name Eishnar Spenie) (1935)
The Symbolic Prophecy of the Great Pyramid (1936)
The Secret Doctrines of Jesus (1937)

Lewis, Ralph Maxwell (1904-1987)

Behold the Sign: A Book on Ancient Symbolism (1944)
The Sanctuary of the Self (1948)
The Conscious Interlude (1957)
Cosmic Mission Fulfilled (1966)
Yesterday Has Much to Tell (1973)
Whisperings of Self: A Collection of Aphorisms Designed to Uplift and Inspire Each Day of the Year (1976)
Through the Mind's Eye (1982)
The Universe of Numbers (1984)
The Immortalized Words of the Past (1986)
Mental Alchemy (1987)

Linn, Denise
Past Lives: Present Dreams: How to Use Reincarnation for Personal Growth (1994)
Sacred Space: Clearing and Enhancing the Energy of Your Home (1996)
The Secret Language of Signs: How to Interpret the Coincidences and Symbols in Your Life (1996)
Quest: A Guide for Creating Your Own Vision Quest (with Meadow Linn) (1997)
Altars: Bringing Sacred Shrines into Your Everyday Life (1999)
Sacred Legacies: Healing Your Past and Creating a Positive Future (1999)
Space Clearing A-Z: How to Use Feng Shui to Purify and Bless Your Home (2001)
Secrets and Mysteries: The Glory and Pleasure of Being a Woman (2002)
Soul Coaching: 28 Days to Discover Your Authentic Self (2003)
How Death Saved My Life – And Other Stories on My Journey to Wholeness (2005)
The Soul Loves the Truth: Lessons Learned on the Path to Joy (2006)
If I Can Forgive, So Can You: My Autobiography of How I Overcame My Past and Healed My Life (2006)
Four Acts of Personal Power: How to Heal Your Past and Create a Positive Future (2007)
The Hidden Power of Dreams: The Mysterious World of Dreams Revealed (2009)
Unlock the Secret Messages of Your Body! The 28-Day Jump-Start Program for Radiant Health and Glorious Vitality (2010)

Lipski, Dr. Elizabeth
Digestive Wellness: How to Strengthen the Immune System and Prevent Disease Through Healthy Digestion (1996)
Leaky Gut Syndrome: What to do About a Health Threat that can Cause Arthrities, Allergies and a Host of Other Illnesses (1998)
Digestive Wellness for Children: How to Strengthen the Immune System and Prevent Disease Through Healthy Digestion (2006)

Lipton, Dr. Bruce (1944-)

The Biology of Belief: Unleashing the Power of Consciousness, Matter and Miracles (2005)
The Wisdom of Your Cells – How Your Beliefs Control Your Biology (2006)
Spontaneous Evolution: Our Positive Future (And a Way to Get There From Here) (with Steve Bhaerman) (2009)

Lodge, Sir Oliver (1851-1940)
The Immortality of the Soul (1908)
The Survival of Man: A Study in Unrecognized Human Faculty (1909)
The Ether of Space (1909)
Reason and Belief (1910)
Raymond, or Life and Death: With Examples of the Evidence for Survival of Memory and Affection After Death (1916)
Christopher: A Study in Human Personality (1919)
The Rationality of Survival in Terms of Physical Science (1925)
Evolution and Creation (1926)
Why I Believe in Personal Immortality (1928)
Phantom Walls (1930)
Demonstrated Survival: Its Influence on Science, Philosophy and Religion (1930)
The Reality of a Spiritual World (1930)
Conviction of Survival (1930)
Religion and the New Science (1932)
My Philosophy, Representing My Views on the Many Functions of the Ether of Space (1933)

Luna, Dr. Luis Eduardo (1947-)
Vegetalismo: Shamanism Among the Mestizo Population of the Peruvian Amazon (1986)
Ayahuasca Visions: The Religious Iconography of a Peruvian Shaman (with Pablo Amaringo) (1991)
Ayahuasca Reader: Encounters With the Amazon's Sacred Vine (with Steven F. White) (2000)
Inner Paths to Outer Space: Journeys to Alien Worlds Through Psychedelics and Other Spiritual Technologies (with Rick Strassman, Slawek Wojtowicz and Ede Frescka) (2008)

Luria, Rabbi Isaac (1534-1572) (books about)
The Rainbow Calendar of Isaac Luria (by Jerome Rothenberg and Harris Lenowitz) (1977)
Isaac Luria and Meister Eckhart: A Comparative Analysis of a Jewish and Christian Mystic (by Andrew J. Keck) (1991)
Tree of Life: Chayyim Vital's Introduction to the Kabbalah of Isaac Luria: The Palace of Adam Kadmon (by Hayyim ben Joseph Vital, et al) (1999)
Kabbalah of Creation: Isaac Luria's Earlier Mysticism (by Hayyim ben Joseph Vital and Eliahu Klein) (2000)
Physician of the Soul, Healer of the Cosmos: Isaac Luria and his Kabbalistic Fellowship (by Lawrence Fine) (2003)

Window of the Soul: The Kabbalah of Rabbi Isaac Luria (1534-1572) (by Hayyim ben Joseph Vital et al) (2006)

From Metaphysics to Midrash: Myth, History, and the Interpretation of Scripture in Lurianic Kabbala (by Shaul Magid) (2008)

M

MacDade, Bonnie (1967-)
Spirit Flight (2011)

Machen, Arthur (1863-1947)
The Great God Pan (1894)
The Inmost Light (1894)
The Shining Pyramid (1895)
The Three Imposters (1895)
The White People (1904)
The Hill of Dreams (1907)
The Great Return (1915)
Far Off Things (1922)
The Secret Glory (1922)
The House of Souls (1922)
Things Near and Far (1923)
The Hill of Dreams (1923)
Dreads and Drolls (1926)
Notes and Queries (1926)
The Children of the Pool (1936)

Macy, Mark (1949-)
Solutions for a Troubled World (1987)
Healing the World and Me (1991)
Miracles in the Storm: Talking to The Other Side With the New Technology of Spiritual Contact

(2001)
Spirit Faces: Truth about the Afterlife (2006)
The Project: The Past, Present, and Future of Humanity (2009)

Madden, Kristin
Pagan Parenting: Spiritual, Magical and Emotional Development of the Child (2000)
Pagan Homeschooling: A Guide to Adding Spirituality to Your Child's Education (2002)
Mabon: Celebrating the Autumn Equinox (2002)
The Book of Shamanic Healing (2002)
The Shamanic Guide to Death and Dying: Meditations, Exercises, Rituals and Ceremonies (2005)
Exploring the Pagan Path: Wisdom from the Elders (2005)
Dancing the Goddess Incarnate: Living the Magic of Maiden, Mother and Crone (with Dorothy Morrison) (2006)
Magickal Crafts (with Liz Roberts) (2006)
Festival Feasts: Pagan Celebration Cookbook (2008)
Magick, Mystery, and Medicine: Advanced Shamanic Healing (2008)
Mabon: Pagan Thanksgiving (2008)
Magic, Mystery and Medicine: Advanced Shamanic Healing (2009)

Maharishi Mahesh Yogi (1917(?)-2008)
Meditation: Easy System Propounded by Maharishi Mahesh Yogi (1962)
The Science of Being and the Art of Living (1963)
Love and God (1965)
Meditations of Maharishi Mahesh Yogi (1968)
On the Bhagavad-Gita: A New Translation with Commentary with Sanskrit Text (1969)
Results of Scientific Research on Transcendental Meditation Programme: Taught by His Holiness Maharishi Mahesh Yogi (1976)
Freedom Behind Bars: Enlightenment to Every Individual and Invincibility to Every Nation (1978)
Building for the Health and Happiness of Everyone: Creating Ideal Housing in Harmony with Natural Law (1998)

Mandino, Og (1923-1996)
The Greatest Salesman in the World (1968)
The Greatest Secret In The World: Featuring Your Own Success Recorder Diary with the Ten Great Scrolls for Success From the Greatest ... (1972)
The Greatest Miracle In The World (1975)
The Christ Commission (1980)
Mission: Success! (1986)
A Better Way To Live (1990)

The God Memorandum: From The Greatest Miracle in the World (1990)
The Return of The Ragpicker (1992)
The Twelfth Angel (1993)
Secrets for Success and Happiness (1995)
Spellbinder's Gift (1995)
The Greatest Mystery in the World: Including a Precious Legacy For All of Us From the Old Ragpicker, Simon Potter (1997)
The Ten Ancient Scrolls for Success: From the Greatest Salesman In The World (1998)

Manning, Matthew (1955-)

The Link: Matthew Manning's Own Story of His Extraordinary Psychic Gifts (1974)
In the Minds of Millions (1977)
The Strangers (1978)
Matthew Manning's Guide to Self Healing (1989)
No Faith Required (1995)
One Foot In the Stars: The Story of the World's Most Extraordinary Healer (with Tessa Rose) (1997)
The Healing Journey: Discover Powerful New Ways to Beat Cancer and Other Serious Illnesses (2001)
Your Mind Can Heal Your Body: How Your Experiences and Emotions Affect Your Physical Health (2007)

Marden, Dr. Orison Swett (1850-1924)

Architects of Fate or, Steps to Success and Power: A Book Designated to Inspire Youth to Character Building, Self-Culture and Nobel Achievement (1897)
The Secret of Achievement: A Book Designated to Teach That the Highest Achievement is That Which Results in Noble Manhood and Womanhood (1898)
Character: The Grandest Thing in the World (1899)
Cheerfulness as a Life Power (1899)
Good Manners: A Passport to Success (with Abner Bayley) (1900)
Success Nuggets (1906)
Optimistic Life, Or, In the Cheering-Up Business (1907)
He Can Who Thinks He Can, and Other Papers of Success in Life (1908)
Peace Power and Plenty (1909)
Do It To a Finish (with Margaret Conolly) (1909)
Everybody Ahead, Or Getting the Most Out of Life (1916)
Making Life a Masterpiece (1916)
The Man You Long to Be (1918)
Love's Way (1919)
The Conquest of Worry (1924)

Margolis, Char (1951-)
Questions from Earth, Answers from Heaven: A Psychic Intuitive's Discussion of Life, Death and What Awaits us Beyond (with Victoria St. George) (1999)
Char: The Medium (with Victoria St. George) (2003)
Life: A Spiritual Intuitive's Collection of Inspirational Thoughts (2004)
Discover Your Inner Wisdom: Using Intuition, Logic and Common Sense to Make Your Best Choices for Life, Health, Finances and Relationships (with Victoria St. George) (2008)
Living in Spirit: Why You and Those You Love Will Never Die (2009)
Love Karma Use Your Intuition to Find, Create and Nuture Love in Your Life (2011)

Marx-Hubbard, Barbara (1929-)
The Evolutionary Journey: A Personal Guide to a Positive Future (1982)
The Hunger of Eve: One Woman's Odyssey Toward the Future (1989)
The Revelation: Our Crisis is a Birth (1993)
The Revelation: A Message of Hope for the New Millennium (1995)
Conscious Evolution: Awakening the Power of Our Social Potential (1998)
Emergence: The Shift from Ego to Essence (2001)
Birth 2012 & Beyond: Humanity's Great Shift to the Age of Consious Evolution (2012)

Maslow, Abraham (1908-1970)
Motivation and Personality (1954)
New Knowledge in Human Values (1959)
Religions, Values and Peak-Experiences (1964)
The Psychology of Science: A Reconnaissance (1966)
Toward a Psychology of Being (1968)
The Farther Reaches of Human Nature (1971)

Masters, Dr. Robert E.L. (1927-2008)
The Anti-Sex: The Belief in the Natural Inferiority of Women: Studies in Male Frustration and Sexual Conflict (1964)
Sex-Driven People: An Autobiographical Approach to the Problem of the Sex-Dominated Personality (1966)
The Varieties of Psychedelic Experience (with Jean Houston) (1966)
Psychedelic Art (with Jean Houston) (1968)
Sexual Self-Stimulation (1967)
Mind Games (with Jean Houston) (1972)
Listening to the Body: The Psychophysical Way to Health and Awareness (with Jean Houston) (1978)
The Goddess Sekhmet: Psychospiritual Exercises of the Fifth Way (1990)
Neurospeak: Transform Your Body, While You Read (1994)
The Way to Awaken: Exercises to Enliven Body, Self and Soul (1997)

Swimming Where Madmen Drown: Traveler's Tales From Inner Space (2002)

Masters, Rev. Roy (1928-)
The Secret of Life and Death (1964)
The Secret of Life (1972)
How to Conquer Suffering Without Doctors (1976)
No One Has to Die! (1977)
The Satan Principle: Life Itself Is Hypnosis: Self-Defense Lessons to Help You Cope With Everyday Pressure (1979)
How to Survive Your Parents: And Not Do to Your Children What Your Parents Did to You (1982)
The Hypnosis of Life: Self Defense Lessons to help You Cope With Everyday Pressure (1988)
Beyond the Known (with Dorothy Baker) (1988)
Understanding Sexuality: The Mystery of Our Lost Identities (with Dorothy Baker) (1988)
The Secret Power of Words: Why Words Affect You So Deeply (with Dorothy Baker) (1988)
Surviving the Comfort Zone (with Dorothy Baker) (1991)
Secrets of a Parallel Universe: Why Our Deepest Problems Hold the Key to Ultimate Personal Success and Happiness (1992)
Finding God in Physics: Einstein's Missing Relative (with Robert Just) (1997)
The Adam and Eve Sindrome (2001)
Hypnotic States of Americans: A Spiritual Survival Manual for Every American Family in a Perilous World (2011)

Mathers, S. L. MacGregor (1854-1918)
The Tarot, Its Occult Significance and Methods of Play (1888)
The Qabbalah Unveiled: Containing the Following Books of the Zohar: The Book of Concealed Mystery, The Greater Holy Assembly and …(1888)
The Key of Solomon the King: Clavicula Solomonis (1889)
The Sacred Magic of Abramelin the Mage (1896)
The Greater Key of Solomon the King: Including a Clear and Precise Exposition of King Solomon's Secret Procedure, Its Mysteries and Magic Rites, Original Plates, Seals, Charms and Talismans (with Lauron William De Laurence) (1914)

Matthews, Caitlin (1952-)
Goddess (1983)
The Elements of the Goddess (1989)
The Celtic Book of the Dead: A Guide for Your Voyage to the Celtic Otherworld (1992)
Encyclopaedia of Celtic Wisdom: The Celtic Shaman's Sourcebook (with John Matthews) (1994)
Singing the Soul Back Home: Shamanism in Daily Life (1995)
The Encyclopedia of Celtic Wisdom: The Celtic Shaman's Sourcebook (with John Matthews) (1996)

While the Bear Sleeps: Winter Tales and Traditions (with Judith Cristine Mills) (1999)
Sophia: Goddess of Wisdom, Bride of God (2001)
King Arthur and the Goddess of the Land: The Divine Feminine in the Mabinogion (2002)
Psychic Shield: The Personal Handbook of Psychic Protection (2006)
Fireside Stories Tales for a Winter's Eve (with Helen Cann) (2007)
King Arthur's Raid on the Underworld: The Oldest Grail Quest (with John Matthews) (2008)

Matthews, John (1948-)
Gawain, Knight of the Goddess: Restoring the Archetype (1990)
The Grail Tradition (1990)
The Winter Solstice: The Sacred Traditions of Christmas (with Caitlin Matthews) (1998)
Quest for the Green Man (2001)
The Celtic Shaman: A Practical Guide (2001)
Taliesin: The Last Celtic Shaman (2002)
Celtic Totem Animals (2002)
The Green Man: Spirit of Nature (2002)
King Arthur: Dark Age Warrior and Mythic Hero (2004)
The Sidhe: Wisdom from the Celtic Otherworld (2004)
Merlin: Shaman, Prophet, Magician (2004)
Book of Arthur: Lost Tales from the Round Table (2005)
The Grail: A Secret History (2006)
Secret Life of Elves and Faeries (2006)

May, Dr. Rollo (1909-1994)
The Meaning of Anxiety (1950)
Man's Search for Himself (1953)
Existence (1956)
The Art of Counseling (1965)
Psychology and the Human Dilemma (1967)
Love and Will (1969)
Power and Innocence: A Search for the Sources of Violence (1972)
The Courage to Create (1975)
Freedom and Destiny (1981)
The Discovery of Being: Writings in Existential Psychology (1983)
My Quest for Beauty (1985)
The Cry for Myth (1991)

McCannon, Tricia
Dialogues With the Angels (1996)
Beings of Light, Worlds in Transition (2004)
Jesus: The Explosive Story of the 30 Lost Years and the Ancient Mystery Religions (2009)

McCartney, Francesca
Intuition Medicine: The Science of Energy (2000)
Body of Health: The Science of Intuition Medicine for Energy and Balance (2005)

McGraw, Dr. Phil (1950-)
Life Strategies: Doing What Works, Doing What Matters (1995)
Relationship Rescue: A Seven Step Strategy for Reconnecting With Your Partner (2000)
Self Matters: Creating Your Life From the Inside Out (2001)
Dr. Phil Getting Real (2001)
The Self Matters Companion: Helping You Create Your Life From the Inside Out (2002)
The Ultimate Weight Solution: The 7 Keys to Weight Loss Freedom (2003)
Family First: Your Step-By-Step Plan for Creating a Phenomenal Family (2004)
The Ultimate Weight Solution Cookbook: Recipes for Weight Loss Freedom (2004)
The Ultimate Weight Solution Food Guide (2004)
Love Smart: Find the One You Want, Fix the One You Got (2005)
Real Life: Preparing for the 7 Most Challenging Days of Your Life (2008)

McKenna, Terence (1946-2000)
The Invisible Landscape: Mind, Hallucinogens, and the I Ching (with Dennis McKenna) (1975)
Psilocybin – Magic Mushroom Grower's Guide (with Dennis McKenna) (1976)
Food of the Gods: The Search for the Original Tree of Knowledge – A Radical History of Plants, Drugs, and Human Evolution (1992)
The Archaic Revival (1992)
Synesthesia (with Timothy C. Ely) (1992)
Trialogues at the Edge of the West: Chaos, Creativity and Resacralization of the World (with R. Sheldrake, R. Abraham and J. Huston) (1992)
True Hallucinations: Being an Account of the Author's Extraordinary Adventures in the Devil's Paradise (1993)
True Hallucinations and the Archaic Revival: Tales and Speculations About the Mysteries of the Psychedelic Experience (1998)
The Evolutionary Mind: Trialogues at the Edge of the Unthinkable (with Rupert Sheldrake and Ralph H. Abraham) (1998)
Food of the Gods: A Radical History of Plants, Drugs, and Human Evolution (1999)
Chaos, Creativity, and Cosmic Consciousness (with Rupert Sheldrake and Ralph H. Abraham) (2001)

McKibben, Bill (1960-)
The End of Nature (1990)
The Age of Missing Information (1992)
Hope, Human and Wild: True Stories of Living Lightly on the Earth (with William K. Stevens)

(1995)
Maybe One: A Personal and Environmental Argument for Single Child Families (1998)
Hundred Dollar Holiday: The Case For a More Joyful Christmas (1998)
Long Distance: Testing the Limits of Body and Spirit in a Year of Living Strenuously (2001)
Enough: Staying Human in an Engineered Age (2003)
Wandering Home: A Long Walk Across America's Most Hopeful Landscape, VT's Champlain Valley and NY's Adirondacks (2005)
The Comforting Whirlwind: God, Job and the Scale of Creation (2005)
Fight Global Warming Now: The Handbook for Taking Action in Your Community (2007)
Deep Economy: The Wealth of Communities and the Durable Future (2007)
American Earth: Environmental Writing Since Thoreau (2008)
The Bill McKibben Reader: Pieces from an Active Life (2008)
Eaarth: Making a Life on a Tough New Planet (2010)
GWR: The Global Warming Reader (2011)

McTaggart, Lynne (1951-)
Kathleen Kennedy: Her Life and Times (1983)
Guide to the Side Effects of Drugs: A Quick Reference to the Most Common Categories of Drugs (1992)
What Doctors Don't Tell You: The Truth About The Dangers Of Modern Medicine (1999)
The Cancer Handbook: What's Really Working (2000)
The Vaccination Bible (2000)
The Field: The Quest for the Secret Force of the Universe (2003)
The Intention Experiment: Using Your Thoughts to Change Your Life and the World (2007)
The Bond: Connecting Through The Space Between Us (2011)

Mead, George Robert Stow (1863-1933)
Simon Magus: The Gnostic Magician (1892)
Orpheus (1895)
Pistis Sophia: A Gnostic Gospel (1896)
Fragments of a Faith Forgotten: The Gnostics, A Contribution to the Study of the Origins of Christianity (1900)
Apollonius of Tyana: The Philosopher-Reformer of the First Century A.D. (1905)
Thrice Greatest Hermes: Studies in Hellenistic Theosophy and Gnosis (1906)
The Gnosis of the Mind (1906)
The Hymns of Hermes: Echoes From the Gnosis (1907)
Doctrine of the Subtle Body in Western Tradition: An Outline of What the Philosophers Thought and Christians Taught on the Subject (1919)
Pistis Sophia: A Gnostic Miscellany (1921)
Gnostic John the Baptizer (1924)

Mehl-Madrona, Dr. Lewis (1954-)
Coyote Medicine: Lessons from Native American Healing (1997)
Coyote Healing: Miracles in Native Medicine (2003)
Coyote Wisdom: The Power of Story in Healing (2005)
Narrative Medicine: The Use of History and Story in the Healing Process (2007)
The Healing Power of Story: The Promise of Narrative Psychiatry (2010)

Metzner, Dr. Ralph (1936-)
Maps of Consciousness: I Ching, Tantra, Tarot, Alchemy, Astrology, Actualism (1971)
Know Your Type: Maps of Identity (1979)
Opening to Inner Light: The Transformation of Human Nature and Consciousness (1986)
The Well of Remembrance: Rediscovering the Earth Wisdom Myths of Northern Europe (1994)
The Unfolding Self: Varieties of Transformative Experience (1998)
Green Psychology – Transforming out Relationship to the Earth (1999)
Sacred Mushroom of Visions: Teonanacatl (2005)
Sacred Vines of Spirits: Ayahuasca (2006)
The Roots of War and Domination (2008)
The Expansion of Consciousness (2008)
Mind Space Time Stream (2009)
Alchemical Divination (2009)
Birth of a Psychedelic Culture: Conversations about Leary, the Harvard Experiments, Millbrook and the Sixties (2010)

Millay, Dr. Jean
Multidimensional Mind: Remote Viewing in Hyperspace (1999)
Radiant Minds: Scientists Explore The Dimensions of Consciousness (with Russell Targ and Dean Radin) (2010)

Millman, Dan (1946-)
Whole Body Fitness: Mind, Body and Spirit (1979)
Way of the Peaceful Warrior: A Book That Changes Lives (1980)
Sacred Journey of the Peaceful Warrior (1991)
No Ordinary Moments: A Peaceful Warrior's Guide to Daily Life (1992)
The Life You Were Born to Live: A Guide to Finding Your Life Purpose (1995)
The Laws of Spirit: Simple, Powerful Truths for Making Life Work (1995)
Everyday Enlightenment: The Twelve Gateways to Personal Growth (1998)
Body Mind Mastery: Creating Success in Sport and Life (1999)
Divine Interventions: True Stories of Mysteries and Miracles That Change Lives (with Doug Childers) (2000)
The Journeys of Socrates (2005)
Living on Purpose: Straight Answers to Life's Tough Questions (2005)

Wisdom of the Peaceful Warrior: A Companion to the Book That Changes Lives (2007)
Bridge Between Worlds: Extraordinary Experiences That Change Lives (with Douglas Childers) (2009)
Peaceful Warrior: The Graphic Novel (with Andrew Winegarner) (2010)
The Four Purposes of Life: Finding Meaning and Direction in a Changing World (2011)

Mindell, Dr. Arnold (1940-)
Dreambody, The Body's Role in Revealing the Self (1982)
River's Way: The Process Science of the Dreambody: Information & Channels in Dream & Bodywork, Psychology and Physics, Taoism and Alchemy (1985)
Working With the Dreaming Body (1985)
The Dreambody in Relationships (1987)
Working on Yourself Alone: Inner Dreambody Work (1990)
Your Body Speaks Its Dream (1991)
Riding the Horse Backwards: Process Work in Theory and Practice (1992)
The Shaman's Body: A New Shamanism for Transforming Health, Relationships, and the Community (1993)
Quantum Mind: The Edge Between Physics and Psychology (2000)
Dreaming While Awake: Techniques for 24-Hour Lucid Dreaming (2000)
The Dreammaker's Apprentice: Using Heightened Status of Consciousness to Interpret Dreams (2001)
The Quantum Mind and Healing: How to Listen and Respond to Your Body's Symptoms (2004)
The Dreaming Source of Creativity: 30 Simple Ways to Have Fun and Work on Yourself (2005)
Earth Based Psychology: Path Awareness from the Teachings of Don Juan, Richard Feynman and Lao Tse (2007)
ProcessMind: A User's Guide To Connecting With The Mind of God (2010)

Mishlove, Dr. Jeffrey (194?-)
The Roots of Consciousness: Psychic Exploration Through History, Science and Experience (1975)
Preliminary Investigation of Events which Suggest the Possible Applied PSI Abilities of Mr. Ted Owens (1978)
PSI Development Systems (1980)
Thinking Allowed: Conversations on the Leading Edge of Knowledge (1992)
The Roots of Consciousness: The Classic Encyclopedia of Consciousness Studies (1993)
The Spiritual Universe (with Fred Alan Wolf and Arthur Bloch) (1997)
The PK Man: A True Story of Mind Over Matter (2000)

Monroe, Robert (1915-1995)
Journeys Out of the Body (1971)
Far Journeys (1985)

Ultimate Journey (1994)

Montgomery, Ruth (1913-2001)
The Gift of Prophecy: The Phenomenal Jean Dixon (1965)
A Search for the Truth (1967)
Here and Hereafter (1968)
Born to Heal: The Astonishing Story of Mr. A and the Ancient Art of Healing With Life Energies (1973)
Companions Along the Way (1974)
The World Before (1976)
Strangers Among Us: Enlightened Beings From a World to Come (1979)
Threshold to Tomorrow (1982)
Aliens Among Us (1985)
Herald of the New Age (with Joanne Garland) (1986)
A World Beyond, A Startling Message From the Eminent Psychic Arthur Ford From Beyond the Grave (with Arthur Ford) (1971)
The World to Come: The Guides' Long-Awaited Predictions for the Dawning Age (1999)

Moody, Dr. Raymond (1944-)
Life After Life: The Investigation of a Phenomenon – Survival of Bodily Death (1976)
Reflections on Life after Life (1977)
Laugh After Laugh: The Healing Power of Humor (1978)
The Light Beyond (with Paul Perry) (1988)
Elvis After Life: Unusual Psychic Experiences Surrounding the Death of a Superstar (1989)
Life Before Life: Regression Into Past Lives (with Paul Perry) (1990)
Coming Back: A Psychiatrist Explores Past-Life Journeys (1991)
Reunions: Visionary Encounters With Departed Loved Ones (with Paul Perry) (1993)
Scrying: A Feminine Form of Divination (1996)
The Last Laugh: A New Philosophy of Near Death Experiences, Apparitions and the Paranormal (1999)
Life After Loss: Conquering Grief and Finding Hope (with Dianne Archangel) (2001)
Reunited: How to Meet Loved Ones Again Who Seem Lost to Death (with Paul Perry) (2006)
Glimpses of Eternity: Sharing a Loved One's Passage From This Life to The Next (with Paul Perry) (2010)

Monti, Dr. Daniel
The Great Life Makeover: A Couples Guide to Weight, Mood and Sex for the Best Years of Your Life – and Your Relationship (2008)
Integrative Psychiatry (with Bernard D. Beitman) (2009)

Moore, Marcia (1929-1979)

Astrology Today – A Socio-Psychological Survey (1960)
Astrology in Action (with Mark Douglas) (1970)
Diet, Sex and Yoga (with Mark Douglas) (1970)
Journeys into the Bright World (with Howard Sunny Alltounian) (1978)

Moore, Mary-Margaret (dictated by Bartholomew)
I Come As a Brother: A Remembrance of Illusions (1986)
From the Heart of a Gentle Brother (1987)
Reflections of an Elder Brother: Awakening From the Dream (1989)
Planetary Brother (1991)
Journeys with a Brother: From Japan to India (1995)

Moore, Dr. Robert (1942-)
The Cult Experience: Responding to the New Religious Pluralism (with J. Gordon Melton) (1982)
King, Warrior, Magician, Lover: Rediscovering the Archetypes of the Mature Masculine (with Douglas Gillette) (1990)
The King Within: Accessing the King in the Male Psyche (with Douglas Gillette) (1992)
The Lover Within: Accessing the Lover in the Male Psyche (with Douglas Gillette) (1993)
The Magician Within: Accessing the Shaman in the Male Psyche (with Douglas Gillette) (1993)
The Warrior Within: Accessing the Knight in the Male Psyche (with Douglas Gillette) (1993)
The Archetype of Initiation: Sacred Space, Ritual Process and Personal Transformation (2001)
The Magician and the Analyst: The Archetype of the Magus in Occult Spirituality and Jungian Analysis (2002)
Facing the Dragon: Confronting Personal and Spiritual Grandiosity (2003)

Moran, Victoria
Compassion: The Ultimate Ethic an Exploration of Veganism (1991)
Love-Powered Diet: When Willpower is Not Enough: Revolutionary Approach to Health Eating and Recovery from Food Addition (1992)
Love Yourself Thin: The Revolutionary Spiritual Approach to Weight Loss (with Sonnet Pierce) (1997)
Shelter for the Spirit: Create Your Own Haven in a Hectic World (1998)
Creating a Charmed Life: Sensible, Spiritual Secrets Every Busy Woman Should Know (1999)
Lit From Within: A Simple Guide to the Art of Inner Beauty (2001)
Fit From Within: 101 Simple Secrets to Change Your Body and Your Life – Starting Today and Lasting Forever (2002)
Younger by the Day: 365 Ways to Rejuvenate Your Body and Revitalize Your Spirit (2005)
Fat, Broke and Lonely No More: Your Personal Solution to Overeating, Overspending and Looking for Love in All the Wrong Places (2007)
Living The Charmed Life: Your Guide to Finding Magic in Every Moment and Meaning in

Every Day (2009)

Morrissey, Dr. Dianne
Anyone Can See The Light How You Can Touch Eternity – And Return Safely (1996)
You Can See the Light: How You Can Touch Eternity – And Return Safely (1997)

Morse, Dr. Melvin
Closer To The Light: Learning from Near Death Experiences of Children (with Paul Perry) (1991)
Transformed By The Light: The Powerful Effect of Near-Death Experiences on People's Lives (with Paul Perry) (1992)
Parting Visions: Uses and Meanings of Pre-Death, Psychic, and Spiritual Experiences (with Paul Perry) (1994)
Where God Lives: The Science of the Paranormal and How Out Brains are Linked to the Universe (with Paul Perry) (2000)

Moses, Harry Morgan
It's So Easy When You Know How (1995)

Moss, Dr. Richard
The I That is We (1981)
How Shall I Live: Transforming Surgery or Any Health Crisis Into Greater Aliveness (1985)
The Black Butterfly: An Invitation to Radical Aliveness (1986)
The Second Miracle: Intimacy, Spirituality, and Conscious Relationships (1995)
Words That Shine Both Ways: Reflections That Reconnect Us to Our True Nature (with Gil Goater) (1998)
The Mandala of Being: Discovering the Power of Awareness (2007)
Inside-Out Healing: Transforming Your Life Through the Power of Presence (2011)

Moss, Robert (1946-)
Conscious Dreaming: A Spiritual Path for Everyday Life (1996)
Dreamgates: An Explorer's Guide to the Worlds of Soul, Imagination, and Life Beyond Death (1998)
Dreaming True: How to Dream Your Future and Change Your Life for the Better (2000)
Dreamways of the Iroquois: Honoring the Secret Wishes of the Soul (2004)
The Dreamer's Book of the Dead: A Soul Traveler's Guide to Death, Dying and the Other Side (2005)
The Three "Only" Things: Tapping the Power of Dreams, Coincidence and Imagination (2007)
The Secret History of Dreaming (2009)

Active Dreaming (2011)

Mother Meera (1960-)
Bringing Down the Light: Journey of a Soul After Death (1990)
Answers (1991)
Answers Part !! (1997)

Mramor, Nancy
Spiritual Fitness: Embrace Your Soul, Transform Your Life (2004)
Top Ten Tips for Lasting Happiness (2011)

Muldoon, Sylvan (1903-1969)
The Case for Astral Projection (1936)
Sensational Psychic Experiences (1941)
Famous Psychic Stories (1942)
Psychic Experiences by Famous People (1948)
The Projection of the Astral Body (1968)
The Phenomena of Astral Projection (with Hereward Carrington) (1969)

Muller, Rev. Wayne
Legacy of the Heart: The Spiritual Advantages of a Painful Childhood (1992)
Darn It!: The History of Romance of Darners (with Stuart Muller) (1995)
How Then, Shall We Live?: Four Simple Questions that Reveal the Beauty and Meaning of Our Lives (1996)
Sabbath: Restoring the Sacred Rhythm of Rest (1999)
Sabbath: Finding Rest, Renewal and Delight in Our Busy Lives (2000)
Learning to Pray: How We Find Heaven on Earth (2003)
Living the Generous Life: Reflections on Giving and Receiving (with Megan Scribner) (2005)
A Life of Being, Having, and Doing Enough (2010)

Murphy, Dr. Joseph (1898-1981)
Peace Within Yourself (1956)
How to Use Your Healing Power (1957)
The Power of Your Subconscious Mind (1963)
The Subconscious Mind: A Source of Unlimited Power (1963)
The Miracle of Mind Dynamics: A New Way to Triumphant Living (1964)
Prayer is the Answer (1965)
The Amazing Laws of Cosmic Mind (1965)
Your Infinite Power to Be Rich (1966)
The Cosmic Power Within You (1968)
Secrets of the I Ching (1970)

Psychic Perception: The Magic of Extrasensory Power (1971)
The Cosmic Energizer: Miracle Power of the Universe (1974)
Within You is the Power: (Around the World With Dr. Murphy) (1977)
These Truths Can Change Your Life (1979)
How to Use the Laws of Mind (1980)

Murray, Margaret (1863-1963)
Elementary Egyptian Grammar (1905)
Elementary Coptic (Hasidic) Grammar (1911)
Legends of Ancient Egypt (1920)
The Witch-Cult in Western Europe (1921)
Egyptian Sculpture (1930)
Egyptian Temples (1931)
God of Witches (1933)
The Splendor That Was Egypt: A General Survey of Egyptian Culture (1949)
The Divine King in England (1954)
The Genesis of Religion (1963)
My First Hundred Years (1963)

Myss, Dr. Caroline (1952-)
Aids: Passageway to Transformation (with Norman Shealy) (1987)
Applying Universal Principles for Spiritual Fitness (1988)
The Creation of Health: Emotional, Psychological and Spiritual Responses that Promote Health and Healing (with Norman Shealy) (1998)
Anatomy of the Spirit: The Seven Stages of Power and Healing (1996)
Why People Don't Heal and How They Can (1997)
Sacred Contracts: Awakening Your Divine Potential (2001)
Invisible Acts of Power: Personal Choices that Create Miracles (2004)
Invisible Acts of Power: Channeling Grace into Your Everyday Life (2005)
Entering the Castle: An Inner Path to God and Your Soul (2007)
Defy Gravity: Healing Beyond the Bounds of Reason (2009)

Naranjo, Dr. Claudio (1932-)
On the Psychology of Meditation (with Robert E. Ornstein) (1971)
The One Quest (1972)
The Healing Journey: New Approaches to Consciousness (1973)
Techniques of Gestalt Therapy (1980)
How to Be: Meditation in Spirit and Practice (1990)
Ennea-Type Structures: Self-Analysis for the Seeker (1990)
Gestalt Therapy: The Attitude and Practice of an Atheoretical Experientalism (1993)
The End of Patriarchy: and the Dawning of a Tri-Une Society (1994)
Character and Neurosis: An Integrative View (1994)
Transformation Through Insight: Enneatypes in Life, Literature, and Clinical Practice (1997)
The Divine Child and the Hero: Inner Meaning in Children's Literature (1999)
The Enneagram of Society: Healing the Soul to Heal the World (2004)
The Way of Silence and the Talking Cure: On Meditation and Psychotherapy (2006)
Healing Civilization: Bringing Personal Transformation into the Societal Realm Through Education and the Integration of the Intra-Psychic Family (2010)

Narby, Dr. Jeremy (1959-)
The Cosmic Serpent: DNA and the Origins of Knowledge (1999)
Shamans Through Time: 500 Years on the Path to Knowledge (with Francis Huxley) (2001)
Intelligence in Nature: An Inquiry into Knowledge (2005)
The Psychotropic Mind: The World According to Ayahuasca, Iboga, and Shamanism (with Jan Kounen and Vincent Ravalec) (2010)

Nash, Carroll B. (1914-1998)
Science of PSI: ESP and PK (1978)
Parapsychology: The Science of Psiology (1986)
Comparison of Responses to ESP and Subliminal Targets (with Catherine S. Nash)
Medical Implications of Parapsychology

Needleman, Jacob (1934-)
The New Religions (1970)
A Sense of the Cosmos: The Encounter of Modern Science and Ancient Truth (1975)
On the Way to Self Knowledge (with Dennis Lewis) (1976)
Understanding the New Religions (with George Baker) (1978)
Consciousness and Tradition (1982)
The Heart of Philosophy (1982)
Lost Christianity: A Journey of Rediscovery to The Centre of Christian Experience (1990)
Money and the Meaning of Life (1991)
The Wisdom of Love: Toward a Shared Inner Search (2001)
The American Soul: Rediscovering the Wisdom of the Founders (2002)
Time and the Soul: Where Has All the Meaningful Time Gone – And Can We Get It Back? (2003)
Why Can't We Be Good? (2007)
The Essential Marcus Aurelius (with John P. Piazza) (2009)
What Is God? (2009)

Neihardt, John (1881-1973)
The Divine Enchantment: A Mystical Poem, and, Poetic Values: Their Reality and Our Need of Them (1900)
A Bundle of Myrrh (1907)
The River and I (1910)
Life's Lure (1914)
The Quest (1916)
Black Elk Speaks: Being the Life Story of a Holy Man of the Oglala Sioux (with Black Elk) (1932)
The Song of the Messiah (1935)
When the Tree Flowered: The Fictional Biography of Eagle Voice, a Sioux Indian (1952)
All is But a Beginning: Youth Remembered 1881-1901 (1972)
Patterns and Coincidences: A Sequel to All is But a Beginning (1973)

Nemeth, Dr. Maria
You and Money: Would it be All Right with You if Your Life Got Easier? (1995)
The Energy of Money: A Spiritual Guide to Financial and Personal Fulfillment (1999)
Mastering Life's Energies: Simple Steps to a Luminous Life at Work and Play (2007)

Newberg, Dr. Andrew (1966-)
Why God Won't Go Away: Brain Science and the Biology of Belief (with Eugene G. D'Aquili and Vince Rause) (2001)
Why We Believe What We Believe: Uncovering Our Biological Need for Meaning, Spirituality and Truth (with Mark R. Waldman) (2007)
Born to Believe: God, Science and the Origin of Ordinary and Extraordinary Beliefs (with Mark Robert Waldman (2007)
How God Changes Your Brain: Breakthrough Findings From a Leading Neuroscientist (with Mark Robert Waldman (2009)
Principles of Neurotheology (2010)
Words Can Change Your Brain: 12 Conversation Strategies to Build Trust, Resolve Conflict, and Increase Intimacy (with Mark R. Waldman) (2012)

Newton, Dr. Michael
Journey of Soul: Case Studies of Life Between Lives (1997)
Destiny of Souls: New Case Studies of life Between Lives (2000)
Life Between Lives: Hypnotherapy for Spiritual Regression (2004)
Memories of the Afterlife: Life Between Lives Stories of Personal Transformation (2009)

Nightingale, Earl (1921-1989)
This Is Earl Nightingale (1969)
The Earl Nightingale Program: Our Changing World (1972)
Earl Nightingale's Greatest Discovery: The Strangest Secret - Revisited (1987)

Northrup, Dr. Christiane
A Healthy Woman's Life: Dr. Christiane Northrup's Seven-Step Program to Creating Health Daily (1998)
Women's Bodies, Women's Wisdom: Creating Physical and Emotional Health and Healing (1998)
The Wisdom of Menopause: Creating Physical and Emotional Health and Healing During the Change (2001)
Mother-Daughter Wisdom: Creating A Legacy of Physical and Emotional Health (2005)
The Wisdom of Menopause Journal: Your Guide to Creating Vibrant Health and Happiness in the Second Half of Your Life (2007)
The Secret Pleasures of Menopause (2008)

Oates, David John
Beyond Backward Masking: Reverse Speech and the Voice of the Inner Mind (with Greg Albrecht) (1987)
Reverse Speech: Hidden Messages in Human Communication (1991)
Reverse Speech: Voices From The Unconscious (1996)
Its Only A Metaphor (2008)
Reverse Speech: A New Theory About Language (2008)

O'Donnell, Michele
Of Monkeys and Dragons: Freedom From the Tyranny of Disease (2001)
The God That We've Created: The Basic Cause of All Disease (2005)
When the Wolf is At the Door: The Simplicity of Healing (2007)
Only Receive: No Barriers, No Boundries
Arise, Shine: Your Time Has Come 365 Daily Inspirations (2011)

O'Leary, Dr. Brian (1940- 2011)
The Making of an Ex-Astronaut (1971)
The Fertile Stars (1981)
Mars 1999 (1987)
Exploring Inner and Outer Space: A Scientist's Perspective on Personal and Planetary Transformation (1989)
The Second Coming of Science: An Intimate Report of the New Science (1993)
Miracle in the Void: Free Energy, UFOs and Other Scientific Revelations (1996)
The Energy Solution Revolution (2009)

Re-Inheriting the Earth: Awakening to Sustainable Solutions and Greater Truths (2010)

Oriah "Mountain Dreamer"
Confessions of a Spiritual Thrillseeker: Medicine Teachings From the Grandmothers (1991)
Dream of Desire: A Collection of Poetry (1995)
The Dance: Moving to the Rhythms of Your True Self (2001)
The Call: Discovering Why You Are Here (2003)
The Invitation: The Poem That Has Touched Lives Around the World (2004)
What We Ache For: Creativity and the Unfolding of Your Soul (2005)
The Dance: Moving to The Deep Rythms of Your Life (2006)

Orloff, Dr. Judith (1951-)
Second Sight (1996)
Dr. Judith Orloff's Guide to Intuitive Healing: Five Steps to Physical, Emotional and Sexual Wellness (2000)
Positive Energy: 10 Extraordinary Prescriptions for Transforming Fatigue, Stress and Fear into Vibrance, Strength and Love (2004)
Emotional Freedom: Liberate Yourself From Negative Emotions and Transform Your Life (2009)

Ornstein, Dr. Robert Evans (1942-)
On the Experience of Time (1969)
The Psychology of Consciousness (1972)
Physiological Studies of Consciousness (with Robert Evan) (1973)
The Mind Field: A Personal Essay (1976)
The Amazing Brain (with Richard F. Thompson) (1984)
Multimind (1986)
The Healing Brain: Breakthrough Discoveries About How the Brain Keeps Us Healthy (with David S. Sobel) (1987)
Healthy Pleasures (with David S. Sobel) (1989)
New World New Mind: Moving Toward Conscious Evolution (with Paul R. Ehrlich) (1989)
The Healing Brain: A Scientific Reader (with Charles Swencionis) (1990)
The Evolution of Consciousness: Of Darwin, Freud, and Cranial Fire: The Origins of the Way We Think (1991)
The Roots of the Self (1993)
The Right Mind (1997)
MindReal: How the Mind Creates Its Own Virtual Reality (2008)
Humanity on a Tightrope: Thoughts on Empathy, Family, and Big Changes for a Viable Future (with Paul Ehrlich) (2010)

Oschman, Dr. James

Energy Medicine: The Scientific Basis (2000)
Energy Medicine in Therapeutics and Human Performance (2003)

Osho (1931-1990)
The Book of Understanding: Creating Your Own Path to Freedom
Being in Love: How to Love with Awareness and Relate Without Fear
Emotional Wellness: Transforming Fear, Anger, and Jealousy into Creative Energy
Essence of Spiritualism: Based on Discourses of Osho and His Three Enlightened Disciples… (with O. Siddhartha, O. Shailendra and O. Priya)
The Spiritual Path: Buddha, Zen, Tao, Tantra
Meetings with Remarkable People
Freedom: The Courage to be Yourself
From Unconsciousness to Consciousness (with Dhyan Khumal and Niket)
Pharmacy for the Soul: A Comprehensive Collection of Meditations, Relaxation, Awareness Exercises andOther Practices for Physical and Emotional Well ..
The Man of Truth: A Majority of One (with Bodhitaru)
The Great Secret: Talks on the Songs of Kabir (with Kabir)
Awareness: The Key to Living in Balance: Insights for A New Way of Living
The Message Beyond Words: A Dialogue with the Lord of Death (et al)

Osteen, Pastor Joel (1963-)
Your Best Life Now: 7 Steps to Living at Your Full Potential (2004)
Become a Better You: 7 Keys to Improving Your Life (2007)
Starting Your Best Life Now: A Guide for New Adventures and Stages on Your Journey (2007)
Your Best Life Now For Moms (2007)
Daily Readings From Become a Better You: 90 Devotions for Improving Your Life Every Day (2008)
The Christmas Spirit: Memories of Family, Friends, and Faith (2010)

Ouspensky, P. D. (1878-1948)
The Symbolism of the Tarot: Philosophy of Occultism in Pictures and Numbers (1913)
Talks with a Devil (1916)
Tertium Organum: The Third Canon of Thought, A Key to the Enigmas of the World (1920)
A New Model of the Universe: Principles of the Psychological Method in Its Application to Problems of Science, Religion and Art (1931)
In Search of the Miraculous: Fragments of an Unknown Teaching (1949)

P

Page, Dr. Christine
The Mirror of Existence: Stepping into Wholeness (1995)
Beyond the Obvious: Bringing Intuition Into Our Awakening Consciousness (1998)
Mind, Body, Spirit Workbook: A Handbook of Health (with Keith Hagenbach) (1999)
Spiritual Alchemy: How To Transform Your Life (2003)
Frontiers of Health: How to Heal the Whole Person (2005)
The Mystery of 2012: Predictions, Prophecies and Possibilities (2007)
2012 and the Galactic Center: Return of the Great Mother (2008)

Palmer, Helen
The Enneagram: Understanding Yourself and the Others in Your Life (1991)
The Enneagram in Love and Work: Understanding Your Intimate and Business Relationships (1995)
The Enneagram Advantage: Putting the Nine Personality Types to Work in the Office (with Paul B. Brown) (1998)
Inner Knowing: Consciousness, Creativity, Insight and Intuition (1998)

Papus (1865-1916)
Contemporary Occultism (1887)
Occultism (1890)
Tarot of the Bohemians: The Most Ancient Book in the World for the Exclusive Use of Initiates (1892)
The Science of Magicians (1892)
The Devil and Occultism (1895)

Systematic Treatise of Practical Magic (1898)
The Qabbalah: Secret Tradition of the West (1903)
The Divinatory Tarot (1909)

Paul, Dr. Margaret
Inner Bonding: Becoming a Loving Adult to Your Inner Child (1992)
Do I Have to Give Up Me To Be Loved by God? (1999)

Peale, Rev. Norman Vincent (1898-1993)
The Art of Living (1937)
Guide to Confident Living (1948)
The Power of Positive Thinking (1952)
Stay Alive All Your Life (1957)
Enthusiasm Makes the Difference (1967)
Norman Vincent Peale's Treasure of Courage and Confidence (1970)
You Can If You Think You Can (1974)
Positive Thinking for A Time Like This (1975)
Positive Imaging: The Powerful Way to Change Your Life (1982)
The True Joy of Positive Living: An Autobiography (1984)
Have a Great Day (1985)
Power of the Plus Factor (1987)
Six Attitudes for Winners (1989)
Reaching Your Potential (1990)
This Incredible Century (1991)

Pearce, Joseph Chilton (1926-)
Exploring the Crack in the Cosmic Egg: Split Minds and Meta-Realities (1974)
Magical Child: Rediscovering Nature's Plan for Our Children (1977)
The Bond of Power: Meditation and Wholeness (1982)
Magical Child Matures (1985)
Evolution's End: Claiming the Potential of Our Intelligence (1992)
The Crack in the Cosmic Egg: Challenging Constructs of Mind and Reality (2002)
The Biology of Transcendence: A Blueprint of the Human Spirit (2002)
Spiritual Initiation and the Breakthrough of Consciousness: The Bond of Power (2003)
The Death of Religion and the Rebirth of Spirit: A Return to the Intelligence of the Heart (2007)

Pearl, Dr. Eric (1955-)
The Reconnection: Heal Others, Heal Yourself (2001)

Pearsall, Dr. Paul (1942-2007)

Super Immunity: Master Your Emotions and Improve Your Health (with Peter D. O'Neill) (1987)

Super Marital Sex: Loving for Life (1987)

Super Joy: Learning to Celebrate Everyday Life (1987)

The Power of the Family: Strength, Comfort, Healing (1990)

The Ten Laws of Lasting Love (1993)

A Healing Intimacy: The Power of Loving Connections (1995)

The Pleasure Prescription: To Love, To Work, To Play, Life in the Balance (1996)

The Heart's Code: Tapping the Wisdom and Power of Our Heart Energy (1998)

Wishing Well: Making Your Every Wish Come True (2000)

Miracle in Maui: Let Miracles Happen in Your Life (2001)

Partners in Pleasure: Sharing Success, Creating Joy, Fulfilling Dreams – Together (2001)

Toxic Success: How to Stop Striving and Start Thriving (2002)

The Beethoven Factor: The New Positive Psychology of Hardiness, Happiness, Healing and Hope (2003)

The Last Self-help Book You'll Ever Need: Repress Your Anger, Think Negatively, Be a Good Blamer and Throttle Your Inner Child (2005)

Awe: The Delights and Dangers of Our Eleventh Emotion (2007)

Pearson, Dr. Caroline S.

The Hero Within: Six Archetypes We Live By (1989)

Educating the Majority: Women Challenge Tradition in Higher Education (1989)

Awakening the Heroes Within: Twelve Archetypes to Help Us Find Ourselves and Transform our World (1991)

Magic at Work: Camelot, Creative Leadership and Everyday Miracles (with Sharon Seivert) (1995)

Invisible Forces II: Harnessing the Power of Archetypes to Improve Your Career and Workplace (1997)

Building Extraordinary Brands Through the Power of Archetypes (2001) (with Margaret Mark)

Introduction to Archetypes in Organizational Settings: A Guide to Interpreting Organizational and Team Culture Indicator Instrument (2003)

Mapping the Organizational Culture (2004) (with John Corlett)

What Story Are You Living?: A Workbork and Guide to Interpreting Results from the Pearson-Marr Archetype Indicator (with Hugh K. Marr) (2007)

The Transforming Leader: New Approaches to Leadership for the Twenty-First Century (2012)

Peck, Dr. M. Scott (1936-2005)

The Road Less Traveled: A New Psychology of Love, Traditional Values and Spiritual Growth (1978)

People of the Lie: The Hope For Healing Human Evil (1983)

The Different Drum: Community Making and Peace (1987)
The Friendly Snowflake: A Fable of Faith, Love and Family (1992)
A World Waiting To Be Born: Civility Rediscovered (1993)
Further Along the Road Less Traveled (1993)
Meditations From the Road (1993)
In Search of Stones: A Pilgrimage of Faith, Reason and Discovery (1995)
Gifts for the Journey: Treasures of the Christian Life (with Marilyn Von Waldner) (1995)
In Heaven As On Earth: A Vision of the Afterlife (1996)
The Road Less Traveled and Beyond: Spiritual Growth in the Age of Anxiety (1997)
Denial of the Soul: Spiritual and Medical Perspectives in Euthanasia and Mortality (1997)
Golf and the Spirit: Lessons for the Journey (1999)
Glimpses of the Devil: A Psychiatrist's Personal Accounts of Possession, Exorcism and Redemption (2005)

Pelletier, Dr. Kenneth (1946-)
Consciousness: East and West (with Charles A. Garfield) (1976)
Mind as a Healer, Mind as a Slayer: A Holistic Approach to Preventing Stress Disorders (1977)
Toward a Science of Consciousness (1978)
Holistic Medicine: From Stress to Optimum Health (1979)
Longevity: Fulfilling Our Biological Potential (1981)
Healthy People in Unhealthy Places; Stress and Fitness at Work (1984)
A New Age: Problems and Potentials (1985)
Sound Mind – Sound Body: A New Model for Lifelong Health (1994)
The Best Alternative Medicine: What Works? What Does Not? (2000)
New Medicine: Complete Family Health Guide – Integrating Complementary, Alternative and Conventional Medicine for the Safest and Most Effective Treatment (2007)

Penczak, Christopher (1973-)
City Magick: Urban Rituals, Spells, and Shamanism (2001)
The Inner Temple of Witchcraft: Magick, Meditation and Psychic Development (2002)
Spirit Allies: Meet Your Team from the Other Side (2002)
Gay Witchcraft: Empowering the Tribe (2003)
Magick of Reiki: Focused Energy for Healing, Ritual, and Spiritual Development (2004)
The Witch's Shield: Protection Magick and Psychic Self-Defense (2004)
The Outer Temple of Witchcraft: Circles, Spells and Rituals (2004)
Temple of Shamanic Witchcraft (2005)
Instant Magick: Ancient Wisdom, Modern Spellcraft (2006)
Sons of the Goddess: A Young Man's Guide to Wicca (2006)
Ascension Magick: Ritual, Myth and Healing for the New Aeon (2007)
The Temple of High Witchcraft: Ceremonies, Spheres, and the Witches' Qabbalah (2007)
The Witches Heart: The Magick of Perfect Love and Perfect Trust (2011)
The Plant Spirit Familiar: Green Totems, Teachers and Healers on the Path of the Witch (2011)

Buddha, Christ, Merlin: Three Wise Men For Our Age (2012)

Pert, Dr. Candace (1946-)
Molecules of Emotion: the Science Behind Mindbody Medicine (1997)
Everything You Need to Know to Feel Go(o)d (2006)

Picucci, Dr. Michael
Complete Recovery: An Expanded Model of Community Healing (1996)
The Journey Toward Complete Recovery: Reclaiming Your Emotional, Spiritual and Sexual Wholeness (1998)
Ritual as Resource: Energy for Vibrant Living (2005)
An Introduction to Focalizing: Organic Solutions to Real-Time Challenges (2007)

Pierrakos, Eva (1915-1979)
Guide Lectures for Self-Transformation (with Guide)
Complete Lectures of the Pathwork
The Pathwork of Self-Transformation (with Guide and Judith Saly)
Surrender to God Within: Pathwork at the Soul Level (with Donovan Thesenga)
Creating Union: The Pathwork of Relationship (with Guide and Judith Saly)
Fear No Evil: The Pathwork Method of Transforming the Laver Self (with Guide and Donovan Thesenga)

Pierrakos, John C. (1921-2001)
The Energy Field in Man and Nature (1971)
The Core of Man (1974)
Anatomy of Evil (1974)
The Case of the Broken Heart (1974)
The Plight of the Modern Woman (1975)
Observations of Group Phenomena and Group Therapy (1975)
Life Functions of the Energy Centers of Man (1975)
Human Energy Systems Theory: History and New Growth Perspectives (1976)
Creative Aspects of the Ego in the Core-Energetic Process (1977)
Core Energetics: Developing the Capacity to Love and Heal (1990)
Eros, Love and Sexuality: The Forces that Unify Man and Woman (1997)

Pike, Albert (1809-1891)
The Meaning of Masonry (1858)
Morals and Dogma of the Ancient and Accepted Scottish Rite of Freemasonry (1872)
Indo-Aryan Deities and Worship as Contained In the Rig Veda (1872)
Lectures of the Arya (1890)
Reprints of Old Rituals

Pizzorno, Joseph
Total Wellness Systems: Improve Your Health by Understanding the Body's Healing (1996)
The Wellness Revolution: How Understanding the Six Roots of Illness Can Change Your Life (1996)
Textbook of Natural Medicine (with Michael T. Murray) (1999)
The Clinician's Handbook of Natural Medicine (with Michael T. Murray and Herb Joiner-Bey) (2002)

Plonka, Lavinia
What Are You Afraid Of: A Body / Mind Guide to Courageous Living (2005)
Walking Your Talk: Changing Your Life Through the Magic of Body Language (2007)
Playing in the Kitchen: Recipes, Stories and Explorations to Feed the Whole Self

Plummer, George Winslow (1876-1944)
Master's Word: A Short Treatise on the Word, the Light and the Self (1913)
A Brief Course in Mediumship (1915)
Rosicrucian Fundamentals: An Exposition of Rosicrucian Synthesis of Religion, Science and Philosophy, in 14 Complete Instructions (1920)
Occult Science (1923)
Consciously Creating Circumstances (1946)
The Art of Rosicrucian Healing (1947)
Principles and Practice for Rosicrucians (1947)

Ponder, Rev. Catherine (1927-)
How to Live a Prosperous Life (1962)
The Prosperity Secrets of the Ages: How to Channel a Golden River of Riches Into Your Life (1964)
Dynamic Laws of Healing (1966)
Prospering Power of Love (1966)
Healing Secrets of the Ages (1967)
Pray and Grow Rich (1968)
The Millionaire from Nazareth: His Prosperity Secrets For You! (1979)
Open Your Mind to Prosperity (1983)
Open Your Mind to Receive (1983)
Dare to Prosper (1983)
The Dynamic Laws of Prosperity (1985)
The Dynamic Laws of Prayer (1987)
A Prosperity Love Story: Rags to Enrichment, A Memoir (2003)
The Dynamic Laws of Prosperities: Giving Makes You Rich (2006)

Potter, Dr. Beverly
Maverick Career Strategies: The Way of the Ronin (1985)
Turning Around: Keys To Motivation and Productivity (1988)
The Way of the Ronin: Riding The Waves of Changes At Work (1988)
Drug Testing At Work: A Guide for Employers (with Sebastian Orfali) (1990)
Brain Boosters: Food and Drugs That Make You Smarter (with Sebastian Orfali and Gini Graham Scott) (1993)
Finding a Path With a Heart: How To Go From Burnout to Bliss (1995)
From Conflict To Cooperation: How to Mediate a Dispute (1996)
The Worrywart's Companion Twenty-One Ways to Soothe Yourself and Worry Smart (1997)
The Healing Magic of Cannabis (with Dan Joy) (1998)
Overcoming Job Burnout: How To Renew Enthusiasm For Work (1998)
Pass The Test: An Employee Guide To Drug Testing (with Sebastian Orfali) (1999)
High Performance Goal Setting: Using Intuition to Conceive and Achieve Your Dreams (2000)
Get Peak Performance Every Day: How to Manage Like a Coach (2004)
Managing Yourself for Excellence: How to Be a Can-Do Person (2009)
Question Authority and Think for Yourself (2012)

Price, Harry (1881-1948)
Revelations of a Spirit Medium (with Eric J. Dingwall) (1922)
Cold Light on Spiritualistic "Phenomena" - An Experiment with the Crewe Circle (with Kegan Paul) (1922)
Stella C. An Account of Some Original Experiments in Psychical Research (1925)
Rudi Schneider: A Scientific Examination of his Mediumship (1930)
Leaves from a Psychic's Case Book (1933)
Confessions of a Ghost-Hunter (1936)
Fifty Years of Psychical Research: A Critical Survey Longmans (1939)
The Most Haunted House in England: Ten Years' Investigation of Borley Rectory (1940)
Search for Truth: My Life for Psychical Research (1942)
Poltergeist Over England: Three Centuries of Mischievous Ghosts (1945)
The End of Borley Rectory (1946)

Price, Henry, Habberley (1899-1984)
Perception (1932)
Truth and Corrigibility (1936)
Hume's Theory of the External World (1940)
Thinking and Representation (1946)
Thinking and Experience and Some Aspects of the Conflict between Science and Religion (1953)
Personal Survival and the Idea of Another World (1953)
Essays in the Philosophy of Religion (1971)

Proctor, Charlene (1959-)
Let Your Goddess Grow!: Seven Spiritual Lessons on Female Power and Positive Thinking! (2005)
The Women's Book of Empowerment: 323 Affirmations That Change Everyday Problems into Moments of Potential (2005)
The Oneness Gospel: Birthing the Christ Consciousness and Divine Human in You (2011)

Pryse, James Morgan (1859-1942)
Reincarnation in the New Testament (1904)
The Sermon on the Mount: and Other Extracts From the New Testament (1904)
The Apocalypse Unsealed: Being an Esoteric Interpretation of the Initiation of Ioannes: Commonly called Revelation of St. John (1910)
The Restored New Testament: the Hellenic Fragments, Freed from the Pseudo-Jewish Interpolations, Harmonized, and done into English ... (1914)

Purce, Jill (1947-)
The Mystic Spiral: Journey of the Soul (1974)

Puthoff, Harold (1936-)
A Perceptual Channel for Information Transfer Over Kilometer Distances: Historical Perspective and Recent Research (with Russel Targ) (1976)

Pythagoras (582-500 B.C.E.) (books about)
A Chronological Account of the Life of Pythagoras, and of Other Famous Men His Contemporaries (by William Lloyd) (1669)
The Golden Verses of Pythagoras and Other Pythagorean Fragments (by Florence Firth and Annie Besant) (1912)
The Golden Verses of Pythagoras (by Antoine Fabre d'Olivet) (1917)
Pythagoras and Early Pythagoreanism (by James A. Philip) (1966)
History of Western Philosophy (by Bertrand Russell) (1972)
Pythagoras (by Dannie Abse) (1979)
Pythagoras: His Life, Teaching and Influence (by Christoph Riedweg) (2005)
Pythagoras: Pioneering Mathematician and Musical Theorist of Ancient Greece (by Dimitra Karamanides) (2006)
Measuring Heaven: Pythagoras and His Influence on Thought and Art in Antiquity and the Middle Ages (by Christiane Joost-Gaugier) (2006)
Pythagoras in Love (by Lee Slonimsky) (2007)
Numerology and the Meaning of Colors as Disclosed Through Vibration of Numbers as Taught by Pythagoras (by L. Dow Balliett) (2008)
Music of Pythagoras: How an Ancient Brotherhood Cracked the Code of the Universe & Lit the

Path from Antiquity to Outer Space (by Kitty Ferguson) (2008)
    Pythagoras: and the Doctrine of Transmigration: Wandering Souls (by James Luchte) (2009)

Index

Haamiah 1
Hacavitz 1
Hades 1
Hades 2
Hagalaz 2
Hagelin, Dr. John 292
Hagelin, John 2
Hagith 2
Hags 3
Hahaiah 3
Hahbwehdiyu 3
Hahiniah 3
Haich, Elisabeth 3
Haich, Elisabeth 292
Hale, Susan 292
Hale, Susan Elizabeth 3
Halexandria Foundation 4
Hall, Manly Palmer 4
Hall, Manly Palmer 292
Hall of Maat 4
Hall of Records 5
Hall of The Slain 5
Halloween 5
Hallucination 5

Hallucinogens 5
Halo 5
Hamadryades 6
Hamakua 6
Hamblin, Henry Thomas 6
Hamblin, Henry Thomas 292
Hameroff, Stuart 6
Hameroff, Stuart 293
Ham-sa 6
Hamsa Hand 7
Hanan Pacha 7
Handfasting 7
Hand of Fatima 7
Hand of Miriam 7
Hand of Mysteries 7
Hanged Man 7
Hanh, Thich Nhat 8
Hanh, Thich Nhat 293
Haniel 8
Hanuman 8
Hapi 8
Harahel 8
Hare 8
Hariel 9

Harman, Willis	9
Harman, Willis	293
Harpies	9
Harris, Alexander	9
Harris, Alexander (book about)	294
Harris, Bertha	10
Hartmann, Dr. Franz	294
Hartmann, Franz	10
Hartmann Grids	10
Harvey, Andrew	10
Harvey, Andrew	294
Hasidism	11
Haskvitz, Sylvia	11
Haskvitz, Sylvia	294
Hastsehogan	11
Hastsezini	12
Hatha	12
Hatha Yoga	12
Hathor	12
Haumea	12
Haunting	12
Haurvatat	13
Hawaiian Gods and Goddesses	13
Ha Wen Neyu	1
Hawkes, Dr. Joyce	295
Hawkes, Joyce	13
Hayagriva	13
HB of L	13
Hcoma	13
Healers	14
Healing Music	14
Heard, Gerald	14
Heard, Gerald	295
Heathen	14
Heather Eaton	iii
   Heather Eaton	viii
Heaven	14
Heavenly Host	15
Hebe	15
Hecate	15
Hecate	15
Hedge Witch	15

Heimdall	16
Heka	16
Heket	16
Hel	16
Hel	16
Helios	16
Hell	17
Hellhound	17
Hells	17
Hephaestus	17
Heptascopy	17
Hera	18
Heracles	18
Herb	18
Herbalism	18
Herbalists	18
Herbal Magic	18
Hercules	19
Hereditary Witch	19
Heresy	19
Heretic	19
Hermes	19
Hermes Trismegistus	19
Hermetic Brotherhood of Luxor	20
Hermeticism	20
Hermeticists	20
Hermit	20
Hermit	20
Hermod	21
Hespere	21
Hesperides	21
Hestia	21
Hex	21
Hexagram	22
Hexagrams	22
Hidden Masters	22
Hierarch	22
Hieroglyphics	22
Hierophant	22
Hierophant	22
Hierophant	23
Hierophany	23

Higher Self	23	Home, Daniel Dunglas	31
High Priestess	23	Homeopathy	31
High Priestess	23	Honorian Alphabet	31
Hi'iaka	23	Hoodoo	31
Hillfolk	24	Hoodoo Sea	31
Hill, Napoleon	24	Hope	32
Hill, Napoleon	295	Horae	32
Hindu Gods and Goddesses	24	Horaios	32
Hinduism	24	Horn	32
Hino	25	Horned God	32
Hippocampus	25	Horniman, Annie	32
Hippogriff	25	Horoscope	33
Hippomancy	25	Horse	33
Hismael	25	Horse Whispering	33
Historians	26	Horus	33
Historical Apparitions	26	Hoturu	33
Hnossa	26	Houngan	33
Hobgoblins	26	Houses of Heaven	34
Hocus Pocus	26	Howard, Vernon	34
Hod	26	Howard, Vernon	296
Hoder	27	HU	34
Hoenir	27	Huacas	34
Holda	27	Huaillepenyi	35
Holi	27	Huallepen	35
Holism	27	Hubbard, L. Ron	35
Holistic	28	Hubbard, L. Ron	297
Holistic Healing	28	Huehuecoyotl	35
Holmes, Ernest	28	Huginn	36
Holmes, Ernest	295	Hugo, Victor	36
Holos University Graduate Seminary	28	Huitzilopochtli	36
Holotropic Breathwork	29	Human Rights Activists	36
Holotropic Communication	28	Huna	37
Holy	29	Hunab Ku	37
Holy Chalice	29	Hun Pic Tok	36
Holy Friday	29	Hurakan	37
Holy Ghost	29	Huxley, Aldous	37
Holy Grail	30	Huxley, Aldous	297
Holy Saturday	30	Huznoth	37
Holy Thursday	30	Hydra	38
Holy Week	30	Hydromancy	38
Holzer, Hans	30	Hygeia	38
Holzer, Hans	296	Hylic	38

Hymen 38
Hymn 38
Hyperborean 38
Hyperesthesia 39
Hyperion 39
Hypnagogic State 39
Hypnos 39
Hypnotherapy 39
Hyslop, Dr. James Hervey 297
Hyslop, James Hervey 39
Iadabaoth 43
Iamblichus 43
IANDS 44
Iao 44
Iapetus 44
IAS D 44
Ibn al-'Arabi, Muhyi al-Din 44
Ica Stones 44
I Ching 43
Ichthus 45
Ichthyomancy 45
Icon 45
Ic Zod Heh Chal 44
Ida 45
Ideoplasm 45
Idlirvirissong 45
Idol 45
Idunn 46
Ietuqiel 46
Igaluk 46
Ignis Fattus 46
Ike 46
Ilamatecuhtli 46
Ilaniel 46
Illapa 46
Illuminati 47
Illumination 47
Illuminism 47
Imagination 47
Imans 47
Imbolc 47
Imhotep 48

Immortality 48
Imperator 48
Imprinting 48
Inanna 48
INARS 49
In Between Worlds 48
Inca 49
Inca Gods and Goddesses 49
Incantation 50
Incarnation 50
Incarnation 50
Inca Worlds 49
Incorporeal 50
Incubus 50
Indigo Children 50
Indra 51
Indrani 51
Inedia 51
Inferno 51
Infinity 51
Ingerman, Sandra 51
Ingerman, Sandra 298
Inguz 52
Initiation 52
Inner Genius 52
Inner Plane Adepti 52
Inner Visions 52
Inspiration 53
Institute for the Study of Human Knowledge 53
Institute of Core Energetics 53
Institute of Noetic Studies 53
Institute of Transpersonal Psychology 54
Instrumental Transcommunication 54
Interconnectedness 54
Interdependence 54
International Association for Near Death Studies 54
International Association for the Study of Dreams 54
International Association of Rubenfeld Synergists 55

International Holistic Health Energy Institute 55
Interspecies Telepathic Communicator   55
Inti 55
Intuition   55
Inuit Gods and Goddesses   56
Invisibility 56
Invisibles, The   56
Invocation 56
Involution 56
Inward Bound   56
Inward Light   56
IONS   56
Ioskeha   57
Iris 57
Iroquois Gods and Goddesses   57
Isa 57
Isa 57
ISHK   57
Ishtar   57
Isis 58
Islam   58
ITC   58
Itzamna   58
Itzpapalotl 59
Itztlacoliuhqui   59
Ivunches   59
Ixchel   59
Ixchup   59
Jack o' Lantern   61
Jacob's Ladder   61
Jaegers, Beverly   61
Jaegers, Beverly   299
Jaina Cross 62
James, William   62
James, William   299
Janmashtami   62
Janus   62
Jarnsaxa   62
Jarnvidjur 62
Jarow, Dr. Rick   299
Jarow, Rick 63
Jehovah   63
Jenkins, John Major   63
Jenkins, John Major   300
Jera   63
Jerusalem 63
Jesodoth   64
Jesus Fish   64
Jesus of Nazareth   64
Jewish New Year   64
Jinni   64
Jinx   64
Jnana   64
Jnana-Dakshinamurti   65
Jnana Yoga 65
Joey Sandy 65
Johannes   65
Johnson, Robert A.   65
Johnson Robert A.   300
Jolkim   65
Jones, Dr. Marc Edmund 301
Jones, Marc Edmund   66
Jord   66
Jormungand   66
Jotunheim 66
Journalists 66
Joyce-Swaim, Elizabeth   67
Joyce-Swaim, Elizabeth   301
Judaism   67
Judgement 68
Judge, William Quan   68
Judge, William Quan   301
Jung, Carl 68
Jung, Dr. Carl Gustav   301
Jungian Analysts   69
Juno   69
Jupiter   69
Jupiter   70
Jupiter   263
Jupiter   266
Jurgenson Frequency   70
Jurgenson, Friedrich   70
Justice   70
Justice   70

351

Juventas 70
Jyeshtha 71
Ka 73
Ka'aba 73
Ka Akua Po 74
Kabalah 74
Kabat-Zinn, Dr. Jon 302
Kabat-Zinn, Jon 74
Kachinas 74
Kaehr, Dr. Shelley 302
Kaehr, Shelley 74
Kahuna 75
Kaku, Dr. Michio 303
Kaku, Michio 75
Kala 75
Kali 75
Kaliya 76
Kali Yuga 76
Kalki 76
Kama 76
Kama 76
Kamaloka 76
Kama Rupa 76
Kami 76
Kan 77
Kanaloa 77
Kane 77
Kano 77
Kan Xib Chac 77
Kapo 77
Kardec, Allan 77
Kardec, Allan 303
Karma 78
Karma Yoga 78
Karmic Debt 78
Karmic Tie 78
Kartikeya 78
Kasl, Charlotte 78
Kasl, Dr. Charlotte 303
Kataskion 79
Katha 79
Katie King 79

Kausitaki 79
Kay Pacha 79
Kedemel 79
Kelly, Edward 79
Kelpie 80
Kemet 80
Kena 80
Keneun 80
Kether 80
Ketu 80
Key of Solomon 80
Key to the Mysteries of the Universe 81
Khaibit 81
Kharitidi, Olga 81
Kharitidi, Olga 303
Khem 81
Khepera 81
Khnemu 82
Khonsu 82
Khopun 82
Khshathra-Vairya 82
Khunrath, Heinrich 82
Kikimora 82
Kilya 83
King Arthur 83
King, Deborah 83
King, Deborah 304
Kingma, Daphne Rose 84
Kingma, Daphne Rose 304
King of the Witches 83
Kingsford, Anna 84
King Solomon 83
Kingston, Karen 84
Kingston, Karen 304
Kinich-Ahau 85
Kircher, Athanasius 85
Kircher, Athanasius (books about) 304
Kirlian Photography 85
Kishar 85
Kisin 86
Kitcki Manitou 86

Knight, Christopher 304
Knight, Gareth 86
Knight, Gareth 305
Knight, JZ 86
Knight, JZ 305
Knights Templar 87
Kolisko Effect 87
Koran 87
Kornfield, Dr. Jack 306
Kornfield, Jack 87
Korotkov, Dr. Konstantin 306
Korotkov, Konstantin 88
Korrigan 88
Kovelman, Dr. Joyce 306
Kovelman, Joyce 88
Koven, Jean-Claude 89
Koven, Jean-Claude 306
Kowalski, Gary 89
Kowalski, Rev. Gary 307
Kraken 89
Krieger, Dolores 89
Krieger, Dolores 307
Krippner, Dr. Stanley 307
Krippner, Stanley 90
Krishna 90
Krishnamurti, Jiddu 90
Krishnamurti, Jiddu 308
Krita Yuga 91
Kriya Yoga 91
KRN 91
Krumm-Heller, Arnold 91
Kshandada-chara 91
Kshitagarbha 91
Kubera 92
Kubera 92
Kubler-Ross, Dr. Elizabeth 308
Kubler-Ross, Elisabeth 92
Kuhlman, Kathryn 92
Kuhlman, Kathryn (books about) 309
Kukulcan 93
Kulagina, Nina 93
Kun 93
Kundalini 93
Kundalini Research Network 93
Kundalini Yoga 94
Kunz, Dora 94
Kunz, Dora 309
Kupala 94
Kupalo 94
Kurma 94
Kurma Purana 95
Kushner, Lawrence 95
Kushner, Rabbi Lawrence 309
Kutiel 95
Kybalion, The 95
Kye ne Bardo 95
LaBerge, Dr. Stephen 310
LaBerge, Stephen 97
Lachesis 97
Lada 98
Lad, Dr. Vasant 310
Lado 98
Lad, Vasant 98
Lady Lovibond 98
Lady of the Lake 98
Laetitia 99
Laguz 99
Lailah 99
Laka 99
Laksmi 99
Lama 99
Lamaism 100
Lamas 100
Lamassu 100
Lamassu 100
Lamen 100
Lamia 100
Lampadomancy 101
Lane, Belden C. 101
Lane, Dr. Belden C. 310
Lang, Andrew 101
Lang, Andrew 311
Lao Tzu 101

Laozi 102
Lares 102
Laskow, Dr. Leonard 311
Laskow, Leonar 102
Latis 102
Latter Day Saints 102
Lattin, Don 311
Lauday 102
Laveau, Marie 103
Law of Attraction 103
Laya 103
Laya Center 103
Laya Yoga 103
LCC 103
LDS 104
Lea 104
Leadbeater, Charles 104
Leadbeater, Rev. Charles 311
Leanan-Sidhe 104
Lecanomancy 104
Leek, Sybil 104
Leek, Sybil 312
Leffas 105
Left Hand Path 105
Legomena 105
Lemegeton 105
Lemures 105
Lemuria 105
Lemuria (Mu) (books about) 312
Lemurian 106
Lenormand, Marie-Anne 106
Lent 106
Leo 106
Leonard, Gladys Osborne 106
Leonardo da Vinci 107
Leonard, R. Cedric 312
Leprechaun 107
Leshy 107
Leucosia 108
Levanah 108
Leviathan 108
Leviathan 108

Levi, Eliphas 108
Levi, Eliphas 313
Levine, Stephen 108
Levine, Stephen 313
Levitation 109
Leviticus 109
Lewis, Dr. Harvey Spencer 313
Lewis, Harvey Spencer 109
Lewis, Ralph Maxwell 109
Lewis, Ralph Maxwell 313
Ley Lines 110
Lha-Mo 110
Li 110
Libanomancy 110
Libation 111
Liberal Catholic Church 111
Liberation 111
Libitina 111
Libra 111
Life after Death 111
Life Between Life 111
Life Reading 111
Life Review 112
Ligeia 112
Lightworker 112
Lilith 112
Lilith 112
Lilith 112
Lilly, William 113
Limbo 113
Lincoln Theatre 113
Lingam 113
Lingam Purana 113
Linn, Denise 114
Linn, Denise 314
Lipski, Dr. Elizabeth 314
Lipski, Elizabeth 114
Lipton, Bruce 114
Lipton, Dr. Bruce 314
List, Guido von 115
Li-Sung 110
Lithomancy 115

Lix 115
Lludd 115
Llyr 115
Loa 115
Loch Ness Monster 116
Lodge 116
Lodge, Sir Oliver 116
Lodge, Sir Oliver 315
Logos 116
Lokapalas 116
Loki 117
Lombroso, Cesare 117
Lomi Lomi 117
Lost Continents 117
Lotus Sutra 117
Lourdes 118
Lovers 118
Lower Spirits 118
Loyalty Islands 118
Lucid Dreaming 118
Lucidity Institute, The 118
Lucifer 119
Lucifer 119
Lucimi 119
Luel 119
Lugh 119
Lughnasadh 119
Luminaries 120
Luminous Phenomena 120
Lumisial 120
Luna 120
Luna, Dr. Luis Eduardo 315
Luna, Luis Eduardo 120
Lunasa 120
Luria, Isaac 121
Luria, Rabbi Isaac (books about) 315
Lustration 121
Lycanthropy 121
Maat 123
Mabinogion, The 123
Mabon 123
Mabon 124

MacDade, Bonnie 317
Macha 124
Machen, Arthur 124
Machen, Arthur 317
Machu Picchu 124
Macumba 124
Macy, Mark 125
Macy, Mark 317
Madden, Kristin 125
Madden, Kristin 318
Madira 125
Maenads 125
Maeve 126
Mafdet 126
Mage 126
Maggidim 126
Maggidim 126
Magi 126
Magi 127
Magic 127
Magical Amulets 127
Magical Correspondences 128
Magical Methods x
Magical Methods 128
Magical Name 128
Magical Square 263
Magical Sword 128
Magical Temple 128
Magical Tools 129
Magic Circle 127
Magician 129
Magician 129
Magic Mirror 127
Magnetic Center 129
Magnetic Currents 129
Magus 129
Mah 130
Maha 130
Mahabharata 130
Mahakala 130
Mahamudra 130
Maharishi 130

Maharishi Mahesh Yogi	131	Mangala	138
Maharishi Mahesh Yogi	318	Mani	138
Mahasaya, Lahiri	131	Manichaeism	138
Maha Shivratri	130	Manifestation	138
Mahatma	131	Manipura	138
Mahatma Gandhi	131	Mani Wheel	138
Mahayana	132	Manjusri	139
Mahish	132	Mannaz	139
Maia	132	Manning, Matthew	139
Maiden	132	Manning, Matthew	319
Maier, Michael	132	Mansions of Heaven	139
Maimonides, Moses	133	Mansions of the Moon	139
Maitreya	133	Mantra	139
Maitri	133	Mantra Yoga	140
Majestas	133	Mara	140
Makara	133	Marah	140
Makia	134	Marden, Dr. Orison Swett	319
Malachy Prophecies	134	Marden, Orison Swett	140
Mal'ak	134	Marduk	141
Malak	134	Margawse	141
Maleficia	134	Margolis, Char	141
Malkuth	134	Margolis, Char	320
Malleus Maleficarum	134	Markandeya Purana	141
Mama	135	Mars	141
Mama Allpa	135	Mars	142
Mama Coca	135	Mars	263
Mama Cocha	135	Mars	265
Mama Quilla	135	Martialis	142
Mama Zara	135	Martinism	142
Mambo	136	Martyr	142
Mammon	136	Maru	142
Mana	136	Marx-Hubbard, Barbara	142
Mana	136	Marx-Hubbard, Barbara	320
Managarm	136	Mary Celeste	143
Manannan	136	Mary Magdalene	143
Manas	136	Masleh	143
Manco Capac	137	Maslow, Abraham	143
Mandala	137	Maslow, Abraham	320
Mandino, Og	137	Mass	144
Mandino, Og	318	Master Djwhal Khul and Master Koot Humi	144
Mandukya	137	Masters	144
Manes	137		

Masters, Dr. Robert E.L.   320
Masters, Rev. Roy   321
Masters, Robert   144
Masters, Roy   144
Masvani   145
Matergabia 145
Materialist   145
Materialization   145
Mathematicians   145
Mathers, Moira   146
Mathers, S. L. MacGregor   146
Mathers, S. L. MacGregor   321
Mati Syra Zemlya   146
Matsya   146
Matsya Purana   146
Matthews, Caitlin   147
Matthews, Caitlin   321
Matthews, John   147
Matthews, John   322
Maudy Thursday   147
Maya   148
Maya   148
Maya Devi 148
Maya Gods and Goddesses   148
Mayahuel   149
Maya Pyramids   149
May, Dr. Rollo   322
May, Rollo 147
McCannon, Tricia 149
McCannon, Tricia 322
McCartney, Francesca   149
McCartney, Francesca   323
McGraw, Dr. Phil   323
McGraw, Phillip   150
McKenna, Terence   150
McKenna, Terence   323
McKibben, Bill   323
McKibben, William   150
McTaggart, Lynne 151
McTaggart, Lynne   324
Mead, George Robert   151
Mead, George Robert Stow   324

Mebahiah   151
Mecca   151
Medical Intuitive   152
Medicina Metallorum   152
Medicine Man   152
Medicine Wheel   152
Meditation 152
Meditation 152
Medium   153
Mediums   153
Medusa   153
Megaera   153
Megalith   153
Mehen   154
Mehet-Weret   154
Mehiel   154
Mehl-Madrona, Dr. Lewis   325
Mehl-Madrona, Lewis   154
Melekim   154
Melpomene   155
Melusine   155
Menehune 155
Menorah   155
Mental Plane   155
Mephistopheles   155
Mercury   156
Mercury   156
Mercury   156
Mercury   264
Mercury   265
Mercy   156
Merfolk   156
Merkaba   156
Merlin   157
Mermaids   157
Mermen   157
Merope   157
Merovingian Dynasty   157
Merrows   158
Merry Meet   158
Merry Part 158
Meskhenet 158

Mesmer, Franz 158
Mesmerism 158
Messiah 159
Metagnomy 159
Metamorphosis 159
Metaphysics 159
Metatron 159
Metempsychosis 159
Methetherial 160
Methods of Prediction 160
Metis 160
Metzner, Dr. Ralph 325
Metzner, Ralph 160
Metztli 160
Michabo 160
Michael 161
Michael 161
Michael 161
Mictlan 161
Mictlantecihuatl 161
Mictlantecuhtli 161
Midgard 162
Midgard Serpent 162
Milam Bardo 162
Millay, Dr. Jean 325
Millay, Jean 162
Miller, Zachary James 162
Millman, Dan 163
Millman, Dan 325
Mimamsa 163
Mimir 163
Min 163
Mind 164
Mind Altering Drugs 164
Mind-Body Energy Medicine 164
Mindell, Arnold 164
Mindell, Dr. Arnold 326
Mindfulness 165
Mind Reading 164
Mind's Eye 164
Minerva 165
Ministers 165

Minotaur 165
Miracle 165
Mishlove, Dr. Jeffrey (194?-) 326
Mishlove, Jeffrey 165
Mishnah 166
Missal 166
Mitchell, Edgar 166
Mithra 166
Mixcoatl 166
MMS 167
Mnemosyne 167
Moai 167
Mohenjo Daro 167
Moirae 167
Mojo 167
Mojo 168
Mokosh 168
Moksha 168
Monad 168
Monasticism 168
Monism 168
Monition 168
Monkey 169
Monolith 169
Monroe, Robert 169
Monroe, Robert 326
Montgomery, Ruth 169
Montgomery, Ruth 327
Monti, Daniel 169
Monti, Dr. Daniel 327
Moody, Dr. Raymond 327
Moody, Raymond 170
Moon 170
Moon 170
Moon 264
Moon 265
Moore, Dr. Robert 328
Moore, Marcia 170
Moore, Marcia 327
Moore, Mary-Margaret 171

Moore, Mary-Margaret (dictated by Bar-

tholomew) 328
   Moore, Robert 171
   Moran, Victoria 171
   Moran, Victoria 328
   Morgawr 172
   Mormonism 172
   Morning Star 172
   Moroni 172
   Morpheus 173
   Morrigan, The 173
   Morrissey, Dianne 173
   Morrissey, Dr. Dianne 329
   Morse, Dr. Melvin 329
   Morse, Melvin 173
   Mortuary Magic 174
   Moses, Harry Morgan 174
   Moses, Harry Morgan 329
   Moses, William Stainton 174
   Moss, Dr. Richard 329
   Moss, Richard 175
   Moss, Robert 175
   Moss, Robert 329
   Most Haunted 175
   Mother 176
   Mother Church 176
   Mother Earth 176
   Mother Meera 176
   Mother Meera 330
   Mother Nature 176
   Mother Teresa 176
   Motivation Management Service Institute 177
   Motto 177
   Mountain Fairies 179
   Mount Etna 177
   Mount Fuji 177
   Mount Kailash 178
   Mount Olympus 178
   Mount Parnassus 178
   Mount Shasta 178
   Mramor, Nancy 179
   Mramor, Nancy 330

Mu 179
Mudra 179
Mueler 179
Muhammad 179
Muladhara 180
Muldoon, Sylvan 180
Muldoon, Sylvan 330
Mullahs 180
Muller, Rev. Wayne 330
Muller, Wayne 180
Multiverse 181
Mummy 181
Munda 181
Muninn 181
Murphy, Bridey 181
Murphy, Dr. Joseph 330
Murphy Joseph 182
Murray, Margaret 182
Murray, Margaret 331
Muses 182
Music Therapy 183
Muspelheim 183
Mut 183
Mut 183
Muta 183
Myers, Frederick 183
Myomancy 184
Myss, Caroline 184
Myss, Dr. Caroline 331
Mystery 184
Mystery Religions 184
Mystery Schools 184
Mystic 185
Mysticism 185
Mystics 185
Myth 185
Mythological Creatures 186
Mythological Places 186
Mythology 185
Naadame 189
Nabi 189
Nabia 189

Nabu	189		Nebo	196
Nachash	190		Nechtan	196
Nadis	190		Necromancer	196
Naenia	190		Necromancy	196
Nagas	190		Necromanteion	197
Nag Hammadi Scrolls	190		Needleman, Jacob	197
Nagomancy	190		Needleman, Jacob	333
Nagua	191		Nefertem	197
Naiads	191		Nehalennia	197
Namaste	191		Nehebkau	197
Namburbi Rituals	191		Nehushtan	198
Nammu	191		Neihardt, John	333
Nanay	191		Neihardt, John G.	198
Nanna	191		Neith	198
Nanna	192		Nekhebet	198
Nanta	192		Nemamiah	199
Nanta	192		Nemesis	199
Napaeas	192		Nemeth, Dr. Maria	333
Naqshbandiyah	192		Nemeth, Maria	199
Narada Purana	192		Nemhain	199
Naranjo, Claudio	192		Nenechen	199
Naranjo, Dr. Claudio	332		Neopaganism	200
Narasimha	193		Neophyte	200
Narby, Dr. Jeremy	332		Neoplatonism	200
Narby, Jeremy	193		Nephelomancy	200
Narcissus	193		Nephesh	200
Narudi	193		Nephilim	200
Nash, Carroll B.	193		Nephthys	200
Nash, Carroll B.	333		Neptune	201
Natal Chart	194		Neptune	201
Natural Magic	194		Nereids	201
Nature Spirits	194		Nereus	201
Nature Worship	194		Nergal	202
Naturopathy	194		Nerthus	202
Nauthiz	195		Neshamah	202
Navagrahas	195		Netzach	202
Navajo Gods and Goddesses	195		New Age	202
Nawao	195		New Age Associations and Societies	203
Nazca Lines	195		Newberg, Andrew	204
NDE	195		Newberg, Dr. Andrew	334
Ndmh	196		Newbrough, John	205
Near Death Experience	196			

New Energy Movement 203
New Physics 204
New Thought 204
Newton, Dr. Michael 334
Newton Institute, The 206
Newton, Isaac 205
Newton, Michael 205
Nguruvilu 206
Niamh 206
Nichols, Ross 207
Nicksa 207
Nictalopes 207
Nidhogg 207
Nidra 207
Nifelheim 207
Nightingale, Earl 208
Nightingale, Earl 334
Nike 208
Niliahah 208
Nimbus 208
Nine Worlds 208
Ningal 209
Ninhursag 209
Ninib 209
Ninurta 209
Nirmana-Kaya 209
Nirvana 209
Njord 210
Nobel Prize Laureates 210
Noetic 210
Nohochacyum 210
Nokomis 210
Norns 210
North Pole 211
Northrup, Christiane 211
Northrup, Dr. Christiane 334
North Star 211
Nostradamus 211
Notarikon 212
Notus 212
Nous 212
Nous 212
Nox 212
Nuada 213
Nucklavee 213
Nuit 213
Numen 213
Numerology 213
Numeromancy 213
Numina 214
Numinous 214
Nushu 214
Nyaya 214
Nyingpo 214
Nymphaeum 214
Nymphs 215
Oannes 217
Oates, David John 217
Oates, David John 335
OBE 217
Obeah 218
OBOD 218
Obsession 218
Occult 218
Occultism 219
Occultists 219
Occult Orders 218
Occult Orders, Brotherhoods and Secret Societies x
Occult Orders, Brotherhoods and Secret Societies 218
Occult Powers 219
Occult Virtues 219
Oceanids 220
Oceanus 220
Och 220
Oculomancy 220
Odhin 220
Odic Force 221
Odin 221
O'Donnell, Michele 221
O'Donnell, Michele 335
Offering 221
Offshore Rio de Janeiro 221

Ogdoas 222
Ogham 222
Ogma 222
Ogre 222
Oimelc 222
Olcott, Henry 222
Old Souls 223
O'Leary, Brian 223
O'Leary, Dr. Brian (1940- 2011) 335
Olga 223
Oliver, John J. 223
Olympian Gods 223
Olympian Spirits 224
Om 225
Om 225
Omacatl 225
Omega Institute for Holistic Studies 225
Omen 225
Ometecuhtli 226
Ometeotl 226
Omeyocan 226
Om Mani Padme Hum 225
Omni 226
Omnipotence 226
Omnipresence 226
Omniscience 226
O'More, Malachy 224
Onatha 226
Oneiromancy 227
Ontology 227
OOBE 227
Oomancy 227
Ophanim 227
Ophians 227
Ophiel 227
Ophites 227
Opiel 227
Opochtli 228
Ops 228
Oracle 228
Orbs 228
Orbs of Light 228
Orcus 228
Ordeals 229
Order 229
Order of Bards, Ovates and Druids 229
Order of Skull and Bones 229
Order of The Stella Matutina 229
Ordo Stella Matutina 229
Ordo Templi Orientis 229
Oreads 230
Oriah "Mountain Dreamer" 230
Oriah "Mountain Dreamer" 336
Orloff, Dr. Judith 336
Orloff, Judith 230
Ormazd 230
Ornithomancy 231
Ornstein, Dr. Robert Evans 336
Ornstein, Robert 231
Orpheus 231
Orpheus 231
Orphic Mysteries 231
Oschman, Dr. James 336
Oschman, James 232
Osho 232
Osho 337
Osiris 232
Ostara 233
Osteen, Joel 233
Osteen, Pastor Joel 337
Otheos 233
Othila 233
OTO 233
Ouija Board 233
Ouroboros 234
Ouspensky, P. D. 234
Ouspensky, P. D. 337
Out of Body Experience 234
Ovates 234
Oversoul 234
Ovinnik 235
Owen, Robert Dale 235

Ox 235
PA 237
Pabid 237
Pachacamac 237
Pacha Mama 237
Pacifica 237
Paddy 238
Padma 238
Padma Purana 238
Pagan 238
Paganism 238
Page, Christine 238
Page, Dr. Christine 338
Pah 239
Palaspas 239
Pallas 239
Pallomancy 239
Palma 239
Palmer, Helen 239
Palmer, Helen 338
Palmistry 240
Palm Sunday 239
Pan 240
Pandora 240
Panpsychism 241
Pantheism 241
Pantheon 241
Pantheon of the Gods 241
Papus 241
Papus 338
Papyrus of Ani 241
Paraatman 242
Paracelsus 242
Paraclete 242
Paradise 242
Paradox 242
Paraiso 242
Paralda 242
Parallel Lives 243
Parallel Universes 243
Paramahamsa 243
Paranormal 243

Parapsychological Association 243
Parapsychologists and Psychic Researchers 243
Parapsychology 243
Parashurama 244
Parasite 244
Pariacaca 244
Parthenope 244
Paruksti 244
Parvati 244
Pasqually, Martinez de 245
Passing Over 245
Passion Sunday 245
Passover 245
Past Life Regression 245
Patecatl 245
Patha 245
Pathworking 245
Paul, Dr. Margaret 339
Paulicians 246
Pauline Arts 246
Paul, Margaret 246
Pawnee Gods and Goddesses 246
Pax 246
Pazuzu 246
Peale, Norman Vincent 247
Peale, Rev. Norman Vincent 339
Pearce, Joseph Chilton 247
Pearce, Joseph Chilton 339
Pearl, Dr. Eric 339
Pearl, Eric 247
Pearsall, Dr. Paul 340
Pearsall, Paul 248
Pearson, Carol 248
Pearson, Dr. Caroline S. 340
Peck, Dr. M. Scott 340
Peck, M. Scott 248
Pedra da Gavea 249
Pegasus 249
Peg Leg Jack 249
Pegomancy 249
Pele 249

Pelletier, Dr. Kenneth 341
Pelletier, Kenneth 249
Pemphredo 250
Penates 250
Penczak, Christopher 250
Penczak, Christopher 341
Pendulum 250
Pentacle 251
Pentagram 251
Pentateuch 251
Pentecost 251
Pentecost 251
People ix
Perception 251
Percipient 252
Perennial Philosophy 252
Persephone 252
Persephone 252
Persian Gods and Goddesses 252
Personality 252
Personology 253
Pert, Candace 253
Pert, Dr. Candace 342
Perth 253
Perun 253
Pesach 253
Peter 254
Pethel 254
Petitioning 254
Pet Psychic 254
Phaistos Disk 254
Phaleg 254
Phantasmata 254
Phantom Ships 254
Pharaoh 255
Phenomenology 255
Philology 255
Philosophers 255
Philosopher's Stone 255
Philosophical and Mystical Movements x
Philosophical and Mystical Movements 256
Philosophical Furnace 256
Philosophy 256
Philtre 256
Phinuit 256
Phobia 257
Phoebe 257
Phoenix 257
Phooka 257
Phosphorus 257
Phronesis 257
Phul 257
Phylactery 258
Phylactery 258
Phyllorhodomancy 258
Phyltotherapy 258
Physicists 258
Picucci, Dr. Michael 342
Picucci, Michael 258
Pierrakos, Eva 259
Pierrakos, Eva 342
Pierrakos, John 259
Pierrakos, John C. 342
Pietas 259
Pike, Albert 259
Pike, Albert 342
Pilgrimage 260
Pillan 260
Pinga 260
Pingala 260
Piper, Leonore 260
Pisces 261
Pistis Sophia 261
Pitris 261
Pitris 261
Pixies 261
Pizzorno, Joseph 261
Pizzorno, Joseph 343
Place Memory 262
Planchette 262
Plane 262
Planes of Existence 262
Planes of Manifestation 262

Planet 263
Planetary Days 262
Planetary Grids 263
Planetary Hours 263
Planetary Seal 263
Planetary Seals and
  Magical Squares 263
Planetary Sigils 264
Planetary Spirits 264
Planets 265
Plant Alchemy 266
Plant Rhys Dwfen 266
Plato 267
Pleiades 267
Plerona 267
Plesithea 267
   Pliny the Elder viii
Pliny the Elder 268
Plonka, Lavinia 268
Plonka, Lavinia 343
Plotinus 268
Ploughing Festival 268
Plummer, George Winslow 269
Plummer, George Winslow 343
Pluto 266
Pluto 269
Pluto 269
Pneuma 269
Pneumatics 269
Pneumatographers 270
Poets 270
Polerian 270
Polerity 270
Poltergeist 270
Polyhymnia 270
Polytheist 270
Pomona 270
Ponder, Catherine 271
Ponder, Rev. Catherine 343
Pono 271
Popol Vuh 271
Poppet 271

Populus 271
Portals 272
Portent 272
Portunes 272
Portunus 272
Poseidon 272
Poseidonis 272
Posidonius 273
Positive Thinking 273
Possession 273
Potameides 273
Potter, Beverly 273
Potter, Dr. Beverly 344
Poughkeepsie Seer 274
Powers 274
Powers 274
Power Spots 274
Practical Qabbalah 274
Prana 274
Pranayama 275
Prayer 275
Prayer Wheel 275
Preachers 275
Precept 275
Precognition 275
Prediction 276
Predictions of Death 276
Pre-Existence 275
Premonition 276
Presence 276
Presentiment 276
Pretas 276
Preternatural 276
Priapus 276
Price, Harry 276
Price, Harry 344
Price, Henry H. 277
Price, Henry, Habberley 344
Priest 277
Priestess 277
Priests 277
Prieure de Sion 277

365

Art and Artists

H

Harman, Bruce
(1958-)   Meditation   Jesus Meditating (20th Century)   harmanvisions.com

Heintz, Joseph (
1598-1609)   Hades The Abduction of Persephone (1605)

Holeman, Daniel B.
(1952-)   Heaven   Welcome Home   awakenvisions.com

Hubner, Julius
(1806-1882)   Melusine   Fair Melusine (1844)   juliushuebner.de

Hughes, Edward Robert
(1851-1914)   Magical Sword Bertuccio's Bride (1845)

Hunt, Lisa
(1967-)   Gorgons   Medusa   lisahuntart.com
   Hags   The Sorceress
   Mama Cocha   Mama Cocha
   Mama Quilla   Mama Quilla
   Merfolk
   Nerthus   Nerthus

I

Ingres, Jean Auguste
(1780-1867)   Hippogriff   Roger Delivering Angelica (1819)

K

Kane, Herb Kawainui
(1928- 2011)   Hawaiian Gods &Godd.   Hawaii herbkanestudio.com

Kaufmann, Isidor
(1854-1921)   Hasidism   Portrait of a Young Boy (20th Century)

Keightley, Thomas
(1789-1872)   Knights Templar   Knights Templar (1852)

Kinkade, Thomas
(1958-2012)   Life Review   Stairway to Paradise (1998)   thomaskinkade.com
    Natural Magic Garden of Prayer (1997)

Knapp, J. A.
(1853-1938)   Invocation   Invocation (19th Century)

L

Lafarge, Jean-Noel Leprechaun   Leprechaun

Lanfranco, Giovanni (
1582-1647)   Ogre   Norandino and Lucina Discovered by the .. (1624)

Laurens, Paul Albert
(1870-1934)   Nymphs-Water Nymphs   Catching Waves (19th Century)

Lawrie, Lee
(1877-1963)   Nabu   Nabu (1939)

Ledoux, Jeanne-Philiberte
(1767-1840)   Lenormand, Marie-Anne   Marie-Anne Lenormand (18th Century)

Leonardo Da Vinci
1452-1519)   Jesus of Nazareth   The Last Supper (1498)   davincilife.com
    Leonardo Da Vinci   Self Portrait (15th Century)

Levi, Eliphas
1810-1875)	Occultism	Occultist and Magician's Pentagram (1855)
   Occult Orders ..Symbol Solomon/Transcendental
         Magic book (1855)

Leyendecker, Joseph
(1875-1951)	Maeve Maeve (1916)

M

Maglioli, Giovanni
(1580-1610)	Mermen	Merman (16th Century)

Mantegna, Andrea
(1431-1506)	Limbo Christ's Descent into Limbo (1468)

Merian, Matthous
(1593-1650)	Maier, Michael Michael Maier (1617)

Michelangelo
(1475-1564)	Healers	The Creation of Adam (1511) michelangelo.com
   Nachash	The Temptation and Fall of Adam and Eve (1508)
   Nehushtan	Nehushtan (Sistine Chapel) (1508)

Millais, Sir John Everett
(1829-1896)	Martyr The Martyr of the Solway (1871)

Miller, Meredith	Inca	Machu Picchu meredithmiller.net
   Nature Spirits Bringers of the Night Rainbow

Moreau, Gustave
(1826-1898)	Juno The Peacock Complaining to Juno (1881)	gustavemoreau.com
   Melpomene	Melpomene (1891)

Mueller, Mickie
(1979-) Lugh Lugh mickiemuellerart.com

Murillo, Bartolome Esteban

(1618-1682) Magi The Adoration of the Magi (1660)
Nimbus The Immaculate Conception (1660)

N

Nattier, Jean Marc
(1685-1766) Juventas Madame de Caumartin as Hebe (1753)

Nesterov, Mikhail
(1862-1942) Hermit Spiritual Hermit (1888)

P

Paciorek, Andy
Gwydion Druid batcow.co.uk
Huginn Corpse Birds (2009)

Park, Andy
(1975-) Mount Olympus Mount Olympus (2005) andyparkart.com

Penrose, James Doyle
(1862-1932) Idunn Idun and the Apples (1890)

Peruzzi, Baldassare
(1481-1537) Muses Muses Dancing with Apollo (16th Century)

Philpot, Glyn Warren
(1834-1937) Heard, Gerald Gerald Heard (1915)

Pietsch, Ludwig
(1824-1911) Norns Norns (1865)

Pogany, Willy
(1882-1955) Hnossa Heimdall and Little Hnossa (1920)

Poortvliet, Rien
(1932-1995) Gnomes Gnomes (1977)

Poussin, Nicolas

(1594-1665)   Helios Helios and Phaeton with Saturn and the Four ..(1635)   nicolaspoussin.org
- Metis   The Infant Jupiter Nutured by the Goat (1638)
- Mount Parnassus   Apollo and the Muses (Parnassus) (1625)

Poynter, Sir Edward
(1839-1919)   Horae Horae Serenae (1894)
- Leucosia   The Siren (1864)
- Nereids   Cave of the Storm Nymphs (1903)

Bibliography

H

Hadas, Moses, Imperial Rome, New York, NY, USA Time-Life Books, , 1965.
Haich, Elisabeth, Initiation, Palo Alto, CA USA, Seed Center, 1974.
Hale, Gill, The Practical Encyclopedia of Feng Shui, New York, NY, USA, Lorenz Books, 1999.
Hartmann, Thom, The Last Hours of Ancient Sunlight – Waking Up to Personal and Global Transformation, Northfield, VT, Mythical Books, 1998.
Hawken, Paul, The Magic of Findhorn: An Eyewitness Account, New York, NY, USA, Bantam Books, 1976.
Holzer, Hans, The Human Dynamo, Millbrae, CA, USA, Celestial Arts, 1977.

K

Kingston, Karen, Creating Sacred Space With Feng Shui, New York , NY, USA, Broadway Books, 1996.
Kornfield, Jack, A Path with Heart: A Guide Through the Perils and Promises of Spiritual Life, CA, USA, A Bantam Book, 1993.
Krishna, Copi, Kundalini: The Evolutionary Energy in Man, Boston, MA, USA, Shambhala, 1997.
Kubler-Ross, Elisabeth, On Death and Dying, New, York , NY, USA, Macmillan Publishing CO. Inc., 1969.

L

Leadbeater, C.W., How Theosophy Came to Me, Wheaton, IL, USA, The Theosophical Publishing House, 1930.
Leadbeater, C.W., Man Visible and Invisible, Wheaton, IL, USA, The Theosophical Publishing

House, 1969.

Leadbeater, C.W., The Chakras, Wheaton, IL, USA, The Theosophical Publishing House, 1987.

Leadbeater, C.W., The Masters and The Path, Chicago, IL, USA, The American Theosophical Society, 1925.

Leek, Sybil, Diary of a Witch: The Private Life of One of the World's Most Famous and Colorful Psychics, New York, NY, USA, Signet Classics, 1969.

Leek, Sybil, Reincarnation: The Second Chance, New York, NY, USA, Stein and Day, 1974.

Leonard, Jonathan Norton, Ancient America, New York, NY, USA, Time-Life Books, 1967.

Lerner, Michael, Spirit Matters, Charlottesville, VA, USA, Hampton Roads Publishing Company, Inc. 2000.

Levi, Eliphas, The History of Magic: Including a Clear & Precise Exposition of Its Procedure, Its Rites and… Los Angeles, CA, USA, Borden Pub. Co.

Levi, Peter, The Cultural Atlas of the World, The Greek World, Richmond, Virginia, USA, Time-Life Inc., 1990.

Lewis, James R., The Dream Encyclopedia, Canton, MI, USA, Visible Ink Press, 2002.

Linn, Denise, Quest: A Guide for Creating Your Own Vision Quest, New York, NY, USA, The Ballentine Publishing Group, 1997.

M

Masters, Robert, The Goddess Sekhmet: Psycho-Spiritual Exercises of the Fifth Way, St. Paul, MN, USA, Llewellyn Pub., 1991.

Matthews, Catilín, The Celtic Tradition, Rockport, MA, USA, Elements Books Inc. 1992.

Matthews, Catilín, The Elements of the Goddess, Dorset, England, Elements Books Inc. Longmead, Shaftesbury, 1989.

Matthews, Catilín and John, The Encyclopaedia of Celtic Wisdom, Rockport, MA, USA, Elements Books, Inc. 1996.

Matthews, John, The Grail Tradition, Longmead, Shaftesbury, Dorset, England, Elements Books Inc., 1990.

Browne, Silvia, Prophesy: What the Future Holds For You, New York, NY, USA, The Penguin Group, 2004.

Matthieu, Richard and Triny Xuan THuan., The Quantum and The Lotus, New York, NY, USA, Three Rivers Press, 2001.

Millman, Dan, The Journeys of Socrates, New York, NY, USA, Harper Collins, 1996.

Monroe, Robert, Journeys Out of the Body, New York, NY, USA, Doubleday, 1971.

Monroe, Robert, Ultimate Journey, New York, NY, USA, Doubleday, 1994.

Moody, Raymond, Jr. Ph.D., M.D., Life After Life, Charlottesville, VA, USA, Hampton Roads Publishing Co. 1975.

Moody, Raymond, Jr. Ph.D., M.D., The Last Laugh: A New Philosophy of Near Death Experiences, Apparitions and the Paranormal, Charlottesville, VA, USA, Hampton Roads Publishing Co. 1999.

Moine, Michele and Degaudenzi, Jean-Louise, Manual de Experimentos Geobiológicos (Original Title: Guide of Géobiologie), Constitution, Barcelona, Spain, Libergraf, 1991.

Montgomery, Ruth, A Search for the Truth, New York, NY, USA, Bantam Books, 1968.

Montgomery, Ruth, Here and Hereafter, Fawcett Crest, 1968.

Montgomery, Ruth, Companions Along the Way, New York, NY, USA, Popular Library Edition, 1976.

Morse, Dr. Melvin, Transformed By The Light: Powerful Effect of Near-Death Experiences on People's Lives, New York, NY, USA, Villard Books, 1992.

Muller, Wayne, How Then Shall We Live? Four Simple Questions That Reveal the Beauty and Meaning of Our Lives, New York, NY, USA, Bantom Books, 1996.

Myss, Caroline, Anatomy of the Spirit: Seven Stages of Power and Healing, New York, NY, USA, Three Rivers Press, 1996.

N

Newton, Michael, Journey of Souls: Case Studies of Life Between Lives, St. Paul, MN, USA, Llewellyn Publications, 1994.

O

O'Hara, Gwydion, The Magick of Aromatherapy, St. Paul, MN, USA, Llewellyn Publications, 1998.

Oxford, The New Oxford Annotated Bible: With the Apocrypha, New York, NY, USA, Oxford University Press Inc., 1973.

P

Peale, Norman Vincent, Power of the Plus Factor, New York, NY, USA, Ballentine Books, 1987.

Peterson, Robert, Out of Body Experiences: How to Have Them & What to Expect, Charlottesville, VA, USA, Hampton Roads Publishing Co. Inc., 1997.

Picknett, Lynn and Prince, Clive, The Templar Revelation: Secret Guardians of the True Identity of Christ, New York, NY, USA, Touchstone, 1998.

Piper, Don, 90 Minutes in Heaven – A True Story of Death and Life, Grand Rapids, MI, USA, Touchstone, 2004.

Webography

H

hafapea.com — Hafapea's Universe – Mythical Beings - Mythology
hagelin.org John Hagelin
haich.de — Elizabeth Haich
halexandria.org — Library of Halexandria – Dan Ward
hallowquest.org.uk — Hallowquest – Shamanic and Celtic Courses, Workshops - Caitlin and John Matthews
halzinabennet.com — Hal Zina Bennet
handfasting.info — Handfasting
handfastings.org — Handfasting
handresearch.com — Hand Analysis and Palm Reading
handwritingpro.com — Handwriting Personality Profile
harmanvisions.com — Bruce Harman (Artist)
haroldsherman.com — Harold Sherman
harryprice.co.uk — Harry Price
harvardsquarelibrary.org — Harvard Square Library
hathayoga.net — Hatha Yoga
hathayogalesson.com — Hatha Yoga Lessons
hauntedamericatours.com — Haunted America Tours
haunteddecatur.com — Haunted Decatur – Lincoln Theater
hauntingholzer.com — Hans Holzer
havurahshirhadash.org — Rabbi Zalman Schachter-Shalomi
HBLU.org — Healing From the Body Level Up – Mind Body Spirit
hds.harvard.edu — Harvard Divinity School

headlesshorseman.co.uk   The Headless Horseman – Online Ghost Guide
healing-arts.org   The Healing Center Online – Metapsycology and TIR - Lewis Mehl-Madrona
healingdeva.com   Alternative Therapies – Healing the Mind, Body and Spirit
healingkeys.com   Healing Keys – Healing the Body Through Mind and Metaphor - Chuck Spezzano
healingstory.org   Healing Story Alliance – Story Telling
healingtouchforanimals.com   Healing Touch for Animals
healingvoice.com   Healing Voice – Jill Purce
heall.com   Health Education Alliance for Life and Longevity
healthsystem.virginia.edu   University of Virginia – Division of Perpetual Studies – Ian Stevenson
heal-thyself.us   Heal Thyself Quantum Clinic
heartgazing.com   Heart Gazing – Awaken Beyond the Mind and Ego - Saniel Bonder
heartmath.org   Institute of Heart Math – Researching Heart Intelligence - Joe Chilton Pearce
heartnetinternational.com   Heart Net International – Carlos Warter
heartofnourishment.com   Heart of Nourishment - Hale Sofia Schatz
helenanelsonreed.com   Helena Nelson Reed (Artist)
helenduncan.org.uk   Helen Duncan
henrysidgwick.com   Henry Sidgwick
henryrhomashamblin.wwwhubs.com   Henry Thomas Hamblin
herbkanestudio.com   Herb Kane (Artist)
herbiebrennan.com   Herbie Brennan
hermetic.com   The Hermetic Library
hermeticfellowship.org   Hermetic Fellowship
hermeticgoldendawn.com   Hermetic Golden Dawn
herowithin.com   Hero Within – Carol S. Pearson
hieronymus-bosch.org   Hieronymus Bosch (Artist)
himalayanacademy.com   Kauai's Hindu Monastery
hindu.com   The Hindu - Newspaper
hindubooks.org   Hindu Books Universe
hinduofuniverse.com   Hindus of Universe – Culture, History, Mythology
hinduism.net   Hinduism
holistic-alt.com   Holistic Philosophy Consultants
holisticboard.org   American Board of Integrative Holistic Medicine
holisticlearningcenter.com   Holistic Learning Center
holisticmedicine.org   American Holistic Medical Association
holisticonline.com   Alternative Holistic Medicine
holisticpr.com   Holistic PR and Marketing – Andrea Adler
holosuniversity.org   Holos University Graduate Seminary – Holistic Medicine – Norman Shealy
holosuniversity.net   Holos University Graduate Seminary – Holistic Medicine - Norman Shealy

holotropic.com Holotropic – Holotropic Breathwork - Christina and Stanislav Grof
holybible.com The Holy Bible
home.marsvenus.com Home Mars Venus – Relationship Advice, Retreats - John Gray
homeopathic.org National Center for Homeopathy
homeopathyhome.com Homeopathy Home
homesthatheal.com Homes That Heal – Bio Biologie
horatiodresser.wwwhubs.com Horatio Dresser
horoscope.com Horoscope
horsewhisperer.com Frank Bell Horse Whisperer
houseofptolemy.org House of Ptolemy
how-to-meditate.org How to Meditate - Guided Meditation Techniques - Buddhist Meditations
huacas.com Sun and Moon Huacas (site in Spanish)
hugo-online.org Victor Hugo
humanitysteam.org Humanities Team – Spiritual Movement
huna.com Ancient Hawaiian Magical Shamanism and Healing
huna.org Hawaiian Huna Village – Alternative or Complementary Healing
hustonsmith.org Huston Smith
hurstwic.org Hurstwic – A Viking Age Living History Society
hyperdictionary.com Hyperdictionary – Online Dictionary

I

iamuniversity.ch I AM University – Ascended Master Training Facility
iands.org International Association for Near-Death Studies
iarp.org The International Association of Reiki Professionals
iarrt.org International Association for Regression Research & Therapies
ias.org International Association of Sufism
ibiblio.org The Ancient Library of Qumran and Modern Scholarship
ibrt.org International Board of Regression Therapy
iching.com I Ching – The Book of Changes
ilanarubelfeld.com Ilana Rubenfeld
ileorunmilaoshun.org Ile Orunmila Oshun – House of Learning and Love – Luisah Teish
illuminati-news.com Illuminati News
iloveulove.com I Love You Love – Unconditional Love - Greg Baer
incaglossary.org Inca Glossary
indiadivine.org India Divine - Encyclopedia of Hinduism, Including Culture, Religion, and Beliefs
indiana.edu Indiana University
indigolife.org Indigo Children
indriesshah.com Indries Shah
inlighttimes.com In Light Times - Nevada Metaphysical Newspaper
innerbonding.com Inner Bonding – Margaret Paul

inner-harmony.org   Inner Harmony – Feng Shui and Space Clearing
innerlight.org.uk   Society of Inner Light
innerself.com   Inner Self – New Attitudes New Possibilities
innersource.net   Inner Source – David Feinstein and Donna Eden
innervisionsworldwide.com   Inner Visions Worldwide – Iyanla Vanzant
innovativehealing.com   Innovative Healing – Elizabeth "Liz" Lipski
innovint.com   Innovations – William "Bill" Guillory
insearchofspirit.com   In Search of Spirit – Philosophy of Spiritualism and Spirit Healing
insightjourneys.com   Insight Journeys – Mysteries and Science – Explore the Connection
inspiredhealth.info   Inspired Health – Nancy Mramor
iswara.com   William Quan Judge
institutespiritualsciences.org   The Institute of Spiritual Sciences – Expansion of Consciousness
integralinstitute.org   Integral Institute – Kenneth "Ken" Wilber
integrallife.com   Integral Life – Free to be Fully Human
integralscience.org   Sacred Science - Essays on Mathematics, Physics and Spiritual Philosophy
integrativemedicine.arizona.edu   Arizona Center for Integrative Medicine
intent.com   Intent – My Path to Wellness
interbeing.org.uk   The Community of Interbeing – Thich Nhat Hanh
interioralignment.com   Interior Alignment – Instinctive Feng Shui – Denise Linn
internationalenneagram.org   International Enneagram
internationalwaterforlifefoundation.org   International Water For Life Foundation – Masaru Emoto
intuition.org   Intuition Network – Jeffrey Mishlove
intuitionmedicine.com   Energy Medicine University – Francesca McCartney
invisibletemple.com   Invisible Temple – Sacred Sites, Sacred Places – Freddy Silva
inwardbound.com   Inward Bound Healing Journeys – David Cumes
irva.org   International Remote Viewing Association
ishk.com   Institute for the Study of Human Knowledge
iskcon.com   International Society for Krishna Consciousness
islam.com   Islam
islam101.net   Islam 101
issseem.org   The International Society for the Study of Subtle Energies and Energy Medicine
ista-usa.org   International Sound Therapy Association
itp.edu   Institute of Transpersonal Psychology
iups.edu   International University of Professional Studies

J

jackkornfield.org   Jack Kornfield
jacobneedleman.com   Jacob Needleman
jacqueslouisdavid.org   Jacques Louis David (Artist)

jacquesreich.com	Jacques Reich (Artist)
jamestissot.org	James Tissot (Artist)
jameswbell.com	James W. Bell - Ancient Sumeria
jan-van-eyck.org	Jan Van Eyck (Artist)
jcf.org	Joseph Campbell Foundation
jean-baptiste-camille-corot.org	Jean Baptiste Corot (Artist)
jeanneachterberg.com	Jeanne Achtenberg
jeanneavery.com	Jeanne Avery
jeannerose.net	Jeanne Rose
jeanshinodabolen.com	Jean Shinoda Bolen
jeff.gaia.com	Jeffrey Mishlove
jennynystrom.se	Jenny Nystrom (Artist)
jeryruhlrobertjohnson.com	Robert Johnson
jewishpeople.com	Jewish People
jewishvirtuallibrary.org	Jewish Virtual Library
jillpurce.com	Jill Purce
jimfitzpatrick.ie	Jim Fitzpatrick (Artist)
jkrishnamurti.org	Jiddu Krishnamurti
jnanayoga.org	Jnana Yoga
joanborysenko.com	Joan Borysenko
joannabarnum.com	Joanna Barnum (Artist)
joannecrabtree.com	Adam Crabtree
joanwanderson.com	Joan Wester Anderson
joelgoldsmith.com	Joel Goldsmith
joelgoldsmithoc.com	Joel Goldsmith – Orange County
joelosteen.com	Joel Osteen
johfra.no.sapo.pt	Johfra Bosschart (Artist)
johnatkinsongrimshaw.org	John A. Grimshaw (Artist)
johndavidson.org	John Davidson
johndee.org	John Dee
johnedward.net	John Edward
johnjoliver.com	John J. Oliver
johnholland.com	John Holland
johnpaulstrain.com	John Paul Strain (Artist)
johnshelbyspong.com	Bishop John Shelby Spong
johnsibbick.com	John Sibbick (Artist)
johnsingersargent.org	John Singer Sargent (Artist)
johnsingletoncopley.org	John Singleton Copley (Artist)
johntenniel.com	John Tenniel (Artist)
johnwelwood.com	John Welwood
johnwilliamgodward.org	John William Godward (Artist)
jonesbrehony.com	Kathleen Brehony

josephinewall.co.uk Josephine Wall (Artist)
josephmurphy.wwwhubs.com Joseph Murphy
josephsmith.com Joseph Smith
josephsmith.net Joseph Smith
joycehawkes.com Joyce Hawkes
judytatelbaum.com Judy Tatelbaum
jules-joseph-lefebvre.org Jules Joseph Lefebvre (Artist)
jwwaterhouse.com John William Waterhouse (Artist)
jzknight.com JZ Knight

K

karma-yoga.net Karma Yoga
katherynalice.com Kathryn Alice
katherynkuhlman.com Kathryn Kuhlman
kelticdesigns.com Jen Delyth (Artist)
kennethcohen.com Kenneth Cohen
kenring.org Kenneth Ring
kenwilber.com Ken Wilber
kevinryerson.com Kevin Ryerson
kindredspirit.co.uk Kindred Spirit – Mind Body and Spirit Magazine
kindredspiritsanimalcommunication.com Kindred Spirits – Animal Communication
kineticchromotherapy.com Kinetic Chromotherapy
kirkjschneider.com Kirk J. Schneider
kirlian.com Kirlian – Energy - Aura Photography
kirlian.org Kirlian Photography – Energy Works
knightstemplar.org Grand Encampment of Knights Templar of the USA
knowledgefiles.com Esoteric Orders
korotkov.org Konstantin Korotkov
kripalu.com Kripalu - Center for Yoga and Health
kristinmadden.com Kristin Madden
krishna.com All About Krishna
kriya.org Kriya Yoga
kriyayoga.com Cyberspace Ashram for Kriya Yoga, God and Love
kriyayogalahiri.com Lahiri Mahasaya
kundalininet.org Kundalini Research Network
kundaliniyoga.com Kundalini Yoga
kundaliniyoga.org Kundalini Yoga

L

laskow.net Healing with Love – Leonard Laskow
laurabergenfortgang.com Laura Bergen Fortgang
laurencekushner.com Laurence Kushner

lauriecabot.com   Laurie Cabot
laviniaplonka.com Lavinia Plonka
law-of-attraction-info.com   Law of Attraction
layayoga.com   Laya Yoga
lds.org   The Church of Jesus Christ of the Latter-Day Saints
learngraphology.com   Learn Graphology
learningmeditation.com   Learning Meditation
leb.net   Kahlil Gibran
lemuria.net   Lemuria
leonardoboff.com   Leonardo Boff
leonardshlain.net   Leonard Shlain
levitation.org   Levitation – Learn How to Self Levitate
lib.byu.edu Harold B. Lee Library
liberalcatholic.org Liberal Catholic Church International
lifeafterlife.com   Life After Life – Raymond Moody
lifecoachtraining.com   Life Coach Training – Patrick "Pat" Williams
life-enthusiast.com   Life Enthusiast – Alternative Natural Health
light.org   Church of Light – C.C. Zain
lightningspiral.com   Lightning Spiral – Pacific Mystery School – Pamela Eakins
lightplanet.com   Light Planet – World Religion
lightworkers.org   Lightworker's Spiritual Social Network
lillian-too.com   Lillian Too – Feng Shui
lindasalvin.com   Linda Salvin
lindaspaintings.com   Linda Rowell-Stevens (Artist)
lisahuntart.com   Lisa Hunt (Artist)
lisairis.bizland.com   Lisa Iris (Artist)
lisawilliamsmedium.com   Lisa Williams
litesofheaven.com   Lites of Heaven – Afterlife Near Death and Out of Body Experiences
livingbeyonddisease.com   Living Beyond Disease – Michelle O'Donnell
livingthefield.com Living the Field – Scientific Study of Spirituality – Lynne McTaggart
livingthequestions.org   Inner Management for Businesses and Org. - Raphael Cushnir
livius.org   Livius – Articles of Ancient History
lizlipski.com   Elizabeth "Liz" Lipski
llewellyn.com   Llewellyn - Carl Llewellyn Weschcke
llewellynencyclopedia.com   Llewellyn Encyclopedia
lojongmindtraining.com   The Tonglen and Mind Training Site (Buddhism)
lomilomi.com   Lomi Lomi – Massage
lomilomi.org   The Hawaiian Lomilomi Association
loresinger.com   Patricia "Trish" Telesco
lorian.org   Lorian Association – David Spangler
lost-civilizations.net   Lost Civilizations
lourdes-france.org Lourdes

loveofsantafe.com Love in Santa Fe - Magazine
lronhubbard.com L. Ron Hubbard
lucidity.com The Lucidity Institute – Stephen LaBerge
luisroyo.com Luis Royo (Artist)
luisahteish.com Luisah Teish
lynnandrews.com Lynn Andrews
lynnrobinson.com Lynn A. Robinson

M

mabinogion.info The Mabinogion
machensoc.demon.co.uk Arthur Machen
machupicchu.org The Machu Picchu Gateway
macyafterlife.wordpress.com Mark Macy
magdalenetours.com Magdalene Tours – Roger Woolger
magialuna.net Magia D' La Luna - Wicca
magritte.com Rene Magritte (Artist)
mahamudracenter.org Mahamudra Meditation Center
maharishi.org Maharishi Mahesh Yogi
mahavana.dhamma.org Dhamma Mahavana Meditation - California Vipassana Center
malindacramer.wwwhubs.com Malinda Cramer
manannan.net The Temple of Manannan Mac Lir
manataka.org American Indian Council
mandalamagazine.org Mandala Magazine – Preservation of the Mahayana Tradition
mandalaproject.org Mandalas
manlyphall.org Manly Palmer Hall
mantra-yoga.com Mantra Yoga
marcusbach.wwwhubs.com Marcus Bach
margotanand.com Margot Anand
marianne.com Marianne Williamson
mariannewilliamson.wwwhubs.com Marianne Williamson
mariayraceburu.com Maria Yraceburu
marinapetro.com Marina Petro (Artist)
marioduguay.com Mario Duguay (Artist)
marilynspoetry.com Marilyn's Inspirational Poetry
mars-venus-counselors.com Mars Venus Counselors – John Gray
martinism.com Martinism
marybakereddylibrary.org Mary Backer Eddy
marymargaretmoore.com Mary-Margaret Moore
masaru-emoto.net Masaru Emoto
masksoftheworld.com Masks of the World
maslow.com Abraham Maslow
massimorighi.com Massimo Righi (Artist)

mastermason.com Master Mason
masterslight.com   Dale Terbrush (Artist)
matthewfox.org   Matthew Fox
mathewmanning.com   Matthew Manning
matrifocus.com   MatriFocus – Web Magazine for Goddess Women
maxinesanders.co.uk   Maxine Sanders
mayacodices.org   Maya Hieroglyphic Codices
maya12-21-2012.com   Official 2012 Maya Calendar Website
mbeinstitute.org   Mary Baker Eddy Institute
medicalacupuncture.org   American Academy of Medical Acupuncture
medicinewheel.com   Medicine Wheel – Native American Spirituality
mediums-spiritguides.com   Mediums and Spirit Guides
mehlmadrona. com   Mehl Madrona
meilach.com   The Spiritual Teaching of William Stainton Moses
melaniegrimes.com   Melanie Grimes
melvinmorse.com Melvin Morse
memetics.com   Memetics – Susan Blackmore
meredithmiller.net   Meredith Miller (Artist)
merkaba.org   The Sacred Merkaba Techniques Website
merovingiandynasty.com   Order of Merovingian Dynasty
merriam-webster.com   Merriam-Webster – Dictionary and Thesaurus
mesoweb.com   Mesoweb – An Exploration of Mesoamerican Cultures
messengersofspirit.ning.com   Messengers of Spirit – Lightworkers Haven
metaphysics.com   University of Metaphysics
meta-religion.com Multidisciplinary View of the Religious, Spiritual and Esoteric Phenomena
metmuseum.org   The Metropolitan Museum of Art
metzneralchemicaldivination.org Metzner Alchemical Divination – Ralph Metzner
michaelgelb.com   Michael Gelb
michaelgurian.com   Michael Gurian
michelangelo.com Michelangelo (Artist)
micheleodonnell.com   Michelle O'Donnell
miguelruiz.com   Miguel Angel Ruiz
million.net Institute for Advanced Studies in Personology and Psychopathology
mindfulnesstapes.com   Mindfulness Meditation – CD's and Tapes – Jon Kabat-Zinn
mishlove.com   Jeffery Mishlove
missionignition.net   Mission Ignition – Geometry, Anthropology and the Art of Consciousness (Bethe Hagens – Artist)
mit.edu   Massachusetts Institute of Technology
mitchellegibsonmd.com   Mitchell Gibson
mitologiachilota.cl Mythology from Chiloe (Chile)
mkaku.org Michio Kaku
mkgandhi.org   Mahatma Gandhi

mmdarshanamerica.com Mother Meera
monroeinstitute.com Monroe Institute – Robert Monroe
montesuenos.org Montesuenos B & B – Brian O'Leary
montyroberts.com Monty Roberts Horse Whispering
moonmavenpublications.com Donna Cunningham
morrisberman.com Morris Berman
mormon.org The Church of Jesus Christ of Later-Day Saints
mormonhaven.com Mormon Haven
mosesmaimonides.com Moses Maimonides
mossdreams.com Robert Moss
mother-god.com A Chapel of Our Mother God – Goddess Mythology
mothermeeraashram.org Mother Meera Ashram
mothermeeraindia.com Mother Meera India
motherteresa.org Mother Teresa
mounisadhu.com Mouni Sadhu
mscottpeck.com M. Scott Peck
muchafoundation.org Alfonse Mucha (Artist)
mudrashram.com Mudrashram Institute of Spiritual Studies
mummiesfilm.com Mummies 3D
mummytombs.com Mummy Tombs
myss.com Caroline Myss
mysteriousbritain.co.uk Mysterious Britain and Ireland – Mysteries, Legends & the Paranormal
mysteriouspeople.com Mysterious People – Strange Powers, Poltergeist Girls, Psychics, Occultists, Feral Children
mystic.wikia.com Mystic Wikia – Wikia Philosophy - Encyclopedia
mysticvoodoo.com Mystic Voodoo
mythencyclopedia.com Myth Encyclopedia
mythinglinks.org Myth*ing Links – Mythology, Fairy Tales and Folklore

N
nag-hammadi.com Nag Hammadi Library
namastecafe.com Namaste Café – Internet Coffee House – Lightworker Network
naphill.org Napoleon Hill
nasa.gov National Aeronautic and Space Administration - USA
native-languages.org Native American Language Net
nativeremedies.com Native Remedies
naturalcures.com Natural Cures
naturalgourmetinstitute.com Natural Gourmet Institute for Health and Culinary Arts – Annemarie Colbin
naturalhistorymag.com National History Magazine
natures-blessings.org Natures Blessings – Healing – Distant Healing - Energy

natures-energies.com — Natures Energies – Discover the Secrets of Feng Shui, Flower Essences, Gem Essences, Protection
naturopathic.org — American Association for Naturopathic Physicians
nautis.com — Nautis Project – About Rupert Sheldrake, CG Jung, Joseph Campbell, & H. Bergson
nderf.org — Near Death Experience Research Foundation
nealedonaldwalsch.com — Neale Donald Walsch
near-death.com — Near Death Experiences and the Afterlife
neardeathsite.com — Near Death Experiences and the Afterlife
neopagan.net — A Very Brief History of Mesopagan Druidism
nessie.co.uk — Legend of Nessie – Loch Ness Monster
netinetifilms.com — Neti Neti Films – About Sri Nisargadatta Maharaj and Stephen Wolinsky
netopus.net — David Cumes
nevillegoddard.com — Neville Goddard
newadvent.org — Catholic Encyclopedia
new-age-spirituality.com — New Age Spirituality - Spiritualism, Psychic Powers, Paranormal
newagespiritualtours.com — New Age Spiritual Tours – Trisha McCannon
newdimensions.org — New Dimensions Media – Changing the World One Broadcast at a Time
newenergymovement.org — The New Energy Movement – Brian O'Leary
newrealitiestv.com — New Realities TV
newthought.com — The Power of Conscious Living – Harry Morgan Moses
newthoughtalliance.org — International New Thought Alliance
newton.ac.uk — Isaac Newton's Institute for Mathematical Sciences
newtoninstitute.org — Newton Institute for Life Between Lives Hypnotherapy – Michael Newton
new-visions.com — Visions of Reality – Elizabeth Joyce
nicolaspoussin.org — Nicolas Poussin (Artist)
nidsci.org — National Institute for Discovery Science – UFO Research
neihardtcenter.org — John Neidhard
nimatullahi.org — The Nimatullahi Sufi Order
nobelprizes.com — Nobel Prizes
noetic.org — The Institute for Noetic Sciences – Edgar Mitchell
noreenrenier.com — Noreen Renier
normanvincentpeale.wwwhubs.com — Norman Vincent Peale
normshealy.com — Normal Shealy
normshealy.net — Normal Shealy
northernway.org — Esoteric Theological Seminary – Online Seminary
nostradamus.org — Nostradamus
notingodsname.com — Not In God's Name – In Search of Tolerance With the Dalai Lama
nouvelle-planete.ch — Nouvelle Planete
nowwhatcoaching.com — Now What Coaching – Laura Berman Fortgang

nqa.org National Qigong (Chi Kung) Association
nrao.edu National Radio Astronomy Universe
numii.net Numii – Serving the Spiritual Search - Living Knowledge Base for Spirituality
nvcaz.com/tucson Non Violent Communication Arizona – Sylvia Haskvitz

O

occultopedia.com Occultopedia - The Occult and Unexplained Encyclopedia
odinsvolk.ca Odin's Volk Asatru – Spiritual and Cultural Organization – Nordic and Germanic
odysseyadventures.ca Odyssey, Adventures in Archeology
ofspirit.com Of Spirit – Healing the Body, Mind and Spirit
ofspiritandsoul.com Of Spirit and Soul
ogham.lyberty.com The Ogham Stone – Ogham Learning Resource
ogmandino.com Og Mandino
om-guru.com Om Guru – Gurus, Saints and Seekers - Hinduism
omsakthi.org Om Sakthi – Spiritual Movement – World Religions
om-sweet-om.net Om Sweet Om – Mystical Hinduism
onegreatspirit.com One Great Spirit – Universal Transformative Spirituality
onespiritinterfaith.org One Spirit – Interfaith Seminary
oriah.org Oriah Mountain Dreamer
oriahmountaindreamer.com Oriah Mountain Dreamer
orisonswettmarden.wwwhubs.com Orison Swett Marden
osho.com Osho
osirisnet.net Osiris Net – Ancient Egypt – Tombs and Mastabas of Ancient Egypt - History
oto.org Ordo Templo Orientis
oto-usa.org Ordo Templo Orientis USA
ourdreamingmind.net Our Dreaming Mind - Dreams
ouspensky.org.uk P. D. Ouspensky
outofthedark.com Out of the Dark - Wicca - Paganism

P

pabloamaringo.com Pablo Amaringo (Artist)
pacificinstitute.org Pacific Institute – Kirk Schneider
pagannews.com Pagan News and Information
paganpresence.com Pagan Presence - Store
paganmystics.ning.com Pagan Mystics Community
paintingdreams.co.uk Wendy Andrew (Artist)
paleothea.com Women in Greek Myths - Mythology
palmistry.com Palmistry – Ghanshyam Birla
pamelaeakins.net Pamela Eakins
pantheism.net World Pantheism

pantheon.org   Encyclopedia Mythica - Mythology
paradigm-sys.com Charles Tart
paralumun.com   Paralumun – New Age Village
paranormalawarenesssociety.org Paranormal Awareness Society
paranormal-encyclopedia.com   Paranormal Encyclopedia
paranormalhelp.com   Life Foundation – Paranormal Help
paranormalplus.com   Paranormal Plus
paranormality.com   Paranormality – A to Z of the Paranormal
parapsych.org   Parapsychological Association
parapsychologylab.com   American Institute of Parapsychology
parapsychology.org   The International Journal of Parapsychology
parsizoroastrianism.com World of Traditional Zoroastrianism
pastlives.net   International Association of Past Life Therapists
pastlives.org   Past Life Regression Therapy
patchadams.com   Patch Adams - Movie
patchadams.org   Patch Adams
pathwork.org   International Pathwork Foundation – Eva Pierrakos
patriciagarfield.com   Patricia Garfield
paulbrunton.org   Paul Brunton Philosophic Foundation
paulocoelho.com   Paulo Coelho
paulpearsall.com Paul Pearsall
thepeacefulwarriormovie.com   The Peaceful Warrior - Movie
peaceinspace.com Peace in Space - Institute for Cooperation in Space
peacexpeace.org   Peace X Peace – Connecting Women for Peace
pedrofigari.com   Pedro Figari (Artist)
peerspirit.com   Peer Spirit – Christina Baldwin
perceivingreality.com   Perceiving Reality - Flash Video on Spirituality, Meaning of Life, Science of Creation
personaltransformation.com   Personal Transformation – Inner Peace and Spiritual Awakening
personology.com   Personology, Research and Development Center
peterpaulrubens.org   Peter Paul Rubens (Artist)
peterrussell.com Peter Russell
peterunderwood.org.uk   Peter Underwood
pflyceum.org   Parapsychology Foundation - Lyceum
phenomenology.org   The World Phenomenology Institute
phenomenologycenter.org Center for Advanced Research in Phenomenology
philcousineau.net Phil Cousineau
philosophyarchive.com   Philosophy Archive – Philosophers and Philosophy
philosophyprofessor.com Philosophy Professor – A Dictionary of Philosophy and Philosophers
phineasquimby..com   Phineas Quimby

phineasquimby.wwwhubs.com   Phineas Quimby
phylliscurott.com Phyllis Curott
pierre-auguste-renoir.org Pierre-Auguste Renoir (Artist)
pietrodabano.net Pietro d'Abano
pitt.edu   University of Pittsburg
planetary-spirit.com   Internet Radio Program with In-Depth Interviews on Spirituality…
planetlightworker.com   Planet Lightworker Magazine
plato.stanford.edu Plato – Stanford Encyclopedia of Philosophy
plumvillage.org   Plum Village Practice Center – Thich Nhat Hanh
pmhatwater.com   Phyllis "P.M.H." Atwater
pov-int.com   Psychology of Vision – Chuck Spezzano
powerlawofattraction.com   Power Law of Attraction
power-of-imagination.com   Power of Imagination – Law of Attraction, Visualization, Meditation
ppquimby.com   Phineas Parkhurst Quimby
prairieghosts.com Prairie Ghosts - American Hauntings
pranayama.org   The Pranayama Institute – Sankara Saranam
prema.exto.org   Win Kuenen (Artist)
probertencyclopaedia.com   Probert Encyclopaedia
prophecykeepers.com   Prophecy Keepers Radio – Prophecies and Predictions - Ancient and Modern Prophets
prosperityproducts.com   Edwene Gaines Seminars
psychcentral.com Psych Central – What is Psychotherapy
psychicchildren.co.uk   Psychic Children – Dolphins, DNA and the Planetary Grid
psychic-experiences.com Psychic Experiences
psychicinvestigators.net   Psychic Investigators into the Paranormal
psychics.co.uk   Psychics and Mediums Network
psychicscience.org Psychic Science – Glossary of Terms in Parapsychology
psychicvista.com Intuitive and Psychic Consultants
psychotherapy.net Online Psychotherapy Magazine
psycotherapyarts.com   Psychotherapy Arts – Adam Crabtree
pumpkinhollow.org   Pumpkin Hollow Retreat Center – Theosophical Foundation

Colophon

Titles: Harrington
Text: Minion Pro

Set in Adobe InDesign

Printed in the USA

www.onespiritpress.com
onespiritpress@gmail.com